STRUCTURED SYSTEM PROGRAMMING

Prentice-Hall International
Series in Computer Science

C. A. R. Hoare, Series Editor

Published

BACKHOUSE, R. C., *Syntax of Programming Languages: Theory and Practice*
DUNCAN, F., *Microprocessor Programming and Software Development*
JONES, C. B., *Software Development: A Rigorous Approach*
WELSH, J., and ELDER, J., *Introduction to PASCAL*
WELSH, J., and MᶜKEAG, M., *Structured System Programming*

Future Titles

de BAKKER, J. W., *Mathematical Theory of Program Correctness*
HENDERSON, P., *Functional Programming: Application and Implementation*
JACKSON, M. A., *System Design*
NAUR, P., *Studies in Program Analysis and Construction*
TENNENT, R., *Principles of Programming Languages*

STRUCTURED SYSTEM PROGRAMMING

by
JIM WELSH
and
MICHAEL M^CKEAG
Queen's University of Belfast
Northern Ireland

Prentice/Hall PHI International

ENGLEWOOD CLIFFS, NEW JERSEY   LONDON   NEW DELHI
SINGAPORE   SYDNEY   TOKYO   TORONTO   WELLINGTON

Library of Congress Cataloging in Publication Data

WELSH, JAMES   1943–
    Structured system programming

    Bibliography: p.
    Includes index
    1. Structured programming.   I. McKeag, R. M.
    II. title
    QA76.6.W464   001.6'42   79-13895
ISBN 0-13-854562-6

British Library Cataloguing in Publication Data

WELSH, JAMES
    Structured system programming
    1. Structured programming
    I. Title   II. McKeag, R. M.
    001.6'42   QA76.6
ISBN 0-13-854562-6

ISBN 0-13-854562-6

PRENTICE-HALL INTERNATIONAL, INC., *London*
PRENTICE-HALL OF AUSTRALIA PTY., LTD., *Sydney*
PRENTICE-HALL OF CANADA, LTD., *Toronto*
PRENTICE-HALL OF INDIA PRIVATE LIMITED, *New Delhi*
PRENTICE-HALL OF JAPAN, INC., *Tokyo*
PRENTICE-HALL OF SOUTHEAST ASIA PTE., LTD., *Singapore*
PRENTICE-HALL, INC., *Englewood Cliffs, New Jersey*
WHITEHALL BOOKS LIMITED, *Wellington, New Zealand*

Typeset by HBM Typesetting Ltd.,
Chorley, Lancashire
Printed and bound in Great Britain
by A. Wheaton and Co. Ltd., Exeter

80 81 82 83 84 5 4 3 2 1

CONTENTS

FOREWORD

The successful programming language is one which guides its user in the construction of successful programs. According to this criterion, the languages Simula and Pascal have proved highly successful in the past ten years. A combination of the merits of these languages has long been the goal of research of Computer Scientists at the Queen's University. An additional objective has been to ensure that a program which simulates a real-time system can be transferred without change to an embedded computer environment to control the real system in real time.

This book reports on the achievement of both these goals. It briefly describes the language Pascal Plus, and then shows how it may be used successfully in the structuring of two systems programs, a compiler and an operating system.

It is particularly appropriate that it should be published in a series which is dedicated to the transformation of computer programming from a craft, carried out in private by a programmer and his computer, to a profession, in which all decisions, designs, and even code, are open to scrutiny by professionally competent colleagues.

C. A. R. HOARE

PREFACE

The purpose of this book is to demonstrate the application of structured programming to the construction of system programs—in particular compilers (which are typical of many similar text-handling programs) and operating systems (which are typical of many real-time systems).

The book begins by summarizing (in Section 1) the structured programming style and notations to be used. Sections 2 and 3 then present the development of a complete compiler and a complete operating system, with working code for each, in a suitable high-level language. The language used is an extended version of the programming language Pascal, known as Pascal Plus. This extended language has been implemented at the Queen's University of Belfast on two different computers, and the programs presented in this book have been compiled and run there. A portable Pascal Plus system is now under preparation. However a reader should be able to implement these programs in any suitable language on his own computer, thereby obtaining some practical experience, as well as theoretical understanding, of structured system programming.

The book should be useful to three classes of reader.

1. For those learning structured programming the book presents two complete case studies of its application to larger programs, showing clearly the particular problems of size which large programs present and how they may be tackled.
2. For those studying compilers or operating systems the book provides a corresponding case study of the implementation of established compiler or operating system techniques within the clear logical framework of a structured program.
3. For professional programmers already engaged in system programming the book demonstrates how structured programming techniques can be

applied successfully in their current area of work, and may encourage them to adopt these techniques if they have not already done so.

Indeed the material of this book has been used many times in courses for professional programmers and for university students, both undergraduate and postgraduate.

We are deeply indebted both to Professor C. A. R. Hoare, who instituted the work described in this book and contributed very many of the techniques we have used, and also to Mr D. W. Bustard, who, by his development, implementation and use of Pascal Plus, has provided the basis of all three sections of this book. In addition we have been considerably influenced in the first section by that classic work *Structured Programming* by Dahl, Dijkstra and Hoare, by Wirth's excellent programming language Pascal, and by Brinch Hansen's and Bustard's extensions to Pascal. The second section builds upon the Pascal compiler developed by Wirth and his team at Zurich, while the final section shows the considerable influence of the T.H.E. Multiprogramming System constructed by Dijkstra and his colleagues in Eindhoven. To these people, and to the UK Science Research Council, International Computers Limited and the Advanced Computer Technology Project of the UK Department of Industry, which supported some of our work on operating systems, we offer our thanks.

The Queen's University of Belfast   J. WELSH
Northern Ireland   R. M. McKEAG

Section 1

STRUCTURED PROGRAMMING

Structured programming has been defined in many ways, with varying degrees of formalization. The approach used in this book is a relatively informal one which is close to that outlined by Dahl, Dijkstra and Hoare in their classic text *Structured Programming*. It involves three essential ingredients:

1. the perception of a logical structure for the program required, which reflects the inherent structure of the problem and the data involved, and any constraints imposed on the solution;
2. the realization of this structure by a systematic process of stepwise refinement, which limits the complexity to be handled at any moment to what can be readily comprehended;
3. the use of a notation which assists the stepwise refinement of the structure required and reinforces this structure in the final program produced.

This section is concerned chiefly with presenting the notation to be used in the subsequent sections, but in doing so it also illustrates the structural decomposition and stepwise refinement techniques.

The notation used is an extended version of the programming language Pascal, and readers familiar with this language may find detailed study of most of this section unnecessary. However, their attention is drawn to the final chapter of the section in which certain language extensions to support abstraction, modular programming and parallelism are introduced.

The section is intended to provide a sufficient understanding of Pascal to enable programs to be read and understood, and to enable use of the language as a notation for program design. It is *not* intended to provide the precise and detailed knowledge required to write compilable Pascal programs.

1

For this the reader is referred to one of the Pascal programming texts listed in the bibliography.

BASIC PROGRAM STRUCTURING

The structured programming demonstrated in this book uses a limited number of basic programming constructs, each expressible in a sequential text notation, as a means of program design *and* documentation.

The form, and limited number, of these constructs enforces a discipline on the structure of programs composed from them. In addition the constructs advocated lend themselves to a programming method, called *stepwise refinement*, which helps the programmer to avoid the problems of complexity which can so easily arise in program development.

The sequential text notation enables the program design to be incorporated in the compilable program text itself, at little extra cost to the programmer; moreover the help which this gives the programmer in debugging creates a positive incentive for him to do so.

In principle there is no reason why the structured-design notation should not be a compilable programming language itself. In fact, the notation used in this book is such a language—an extended version of the programming language Pascal known as Pascal Plus. The advantages of using a compilable structured language are obvious—the design and coding processes are merged, and the consistency of program structure can be checked by the compiler, not just the programmer. However, even without such a compiler the advantages of designing a program in structured notation and then transcribing it into the available compilable code are considerable, and most of the practical disadvantages which an unstructured approach to coding creates are avoided.

Basic Programming Constructs

Basic actions

A program is composed of basic data-manipulating actions such as *assignment*, *input* and *output* of data values.

In Pascal an assignment of a value to a variable is denoted by

$$variable := expression$$

where the expression is composed from variable and constant operands using familiar operators such as $+$, $-$, $*$ etc. (The full range of operands appropriate to various types of data values is discussed more fully in subsequent sections.) Simple examples of assignment statements are

$i := 7$
$circumference := 3.14159 * diameter$
$count := count + 1$

Input and output in Pascal are based on the concept of *sequential files*, from which values may be *read*, or to which values may be written. Legible character input and output involve *text files*, which are sequential files of characters, with a superimposed line structure.

Values for variables $v1$, $v2$, ... may be read from an input text file by a statement of the form

$read (v1, v2, ...)$

Subsequent alignment of the input text file at the start of the next line may be achieved by using the alternative form

$readln (v1, v2, ...)$

or by subsequent use of the form

readln

When the last character of the current line of input has been read, the predicate

eoln

is true, otherwise it is false. When the input file has been exhausted the predicate

eof

is true, otherwise it is false.

Values $v1$, $v2$, ... may be written to an output text file by a statement of the form

$write (v1, v2, ...)$

Subsequent alignment of the output file at the start of a new line may be achieved by using the alternative form

$$writeln \ (v1 \ , \ v2 \ , \ \ldots \ )$$

or by subsequent use of the form

$$writeln$$

The number of characters written to a file for each value output may be controlled by a *field width* w following the value, thus

$$write \ (\ v1 \ : \ w1 \ , \ v2 \ : \ w2 \ , \ \ldots \ )$$

Sequential composition

The sequential execution of a number of actions $A, B, C, \ldots$, can be written in sequential text simply as

$$A \ ; \ B \ ; \ C \ ; \ \ldots$$

When the composite action is to be regarded as a single component of some larger structure, brackets such as **begin** . . . **end** may be introduced:

begin $A \ ; \ B \ ; \ C \ ; \ D$ **end**

Selection

Selection between two alternative actions A,B, on some conditions Q, can be written in sequential text as

if Q **then** A **else** B

More complex selections can always be expressed as a combination of **if** . . . **then** . . . **else** constructs. Two special cases may be singled out for special notation, as in Pascal

(a) when one of the alternative actions is null the reduced form

if Q **then** A

may be used;

(b)   when selection between a set of actions A, B, C, ... has to be made according to corresponding values $a,b,c,$ ... of some selector expression Q the **case** notation may be used, viz.:

> **case** Q **of**
> $\quad a : A$;
> $\quad b : B$;
> $\quad c : C$;
> $\quad$ . . .
> **end**

Repetition

Repetition of some action A while some condition Q remains true can be written in sequential text as

> **while** Q **do** A

More complex repetitions can be expressed as combinations of the **while** and **if** ... **then** ... **else** constructs. Pascal, however, isolates two special cases for which an alternative notation is provided:

(a)   when the repeated action is to be executed at least once, and the terminating condition may be undefined initially, the construct

> **repeat** A **until** Q

may be used;

(b)   when the number of iterations is known at the start of repetition, and perhaps a corresponding counting variable is required, the constructs

> **for** $v := i$ **to** f **do** A
> **for** $v := i$ **downto** f **do** A

may be used. These cause the action A to be repeatedly executed while variable v takes successive (ascending or descending) values from initial value i to final value f.

Combining the constructs

A noticeable feature of the constructs given above is that each defines a control structure with a single entry and single exit point. It is this property that makes them simple but powerful building blocks for more complex control structures, and ensures that the resultant structure remains comprehensible to our limited human intellect.

When using the sequential text notation to define a complex control structure, careful layout and indentation may be used to emphasize the structure involved. For example, the code fragment

> **if** . . .
> **then**
> > **begin**
> > > . . . ;
> > > . . . ;
> > > . . .
> > **end**
> **else**
> > **while** . . .**do** . . .
> > > . . . ;

clearly involves two alternative paths, one of which is a simple composition of three component actions, the other a repetition of a single action.

Realizing structure by jumps

If a structured notation such as that outlined above is not available as a compilable programming language the approach recommended is to design the program required in a structured notation and then transcribe this into whatever language is available, incorporating the structured text as comment alongside the corresponding code. The constructs described can be realized in any sequential programming language that provides

(a) a conditional jump instruction, say **if** Q **goto** L

(b) an unconditional jump, say **goto** L

For example, sequential execution of A ; B ; C . . . is achieved without any explicit control structure, simply by juxtaposing the code for the component actions $A, B, C, . . .$

The construct

> **if** Q **then** A **else** B

is achieved by a code structure

> if $\overline{Q}$ goto F
> A
> goto E
> $F : B$
> $E : \ldots$

where $\overline{Q}$ denotes the negation of condition Q.
The construct

> **while** Q **do** A

is achieved by

> S : if $\overline{Q}$ goto E
> A
> goto S
> $E : \ldots$

Similar coding conventions can readily be devised for the other selective and repetitive constructs. Transcription of a program in structured notation then reduces to a mechanical application of these coding templates to each occurrence of the corresponding constructs.

In this book **goto** statements are very occasionally used to exit from a piece of program where there is no suitable structured notation for this in Pascal Plus.

Stepwise Refinement

In structured programming a complex program is composed by a process of *stepwise refinement*. With this technique programming proceeds from the initial program concept to the final program text by a series of steps. At each step a single program component is considered and rewritten, using one or more of the basic constructs and introducing new components for further refinement as required. Each new component is then considered in subsequent steps until no further refinement is required. In this way a complex program structure is built up in a systematic fashion, and the complexity which the programmer has to face at any moment is limited to the component currently being refined.

The technique, and the use of the constructs introduced above, is best demonstrated by a simple programming example (taken, with permission, from Jackson's *Principles of Program Design*; copyright by Academic Press Inc. (London) Ltd.)

Given a procedure *write(I)* which prints an integer *I* on the current output line, and *writeln* to take a new output line, we wish to construct a piece of program which will print the lower triangle of a multiplication table of numbers up to a given *N*.

For example, if *N* = 4 the output should be

```
1
2   4
3   6   9
4   8   12   16
```

We will assume there is sufficient printing width for the table required.

Stepwise refinement starts from an initial program concept which in this case might be expressed as

print multiplication table (N)

Realizing that the required table involves *N* printed lines, we might refine this initial concept as a loop which prints lines one by one:

```
lineno := 1 ;
while lineno ⩽ N do
begin
    write one line ;
    writeln ;
    lineno := lineno + 1
end
```

The step *write one line* now has to be considered. This too is clearly a loop which prints values one by one. The number of values to be printed equals the line number, so we have

```
colno := 1 ;
while colno ⩽ lineno do
begin
    write one value ;
    colno := colno + 1
end
```

Finally we consider the value to be printed in each column. This is clearly the product of the line and column numbers, so the step *write one value* is trivially programmed in Pascal as:

> *write (lineno * colno)*

Putting these together we have a complete program fragment:

```
lineno := 1;
while lineno ≤ N do
begin
    {write one line}
    colno := 1;
    while colno ≤ lineno do
    begin
        {write one value}
        write (lineno * colno) ;
        colno := colno + 1
    end ;
    writeln ;
    lineno := lineno + 1
end
```

An equivalent program, using **for** loops rather than **while** loops, could be produced by an equivalent sequence of steps.

Note that the intermediate abstractions have been retained in the form of comments, thereby enabling the program to be more easily understood and more readily amended. In Pascal comments are enclosed in braces { }, but when these are not available the delimiters (* *) are used.

BASIC DATA STRUCTURING

The problems of designing and documenting the data manipulated by a program are similar to those of programming the manipulation itself. Again the approach taken in this book is to use a limited set of basic data constructs, expressible in sequential text notation, to define a transparent logical structure for the data involved. As we shall see, many of these constructs are direct analogs of those used in program structuring. They represent an extension of the traditional concept of *type*, whose rôle in programming we first clarify.

The Concept of *Type* in Programming Languages

Most high-level programming languages enforce a type specification of the data items manipulated by a program. In Pascal, for example, variables must be declared before use, by declarations such as:

$$\textbf{var } a,b,c : integer ;$$
$$x1,x2,discriminant : real ;$$

The rôle played by the types specified is based on the following principles:

(a)   The type of a data item determines the range of values which it may take, and the range of operations which may be applied to it.

(b)   Each data item has a single type.

(c)   The type of a data item denoted by a constant, variable or expression in the language is apparent, i.e. it can be deduced solely from its form or context, without any knowledge of the particular values it may take during execution of the program.

(d)   Each operator in the language requires operands of specified types and produces a result of specified type.

By providing a range of types, with appropriate operators, a programming language enables the programmer to describe his data manipulation in terms natural to the data, rather than in terms of the machine representation ultimately involved.

By enforcing the constraints listed above, the language (or its implementation) also protects the programmer from describing illogical combinations of data and operations, a protection not available at machine level.

Effective data structuring requires an adequate range of constructs for defining appropriate data types. The notations used in this book are introduced in the following sections, together with an indication of how values of these types may be represented in computer storage.

Unstructured Types

Definition of unstructured types

Just as program structures are composed ultimately of unstructured operations, such as assignment or input/output, all data are built up from unstructured components of some *unstructured type*. We have three useful classes of unstructured type.

1. *Primitive types*

    These are types which may be taken as given by a programming language or a computer; *integer, real, chara*cter and *Boolean* are examples of primitive types.

2. *Enumerations*

    When data items take a limited range of values, which do not correspond directly to any primitive type, it is convenient to regard them as of a type that we define by enumerating the names of its values. For example,

    type *suit* = (*club, diamond, heart, spade*);

    The value identifiers introduced—*club, diamond, heart*, and *spade*—act as constants of the type, denoting the only values which data items of type *suit* can take.

    type *primary color* = (*red, yellow, blue*) ;
    day of week   = (*Sunday, Monday, Tuesday, Wednesday, Thursday, Friday, Saturday*) ;
    marital status   = (*single, married, widowed, divorced*) ;

    An intrinsic ordering between the values of the type is assumed in Pascal. Ordering operators ($<$, $\leqslant$, etc.) can then be used for the comparison of such values.

3. *Subranges*

    When a data item takes a range of values which is a subrange of the values described by some existing unstructured type it is useful to define its type as a subrange of the existing type. For example,

    type *year*   = 1900 . . 1999;
    day of month = 1 . . 31 ;
    workday   = *Monday* . . *Friday* ;

    Having introduced such types we can declare variables of these types in the usual way

    var *trumps* : *suit* ;
    arrival, departure : *day of month* ;
    y : *year* ; *d* : *day of week* ;
    ms : *marital status*

Manipulation of unstructured types

Primitive types such as *real* and *integer* tend to have special operators associated with them (+, −, ∗,/, etc.) but the following are common to unstructured types in general.

1. *Assignment*   For example,

$$pc := yellow \; ;$$
$$y := 1927 \; ;$$
$$arrival := departure$$

2. *Comparison*

   (a)   equality testing, for example

   if *arrival* = *departure* **then** . . .
   if *trumps* ≠ *spade* **then** . . .

   (b)   ordering, for example,

   if (*d* ⩾ *Monday*) **and** (*d* ⩽ *Friday*) **then** . . .

   Because of character set limitations, the program listings in this book represent the three symbols ⩽ ⩾ ≠ by <=, >=, <> respectively.

3. *Case discriminations*

   For unstructured data items that take a limited range of values the **case** construct is extremely useful. For example,

   case *d* **of**
   Sunday : . . .
   Monday, Tuesday, Wednesday,
       Thursday, Friday : . . .
   Saturday : . . .
   end

Representation of unstructured types

1. *Primitive types* have in general a representation dictated by the hardware facilities of the computer involved.

2. *Enumerated types*   The *standard* representation is to map the values, in the order of their enumeration, onto machine integers $0 \: .. \: n-1$ (where *n* is the number of values, or *cardinality*, of the type). For example,

red	0
yellow	1
blue	2

3. *Subrange types*   The *standard* representation is to give each value the same representation as it has in the original type. Converting values between these two types then involves no physical operation.

Symbolic constants

The enumerated type enables meaningful identifiers to be used for each constant value of type. It is often an aid to program clarity and adaptability to denote constant values of other types by identifiers as well. In Pascal this can be done by means of constant definitions, such as the following:

$$\begin{aligned} \textbf{const } pi &= 3.14159 \text{ ;} \\ terminator &= '\ .\ ' \text{ ;} \\ separator &= '\ ,\ ' \text{ ;} \end{aligned}$$

Records

Definitions of records

The brackets **begin . . . end** were introduced to denote a sequence of actions grouped to form a single composite action. Often we find that a number of data items, distinct in nature and perhaps in type, are similarly grouped together to form a composite data item. We may regard the latter as having a type which is the *cartesian product* of the types of its components, and we adopt a notation for the definition of such types as follows:

Given types

$$month = (Jan,Feb,Mar,Apr,May,Jun,Jul,Aug,Sep,Oct,Nov,Dec) \text{ ;}$$
$$dayofmonth = 1 .. 31 \text{ ;}$$
$$year = 1900 .. 1999 \text{ ;}$$

we define a type

$$date = \textbf{record } m : month \text{ ; } d : dayofmonth \text{ ; } y : year \textbf{ end}$$

Our definition specifies the type of each component or *field*, and introduces selector identifiers to distinguish between them.
Another example, from mathematics, might be:

$$\textbf{type } complex = \textbf{record } realpart, imagpart : real \textbf{ end}$$

Manipulation of records

For the following examples assume variables *day* : *date* ; *c* : *complex* .

The operations useful in manipulating records are *assignment* plus the following:

1. *Selection*   To denote a particular component of a record variable we qualify the variable name by .component selector. For example,

    > *c.imagpart*
    > *day.m*

2. *Selective updating*   To denote the changing of an individual component value within a record variable, leaving all other components unchanged, we use the assignment operator with the component selector on the left-hand side. For example,

    > *c.imagpart* := 2.0 ;
    > *day.y* := 1904

3. *The* **with** *notation*   In processing a record value it is often necessary to make several references to its components within a small region of code. For this purpose a **with** construction is used of the form

    > **with** *r* **do** *S*

    Within statement *S* any occurrence of an appropriate component selector is taken to refer to the corresponding component of record value *r*. For example,

    > **with** *c* **do**
    > **begin**
    >   *realpart* := 0.0 ;
    >   *imagpart* := − *imagpart*
    > **end**

    means the same as

    > **begin**
    >   *c.realpart* := 0.0 ;
    >   *c.imagpart* := − *c.imagpart*
    > **end**

Representation of records

The standard method juxtaposes values of components in consecutive storage regions, either

1. *unpacked*—each component occupying an integral number of words:

(Mar, 7, 1908)   *m* | 2 |
                       d | 7 |
                       y | 1908 |

or

2. *packed*—each component occupies only enough bits for its representation and components are directly juxtaposed:

(Mar, 7, 1908) | 2 | 7 | 1908 |
                   4   5   11

In Pascal a packed representation is denoted by preceding the word **record** by the word **packed** in the record type definition. For example,

> **type** *date*1 = **packed record**
> > *m* : *month* ;
> > *d* : *dayofmonth* ;
> > *y* : *year*
>
> **end**

Whereas a value of type *date* would usually occupy three words in memory a value of type *date*1 would occupy only one or two.

Unions

Definition of union types

The **if** . . . **then** . . . **else** construct expresses an action as one of two (or more) alternative actions. We sometimes find a data object which takes two or more alternative forms during its lifetime. It is useful to regard such an object as having a type which is the union of the types of its alternative forms.

Consider for example the register of all cars in a country. Cars are distinguished either as local cars owned by residents of the country, or as foreign cars currently visiting the country. For local cars the data recorded are as follows

```
type localcar = record make: manufacturer ;
                      regnumber :carnumber ;
                      owner :person ;
                      firstreg :date
              end
```

For foreign cars the data recorded are as follows

```
type foreigncar = record make :manufacturer ;
                        regnumber :carnumber ;
                        origin :country
                end
```

A data type covering both kinds of car may be regarded as the *union* of these two types. Such unions are catered for in Pascal by extension of the record concept to allow *variant parts*. A variant part consists of an explicitly declared tag field followed by field lists corresponding to possible values of this tag field.

For example the union type *car* would be defined in Pascal as follows:

```
carkind = (local,foreign) ;
car = record
            make : manufacturer ;
            regnumber : carnumber ;
            case kind : carkind of
            local : (owner : person ;
                     firstreg : date) ;
            foreign : (origin : country)
      end
```

Manipulation of union types

Manipulation of union types, or records with variant parts, may be expressed in the same notation as for simple records. For example, the tag field *kind* of a variable *c* of type *car* and the variant fields *owner* etc. can be denoted by *c.kind*, *c.owner*, etc.

However, reference to a variant field *c.owner* is valid only when *c* has the corresponding variant form, i.e. when *c.kind* = *local*. Use of the **case** statement with the normal **with** statement does reduce the likelihood of error in this respect. For example,

```
with c do
begin
    . . .
    case kind of
    local : begin
                owner := . . .
                firstreg := . . .
            end ;
    foreign : origin := . . .
    end ;
    . . .
end
```

Representation of union types

Representation of unions or variant records is the same as that for simple records, except that the fields of alternative variants share the same storage, since only one variant exists at any moment.

The values of the alternative types may occupy different amounts of storage. It may sometimes be necessary to pad out shorter values to equalize the lengths. For example,

a local car

make	Mini
regnumber	GOI 4030
tag	local
owner	BLOGGS
firstreg	Sep 1 1973

a foreign car

make	Fiat
regnumber	37-27-193
tag	foreign
origin	Italy
	(padding)

Arrays

Definition of arrays

We often find that a number of data items, identical in nature and type, are grouped to form a composite data item. When the number of items is predetermined, and the individual items are distinguishable by a corresponding subscript value, the composite data item may be thought of as an *array*, whose component items are called *elements*. An array type may be defined in the general form

array [*subscript range*] of *elementtype*

For example,

$$\textbf{type} \quad vector = \textbf{array} \; [1 \, . \, . \, 30] \; \textbf{of} \; real \; ;$$
$$punchcard = \textbf{array} \; [1 \, . \, . \, 80] \; \textbf{of} \; char \; ;$$
$$hoursworked = \textbf{array} \; [dayofweek] \; \textbf{of} \; 0 \, . \, . \, 24 \; ;$$

Manipulation of arrays

Besides *assignment*, arrays may be manipulated by

1. *Selection*   The element of an array A corresponding to a subscript value x is denoted by $A[x]$.
   The selection operation is called subscripting.
2. *Selective updating*   To change the value of the array element corresponding to a particular subscript value, leaving other element values unchanged, we write

$$A[x] := r$$

Representation of arrays

Standard unpacked representation allocates one or more whole words to each element of the array. The address of a particular element is then given by

(a)   reduce subscript by value of its lower bound

(b)   multiply by number of words for each element

(c)   add address of first element.

Packed representations in which more than one element share a word may be devised with more complex addressing mechanisms.

In Pascal a packed representation can be requested by preceding the word **array** with the word **packed**, e.g.

$$name = \textbf{packed array} \; [1 \, . \, . \, 12] \; \textbf{of} \; char$$

Strings

Packed arrays of characters are given special status in Pascal and known as *strings*. Certain additional operations are provided for string types as follows:

1. *Construction* of string constants is denoted by enclosing a sequence of characters in quotes

$$'JOHN \; P \; SMITH'$$

A sequence of n characters thus denoted is assumed to be of type **packed array** $[1 .. n]$ **of** *char*.

2. *Tests of equality and ordering* are allowed on string types by the operators $=, \neq, <, \leqslant, \geqslant, >$. For example,

if name1 $=$ 'JOHN P SMITH' then . . .

Ordering is by normal lexicographic conventions.

3. *Output* of strings is accomplished by the standard procedure *write*.

These operations are not allowed on any other array types.

Sets

Definition of sets

We have defined the concept of type as the set of values which an object of that type may take. In mathematics the *powerset* of a set is the set of all subsets of that set. Correspondingly we can define a powerset type as a type whose values are all possible sets of values of some other type, the *base* type.

For example given

type primarycolor $=$ (red,yellow,blue)

we can define

color $=$ set of primarycolor

The type *color* then has values

[*red,yellow,blue*]	(the universal set of colors)
[*red,yellow*]	
[*red,blue*]	
[*yellow,blue*]	
[*red*]	
[*yellow*]	(unit or singleton sets)
[*blue*]	
[ ]	(the empty set)

Another example of data of set type is the outstanding calls on an elevator in a multistorey building. For example,

type floor $=$ (first,second,third,fourth);
elevatorcall $=$ set of floor

Manipulation of sets

Apart from assignment and test of equality a wide variety of basic operations is available for sets.

1. *Construction*

    (a) By enumeration of members. For example,
    [*red,yellow*]
    [*first*]
    [   ]

    (b) By subrange. For example,

    [*first . . third*]

2. *Membership testing*

    (a) *a* **in** *s*   gives *true* if *a* is a member of *s*,
    false otherwise

    (b) *s*1 ⩽ *s*2   gives *true* if all members of *s*1 are members of *s*2,
    false otherwise

3. *Set arithmetic*

    (a) *s*1 + *s*2   denotes the *union* of *s*1 and *s*2, i.e. the set of all values which are *either* in *s*1, *or* in *s*2, *or* in both,
    (b) *s*1 * *s*2   denotes the intersection of *s*1 and *s*2, i.e. the set of all values which are in *s*1 *and s*2 ;
    (c) *s*1 − *s*2   denotes the *relative complement,* i.e. the set of values which are in *s*1 but *not in s*2.

Representation of sets

Provided the base type is not too large, powerset types are conveniently represented by *bit* patterns containing one bit for each potential member of the set. This bit takes value 1 if the base value is a member, value 0 if it is not. For example,

type *color* (see p. 19) is representable by 3 bits

101   represents   [*red,blue*]
010   represents   [*yellow*]
000   represents   [   ]

This representation allows efficient implementation of most of the basic operations postulated, by use of the logical and shift instructions provided on most machines.

Dynamic Structures

A simple example

The constructs already introduced enable the description of data structures whose form and size are predetermined, and remain fixed throughout their lifetime. As such the constructs are easily and efficiently incorporated in a compilable programming language such as Pascal. In other languages they can be realized by fixed storage structures and appropriate code based on the representations suggested.

Other data structures *vary* in size and form during their lifetime. These too can be described and manipulated in an appropriate abstract notation. For example we might define a *stack S*, of items of some given type, by a declaration of the form

$$S : \textbf{stack of } itemtype$$

The only operations permitted on this stack might be

(a) the addition, or "pushing", of a new topmost item i, which we denote by

$$S.push(i)$$

(b) the removal, or "popping", of the topmost item to a variable i, which we denote by

$$S.pop(i)$$

(c) testing if the stack is empty, which we denote by

$$S.empty$$

The way in which these operations are best realized depends critically on the nature and size of the items to be stacked and whether any useful upper bound can be placed on the maximum length of the stack.

The same is true of other dynamic structures, trees, lists, etc., which arise in programming. An abstract notation for them is readily devised, but the most appropriate implementation will depend on characteristics of each particular application.

It is therefore impractical to build the abstract description of such structures into a general-purpose compilable programming language. Any general implementation chosen is likely to be unsatisfactory for particular applications. Instead a general-purpose language should provide facilities for the realization of such structures by the programmer himself.

To this end Pascal provides the *pointer* mechanism, which allows the creation of chained representations of structures in dynamically allocated storage.

Pointers in Pascal

A Pascal program may define a pointer type by a type declaration of the form

$$P = \uparrow T$$

where T is the type of object which values of type P may reference, or point to. Since these objects themselves usually contain pointers of type P, so allowing chaining, the definition of T is allowed to follow that of P

$$\textbf{type } P = \uparrow T ;$$
$$T = \textbf{record}$$
$$I : item ;$$
$$Next : P$$
$$\textbf{end}$$

The declaration of a pointer variable thus

$$\textbf{var } p : P$$

does not itself create an object to which p points, only the capability of doing so. Creation of such an object is achieved by use of the built-in procedure *new*, called as follows

$$new\ (p)$$

The effect is to create, in available storage, an object of type T, and set the pointer variable p to point to it. Thereafter this object, or dynamically allocated variable, may be referenced by writing $p \uparrow$. For example,

$$p \uparrow .I := I1$$

Apart from creation by means of *new*, and the use of the $\uparrow$ notation, pointer values may be copied, and tested for equality. To indicate that a pointer does not point to anything a special value **nil** is provided, and this can be assigned to variables of any pointer type. For example,

p := **nil** ; ...
if $p \neq$ **nil then** ...

Once created by *new*, a dynamically allocated variable remains in existence until it is explicitly destroyed by a call to the built-in procedure *dispose*, thus:

dispose (p) ;

where p is a pointer value currently referencing, or pointing to, the variable to be destroyed. Note that the lifetime of dynamically allocated variables is not related either to the block in which they are created or to the block in which pointer variables referencing them are declared. It is the programmer's responsibility to ensure that all dynamically allocated variables are disposed of, if storage economy is to be maintained. It is also his responsibility to ensure that a variable that has been disposed of is never referred to again.

The listings in Sections 2 and 3 are limited to a restricted character set and use the symbol $\wedge$ in place of $\uparrow$.

Implementing a stack in Pascal

The use of the pointer facility to implement the abstract stack structure outlined above would be as follows.

A pointer type enabling the representation of a chain of items is introduced thus

type *stackp* = $\uparrow$ *stackr* ;
        stackr = **record**
                    item : *itemtype* ;
                    previousitem : *stackp*
               end

A stack is then represented by the pointer to its topmost item, which we shall declare

var *topmost* : *stackp*

The operation *push(i)* can then be realized by the following code, where p is a working variable of type *stackp*

$new(p)$;
with p ↑ **do begin**
        $item := i$;
        $previousitem := topmost$
      end ;
$topmost := p$

The operation $pop(i)$ is realized as follows

$p := topmost$;
$i := topmost$ ↑ $.item$;
$topmost := topmost$ ↑ $.previousitem$;
$dispose(p)$

The emptiness of the stack at any moment can be tested by

$topmost =$ **nil**

Initially, of course, the stack must be empty; this is accomplished by the initializing code:

$topmost :=$ **nil**

and, when use of the stack is complete, the storage occupied by any residual "unpopped" items should be recovered by the following code:

while $topmost \neq$ **nil do**
begin
  $p := topmost$;
  $topmost := topmost$ ↑ $.previousitem$;
  $dispose(p)$
end

BLOCK STRUCTURING

The basic tenet of structured programming is that the structure of a program and its data should reflect the structure inherent in the problem that the program is designed to solve. It follows that in the stepwise refinement of a program we should seek to develop both code and data together in such a way as to reflect the structure of the component we are refining. The unit of construction that we use is the *block*, which introduces some data and also the actions that are performed on it. There are several forms that blocks can take.

Procedures

A *procedure* consists of a block preceded by a heading which associates a name with the block. Thus the finalization associated with the stack in the last example can be defined as a procedure.

```
procedure release ;
  var p: stackp ;
  begin
    while topmost ≠ nil do
      begin
        p := topmost ;
        topmost := p ↑ .previousitem ;
        dispose(p)
      end
  end
```

Executing a statement consisting of the procedure name

$$... ; release ; ...$$

has the effect of executing the procedure block and is known as *invoking* or *calling* the procedure.

Value parameters

The operation *push*, from the example of the programmer-defined stack, can also be implemented as a procedure but in this case the value of the item to be pushed onto the stack must be supplied to the procedure. This is achieved by specifying a *formal parameter i* in the definition of the procedure

```
procedure push (i: itemtype) ;
  var p: stackp ;
  begin
    new(p) ;
    with p ↑ do begin item :=i; previousitem := topmost end ;
    topmost := p
  end
```

and by supplying a corresponding *actual parameter* in the call of the procedure

$$\ldots ; push(j) ; \ldots$$

When the procedure is called, a variable *i* is created, corresponding to the formal parameter, and is assigned the value of the corresponding actual parameter *j*, which may be any expression that yields a value of type *itemtype*. An actual parameter, such as this, that must yield a value, is called a *value parameter*.

Variable parameters

The operation *pop* may also be written as a procedure but, as the purpose of this operation is to *return* a value to the calling program, the latter must specify as an actual parameter the name of the variable to which the result is to be assigned; such a parameter is called a *variable parameter*. The declaration of the corresponding formal parameter is prefaced by **var** as in the following example.

```
procedure pop (var i: itemtype) ;
  var p: stackp ;
  begin
  p := topmost ;
  with p ↑ do begin i := item ; topmost := previousitem end ;
  dispose(p)
  end
```

When the procedure is called,

$$\ldots ; pop(j) ; \ldots$$

all operations referring to *i* within the procedure in fact operate on the variable *j*—in this case the actual parameter must be a *variable* of type *itemtype*.

Functions

The stack operation *empty*, which returns a Boolean value when it is executed, may be defined as a *function* which in form closely resembles a procedure but returns a single value as the result of its execution.

```
function empty: Boolean ;
  begin empty := (topmost = nil) end
```

The function is called by using its name as an operand in an expression, e.g.

$$\ldots ; \textbf{if } empty \textbf{ then} \ldots ;$$

Evaluation of an expression containing a function call causes the function block to be executed. The value assigned to the function name during this execution is then used as the corresponding operand value in the expression evaluation. Functions, like procedures, may have parameters.

Lifetime and scope

In each of the procedures *release*, *push*, and *pop* programmed earlier, a variable *p* is declared within the procedure block itself. This indicates that the variable is used only within the procedure and is of no significance outside the procedure block. The variable is said to be *local* to the procedure in this case. Using the same name, *p*, for the local variables of the three procedures does not imply any relationship between the variables themselves.

In contrast, all the procedures make use of the same variable *topmost*, which points to the top of the stack on which they operate. The declaration of this variable must be such that the name *topmost* denotes the *same* variable in all the procedures.

The definitions of blocks as they appear in the program text are nested—the definition of any block may contain further block definitions within it. This textual or *static* nesting is used to determine the accessibility of the identifiers introduced in blocks, as follows. The accessibility or *scope* of each identifier is limited to the block in which it is defined or declared, including any local blocks. Thus no identifier may be used outside the block in which it is defined or declared.

In each of the procedures *release*, *push* and *pop* above, the variable *p* is declared within the procedure block and can be used only within that procedure—it is not accessible to the enclosing block. However, the variable *topmost* is presumably declared in the enclosing block and is therefore accessible within the procedure *release*, and within any other procedures that manipulate the stack which *topmost* represents.

When an identifier is defined in two or more nested blocks, the innermost accessible definition applies to each particular use of that identifier.

On entry to a block, the variables declared there come into being, and the compound statement that constitutes the body of the block is executed; then, on exit from the block, the variables cease to exist. Thus the lifetimes of the variables declared within, or *local* to, a block are limited to the lifetime of that block. Also, within one block other blocks may be entered, perhaps by procedure calls, and the lifetimes of the latter are nested within the lifetime of the former. This nesting of lifetimes, which depends on the sequence in which blocks are invoked, is known as *dynamic* nesting.

Recursion

The body of a procedure may contain calls on that procedure and this *recursive* use of a procedure, or of a function, can be very valuable when programming a problem that is inherently recursive. As a simple example consider a procedure to reverse a sequence of characters terminated by an asterisk.

```
procedure reversesequence ;
    var c: char ;
    begin
        read(c) ;
        if c ≠ '*' then reversesequence ;
        write(c)
    end
```

When this procedure is called to reverse a sequence '*xyz**' a variable c comes into being and the compound statement reads 'x' into c and then calls the procedure again to reverse the remaining sequence 'yz*'; when this has been done the string '*zy' will have written been out and finally the 'x' can be written out from the variable c. Thus when the asterisk is being processed there will be four nested instances of the procedure in being, each with its own local variable c holding one of the four characters of the string.

In the example above, the recursive procedure *reversesequence* calls itself directly. In some cases two procedures A and B are mutually recursive, i.e. procedure A calls procedure B which in turn calls procedure A. . . . Most Pascal compilers require that the parameter list of a procedure is specified before any call of the procedure in the program text. For mutually recursive procedures this is accomplished as follows:

```
procedure B (parameter list of B) ; forward ;
procedure A (parameter list of A);
    begin
        .
        .
        B ( )
        .
        .
    end ;

procedure B ;
    begin
        .
        .
        A ( )
        .
        .
    end ;
```

The first declaration of B defines its parameter list and indicates that the definition of its action will be given later. The second declaration of B provides this definition, but the parameter list details need not be repeated.

Envelopes

Returning to the example of the stack we may illustrate another use of block structure. The realization of the stack that we have programmed so far has the following overall form.

> **type** *stackp* = ...
> **var** *topmost* : *stackp* ;
> **procedure** *push* (*i: itemtype*) ;
>
> ...
>
> **procedure** *pop* (**var** *i: itemtype*) ;
>
> ...
>
> **function** *empty* : *Boolean* ;
>
> ...
>
> **procedure** *release* ; ...

While the implementation details of the stack operations are hidden within the procedures, the realization still has the following disadvantages.

(a) The variable *topmost* and the types defining it are shared by all the procedures and must be declared in a block enclosing their definition. This means that *topmost* is also accessible to the code that uses these procedures.

(b) These procedures depend on some initialization of *topmost* being made before they are used by that code.

(c) To ensure that any residual storage used by the stack is recovered, the procedure *release* must be called after the user's code has been executed.

Ideally we should like to define our stack by a block that would hide completely the data used to implement the stack from the using code; this block would guarantee its initialization and finalization before and after the using code has access to the visible operations.

For this purpose, we introduce a further block structure to our notation, and to Pascal, called an *envelope*. An envelope defines

(a) a data structure;

(b) the operations that can be applied to the data structure, as procedures and functions; and

(c) the initial and final actions that must be applied to the data structure at the moments of its creation and destruction.

For the stack example the appropriate envelope would be as follows:

> **envelope** *stack* ;
> **type** *stackp* = ↑ *stackr* ;
>   *stackr* = **record**
>   *item*: *itemtype* ;
>   *previousitem*: *stackp*
>   **end** ;
> **var** *topmost*: *stackp* ;
> **procedure** **push* (*i*: *itemtype*) ;
>   ... *defined as before* ... ;
> **procedure** **pop* (**var** *i*: *itemtype*) ;
>   ... *defined as before* ... ;
> **function** **empty*: *Boolean* ;
>   ... *defined as before* ... ;
> **procedure** *release* ;
>   ... *defined as before* ... ;
> **begin**
>   *topmost* := **nil** ;
>   *** ;
>   *release*
> **end**

An envelope may be thought of as being a data type with associated code, instances of which can be declared at the head of a block as follows.

> **instance** *S*: *stack*

The effect of this is that the variable *topmost* comes into being and the compound statement that forms the body of the envelope is executed. Firstly *topmost* is initialized; secondly the *inner* statement (represented by ***) is encountered; and finally the procedure *release* is invoked. The effect of the *inner* statement is to execute the rest of the block in which *S*, the instance of the envelope, is declared; during the execution of this block the starred identifiers of the envelope are accessible using the normal dot notation or **with** notation.

> **if** *S.empty* **then** ... **else** ...
> **with** *S* **do begin** ... ; *push*(*j*) ; ... ; *pop*(*j*) ; ... **end**

Starred variables of an envelope may be accessed but not assigned, thereby protecting their integrity. Envelopes, like procedures and functions, may have parameters; however they may not assign values to any global variables.

It is often convenient to be able to declare several instances, thus:

> **instance** *S,T* : *stack* ;

or even an array of envelope instances, thus:

> **instance** *A* : **array** [1 .. 10] **of** *stack* ;

If just one instance of an envelope is required, the definition and declaration may be combined into a single *module* using the notation:

> **envelope module** *S* ;
> **type** *stackp* = ↑ *stackr* ;
>   *stackr* = **record**
>   *item*: *itemtype* ;
>   *previousitem*: *stackp*
>   **end** ;
> **var** *topmost* : *stackp* ;
> ... *procedures defined as before* ...
> **begin**
>   *topmost* := *nil* ;
>   *** ;
>   *release*
> **end**

The attraction of the envelope structure is that it enables us to distinguish between, on the one hand, the declaration and use of an abstract data structure such as a stack, and, on the other hand, the concrete representation of that data structure as a linked list, or whatever representation has been chosen. The block which declares and uses an instance of the envelope has, and needs, no knowledge of that representation. It manipulates the instance purely in terms of the abstract properties presented by the starred identifiers.

The Program

A complete Pascal program is a block preceded by a heading and followed by a full stop. For example, the complete program to reverse a sequence of characters using recursion is as follows.

> **program** *reversal* (*input,output*) ;
> **procedure** *reversesequence* ;
>   **var** *c*: *char* ;
>   **begin**

```
        read(c) ;
        if c ≠ '*' then reversesequence ;
        write(c)
      end ;
   begin
      reversesequence
   end.
```

The same program, but using an explicit stack of characters, is as follows.

```
      program reversal (input,output) ;
        type itemtype = char ;
        var c: itemtype ;
        envelope module S ;
          ⋮
          . . . as already programmed . . .
          ⋮
        begin
          repeat read(c) ; S.push(c) until c = '*' ;
          repeat S.pop(c) ; write(c) until S.empty
        end.
```

Processes

To design an operating system we need to extend our notation further; unlike most programs, which are sequential, an operating system involves a fair degree of parallelism: at any moment there may be in the computer several users' programs and also a number of other programs performing such services as controlling peripheral devices: all these programs may be proceeding in parallel (if there are enough processors, and in quasi-parallel otherwise) and each of these programs we term a *process*. We therefore extend our sequential programming language with notations to define processes and to declare instances of them. Each process is defined as an ordinary Pascal block preceded by a heading, which may have parameters:

```
      process producer ;
        var i: itemtype ;
        begin
          repeat
            produce item i ;
            put i into buffer
          until switch off
        end
```

and instances of a process may be declared as follows:

instance *P*: **array** [1 .. 3] **of** *producer*

If only one instance is required, the definition and declaration may be combined into a single module:

process module *P* ;
  var *i*: *itemtype* ;
  begin
    repeat
      produce item i ;
      put i into buffer
    until *switch off*
  end

If, for example, we wish to simulate the actions of three producers, which are producing items to be put into some common buffer, and four consumers, which are getting items from the buffer for consumption, we may define a process to model a producer and declare three instances of it (as above), and we may declare four instances of a process that models the actions of a consumer.

program *producers and consumers* ;
  {*declaration of a data structure to represent a buffer*} ;
  process *producer* ;
  var *i*: *itemtype* ;
  begin
    repeat
      produce item i ;
      put i into buffer
    until *switch off*
  end ;
  process *consumer* ;
  var *i*: *itemtype* ;
  begin
    repeat
      get i from buffer ;
      consume item i
    until *switch off*
  end ;
  instance

> *P*: **array** [1 .. 3] **of** *producer* ;
> *C*: **array** [1 .. 4] **of** *consumer* ;
> **begin**
>   {*initialization of program*} ;
>   *** ;
>   { *finalization of program*}
> **end**.

The seven producer and consumer processes are activated when the *inner* statement of the program block is encountered. They then proceed in parallel with one another until they terminate, whereupon the finalization of the program block is performed.

   Associated with each process is a priority represented by a non-negative integer value; this is used to determine which process should run next if there are insufficient processors to run all the processes simultaneously. A process may set its priority to some value, *p* say, by a call on a procedure *setpriority*(*p*); the smaller the value of *p* the higher is the priority.

Monitors

The processes of a program are not usually entirely independent of one another: in the previous example the seven producers and consumers all accessed the common buffer. Chaos would result if processes were able to access such global data in an unregulated manner and so we define the buffer, together with the operations, *put* and *get*, that may be performed on it and also its initialization and finalization, in the form of an envelope—but this envelope, being shared, must have the property, termed *mutual exclusion*, that only one process at a time may be executing one of its procedures: this form of envelope is called a *monitor*. Monitors are defined and declared in the same way as envelopes.

> **monitor module** *buffer* ;
>   **var** *item*: **array** [1 .. 100] **of** *itemtype* ;
>   *putcount*, *getcount*: *integer* ;
>   **procedure** *put (*i*: *itemtype*) ;
>   **begin**
>   **if** *putcount* − *getcount* = 100 **then** *wait until not full*;
>   *item* [*putcount* **mod** 100 + 1] := *j* ;
>   *putcount* := *putcount* + 1
>   **end** ;
>   **procedure** *get (**var** *i*: *itemtype*) ;
>   **begin**
>   **if** *putcount* − *getcount* = 0 **then** *wait until not empty* ;

$$i := item \; [getcount \; \textbf{mod} \; 100 + 1] \; ;$$
$$getcount := getcount + 1$$
end ;
begin *putcount* $:= 0$; *getcount* $:= 0$; *** **end**

Now *put i into buffer* and *get i from buffer* can be replaced by *buffer.put(i)* and *buffer.get(i)* respectively. Thus the only way in which a process may access global variables is indirectly, through a procedure or function of a monitor. Mutual exclusion can be enforced by suitable code on entry to and exit from monitor procedures and functions.

To ease implementation, instances of monitors and processes may be declared only within monitors (and the complete program block is deemed to be a monitor). Thus there is no dynamic creation of processes and so each process can be assigned enough space for its stack before execution, providing a limit is placed on the depth of procedure and function recursion allowed.

Conditions

Because a monitor is used by more than one process it is feasible for a process that is unable to continue (e.g. a producer that finds the buffer full) to wait until it is enabled to continue by some other process (e.g. a consumer that removes an item from the buffer). Therefore, for each condition (e.g. that the buffer be not full) that must hold before a process can continue, we introduce a queue on which processes can wait until signaled to continue by other processes. In our example we declare two such condition queues:

instance *notfull, notempty: condition*

and we replace *wait until not full* and *wait until not empty* by *notfull.wait* and *notempty.wait* respectively, and at the end of *put* and *get* we add *notempty. signal* and *notfull.signal* respectively. When a process waits, it is appended to its condition queue and the exclusion on the monitor is released. When a process signals, it immediately passes control to the process at the head of the condition queue and is delayed until the awoken process has released the exclusion on the monitor; a signal has no effect if no process is waiting on the condition queue.

Normally a signal will cause the longest waiting process to be resumed and this is a good simple scheduling strategy that prevents a process from being overtaken indefinitely often. However, there are many cases where this is inadequate and so, to give closer control over the scheduling strategy, we introduce a version of the wait operation, *pwait*, that specifies a priority in the form of a non-negative integer parameter so that processes are queued in order of decreasing priority (the smaller the integer, the higher the priority). We also permit a process to determine the *length* of a condition queue and, if the queue is not empty, the *priority* of the process at the head of it. For example, a process might wish to wait on a condition queue, *c*, only if its priority, represented by *p*, is lower than that of the process (if any) at the head of the queue.

$$\text{if } c.length > 0 \text{ then if } c.priority < p \text{ then } c.pwait(p)$$

As an example of a very simple operating system scheduler, consider a monitor to schedule the use of a single lineprinter which different processes wish to use from time to time. To record the availability of the device we need a Boolean variable, *free*, and to delay processes wishing to use the printer when it is unavailable we require a condition queue, *released*; we provide the processes with two procedures, *acquire* and *release*.
Our scheduler is programmed as follows:

```
monitor module lpscheduler ;
  var free: Boolean ;
  instance released: condition ;
  procedure *acquire ;
    begin
      if not free then released.wait ;
      free := false
    end ;
  procedure *release ;
    begin
      free := true ;
      released.signal
    end ;
  begin
    free := true ;
    ***
  end
```

Each process can then bracket its use of the lineprinter between calls on *lpscheduler.acquire* and *lpscheduler.release*.

Section 2

A STRUCTURED COMPILER

The primary objective of this section is to illustrate the application of structured programming techniques to the construction of a compiler for a small programming language. Where specific compilation techniques are used they are introduced in simple terms.

The first chapter presents an informal specification of the compiler to be constructed, and serves both to define the nature of a compiler and to identify the significant factors that influence its construction. Subsequent chapters trace the step-by-step refinement of a compiler program which meets these requirements.

There is a gradual increase in "pace" in the discussion of design and programming decisions throughout the section. In the early chapters the pace is gentle, allowing the reader to become accustomed to the problems of compilation and the style of programming in use. In later chapters the pace quickens with only some of the programming decisions being discussed in detail. However the program listings incorporated in each chapter show the complete final outcome of the design and programming strategy.

THE COMPILER SPECIFICATION

A compiler is a computer program which accepts as input another program expressed in a given language (which we call the *source* language), and produces as output an equivalent program in another language (the *object* or *target* language), together with a listing of the source program input.

The Input

At first sight the input which a compiler is required to handle is perfectly defined, since the source-language definition determines exactly the set of programs for which the compiler may be asked to generate equivalent object code. However a practical compiler is expected not only to generate object code for the correct programs of the source language, but also to diagnose faults in incorrect ones. In practice therefore all inputs to a compiler must be accepted and treated in some appropriate manner.

The source-language definition remains the central component of the compiler writer's specification. Definition of the structure or syntax of programs is well understood and a standard notation—the so-called *Backus-Naur Form* or *BNF*—is widely used in language definitions. Formal definition of the meaning or semantics given to programs, and the semantic constraints which the language rules impose, is a more difficult problem and no generally accepted method has so far emerged.

A definition of the model language whose implementation we shall consider is given in the next chapter. The definition takes the form of a formal syntax description, using an augmented BNF notation, accompanied by an informal semantic description in natural language. The language defined, which we call Mini-Pascal, is a small subset of the Pascal language and its definition is derived directly from the Pascal Report. As we shall see the formal syntax definition greatly assists the compiler writer in determining the structural framework of the compiler, while the informal description of semantics leaves a much greater burden on him in the realization of semantic analysis and object-program generation.

The Output

The output from a compiler comes in two parts—the object program generated and the program listing. Remembering that the compiler will deal with more incorrect than correct programs, the qualities of the program listing and error messages produced may be as important as those of the object code.

The program listing

The source-program listing output by the compiler provides

(a) a confirmation, and permanent visual record, of the source program compiled;
(b) an indication of all errors detected by the compiler.

The exact form in which these are provided is usually left to the compiler writer to determine. Doing so is a straightforward, if sometimes neglected, exercise in man/machine engineering.

The user programmer expects the compiler

(a) to enforce every language rule;
(b) to find all violations of the language rules in a single compilation run;
(c) to generate no spurious or misleading error reports due to preceding errors.

Achieving (b) and (c) implies that the compiler must resume compilation immediately after detecting each error as if the error had not existed. Clearly this is an impossible task in some situations. However, this need for *error recovery* is a dominant influence on the compiler design.

The object program generated

The object program output by the compiler is expressed in a precisely defined language, e.g. the machine language of the object machine, but the compiler writer is left the freedom to choose the way in which source-language features are expressed in the object language. He does so subject to specifiable requirements of the object program produced, e.g.

(a) its compactness or storage economy;
(b) its speed in execution;
(c) the security against run-time errors which it provides;
(d) the run-time diagnostic facilities which it provides.

It is soon apparent, however, that some of these desirable characteristics of the object program are mutually conflicting, and cannot all be realized in a single object-program form. The code generated by any particular compiler represents some compromise between them, according to the particular priorities adopted in its construction. In the Mini-Pascal compiler the generation of compact, reasonably efficient machine code for a realistic machine will be illustrated. Details of the machine will be given later.

Specified Design Constraints

Like any other program a compiler may be subject to constraints on its design and implementation. These constraints stem from the general objectives of software construction such as:

Reliability

Compiler reliability is not achieved by techniques peculiar to compiler construction. It results rather from a simple well-structured design, which gives a logical separation of concerns, and the use of simple well-understood techniques for their realization. The rôle played by modular development, and modular testing, in achieving reliability is well illustrated by the Mini-Pascal compiler.

Efficiency

Efficiency requirements of object programs were mentioned as part of the compiler's output specification. However, if a compiler is used as frequently as the programs which it produces, then its own efficiency becomes significant. Compiler efficiency involves three factors:

(a)   speed of compilation;

(b)   storage used during compilation;

(c)   backing store usage during compilation.

All three factors warrant economy in the construction of a compiler. Compilers are often constructed as multi-pass systems for reasons of language design, main storage limitation, or conceptual simplicity. However the backing store transfers involved in multi-pass compilation are a very significant overhead in many environments. As we shall see, the conceptual simplification of the compilation process into several component processes can be achieved without enforcing multi-pass operation on the compiler which carries it out.

Flexibility

Flexibility is a particular virtue in system programs whose useful lifetime may span many changes in their working environment.

An obvious flexibility for a compiler is a capacity to generate object code for a totally different target machine. Much of the effort of writing a compiler for a given language is machine independent, but if this commonality of effort is to be fully exploited in producing compilers for other machines a compiler structure which separates the machine-dependent and machine-independent aspects must be chosen at an early stage in the design.

A less radical but commonly required flexibility in system software is device independence. If the environment in which the compiler runs does not support device independent I/O, then it must be realized within the compiler itself. The ease with which this can be done is again dependent on the degree to which the chosen compiler structure isolates the device dependencies within the overall compilation process.

To illustrate the influence which such considered flexibility may have on a program's development, both the above will be incorporated in the specification of the Mini-Pascal compiler.

A Specification Summary

In summary the specification we adopt for the Mini-Pascal compiler is as follows:

(a) it must compile the language Mini-Pascal as defined in the language definition which follows;
(b) it must achieve an acceptable level of error recovery;
(c) it must generate reasonably efficient machine code for the chosen target computer;
(d) it must be reliable;
(e) it should be reasonably efficient in time, storage and backing-store utilization;
(f) it should be adaptable to
   (i) a variety of I/O devices on the given machine,
   (ii) generation of object code for different machines.

DEFINITION OF MINI-PASCAL

Introduction

Mini-Pascal is a small subset of the language Pascal, defined for two purposes:

(a) as a suitable language for teaching the elementary principles of computer programming;
(b) as a suitable language for illustrating the techniques and problems of compiler construction.

This definition is intended therefore as a model of the language definitions which programmers must be able to read, and on which compiler writers must base the compilers which they construct. Its form and content are derived directly from the *Pascal User Manual and Report* by Jensen and Wirth.

Summary of the Language

An algorithm or computer program consists of two essential parts, a description of *actions* which are to be performed, and a description of the *data* which are manipulated by these actions. Actions are described by *statements*, and data are described by *declarations*.

The data are represented by values of *variables*. Every variable occurring in a statement must be introduced by a *variable declaration* which associates an identifier and a data type with that variable. The *data type* essentially defines the set of values which may be assumed by that variable.

The basic data types are the standard types: *Boolean, integer, char*. Except for the type Boolean, their values are not denoted by identifiers, but instead by numbers and quotations respectively. These are syntactically distinct from identifiers. The set of values of type char is the character set available on a particular installation.

A type may also be an *array type*, each value of which comprises a number of components all of the same component type. A component is selected by a *computable index*, whose range is indicated in the array type definition and which must be of the type integer. Given a value of the index range, an indexed variable yields a value of the component type.

The most fundamental statement is the *assignment statement*. It specifies that a newly computed value is to be assigned to a variable (or components of a variable). The value is obtained by evaluating an *expression*. Expressions consist of variables, constants, and operators operating on the denoted values and producing new values. Mini-Pascal defines a fixed set of operators, each of which can be regarded as describing a mapping from the operand types into the result type. The set of operators is subdivided into groups as follows:

1. *arithmetic operators* of addition, subtraction, inversion, multiplication and division;
2. *Boolean operators* of negation, union (or), and conjunction (and);
3. *relational operators* of equality, inequality, ordering.

A program has at its disposal an *input device* and an *output device*. The input device is capable of delivering information to the program in the form of a continuous character stream. The output device is capable of receiving information from the program in the form of a continuous character stream. Transfer of information from or to the input or output devices is caused by *read* or *write statements* within the program.

The *procedure statement* causes the execution of the designated procedure (see below). Assignment, read, write, and procedure statements are the components or building blocks of *structured statements*, which specify sequential, selective, or repeated execution of their components. Sequential execution of statements is specified by the *compound statement*, conditional or selective execution by the *if statement*, repeated execution by the *while statement*.

A statement can be given a name (identifier), and be referenced through that identifier. The statement is then called a *procedure*, and its declaration is a *procedure declaration*. Such a declaration may additionally contain a set of variable declarations, or further procedure declarations, to form a *block*. Since procedures may thus be declared within the blocks defining other procedures, blocks may be nested. This nested block structure determines the range of use, or *scope*, of the identifiers denoting variables, procedures, types and constant values, and also determines the *lifetime* of variables.

Notation, Terminology and Vocabulary

According to traditional Backus–Naur form, syntactic constructs are denoted by English words enclosed between the angular brackets $\langle$ and $\rangle$. These words also describe the nature or meaning of the construct, and are used in the accompanying description of semantics. In our extension of BNF possible repetition of a construct zero or more times is indicated by enclosing the construct within braces { and }. The symbol $\langle empty \rangle$ denotes the null sequence of symbols.

The basic vocabulary of Mini-Pascal consists of basic symbols classified into letters, digits, and special symbols.

$\langle letter \rangle ::=$ $\quad A|B|C|D|E|F|G|H|I|J|K|L|M|N|O|P|Q|R|S|$
$\quad\quad\quad\quad\quad\quad T|U|V|W|X|Y|Z|a|b|c|d|e|f|g|h|i|j|k|l|m|n|$
$\quad\quad\quad\quad\quad\quad o|p|q|r|s|t|u|v|w|x|y|z|$

$\langle digit \rangle ::=$ $\quad 0|1|2|3|4|5|6|7|8|9$

$\langle special\ symbols \rangle ::=$ $\quad +\ |\ -\ |\ *\ |\ =\ |\ <>\ |\ <\ |\ >\ |\ <=\ |\ >=\ |$
$\quad\quad\quad\quad\quad\quad\quad\quad (\ |\ )\ |\ [\ |\ ]\ |\ :=\ |\ .\ |\ ,\ |\ ;\ |\ :\ |\ ..\ |\ \textbf{div}\ |\ \textbf{or}\ |$
$\quad\quad\quad\quad\quad\quad\quad\quad \textbf{and}\ |\ \textbf{not}\ |\ \textbf{if}\ |\ \textbf{then}\ |\ \textbf{else}\ |\ \textbf{of}\ |\ \textbf{while}\ |\ \textbf{do}\ |$
$\quad\quad\quad\quad\quad\quad\quad\quad \textbf{begin}\ |\ \textbf{end}\ |\ \textbf{read}\ |\ \textbf{write}\ |\ \textbf{var}\ |\ \textbf{array}\ |$
$\quad\quad\quad\quad\quad\quad\quad\quad \textbf{procedure}\ |\ \textbf{program}$

Identifiers

Identifiers denote constants, types, variables, and procedures. Their association must be unique within the block in which they are declared (see Procedure Declarations and Programs below).

$\quad\quad\quad\quad \langle identifier \rangle ::= \langle letter \rangle\{\langle letter\ or\ digit \rangle\}$
$\quad\quad\quad\quad \langle letter\ or\ digit \rangle ::= \langle letter \rangle\ |\ \langle digit \rangle$

Constants

Constants are the particular values which variables of the basic types, *integer*, *char* and *Boolean* may take.

The usual decimal notation is used for those natural numbers which are constants of the data type *integer*

$$\langle integer\ constant \rangle ::= \langle digit \rangle \{ \langle digit \rangle \}$$

Examples

$$0 \quad 1 \quad 100$$

The constants of the data type *char* are denoted by the character involved enclosed in quote marks. If the character is itself a quote mark the quote mark is written twice

$$\langle character\ constant \rangle ::= {}'\langle any\ character\ other\ than\ '\rangle'\ |\ '\ '\ '\ '$$

Examples

$$'A' \quad ';' \quad '\ ' \quad ''''$$

The constants of the data type *Boolean* are denoted by the identifiers *true* and *false*. These are the only constant identifiers in Mini-Pascal:

$$\langle constant\ identifier \rangle ::= \langle identifier \rangle$$
$$\langle constant \rangle ::= \langle integer\ constant \rangle\ |\ \langle character\ constant \rangle\ |$$
$$\langle constant\ identifier \rangle$$

Data Types

A data type determines the set of values which variables of that type may assume

$$\langle type \rangle ::= \langle simple\ type \rangle\ |\ \langle array\ type \rangle$$

Simple types

$$\langle simple\ type \rangle ::= \langle type\ identifier \rangle$$
$$\langle type\ identifier \rangle ::= \langle identifier \rangle$$

The following types are standard in Mini-Pascal:

integer   The values are a subset of the whole numbers defined by individual implementations. Its values are denoted as described under Constants.

Boolean Its values are the truth values denoted by the identifiers *true* and *false*.

char Its values are a set of characters determined by particular implementations. They are denoted by the characters themselves enclosed within quotes. Characters which are letters or digits are ordered in a manner consistent with alphabetic or numeric ordering. Thus

$$'A' < 'B' < 'C' \ldots$$
$$'0' < '1' < '2' \ldots$$

Array types

An array type is a structure consisting of a fixed number of components which are all of the same type, called the *component type*. The elements of the array are designated by indices, values belonging to a certain *index range*. The array type definition specifies the component type as well as the index range.

⟨*array type*⟩ ::= **array** [⟨*index range*⟩] **of** ⟨*component type*⟩
⟨*index range*⟩ ::= ⟨*unsigned integer*⟩ . . ⟨*unsigned integer*⟩
⟨*component type*⟩ ::= ⟨*simple type*⟩

Examples

array [1 . . 100] **of** *integer*
array [1 . . 80] **of** *char*

Declarations and Denotations of Variables

Variable declarations consist of a list of identifiers denoting the new variables, followed by their type.

⟨*variable declaration*⟩ ::= ⟨*identifier*⟩{,⟨*identifier*⟩} : ⟨*type*⟩

Examples

x,y,z: *integer*
i,j: *integer*
p,q: *Boolean*
a: **array** [0 . . 63] **of** *integer*

Denotations of variables designate either an entire variable or an indexed variable. Variables occurring in the examples in subsequent sections are assumed to be declared as indicated above.

⟨*variable*⟩ ::= ⟨*entire variable*⟩ | ⟨*indexed variable*⟩

Entire variables

An entire variable is denoted by its identifier.

⟨*entire variable*⟩ ::= ⟨*variable identifier*⟩
⟨*variable identifier*⟩ ::= ⟨*identifier*⟩

Indexed variables

A component of an array variable is denoted by the variable followed by an index expression.

⟨*indexed variable*⟩ ::= ⟨*array variable*⟩ [⟨*expression*⟩]
⟨*array variable*⟩ ::= ⟨*entire variable*⟩

The type of the index expression must be integer and its value must lie in the range defined by the array type.

Examples

$a[12]$
$a[i+j]$

Expressions

Expressions are constructs denoting rules of computation for obtaining values of variables and generating new values by the application of operators. Expressions consist of operands (i.e. variables and constants) and operators.

The rules of composition specify operator *precedences* according to four classes of operators. The operator **not** has the highest precedence, followed by the multiplying operators, then the adding operators, and finally, with the lowest precedence, the relational operators. Sequences of operators of the same precedence are executed from left to right. The rules of precedence are reflected by the following syntax.

⟨*factor*⟩ ::= ⟨*variable*⟩ |⟨*constant*⟩ |(⟨*expression*⟩) |
    not ⟨*factor*⟩
⟨*term*⟩ ::= ⟨*term*⟩{⟨*multiplying operator*⟩ ⟨*factor*⟩}
⟨*simple expression*⟩ ::= ⟨*sign*⟩ ⟨*term*⟩{⟨*adding operator*⟩ ⟨*term*⟩}
⟨*expression*⟩ ::= ⟨*simple expression*⟩ |
    ⟨*simple expression*⟩ ⟨*relational operator*⟩ ⟨*simple expression*⟩
⟨*multiplying operator*⟩ ::= * | **div** | **and**
⟨*sign*⟩   ::= + | − | ⟨*empty*⟩
⟨*adding operator*⟩   ::= + | − | **or**
⟨*relational operator*⟩   ::= = | <> | < | > | <= | >=

Examples

Factors	x
	15
	$(x+y+x)$
	not p
Terms	$x * y$
	$(x<=y)$ **and** $(y<z)$
Simple expressions	$x+y$
	$-x$
	$i * j + 1$
Expressions	$x = 1$
	$p <= q$
	$(i < j) = (j < k)$

Operators

The operator **not**
The operator **not** denotes negation of its Boolean operand.

Multiplying operators

Operator	Operation	Type of operands	Type of result
*	multiplication	both integer	integer
div	division with truncation	both integer	integer
and	logical "and"	both Boolean	Boolean

Adding operators

Operator	Operation	Type of operands	Type of result
+	addition	both integer	integer
−	subtraction	both integer	integer
or	logical "or"	both Boolean	Boolean

When used with one (integer) operand only, − denotes sign inversion, and + denotes the identity operation.

Relational operators

Operator	Type of operands	Result
= <> < > <= >=	both integer or both char	Boolean

The operators $<>$, $<=$, $>=$ stand for unequal, less or equal, and greater or equal respectively.

Statements

Statements specify actions of a computer, and are *executable*.

$$\langle statement \rangle ::= \langle simple\ statement \rangle \,|\, \langle structured\ statement \rangle$$

Simple statements

A simple statement is a statement which does not contain another statement.

$$\langle simple\ statement \rangle ::= \langle assignment\ statement \rangle \,|$$
$$\langle procedure\ statement \rangle \,|\, \langle read\ statement \rangle \,|\, \langle write\ statement \rangle$$

Assignment statements

The assignment statement replaces the current value of a variable by a new value denoted by an expression.

$$\langle assignment\ statement \rangle ::= \langle variable \rangle := \langle expression \rangle$$

The variable and the expression must be of identical type.

Examples

$$x := y+z$$
$$p := (1 <= i)\ \textbf{and}\ (i < 100)$$

Procedure statements

A procedure statement executes the procedure denoted by the procedure identifier.

$$\langle procedure\ statement \rangle ::= \langle procedure\ identifier \rangle$$

Examples

> *next*
> *Transpose*

Read statements

A read statement transfers values from the input device to one or more specified variables of the program

> ⟨*read statement*⟩ ::= **read** (⟨*input variable*⟩{,⟨*input variable*⟩})
> ⟨*input variable*⟩ ::= ⟨*variable*⟩

Each input variable must be of type integer or of type char. Values are transferred from the input device in the order in which the variables appear in the read statement. For a variable of type char the value transferred is the next character from the input device. For a variable of type integer the value transferred is that denoted by a sequence of characters from the input device. This sequence of characters must conform to the syntax for integer constants given above optionally preceded by a + or − sign and/or an arbitrary number of blanks. Successive integer values must be separated by at least one blank character.

Write statements

A write statement transfers values from the program to the output device

> ⟨*write statement*⟩ ::= **write** (⟨*output value*⟩{,⟨*output value*⟩})
> ⟨*output value*⟩ ::= ⟨*expression*⟩

Each output value must be an expression of type char, or of type integer. Values are transferred to the output device in the order in which they appear in the write statement. A value of type char is transferred as the single character denoted. A value of type integer is transferred as the sequence of decimal digits denoting its value, preceded by a − sign when appropriate, and possibly some blanks. The length of the sequence of characters transferred is a constant sufficiently large to accommodate all integers representable on the object machine.

Structured statements

Structured statements are constructs composed of other statements which have to be executed either in sequence (compound statement), conditionally (if statements), or repeatedly (while statements).

> ⟨*structured statement*⟩ ::= ⟨*compound statement*⟩ |
> ⟨*if statement*⟩ | ⟨*while statement*⟩

Compound statements

The compound statement specifies that its component statements are to be executed in the same sequence as they are written. The symbols **begin** and **end** act as statement brackets.

⟨*compound statement*⟩ ::= **begin** ⟨*statement*⟩{;⟨*statement*⟩} **end**

Example

begin $z := x$; $x := y$; $y := z$ **end**

If statements

The if statement specifies that a statement be executed only if a certain condition (Boolean expression) is true. If it is false, then the statement following the symbol **else** is to be executed; or if there is no **else**, no action is performed.

⟨*if statement*⟩ ::= **if** ⟨*expression*⟩ **then** ⟨*statement*⟩ |
    if ⟨*expression*⟩ **then** ⟨*statement*⟩ **else** ⟨*statement*⟩

The expression between the symbols **if** and **then** must be of Boolean type.

Example

if $x < 1$ **then** $z := x + y$ **else** $z := 1$

Note   The syntactic ambiguity arising from the construct

if ⟨*expression-1*⟩ **then** **if** ⟨*expression-2*⟩ **then** ⟨*statement-1*⟩
    else ⟨*statement-2*⟩

is resolved by interpreting the construct as equivalent to

if ⟨*expression-1*⟩ **then**
begin if ⟨*expression-2*⟩ **then** ⟨*statement-1*⟩ **else** ⟨*statement-2*⟩
end

i.e., the **else** matches the closest unmatched **then.**

While statements

⟨*while statement*⟩ ::= **while** ⟨*expression*⟩ **do** ⟨*statement*⟩

The expression controlling repetition must be of type Boolean. The statement is repeatedly executed until the expression becomes false. If its value is false at the beginning, the statement is not executed at all.

Procedure Declarations

Procedure declarations define parts of a program and associate identifiers with them so that they can be activated by procedure statements.

⟨*procedure declaration*⟩ ::= ⟨*procedure heading*⟩ ⟨*block*⟩
⟨*block*⟩ ::= ⟨*variable declaration part*⟩
⟨*procedure declaration part*⟩
⟨*statement part*⟩

The *procedure heading* specifies the identifier naming the procedure.

⟨*procedure heading*⟩ ::= **procedure** ⟨*identifier*⟩ ;

The *variable declaration part* contains all variable declarations within the procedure block.

⟨*variable declaration part*⟩ ::= ⟨*empty*⟩ |
var ⟨*variable declaration*⟩{;⟨*variable declaration*⟩} ;

The *procedure declaration part* contains all procedure declarations within the procedure block.

⟨*procedure declaration part*⟩ ::= {⟨*procedure declaration*⟩;}

The *statement part* specifies the algorithmic actions to be executed upon an activation of the procedure by a procedure statement.

⟨*statement part*⟩ ::= ⟨*compound statement*⟩

Identifiers introduced in the variable and procedure declaration parts are *local* to the procedure block, which is called the *scope* of these identifiers. More precisely the scope of an identifier declaration is defined as follows:

(a) The scope of an identifier declaration is the block in which the declaration occurs, and all blocks enclosed in that block, subject to rule (b) which follows.

(b) When an identifier declared in block *A* is redeclared in some block *B* enclosed by *A*, block *B* and all blocks enclosed by it are excluded from the scope of the identifier's declaration in *A*.

An identifier may have at most one declaration in any block, and may be used only within the scope of such a declaration.

Variables declared in a block are created at the beginning of each execution of that block, and cease to exist when its execution is complete. Their values are undefined at the beginning of each execution of the block.

The use of a procedure identifier in a procedure statement within its declaration specifies *recursive* execution of the procedure.

Programs

A Mini-Pascal program has the form of a procedure declaration, except that its heading uses the word *program* instead of *procedure*, and its block is followed by a period.

⟨*program*⟩ ::= ⟨*program heading*⟩ ⟨*block*⟩ .
⟨*program heading*⟩ ::= **program** ⟨*identifier*⟩ ;

The identifier following the symbol **program** is the program name; it has no further significance inside the program.

Identifiers declared within the program block are called *global*, since their scope comprises the program block and all enclosed procedure blocks, except those in which they are redeclared.

Variables declared in the program block are created at the beginning of execution of the program, i.e. of its statement part, and remain in existence throughout its execution.

The standard identifiers *integer, char, Boolean, false* and *true* have a scope which encloses the program block, and are thus usable throughout the program, except in blocks where they are redeclared.

SOURCE HANDLING

Isolating Device Dependencies

Our initial concept of a compiler was a program which takes a source program as input and produces an object program and a listing as output. Our first formal expression of the compiler's structure might thus be

compiler (*source program*) (*object program, listing*)

where

1. *source program* denotes the program to be compiled;
2. *object program* denotes the translated program;
3. *listing* denotes the program listing produced.

All three of these involve physical representation on some input, output or storage media. Their format is in general dependent on the devices or media involved. Since device independence was identified as an objective for the compiler a logical refinement on this first model is to isolate the device dependencies from the compiler proper, by introducing

1. An *input handler*   which converts the device-dependent source into a device-independent form.
2. An *output handler* which composes a device-oriented listing format by collating the source program input with the errors detected by the compiler proper.
3. A *code handler*   which constructs a device-oriented representation of the object program from the device-independent object code emitted by the compiler proper.

This separation of device-dependent functions gives us a revised model of our compiler structure which is as follows:

> *input handler* (*source program*)(*character stream*)
> *compiler* (*character stream*)(*errors, object code*)
> *output handler* (*source program, errors*)(*listing*)
> *code handler* (*object code*)(*object program*)

The notation used is not intended to imply the order in which these activities take place. They might proceed in sequence, in parallel, or by appropriate interleaving of their component actions. That remains to be determined. What the model has achieved is the separation of the device-dependent activities from the process of compilation proper. If this modularity can be carried into the final compiler program a sound basis for device independence will be achieved.

Realizing such modular structure involves

(a) defining precisely the communication interfaces between the modules;
(b) choosing program structures to represent them;
(c) proceeding with the refinement of the individual modules.

However, attempting to do so for the compiler model given above quickly reveals a practical flaw in the suggested structure.

Both the *input handler* and the *output handler* process the device-dependent representation of the input source program. Practicalities of course dictate that input from a physical device such as a card reader should take place once only. Likewise simple efficiency considerations suggest that any internal saving and re-scanning of the source representation must be avoided whenever possible. The input and output handlers could share a single scan of the source input through a shared line buffer and an appropriate access protocol. But the need for such a shared structure calls into question the practical independence of the input and output handlers.

An alternative is to revise our compiler model, merging the activities of the input and output handlers into a single *source handler*. It is then a question internal to the *source handler* how the input and listing device pair should co-operate.

Our compiler model now has the form

source handler (*source program, errors*)(*character stream, listing*)
compiler (*character stream*)(*errors, object code*)
code handler (*object code*)(*object program*)

We will find that this model remains a valid basis of all subsequent compiler development. It is not appropriate to consider the compiler/code handler interface further at this stage, but we shall proceed to define the source handler/compiler interface and then to develop each module in turn.

Defining the Source Handler/Compiler Interface

The *source handler/compiler* interface involves the transmission of the source character stream from the *source handler* to the *compiler*, and the transmission of error reports from the *compiler* to the *source handler*.

Consider the source character stream first.

Simple efficiency considerations suggest that the compiler should scan the individual characters in the source character stream once only, presumably in left-to-right order. A sufficient interface therefore is that the source handler makes available to the compiler the "current" character in the source stream, say as a variable

$$ch : char ;$$

together with the ability to replace this character by its successor when the compiler wishes. This could be provided as a procedure

procedure *Nextch* ;

Now consider the error reporting. For each error detected the compiler must report to the source handler the *nature* and *position* of the error.

For the nature of the error we shall adopt a simple numeric code, at the interface level. Whether this code is translated into an explicit text message by the source handler is a listing design decision which affects only the source handler.

It is important to realize that the position of the error is not necessarily related to the current character position in the source character stream. Since we should make no assumptions as to how the compiler actually detects errors in this stream, it may be any position in the stream already scanned by the compiler.

The compiler could keep track of the ordinal position of each character in the source stream scanned and express each error position in terms of these. Equally the source handler could relate an ordinal character position to whatever line or text structure it scanned in the original source program.

A little consideration however shows that it is more efficient for the source handler to make available with each character in the source stream a corresponding position value which the compiler may record. This is more efficient because

(a)   the source handler must maintain some such positional coordinates anyhow;

(b)   the compiler need only copy this position at those points to which a subsequent error report may refer.

So we first extend our source character stream interface by a variable

> *positionnow* : *textposition* ;

and then the error reporting interface is easily provided as a procedure

> **procedure** *Error* (*errorcode* : *integer* ;
> *errorposition* : *textposition*) ;

The total interface described can be implemented by declaring the source handler as a module with the structure shown

> **envelope module** *source* ;
> **type**
>   **textposition* = ... ;
> **var**
>   **ch* : *char* ;
>   **positionnow* : *textposition* ;

procedure *Nextch ;

. . .

procedure *Error (errorcode : integer ;

errorposition : textposition) ;

. . .

begin
    {initialize I/O} ;
    *** ;
    {finalize I/O}
end ;

Any use of a source handler's facilities by the compiler must be preceded by some initialization, and followed by some finalization, of the source handler's I/O activities. This bracketing is assured by the use of the inner mechanism in the source-handler body.

Programming the Source Handler

The keynote in programming the facilities provided within the source handler must be efficiency, since the overall efficiency of a compiler is determined largely by the efficiency of its character handling. It is crucial, therefore, that the normal repetitive actions provided by the source handler, primarily the *Nextch* procedure, be programmed as efficiently as possible. With this in mind, the internal structure of the source handler is now considered.

A first model for the action of *Nextch* might be

if current character is last in line
then begin
    list this line ;
    read next line
    end ;
update ch , position for next character

As was anticipated, the position made available to the compiler can also be used within the source handler to control character transmission.

For a line-by-line text format a text position involves a line identity or number, and a character position within the line. Assuming a maximum line length *maxline* we might define a type

charposition = 1 .. maxline

and hence

> *textposition* = **record**
>> *linenumber* : 0 . . 99999 ;
>> *charnumber* : *charposition*
>
> **end**

The line buffer used to hold the source line under scan can now be declared as a variable

> *line* : **packed array** [*charposition*] **of** *char* ;

For some input devices the actual line in the line buffer at any moment may be less than the maximum length, or the first actual character may be preceded by one or more "red-tape" characters which do not form part of the source input. It is convenient to introduce auxiliary variables

> *firstinline* ; *lastinline* : *charposition* ;

to delimit the significant contents of the line buffer at any time.

With these decisions our first model for *Nextch* is easily translated into

> **procedure** *Nextch* ;
>> **begin**
>>> **with** *positionnow* **do**
>>> **begin**
>>>> **if** *charnumber* = *lastinline*
>>>> **then begin**
>>>>> *List this line* ;
>>>>> *Read next line* ;
>>>>> *linenumber* := *linenumber*+1 ;
>>>>> *charnumber* := *firstinline*
>>>>
>>>> **end**
>>>> **else** *charnumber* := *charnumber*+1 ;
>>>> *ch* := *line* [*charnumber*]
>>>
>>> **end**
>>
>> **end** ;

To complete the programming of *Nextch* it remains to refine the actions *List this line* and *Read next line*. However, since these actions

(a) involve the mechanics of actual device manipulation, and

(b)   are also required in the initialization and finalization of the source handler activities,

it is prudent to abstract them as procedures to be called from *Nextch*, and elsewhere as required.

Read next line is a straightforward device-handling procedure which

(a)   transfers the next input record to the line buffer, and
(b)   sets the markers *firstinline*, *lastinline* appropriately.

The dynamic setting of the markers *firstinline*, *lastinline* enables leading and trailing blanks to be "stripped" by a fast scan within *Read next line*, rather than a slow scan

$$\textbf{while } ch = ' \quad ' \textbf{ do } nextch$$

within the compiler proper.

Listthisline depends on the error collection and collation mechanisms chosen. These we consider next.

We will assume that the compiler reports most errors relating to a particular line before moving to the next line, a reasonable assumption for a language such as Mini-Pascal. In this case error-message lines which are interleaved with the source-program text give the most convenient listing format, both from the compiler's and the user's viewpoint. Those messages which refer to a point in the immediately preceding source line can do so by a simple position marker, while those which refer to an earlier line may do so by means of line numbers included in the listing, as the following listing excerpt suggests:

```
 ..  . . . . . . . .
 27   A := A+1 ;
 28   B = B*−A
*****       ↑ ERROR . . .
*****                ↑ ERROR . . .
*****   ERROR . . .   ON LINE 24
```

Thus the source handler needs to accept the hold error reports during the processing of each line, for printout when the end of the line is reached. In these circumstances it is reasonable to set a fairly small upper limit on the number of errors reported during any line. If the compiler exceeds this limit it is more likely that the compiler has failed to recover from one of the first errors reported, and so generated a welter of spurious messages, than that so many genuine independent errors exist. Of course the compiler must tell the user when such messages have been suppressed. So given a limit *errmax* we introduce an array to hold the error code/position pairs:

errorlist : **array** [1 .. *errmax*] **of record**
                              errorposition : *textposition* ;
                              errorcode : *integer*
         end ;

a counter to indicate the number of errors collected so far since the last end of line

errinx : 0 .. *errmax* ;

and finally a flag to indicate when error overflow, with the consequent suppression of further errors, has occurred during processing of a given line

erroroverflow : *Boolean* ;

Besides the individual error reports interleaved with the program text it is useful to provide the user with a summary count of errors reported at the end of the compilation listing. For this purpose we introduce one additional variable

errorcount : *integer* ;

With these decisions the error-collecting procedure *Error*, and the listing procedure *Listthisline*, are both easily programmed. Likewise the initialization and finalization of the source-handler activities are readily programmed, involving only the printing of listing headers and trailers, and the suitable initialization of the variables introduced. Listing 1 shows the complete source handler, using Pascal's standard input and output facilities to realize source input and listing output.

    Test 1 which follows shows a simple driver program used to test the source-handler module, and the output produced from a carefully chosen sequence of input lines. (The driver program makes use of a module inclusion facility provided by the Queen's University Pascal Plus compiler, to extract the source module from the specified library file called Listing 1.)

Listing 1

```
ENVELOPE MODULE SOURCE ;

    (* THE SOURCEHANDLER ENABLES SOURCE TEXT INPUT AND SOURCE LISTING  *)
    (* GENERATION THROUGH THE FOLLOWING ACCESSIBLE PROCEDURES :         *)
    (*                                                                  *)
    (*                                                                  *)
    (* NEXTCH    THIS PROCEDURE READS THE NEXT SOURCE CHARACTER FROM    *)
    (*           THE INPUT STREAM, COPIES IT TO THE OUTPUT STREAM,      *)
    (*           AND LEAVES ITS VALUE IN THE ACCESSIBLE VARIABLE CH .   *)
    (*           THE POSITION OF THE CHARACTER WITHIN THE INPUT TEXT    *)
    (*           IS MAINTAINED IN THE ACCESSIBLE VARIABLE POSITIONNOW . *)
    (*           ENDS OF LINE ARE TRANSMITTED AS BLANK CHARACTERS.      *)
    (*                                                                  *)
    (*                                                                  *)
    (* ERROR     THIS PROCEDURE ENABLES THE ANALYSIS PROCESSES TO       *)
    (*           RECORD ERROR CODE / TEXTPOSITION PAIRS FOR             *)
    (*           PRINTOUT DURING LISTING GENERATION.                    *)
    (*                                                                  *)
    (*                                                                  *)
    (* PROPER INITIALIZATION AND FINALIZATION OF THE SOURCE HANDLING    *)
    (* PROCESS IS ENSURED BY THE SOURCEHANDLER BODY, WHICH ENVELOPES    *)
    (* THE BODY OF THE BLOCK INVOKING IT, BY THE 'INNER' MECHANISM      *)

CONST

    ERRMAX = 6 ;
    MAXLINE = 101 ;

TYPE

    CHARPOSITION = 1..MAXLINE ;

   *TEXTPOSITION = RECORD
                         LINENUMBER : 0..99999 ;
                         CHARNUMBER : CHARPOSITION
                   END ;

VAR

   *CH: CHAR ;
   *POSITIONNOW : TEXTPOSITION ;

    LINE : PACKED ARRAY [CHARPOSITION] OF CHAR ;
    FIRSTINLINE,LASTINLINE : CHARPOSITION :

    ERRORCOUNT : INTEGER ;
    ERRINX : 0..ERRMAX ;
    ERROROVERFLOW : BOOLEAN ;
    ERRLIST : ARRAY [1..ERRMAX] OF
                RECORD
                    ERRORPOSITION : TEXTPOSITION ;
                    ERRORCODE : INTEGER
                END :
```

```
PROCEDURE READNEXTLINE ;

  VAR
     I : CHARPOSITION ;

  BEGIN
     I := 1 ; FIRSTINLINE := I ;
     WHILE NOT EOLN DO BEGIN READ(LINE[I]) ; I:=I+1 END ;
     LINE[I] := ' ' ; LASTINLINE := I ;
     READLN
  END (* READNEXTLINE *) ;


PROCEDURE LISTTHISLINE ;

  VAR
     I : CHARPOSITION ;

  PROCEDURE LISTERRORS ;
     VAR
        K  : 1..ERRMAX ;
     BEGIN
        ERRORCOUNT := ERRORCOUNT + ERRINX ;
        FOR K := 1 TO ERRINX DO
           WITH ERRLIST[K] DO
           BEGIN
              WRITE('*****   ') ;
              IF ERRORPOSITION.LINENUMBER <> POSITIONNOW.LINENUMBER
              THEN WRITE( 'ERROR',ERRORCODE:4,
                          ' AT CHARACTER',
                          ERRORPOSITION.CHARNUMBER-FIRSTINLINE+1:3,
                          ' OF LINE',
                          ERRORPOSITION.LINENUMBER:6)
                 ELSE WRITE( '^ERROR':ERRORPOSITION.CHARNUMBER-FIRSTINLINE+6,
                          ERRORCODE:4) ;
              WRITELN
           END ;
        IF ERROROVERFLOW
        THEN WRITELN('*****   FURTHER ERRORS SUPPRESSED') ;
        WRITELN ;
        ERRINX := 0 ; ERROROVERFLOW := FALSE
     END (* LISTERRORS *) ;

  BEGIN
     WRITE(POSITIONNOW.LINENUMBER:5,'   ') ;
     FOR I := FIRSTINLINE TO LASTINLINE DO WRITE(LINE[I]) ;
     WRITELN ;
     IF ERRINX > 0 THEN LISTERRORS
  END (* LISTTHISLINE *) ;
```

```
PROCEDURE *NEXTCH ;

   BEGIN
      WITH POSITIONNOW DO
      BEGIN
         IF CHARNUMBER = LASTINLINE
         THEN
         BEGIN
            LISTTHISLINE ;
            READNEXTLINE ;
            LINENUMBER := LINENUMBER+1 ;
            CHARNUMBER := FIRSTINLINE
         END
         ELSE CHARNUMBER := CHARNUMBER+1 ;
         CH := LINE[CHARNUMBER]
      END
   END (* NEXTCH *) ;


PROCEDURE *ERROR ( CODE : INTEGER ; POSITION : TEXTPOSITION ) ;

   BEGIN
      IF ERRINX = ERRMAX
      THEN ERROROVERFLOW := TRUE
      ELSE
      BEGIN
         ERRINX := ERRINX+1 ;
         WITH ERRLIST[ERRINX] DO
         BEGIN
            ERRORCODE := CODE ;
            ERRORPOSITION := POSITION
         END ;
      END
   END (* ERROR *) ;



BEGIN
   WRITELN('LISTING PRODUCED BY MINI-PASCAL COMPILER MK 1') ;
   WRITELN ; WRITELN ;
   READNEXTLINE ;
   WITH POSITIONNOW DO
   BEGIN
      LINENUMBER := 0 ;
      CHARNUMBER := FIRSTINLINE ;
      CH := LINE[CHARNUMBER]
   END ;
   ERRORCOUNT := 0 ; ERRINX := 0 ; ERROROVERFLOW := FALSE ;

   *** (* EXECUTE COMPILER *) ;

   LISTTHISLINE ;
   WRITELN ; WRITELN ; WRITE('COMPILATION COMPLETED :') ;
   IF ERRORCOUNT = 0
   THEN WRITE(' NO')
   ELSE WRITE(ERRORCOUNT:5) ;
   WRITELN(' ERRORS REPORTED')
END (* SOURCE MODULE *) ;
```

Test 1

PASCAL PLUS COMPILER

```
 0   3300  PROGRAM TESTSOURCE (INPUT,OUTPUT) ;
 1
 2              ENVELOPE MODULE SOURCE = LISTING1 IN LIBRARY ;
 3
 4   3723      VAR  LASTQUERY : SOURCE.TEXTPOSITION ;
 5
 6   3738      BEGIN
 7   3738        REPEAT
 8   3738          IF SOURCE.CH = '*'
 9   3738          THEN SOURCE.ERROR(1,SOURCE.POSITIONNOW)
10   3748          ELSE IF SOURCE.CH = '?'
11   3750              THEN LASTQUERY := SOURCE.POSITIONNOW
12   3753              ELSE IF SOURCE.CH = '!'
13   3758                  THEN SOURCE.ERROR(2,LASTQUERY) ;
14   3769          SOURCE.NEXTCH
15   3769        UNTIL SOURCE.CH='.'
16   3770      END.
```

```
COMPILATION COMPLETE :       NO ERRORS REPORTED
COMPILATION TIME      =      439 MILLISECONDS
SOURCE PROGRAM        =      188 LINES
OBJECT PROGRAM        =      3830 WORDS
```

LISTING PRODUCED BY MINI-PASCAL COMPILER

```
 0   THE FIRST LINE
 1   A LINE WITH NO ERRORS
 2   A LINE WITH *NE ERROR
*****              ^ERROR   1

 3   A LINE WITH TW* ERR*RS
*****              ^ERROR   1
*****                ^ERROR   1

 4   A LINE WITH SIX ERR*RS  *     *       *  **
*****              ^ERROR   1
*****                ^ERROR   1
*****                  ^ERROR   1
*****                        ^ERROR   1
*****                          ^ERROR   1
*****                            ^ERROR   1
```

```
    5   A LINE WITH L*TS *F ERR*RS  *  *  *  *  *  *  *  *  *  *
*****                 ^ERROR   1
*****                   ^ERROR    1
*****                     ^ERROR    1
*****                       ^ERROR    1
*****                         ^ERROR    1
*****                           ^ERROR    1
*****   FURTHER ERRORS SUPPRESSED

    6   * A LINE WITH AN ERROR IN THE FIRST CHARACTER POSITION
*****   ^ERROR   1

    7   A LINE WITH A RETROS?ECTIVE ERROR, DETECTED ON THE SAME LINE !
*****                        ^ERROR    2

    8   A LINE WITH A RETROS?ECTIVE ERROR,
    9                          DETECTED ON THE NEXT LINE !
*****   ERROR   2 AT CHARACTER 21 OF LINE      8

   10   A RETROS?ECTIVE ERROR WITH OTHER ERR*RS BEF*RE ITS DETECTION!
*****                                    ^ERROR    1
*****                                        ^ERROR   1
*****              ^ERROR    2

   11   THE LAST LINE.


COMPILATION COMPLETED :   21 ERRORS REPORTED
```

Exercise 1   Modify the source-handler module in Listing 1 to screen the leading and trailing blanks on each input line from the attention of the compiler proper.

LEXICAL ANALYSIS

Splitting the Compiler Proper

Isolation of device dependencies left us with a compiler proper of the form

$$compiler\ (character\ stream)(errors,\ object\ code)$$

The two outputs *errors* and *object code* reflect the compiler's underlying twin purposes which are

(a)   to determine if the input program is error free, and to diagnose the errors therein if it is not, and

(b)   to generate an equivalent object code program.

In practice action (b) may be conditional on action (a) finding the program error free, but in any case should make use of the program analysis which (a) must involve. This leads immediately to a subdivision of the compiler process, thus

> *analyzer* (*character stream*)(*errors, analyzed program*)
> *generator* (*analyzed program*)(*object code*)

where *analyzed program* is some representation produced by the analyzer, enabling the generator to produce the object code required.

This splitting of our compiler into *analyzer* and *generator* processes contributes to the objective of achieving flexibility in the form of object code generated. The analyzer in effect represents those aspects of compilation which are machine- or object-code-independent, and its output, the *analyzed program*, can be thought of as a machine-independent expression of the program's meaning or effect. In contrast, the generator must convert this output into a form which is totally dependent on the object machine code, and thus embodies those parts of the compiler which must change when the object code required is changed. The separation is thus not just a conceptual one but a practical means of achieving the flexibility required within the final compiler program. We adopt therefore a two-module structure for the compiler proper, comprising an *analyzer module* and a *generator module*, whose mutual interface, the *analyzed program*, should permit the generation of a variety of object codes by the generator, without any alteration to the analyzer.

Having made this decision, our next step in principle should be to define the *analyzed program* interface before proceeding with the refinement of either the analyzer or generator module. In practice, however, so much of the analyzer is independent of this interface that it is convenient to postpone its definition to a later stage, proceeding for the moment with the development of an open-ended analyzer module of the form

> *analyzer* (*character stream*)(*errors,*   ?   )

Splitting the Analyzer

The primary task of the *analyzer* is to apply the rules of the language definition to the input source program, so determining any errors which exist within it, and its meaning. Our definition distinguishes in form between the (formally expressed) syntax rules, such as

> ⟨*assignment statement*⟩ ::= ⟨*variable*⟩ := ⟨*expression*⟩

and the (informally expressed) semantic rules, such as

"The variable and the expression must be of identical type",

whose enforcement depends on the contextual information established by previous declarations, etc. Since application of the semantic rules depends on prior application of the syntax rules, a logical and commonly made separation of analyzer activities is as follows:

> *syntax analyzer* (*character stream*)(*syntax errors, program syntax*)
> *semantic analyzer* (*program syntax*)(*semantic errors,*   ?   )

In practice a further distinction is usually made within the *syntax analyzer* between the analysis of those sequences of characters which form the individual *symbols* of the program, i.e. identifiers, constants, reserved words etc., and the analysis of the sequence of symbols itself. This distinction is not particularly reflected in the formal language definition, but follows rather from our intuitive conception of program composition in which we regard the symbols as the indivisible atomic building blocks, whose actual representation as character sequences is a mere clerical detail. The symbol-recognition process is usually known as *lexical analysis* or *lexical scanning*, so our model of the overall analysis process is now

> *lexical scanner* (*character stream*)(*lexical errors, symbol stream*)
> *syntax analyzer* (*symbol stream*)(*syntax errors, program syntax*)
> *semantic analyzer* (*program syntax*)(*semantic errors,*   ?   )

This separation of the lexical scanning process has some significance in achieving inter-machine flexibility; while the "language" as such should not change from one machine to another the character set available for its representation may do so, and thus enforce variations in the symbol representations, or "dialects". This character-set dependence is usefully isolated within the lexical scanner.

For this reason, and because of the simplicity of its relationship with the syntax analyzer, we can readily choose to retain the separation of the lexical scanner within the analyzer module of the final compiler program.

Defining the Lexical Scanner Interface

The function of the *lexical scanner* is to transform the character stream transmitted by the *source handler* into a symbol stream suitable for analysis by the *syntax analyzer*. Again we assume that the syntax analyzer will scan the symbols in the symbol stream once only from left to right (a more significant assumption in this case, as we shall see). An adequate interface is that the lexical scanner makes available to the syntax analyzer the "current" symbol in the input symbol stream, together with the ability to replace this symbol by its successor when the syntax analyzer wishes.

What is a symbol? Our intuitive definition of symbols as the words from which a program is composed suggests that a symbol is an identifier, a constant, or one of the special symbols defined in the language definition. We can thus define the range of "values" which a symbol may take as an enumerated type

$$symboltype \; = \; (identifier, \; integer \; constant, \; char \; constant,$$
$$notop, \; andop, \; orop, \ldots \ldots)$$

The suggested interface for the *lexical scanner* is then provided by a variable representing the current symbol

$$symbol \; : \; symboltype \; ;$$

and a procedure which replaces the current symbol by its successor

procedure *Nextsymbol* ;

The syntax analyzer which receives these symbols may subsequently wish to report errors relating to them directly to the source handler, and requires some text position coordinates to do so. The syntax analyzer should not assume that the current position indicated by the source handler is that of the current symbol offered by the lexical scanner. Instead we will require the lexical scanner to make available a text position for each symbol, as an additional variable

$$symbolposition \; : \; textposition \; ;$$

When necessary the syntax analyzer may use this value in reporting errors to the source handler.

The interface so far defined is sufficient for the process of syntax analysis itself. However the process of semantic analysis will require additional knowledge of user-defined symbols, viz. the spelling of each identifier, and the value denoted by each integer or character constant. Whatever interface we define between the syntax and semantic analyzers must transmit this information, and hence the lexical scanner must enable the syntax analyzer to do so. We extend the interface therefore with additional variables

spelling : *alfa* ;
constant : *integer*;

which, respectively, give the relevant identifier spelling when *symbol* = *identifier*, and the equivalent integer value when *symbol* = *integerconstant* or *charconstant*. The type *alfa* must provide some means of representing identifier spellings.

The total interface described can be implemented as a module with the structure shown below. The module structure serves to protect the accessible variables from external assignment and to provide and protect the permanent tables which the scan process presumably requires.

envelope module *scan* ;
var *symbol : *symboltype* ;
*spelling : *alfa* ;
*constant : *integer* ;
*symbolposition : *textposition* ;
procedure *Nextsymbol ;
. . .

Programming the Lexical Scanner

The lexical scanner's function, implemented by its single procedure *Nextsymbol*, is defined by the syntax rules given for special symbols, identifiers and constants in the language definition. We will find however that this definition is incomplete and must be augmented to enable a working lexical scanner to be programmed.

For a free-format language successive calls to the lexical scanner must deal not only with the characters that actually compose the language symbols but also those characters, such as blanks, that are allowed to occur between. The usual rule adopted for Pascal-like languages is that any arbitrary number of blanks may occur between, but not within, the symbols of the program. This might be represented by an additional syntax rule

⟨*symbol*⟩ ::= {⟨*separator*⟩} ⟨*proper symbol*⟩
⟨*separator*⟩ ::= ⟨*blank*⟩
⟨*proper symbol*⟩ ::= ⟨*identifier*⟩ | ⟨*integer constant*⟩ |
⟨*character constant*⟩ | ⟨*special symbol*⟩

This new syntax rule for ⟨*symbol*⟩ leads us intuitively to a corresponding coding for the *Nextsymbol* scan process as follows:

```
procedure Nextsymbol ;
  begin
    with source do
    begin
      while ch = '  ' do Nextch ;
      symbol position := position now ;
      scan proper symbol
    end
  end ;
```

We have assumed that each call of Nextsymbol expects *source.ch* to contain the first possible character of the next symbol already, and leaves in *source.ch* the first character which follows that symbol.

Now consider the representation of the various proper symbols. The language definition represents the special symbols **div, not, begin** etc. as sequences of bold face lower-case letters. Within the printable character sets of most machines such a representation is impossible. The alternatives open to the implementor are

(a) to require the users to distinguish such symbols in some way;
(b) to require no distinction other than context between these symbols and identifiers of the same spelling;
(c) to require no physical distinction between these symbols but to forbid the use of identifiers of the same spelling.

Making choice (c) as the simplest solution acceptable to most users, we correspondingly revise our syntax rules as follows:

$$\langle proper\ symbol \rangle ::= \langle identifier\ or\ reserved\ word \rangle \mid$$
$$\langle integer\ constant \rangle \mid \langle character\ constant \rangle \mid$$
$$\langle special\ symbol \rangle$$
$$\langle identifier\ or\ reserved\ word \rangle ::= \langle letter \rangle \{ \langle letter \rangle \mid \langle digit \rangle \}$$
$$\langle special\ symbol \rangle ::= + \mid - \mid * \mid \ldots \mid ; \mid :$$

Identifiers and reserved words are no longer syntactically distinguished. Correspondingly our scanner will distinguish them only by a secondary process after their character-by-character scan is complete.

With these changes our definition of proper symbols is readily translatable into an equivalent *scan proper symbol* process.

Rewriting the definition yet again in the form

⟨*proper symbol*⟩ ::= ⟨*identifier or reserved word*⟩ |
⟨*integer constant*⟩ |
⟨*character constant*⟩ |
< = | <> | < |
> = | > |
:= | : |
+ |
− |
* |
= |
(|
) |
[|
] |
. |
; |

we see that the alternatives on each line are completely distinguished from those on other lines by the first character involved, and that the occurrence of any other character other than these shown cannot represent a legal symbol at all. This leads us immediately to a code structure for the process *scan proper symbol* as follows

```
case ch of
'A' .. 'Z'   : scan identifier or reserved word ;
'0' .. '9'   : scan integer constant ;
''''         : scan character constant ;
'<'          : scan <>,<= or < symbol ;
'>'          : scan >= or > symbol ;
':'          : scan := or : symbol;
'+'          : scan + symbol ;
..........   : .........
';'          : scan ; symbol ;
other chars  : scan illegal symbol
end
```

The process *scan identifier or reserved word* must implement the structural rule

⟨*identifier or reserved word*⟩ ::= ⟨*letter*⟩{⟨*letter*⟩ | ⟨*digit*⟩}

When the existence of the initial letter has been established by the case construct, this is programmable as

> *Nextch* ;
> **while** *ch is letter or digit* **do** *nextch*

or, more neatly, as

> **repeat** *Nextch* **until** *ch is not a letter or digit*

But the scan process must also implement

(a) the distinction between identifiers and reserved words;
(b) the recording of identifier spellings.

How should spellings be represented by the type *alfa* assumed earlier? The language rules put no limit on the length of identifiers, but it is common for identifier implementations to impose some limit *alfalength* on their (significant) length (i.e. identifiers must differ in the first *alfalength* characters if they are to be considered as distinct). The analyzer then has only to retain the first *alfalength* characters as the spelling of each identifier, where the limit *alfalength* is chosen to give the most efficient copying and comparison of spellings consistent with the user's need for a reasonable significant length for his identifiers.

Having decided how spellings are represented the *"scan identifier or reserved word"* process may be elaborated as follows:

```
begin
    k := 0 ; spelling := '    ' ;
    repeat
        if k < alfalength then
        begin k := k+1 ; spelling [k] := ch end ;
        Nextch
    until ch is not a letter or digit ;
    decide if spelling is identifier or reserved word
end
```

Deciding whether the spelling represents an identifier or a reserved word is a straightforward table-look-up process. However, since up to 50% of symbols in a program fall into this category it is important that the look-up be efficiently programmed. The scanner in Listing 2 uses a look-up table which is sorted and indexed by actual spelling length, so that each spelling is compared only with those reserved words of the same actual length. To give a fast search loop with a single terminating condition an additional table position is left at the end of each sequence of words of given length, with preset symbol value *identifier*. The spelling scanned is inserted at this position before the search loop is entered. If no preceding entry gives a match the loop will terminate at this entry, and return the symbol value *identifier* as required:

wordsymbol [(*index of last wordsymbol of length k*)+1].*spelling* := *spelling* ;
I := *index of first wordsymbol of length k* ;
while *wordsymbol* [*I*].*spelling* ≠ *spelling* **do** *I* := *I* + 1 ;
symbol := *wordsymbol* [*I*].*value* ;

The process *scan integer constant* implements the structural rule
⟨*integer constant*⟩ ::= ⟨*digit*⟩{⟨*digit*⟩}

which again is readily programmed as

repeat *Nextch* **until** *ch is not a digit*

Computation of the integer value equivalent to the constant scanned is readily incorporated in this loop, the only complication being that the scanner must guard against sequences of digits which denote values beyond the machine limit for integers.

The other scanning processes within the case discrimination are equally easily programmed. Listing 2 shows the resultant code for each. Test 2 which follows it shows a suitable driver program to test the lexical scanner, and the output produced from an input program which demonstrates the complete range of Mini-Pascal symbols.

Listing 2

```
ENVELOPE MODULE SCAN ;

    (* THE SCAN MODULE ENABLES THE LEXICAL SCANNING OF SYMBOLS IN THE    *)
    (* SOURCE STREAM THROUGH THE ACCESSIBLE PROCEDURE NEXTSYMBOL         *)
    (*                                                                    *)
    (*       (THE MODULE STRUCTURE IS USED ONLY TO PROTECT THE          *)
    (*        PERMANENT TABLES WHICH THIS PROCEDURE REQUIRES)           *)
    (*                                                                    *)
    (* WHEN CALLED, NEXTSYMBOL SCANS THE NEXT LANGUAGE SYMBOL IN THE     *)
    (* INPUT STREAM AND RETURNS A REPRESENTATION OF IT IN THE            *)
    (* FOLLOWING ACCESSIBLE VARIABLES :                                 *)
    (*                                                                    *)
    (*                                                                    *)
    (*    SYMBOL      IN ALL CASES SYMBOL REPRESENTS THE SYMBOL          *)
    (*                SCANNED, AS DEFINED BY THE TYPE SYMBOLTYPE          *)
    (*                                                                    *)
    (*                                                                    *)
    (*    SPELLING    WHEN SYMBOL = IDENT , SPELLING HOLDS THE           *)
    (*                (SIGNIFICANT) CHARACTERS OF THE IDENTIFIER         *)
    (*                SCANNED                                            *)
    (*                                                                    *)
    (*                                                                    *)
    (*    CONSTANT    WHEN SYMBOL = INTCONST OR CHARCONST, CONSTANT      *)
    (*                HOLDS THE INTEGER REPRESENTATION OF THE CONSTANT    *)
    (*                                                                    *)
    (*                                                                    *)
    (* THE STARTING POSITION OF THE SYMBOL SCANNED IS LEFT IN            *)
    (* THE ACCESSIBLE VARIABLE SYMBOLPOSITION                           *)
    (*                                                                    *)
    (* THE SCANNER REPORTS ERRORS WITH THE FOLLOWING CODES              *)
    (*                                                                    *)
    (* 1 .... INTEGER CONSTANT TOO LARGE                                *)
    (* 2 .... CHARACTER CONSTANT INCOMPLETE                             *)


CONST

    NOWORDSYMBOLS = 26 ;


VAR

   *SYMBOL : SYMBOLTYPE ;
   *CONSTANT : INTEGER ;
   *SPELLING : ALFA ;

   *SYMBOLPOSITION : SOURCE.TEXTPOSITION ;


   WORDSYMBOLS : ARRAY[ 1..NOWORDSYMBOLS] OF
                      RECORD
                            SYMBOLSPELLING   : ALFA ;
                            SYMBOLVALUE : SYMBOLTYPE
                      END ;
   LASTOFLENGTH : ARRAY[0..ALFALENGTH] OF 0..NOWORDSYMBOLS ;
```

```
PROCEDURE *NEXTSYMBOL ;

    VAR
        K : 0..ALFALENGTH ;
        I : 1..NOWORDSYMBOLS ;
        DIGIT : 0..9 ;

    BEGIN (* NEXTSYMBOL *)

        WITH SOURCE DO
        BEGIN
            (* READ CHARACTER BY CHARACTER UNTIL NEXT
               SIGNIFICANT CHARACTER                        *)
            WHILE CH = ' ' DO NEXTCH ;
            SYMBOLPOSITION := POSITIONNOW ;
            CASE CH OF

            'A','B','C','D','E','F','G','H','I',
            'J','K','L','M','N','O','P','Q','R',
            'S','T','U','V','W','X','Y','Z' :

                (* ANALYSIS OF AN IDENTIFIER OR WORD SYMBOL    *)

                BEGIN
                    K := 0 ; SPELLING := '          ' ;
                    REPEAT
                        IF K < ALFALENGTH THEN
                        BEGIN
                            K := K+1 ; SPELLING[K] := CH
                        END ;
                        NEXTCH
                    UNTIL ((CH<'0') OR (CH>'9')) AND ((CH<'A') OR (CH>'Z')) ;
                    WORDSYMBOLS[LASTOFLENGTH[K]].SYMBOLSPELLING := SPELLING ;
                    I := LASTOFLENGTH[K-1]+1 ;
                    WHILE WORDSYMBOLS[I].SYMBOLSPELLING<>SPELLING DO I:=I+1 ;
                    SYMBOL := WORDSYMBOLS[I].SYMBOLVALUE
                END ;

            '0','1','2','3','4',
            '5','6','7','8','9':

                (* ANALYSIS OF AN INTEGER CONSTANT        *)

                BEGIN
                    CONSTANT := 0 ;
                    REPEAT
                        DIGIT := ORD(CH)-ORD('0') ;
                        IF (CONSTANT < MAXINT DIV 10) OR
                           (CONSTANT = MAXINT DIV 10) AND
                           (DIGIT <= MAXINT MOD 10)
                        THEN CONSTANT := 10*CONSTANT + DIGIT
                        ELSE
                        BEGIN
                            ERROR(1,POSITIONNOW) ;
                            CONSTANT := 0
                        END ;
                        NEXTCH
                    UNTIL (CH<'0') OR (CH>'9') ;
                    SYMBOL := INTCONST
                END ;
```

```
''''  :

  (* ANALYSIS OF A CHARACTER CONSTANT  *)

  BEGIN
     NEXTCH ;
     IF CH = ''''  THEN
     BEGIN
        NEXTCH ;
        IF CH <> ''''  THEN ERROR(2,POSITIONNOW)
     END ;
     CONSTANT := ORD(CH) ;
     NEXTCH ;
     IF CH <> ''''
     THEN ERROR(2,POSITIONNOW)
     ELSE NEXTCH ;
     SYMBOL := CHARCONST
  END ;


  (* 2-CHARACTER OPERATOR/DELIMITERS *)

':'  :
  BEGIN
     NEXTCH ;
     IF CH = '='
     THEN BEGIN SYMBOL := BECOMES ; NEXTCH END
     ELSE SYMBOL := COLON
  END ;
'.'  :
  BEGIN
     NEXTCH ;
     IF CH = '.'
     THEN BEGIN SYMBOL := THRU ; NEXTCH END
     ELSE SYMBOL := PERIOD
  END ;
'<'  :
  BEGIN
     NEXTCH ;
     IF CH='='
     THEN BEGIN SYMBOL := LEOP ; NEXTCH END
     ELSE
        IF CH = '>'
        THEN BEGIN SYMBOL := NEOP ; NEXTCH END
        ELSE SYMBOL := LTOP
  END ;
'>'  :
  BEGIN
     NEXTCH ;
     IF CH='='
     THEN BEGIN SYMBOL := GEOP ; NEXTCH END
     ELSE SYMBOL := GTOP
  END ;
```

```
              (* 1-CHARACTER OPERATOR/DELIMITERS *)

    '+'  : BEGIN SYMBOL := PLUS ; NEXTCH END ;
    '-'  : BEGIN SYMBOL := MINUS ; NEXTCH END ;
    '*'  : BEGIN SYMBOL := TIMES ; NEXTCH END ;
    '='  : BEGIN SYMBOL := EQOP ; NEXTCH END ;
    '('  : BEGIN SYMBOL := LEFTPARENT ; NEXTCH END ;
    ')'  : BEGIN SYMBOL := RIGHTPARENT ; NEXTCH END ;
    '['  : BEGIN SYMBOL := LEFTBRACKET ; NEXTCH END ;
    ']'  : BEGIN SYMBOL := RIGHTBRACKET ; NEXTCH END ;
    ','  : BEGIN SYMBOL := COMMA ; NEXTCH END ;
    ';'  : BEGIN SYMBOL := SEMICOLON ; NEXTCH END ;


              (* OTHER ILLEGAL CHARACTERS *)

    '#','/','!','^','\','&','@','$','_','%','?','"' :

        BEGIN
            SYMBOL := OTHERSY ;
            NEXTCH
        END ;

    END (* CASE *)

  END

END (* NEXTSYMBOL *) ;




BEGIN

    (* INITIALIZE WORD SYMBOL TABLES *)

    LASTOFLENGTH[0] := 0 ;

    WITH WORDSYMBOLS[1] DO
    BEGIN SYMBOLSPELLING:='          ' ; SYMBOLVALUE:=IDENT END ;
    LASTOFLENGTH[1] := 1 ;

    WITH WORDSYMBOLS[2] DO
    BEGIN SYMBOLSPELLING:='IF        ' ; SYMBOLVALUE:=IFSY END ;
    WITH WORDSYMBOLS[3] DO
    BEGIN SYMBOLSPELLING:='DO        ' ; SYMBOLVALUE:=DOSY END ;
    WITH WORDSYMBOLS[4] DO
    BEGIN SYMBOLSPELLING:='OF        ' ; SYMBOLVALUE:=OFSY END ;
    WITH WORDSYMBOLS[5] DO
    BEGIN SYMBOLSPELLING:='OR        ' ; SYMBOLVALUE:=OROP END ;
    WITH WORDSYMBOLS[6] DO
    BEGIN SYMBOLSPELLING:='          ' ; SYMBOLVALUE:=IDENT END ;
    LASTOFLENGTH[2] := 6 ;
```

```
      WITH WORDSYMBOLS[7] DO
      BEGIN SYMBOLSPELLING:='END      ' ; SYMBOLVALUE:=ENDSY END ;
      WITH WORDSYMBOLS[8] DO
      BEGIN SYMBOLSPELLING:='VAR      ' ; SYMBOLVALUE:=VARSY END ;
      WITH WORDSYMBOLS[9] DO
      BEGIN SYMBOLSPELLING:='DIV      ' ; SYMBOLVALUE:=DIVOP END ;
      WITH WORDSYMBOLS[10] DO
      BEGIN SYMBOLSPELLING:='AND      ' ; SYMBOLVALUE:=ANDOP END ;
      WITH WORDSYMBOLS[11] DO
      BEGIN SYMBOLSPELLING:='NOT      ' ; SYMBOLVALUE:=NOTOP END ;
      WITH WORDSYMBOLS[12] DO
      BEGIN SYMBOLSPELLING:='         ' ; SYMBOLVALUE:=IDENT END ;
      LASTOFLENGTH[3] := 12 ;

      WITH WORDSYMBOLS[13] DO
      BEGIN SYMBOLSPELLING:='THEN     ' ; SYMBOLVALUE:=THENSY END ;
      WITH WORDSYMBOLS[14] DO
      BEGIN SYMBOLSPELLING:='ELSE     ' ; SYMBOLVALUE:=ELSESY END ;
      WITH WORDSYMBOLS[15] DO
      BEGIN SYMBOLSPELLING:='READ     ' ; SYMBOLVALUE:=READSY END ;
      WITH WORDSYMBOLS[16] DO
      BEGIN SYMBOLSPELLING:='         ' ; SYMBOLVALUE:=IDENT END ;
      LASTOFLENGTH[4] := 16 ;

      WITH WORDSYMBOLS[17] DO
      BEGIN SYMBOLSPELLING:='BEGIN    ' ; SYMBOLVALUE:=BEGINSY END ;
      WITH WORDSYMBOLS[18] DO
      BEGIN SYMBOLSPELLING:='WHILE    ' ; SYMBOLVALUE:=WHILESY END ;
      WITH WORDSYMBOLS[19] DO
      BEGIN SYMBOLSPELLING:='ARRAY    ' ; SYMBOLVALUE:=ARRAYSY END ;
      WITH WORDSYMBOLS[20] DO
      BEGIN SYMBOLSPELLING:='WRITE    ' ; SYMBOLVALUE:=WRITESY END ;
      WITH WORDSYMBOLS[21] DO
      BEGIN SYMBOLSPELLING:='         ' ; SYMBOLVALUE:=IDENT END ;
      LASTOFLENGTH[5] := 21 ;

      WITH WORDSYMBOLS[22] DO
      BEGIN SYMBOLSPELLING:='         ' ; SYMBOLVALUE:=IDENT END ;
      LASTOFLENGTH[6] := 22 ;

      WITH WORDSYMBOLS[23] DO
      BEGIN SYMBOLSPELLING:='PROGRAM  ' ; SYMBOLVALUE:=PROGRAMSY END ;
      WITH WORDSYMBOLS[24] DO
      BEGIN SYMBOLSPELLING:='         ' ; SYMBOLVALUE:=IDENT END ;
      LASTOFLENGTH[7] := 24 ;

      WITH WORDSYMBOLS[25] DO
      BEGIN SYMBOLSPELLING:='PROCEDUR' ; SYMBOLVALUE:=PROCSY END ;
      WITH WORDSYMBOLS[26] DO
      BEGIN SYMBOLSPELLING:='         ' ; SYMBOLVALUE:=IDENT   END ;
      LASTOFLENGTH[8] := 26 ;


      NEXTSYMBOL ; (* MAKE FIRST SYMBOL AVAILABLE *)

      *** (* EXECUTE ANALYZER *)

END (* SCAN.MODULE *) ;
```

Test 2

```
0    3300  PROGRAM TESTSCAN (INPUT,OUTPUT,SYMBOLS) ;
1
2              ENVELOPE MODULE SOURCE = LISTING1 IN LIBRARY ;
3
4    3650  CONST ALFALENGTH = 8 ;
5
6              TYPE ALFA = PACKED ARRAY [1..ALFALENGTH] OF CHAR ;
7
8                   SYMBOLTYPE = (IDENT,INTCONST,CHARCONST,
9                                 NOTOP,ANDOP,OROP,
10                                TIMES,DIVOP,PLUS,MINUS,
11                                LTOP,LEOP,GEOP,GTOP,NEOP,EQOP,
12                                RIGHTPARENT,LEFTPARENT,LEFTBRACKET,RIGHTBRACKET,
13                                COMMA,SEMICOLON,PERIOD,COLON,BECOMES,THRU,
14                                PROGRAMSY,VARSY,PROCSY,ARRAYSY,OFSY,
15                                BEGINSY,ENDSY,IFSY,THENSY,ELSESY,WHILESY,DOSY,
16                                READSY,WRITESY,
17                                OTHERSY) ;
18
19             ENVELOPE MODULE SCAN = LISTING2 IN LIBRARY ;
20
21   4386  VAR SYMBOLS : TEXT ;
22
23   4425  BEGIN
24
25   4425      WRITELN(SYMBOLS,'SYMBOLS SCANNED :') ;
26   4436      WRITELN(SYMBOLS) ;
27
28   4442      REPEAT
29
30   4442         CASE SCAN.SYMBOL OF
31   4444             IDENT       : WRITELN(SYMBOLS,'IDENTIFIER ',SCAN.SPELLING) ;
32   4460             INTCONST    : WRITELN(SYMBOLS,'INTEGER',SCAN.CONSTANT) ;
33   4475             CHARCONST   : WRITELN(SYMBOLS,'CHARACTER ',CHR(SCAN.CONSTANT)) ;
34   4494             NOTOP       : WRITELN(SYMBOLS,'NOT') ;
35   4506             ANDOP       : WRITELN(SYMBOLS,'AND') ;
36   4518             OROP        : WRITELN(SYMBOLS,'OR') ;
37   4530             TIMES       : WRITELN(SYMBOLS,'*') ;
38   4542             DIVOP       : WRITELN(SYMBOLS,'DIV') ;
39   4554             PLUS        : WRITELN(SYMBOLS,'+') ;
40   4566             MINUS       : WRITELN(SYMBOLS,'-') ;
41   4578             LTOP        : WRITELN(SYMBOLS,'<') ;
42   4590             LEOP        : WRITELN(SYMBOLS,'<=') ;
43   4602             GEOP        : WRITELN(SYMBOLS,'>=') ;
44   4614             GTOP        : WRITELN(SYMBOLS,'>') ;
45   4626             NEOP        : WRITELN(SYMBOLS,'<>') ;
46   4638             EQOP        : WRITELN(SYMBOLS,'=') ;
47   4650             RIGHTPARENT : WRITELN(SYMBOLS,')') ;
48   4662             LEFTPARENT  : WRITELN(SYMBOLS,'(') ;
49   4674             RIGHTBRACKET : WRITELN(SYMBOLS,']') ;
50   4686             LEFTBRACKET : WRITELN(SYMBOLS,'[') ;
```

```
51   4698            COMMA        : WRITELN(SYMBOLS,',') ;
52   4710            SEMICOLON    : WRITELN(SYMBOLS,';') ;
53   4722            PERIOD       : WRITELN(SYMBOLS,'.') ;
54   4734            COLON        : WRITELN(SYMBOLS,':') ;
55   4746            BECOMES      : WRITELN(SYMBOLS,':=') ;
56   4758            THRU         : WRITELN(SYMBOLS,'..') ;
57   4770            PROGRAMSY    : WRITELN(SYMBOLS,'PROGRAM') ;
58   4782            VARSY        : WRITELN(SYMBOLS,'VAR') ;
59   4794            PROCSY       : WRITELN(SYMBOLS,'PROCEDURE') ;
60   4806            ARRAYSY      : WRITELN(SYMBOLS,'ARRAY') ;
61   4818            OFSY         : WRITELN(SYMBOLS,'OF') ;
62   4830            BEGINSY      : WRITELN(SYMBOLS,'BEGIN') ;
63   4842            ENDSY        : WRITELN(SYMBOLS,'END') ;
64   4854            IFSY         : WRITELN(SYMBOLS,'IF') ;
65   4866            THENSY       : WRITELN(SYMBOLS,'THEN') ;
66   4878            ELSESY       : WRITELN(SYMBOLS,'ELSE') ;
67   4890            WHILESY      : WRITELN(SYMBOLS,'WHILE') ;
68   4902            DOSY         : WRITELN(SYMBOLS,'DO') ;
69   4914            READSY       : WRITELN(SYMBOLS,'READ') ;
70   4926            WRITESY      : WRITELN(SYMBOLS,'WRITE') ;
71   4938            OTHERSY      : SOURCE.ERROR(10,SCAN.SYMBOLPOSITION)
72   4945          END ;
73
74   4991          SCAN.NEXTSYMBOL
75
76   4991      UNTIL SCAN.SYMBOL=PERIOD
77
78   4992    END.


COMPILATION COMPLETE :       NO ERRORS REPORTED
COMPILATION TIME     =     1808 MILLISECONDS
SOURCE PROGRAM       =      547 LINES
OBJECT PROGRAM       =     5153 WORDS
```

LISTING PRODUCED BY MINI-PASCAL COMPILER MK 1


```
 0    PROGRAM SYMBOLS ;
 1    VAR I,J : INTEGER ;
 2       A : ARRAY [1..10] OF CHAR ;
 3    PROCEDURE P ;
 4      VAR J : INTEGER ;
 5      BEGIN
 6        READ(J) ;
 7        I := I+I-I*I DIV I ;
 8        IF (J=I) OR NOT (J<>I) THEN A[I]:=' ' ELSE A[I]:=''' ;
*****                                                    ^ERROR   2

 9        WRITE(A[I]) ;
10        I := I+1
11      END ;
12    BEGIN
13      I := 1 ; J := 10000000;
*****                          ^ERROR   1

14      WHILE (I>0)AND(I<11)OR(I>=1)AND(I<=10) DO P ;
15      WRITE(J)
16      &   "   %   ^   #   $
*****    ^ERROR   10
*****        ^ERROR   10
*****            ^ERROR   10
*****                ^ERROR   10
*****                    ^ERROR   10
*****                        ^ERROR   10

17      !   \   @   _   ?
*****    ^ERROR   10
*****        ^ERROR   10
*****            ^ERROR   10
*****                ^ERROR   10
*****                    ^ERROR   10

18    END.
```


COMPILATION COMPLETED :   13 ERRORS REPORTED

SYMBOLS SCANNED :

PROGRAM
IDENTIFIER SYMBOLS
;
VAR
IDENTIFIER I
,
IDENTIFIER J
:
IDENTIFIER INTEGER
;

IDENTIFIER A	IF	IDENTIFIER I	(
:	(	:=	IDENTIFIER I
ARRAY	IDENTIFIER J	IDENTIFIER I	<=
[	=	+	INTEGER 10
INTEGER 1	IDENTIFIER I	INTEGER	·)
..	)	END	DO
INTEGER 10	OR	; ·	IDENTIFIER P
]	NOT	BEGIN	;
OF	(	IDENTIFIER I	WRITE
IDENTIFIER CHAR	IDENTIFIER J	:=	(
;	<>	INTEGER 1	IDENTIFIER J
PROCEDURE	IDENTIFIER I	;	)
IDENTIFIER P	)	IDENTIFIER J	END
;	THEN	:=	
VAR	IDENTIFIER A	INTEGER 0	
IDENTIFIER J	[	;	
:	IDENTIFIER I	WHILE	
IDENTIFIER INTEGER	]	(	
;	:=	IDENTIFIER I	
BEGIN	CHARACTER	>	
READ	ELSE	INTEGER 0	
(	IDENTIFIER A	)	
IDENTIFIER J	[	AND	
)	IDENTIFIER I	(	
;	]	IDENTIFIER I	
IDENTIFIER I	:=	<	
:=	CHARACTER '	INTEGER 11	
IDENTIFIER I	;	)	
+	WRITE	OR	
IDENTIFIER I	(	(	
-	IDENTIFIER A	IDENTIFIER I	
IDENTIFIER I	[	>=	
*	IDENTIFIER I	INTEGER 1	
IDENTIFIER I	]	)	
DIV	)	AND	
IDENTIFIER I	;		
;			

Exercise 2 Modify the lexical scanner in Listing 2 to allow comments of the form

$$\{ \cdots \cdots \}$$

to precede any Mini-Pascal symbol. Why is it more difficult for comments of the form

$$(* \cdots \cdots *)$$

to be allowed?

SYNTAX ANALYSIS

Separating Syntax and Semantics

The remaining components of the analysis process were identified as

    syntax analyzer (symbol stream)(syntax errors, program syntax)

    semantic analyzer (program syntax)(semantic errors,   ?   )

Before further development can take place some decision must be taken on the structural relationship between these processes. The factors affecting this decision are as follows:

(a) The language features of Mini-Pascal do not require that semantic analysis of the program as a whole should follow its syntax analysis— they can take place in *parallel*, and efficiency considerations dictate that they should.

(b) The project constaints do not, as in the case of the source handler, the generator and the scanner, require the physical separation of the syntax and semantic analysis code. This choice can be made purely on the inherent nature of the two processes and their mutual interaction.

(c) The conceptual interface *program syntax* is some representation of the significant program structure, usually referred to as a syntax tree. A common property of such recursive tree structures is that the sequence of control involved in their "consumption" (in our case, by semantic analysis) either mirrors exactly, or is an exact subset of, the sequence of control which creates them (in our case, syntax analysis). Where these take place in parallel a common controlling code structure can suffice.

The way forward therefore is not to define any explicit interface at this stage, but to construct the code structure necessary for syntax analysis and then to add to this syntactic skeleton the meat of semantic analysis. The end product will be a single module which carries out both syntax and semantic analysis.

Programming the Syntax Analyzer

In the previous chapter we intuitively translated the syntax rules for symbols into equivalent fragments of scanner code. A similar technique can be used to construct a syntax analyzer from the remaining syntax rules of the language. Thus, from the syntax rule for ⟨*program*⟩

$$⟨program⟩ ::= \textbf{program} ⟨identifier⟩ ; ⟨block⟩.$$

we can formulate a procedure for the analysis of a program as:

```
procedure program ;
    begin
        accept (programsy) ;
        accept (identifier) ;
```

```
            accept (semicolon) ;
            block ;
            accept (period)
         end ;
```

where *accept* is a procedure which checks that the current symbol is that specified and scans to the next, otherwise it reports a syntax error:

```
         procedure accept (expected symbol : symbol type) ;
            begin
            if scan.symbol = expected symbol
            then scan.nextsymbol
            else source.error (      )
         end ;
```

The procedure for the analysis of a ⟨block⟩ is similarly derived from the corresponding syntax rule

```
         ⟨block⟩ ::= ⟨variable declaration part⟩
                     ⟨procedure declaration part⟩
                     ⟨statement part⟩
```

leading to a procedure:

```
         procedure block ;
            begin
            variable declaration part ;
            procedure declaration part ;
            statement part
         end ;
```

Since these are the only calls on the procedures *variable declaration part*, *procedure declaration part* and *statement part* which occur, they could be replaced by the procedure bodies themselves, and the procedures dropped from the analyzer. However, in this case their retention gives a useful structural separation of the very different activities of dealing with variable declarations, procedure declarations, and statements.

We could continue developing syntax-analysis procedures in this way, one for each syntax rule in the language definition. It is clear however that each procedure developed is a direct "translation" of the corresponding syntax rule. Before continuing, therefore, it is worthwhile to formulate a set of rules for the translation process.

Each syntax rule takes the form

$$\langle syntactic\ construct \rangle ::= allowable\ form$$

where the allowable form is expressed in terms of

(a)   the basic symbols of the language, which we will denote for the present by lower case letters, $a, b, \ldots$;
(b)   other syntactic constructs $\langle A \rangle$, $\langle B \rangle$, $\ldots$;
(c)   the meta-symbols | and { } denoting selection and possible repetition.

Our objective is to translate the syntax rule for each syntactic construct into a *procedure* of the same name, whose action is to analyze the incoming sequence of symbols, and verify that it is of the corresponding allowable form, reporting errors if it is not. More precisely, the procedure corresponding to a syntactic construct $\langle S \rangle$

(a)   assumes initially that scan.symbol contains the first symbol of an S ;
(b)   causes the input of the longest sequence of symbols which are of form S, reporting an error if no such sequence is found ;
(c)   leaves in *scan.symbol* the first symbol which does not belong to S .

The body of the procedure required is clearly some transformation of the allowable form appearing in the syntax rule, so we can depict our translation process as converting a syntax rule

$$\langle S \rangle ::= \alpha$$

into an equivalent procedure

procedure S ;
    begin
       $T(\alpha)$
    end ;

The transformation T is defined by a series of rules as follows:

1.   If the allowable form α is a single symbol of the language, the action required is to inspect the current input symbol, and if it is the allowed symbol then scan to the next symbol, otherwise report an error. Assuming the procedure *accept* defined above, our first transformation rule is thus
    Rule 1 $T(\alpha) \rightarrow accept\ (\alpha)$

2. If the allowable form is itself a single syntactic construct, $\langle A \rangle$ say, the action required is simply a call to the corresponding procedure A. Hence rule 2:

Rule 2 $T(\langle A \rangle) \rightarrow A$

3. If the allowable form is a sequence of symbols and syntactic constructs the action required is clearly the corresponding sequence of actions appropriate to each. Hence rule 3 :

Rule 3 $T(\alpha_1 \alpha_2 \ldots \alpha_n) \rightarrow$ **begin**
$$T(\alpha_1) \ ;$$
$$T(\alpha_2) \ ;$$
$$\vdots$$
$$T(\alpha_n)$$
        end ;

4. If the allowable form consists of a number of alternative forms $\alpha \,|\, \beta \,| \ldots |\, \delta$, the action required is clearly some selection between the actions appropriate to each alternative

      case   ?   **of**
        ? : $T(\alpha)$;
        ? : $T(\beta)$;
       .. : ... ;
        ? : $T(\delta)$
      end

On what basis is the selection made? In the lexical scanner the corresponding decision was made on the value of the current input character, which was necessarily the first character of the symbol under scan. Analogously the choice here should be made on the basis of the current input symbol. If we define those symbols which can begin a sequence of symbols of form α as *Startersof*(α), the necessary transformation seems to be

Rule 4 $T(\alpha \,|\, \beta \,| \ldots |\, \delta) \rightarrow$ **case** *scan.symbol* **of**
                Startersof(α) : $T(\alpha)$;
                Startersof(β) : $T(\beta)$;
                $\vdots$
                Startersof(δ) : $T(\delta)$
            end

We note however that if this is to be a deterministic **case** statement we must insist on the following condition:

Condition (a)   No symbol may be a starter of more than one of the alternatives of each allowable form.

Even this condition is insufficient if one of the alternatives is ⟨*empty*⟩, or allows an empty sequence of symbols.

The analyzer's action for an ⟨*empty*⟩ alternative of an allowable form S is to accept no symbols. This action should be taken when the next symbol is a follower of the allowable form, i.e.

$$T(\alpha \mid \beta \mid \ldots \mid \langle empty \rangle) \rightarrow \textbf{case } scan.symbol \textbf{ of}$$
$$Startersof(\alpha) : T(\alpha) ;$$
$$Startersof(\beta) : T(\beta) ;$$
$$\vdots$$
$$Followersof(S) :$$
$$\textbf{end}$$

Hence we must have condition (b):

Condition (b)   No symbol may be both a possible starter and a possible follower of an allowable form which has an empty alternative.

The **case** construct used in Rule 4 neatly expresses a choice between any number of alternatives. If only two alternatives exist it may of course be re-expressed as an **if . . then . . else,** and if one of these alternatives is empty it reduces to a simple **if . . then . .**

5.   If the allowable form involves a possible repetition, { }, the action required is clearly a loop. As in the lexical scanner the criterion for loop termination is again based on the current symbol, hence Rule 5:

Rule 5 $T(\{\alpha\}) \rightarrow \textbf{while } scan.symbol \textbf{ in } Startersof(\alpha)$
$$\textbf{do } T(\alpha)$$

Note that since a repetitive form { } is possibly empty, condition (b) again applies. Those repetitions that cannot be empty are written in the syntax rules $\alpha\{\alpha\}$, which transforms to

begin
$T(\alpha)$;
while . . . **do** $T(\alpha)$
end

In Pascal this may be rewritten:

repeat $T(\alpha)$ **until not** (*scan symbol* **in** *Startersof*(α))

Rules 1–5 enable the translation of the set of syntax rules defining a language into an equivalent set of syntax procedures. The ultimate objective, viz. the analysis of programs of the language, is then achieved by a call to the procedure corresponding to the syntax rule for ⟨*program*⟩. This procedure of course calls other procedures, which in turn call others, so producing a gradual tracing of the conceptual syntax tree of the program being analyzed, accompanied by a symbol-by-symbol acceptance of the program each time a "leaf"of the tree is identified. For those constructs which are nested or recursive in form, e.g. *expressions, statements*, the procedures automatically call themselves recursively to deal with nested instances of their allowable forms. Because of its inherently recursive nature, and the fact that analysis proceeds from the *top* (⟨*program*⟩) of the syntax tree to its *bottom* (the actual symbols), such an analyzer is referred to as a *recursive-descent analyzer*.

The analyzer operates in a deterministic manner, determining the appropriate analysis path by inspection of the current input symbol, provided each of the underlying syntax rules fulfils conditions (a) and (b). A set of syntax rules meeting these conditions constitutes what is known as an LL(1) grammar. Many simple programming languages can be defined by such a grammar.

Constructing the syntax analyzer for Mini-Pascal now involves the systematic application of rules 1–5 to the syntax rules appearing in the language definition, with a preliminary check that conditions (a) and (b) are fulfilled where appropriate. The following table shows the syntax rules as they appear in the definition, but sorted in an order appropriate to recursive descent.

Table showing Syntax of Mini-Pascal in recursive descent order

⟨*program*⟩ :: = **program** ⟨*identifier*⟩; ⟨*block*⟩.
⟨*block*⟩ :: = ⟨*variable declaration part*⟩
⟨*procedure declaration part*⟩
⟨*statement part*⟩

⟨*variable declaration part*⟩ :: = ⟨*empty*⟩ |
     var ⟨*variable declaration*⟩;
      {⟨*variable declaration*⟩;}
⟨*variable declaration*⟩ :: = ⟨*identifier*⟩ {,⟨*identifier*⟩}: ⟨*type*⟩
⟨*type*⟩ :: = ⟨*simple type*⟩ |⟨*array type*⟩
⟨*array type*⟩ :: = **array** [⟨*index range*⟩] of ⟨*simple type*⟩
⟨*index range*⟩ :: = ⟨*integer constant*⟩ .. ⟨*integer constant*⟩
⟨*simple type*⟩ :: = ⟨*type identifier*⟩
⟨*type identifier*⟩ :: = ⟨*identifier*⟩

⟨*procedure declaration part*⟩ :: = {⟨*procedure declaration*⟩;}
⟨*procedure declaration*⟩ :: = **procedure** ⟨*identifier*⟩; ⟨*block*⟩

⟨*statement part*⟩ :: = ⟨*compound statement*⟩
⟨*compound statement*⟩ :: = **begin** ⟨*statement*⟩{;⟨*statement*⟩} **end**
⟨*statement*⟩ :: = ⟨*simple statement*⟩ |⟨*structured statement*⟩
⟨*simple statement*⟩ :: = ⟨*assignment statement*⟩ |⟨*procedure statement*⟩ |
       ⟨*read statement*⟩ |⟨*write statement*⟩
⟨*assignment statement*⟩ :: = ⟨*variable*⟩ : = ⟨*expression*⟩
⟨*procedure statement*⟩ :: = ⟨*procedure identifier*⟩
⟨*procedure identifier*⟩ :: = ⟨*identifier*⟩
⟨*read statement*⟩ :: = **read** (⟨*input variable*⟩{,⟨*input variable*⟩})
⟨*input variable*⟩ :: = ⟨*variable*⟩
⟨*write statement*⟩ :: = **write** (⟨*output value*⟩{,⟨*output value*⟩})
⟨*output value*⟩ :: = ⟨*expression*⟩
⟨*structured statement*⟩ :: = ⟨*compound statement*⟩ |⟨*if statement*⟩ |
       ⟨*while statement*⟩
⟨*if statement*⟩ :: = **if** ⟨*expression*⟩ **then** ⟨*statement*⟩ |
   if ⟨*expression*⟩ **then** ⟨*statement*⟩ **else** ⟨*statement*⟩)
⟨*while statement*⟩ :: = **while** ⟨*expression*⟩ **do** ⟨*statement*⟩

⟨*expression*⟩ :: = ⟨*simple expression*⟩ |
     ⟨*simple expression*⟩ ⟨*relational operator*⟩ ⟨*simple expression*⟩
⟨*simple expression*⟩ :: = ⟨*sign*⟩ ⟨*term*⟩ {⟨*adding operator*⟩ ⟨*term*⟩}
⟨*term*⟩ :: = ⟨*factor*⟩{⟨*multiplying operator*⟩ ⟨*factor*⟩}
⟨*factor*⟩ :: = ⟨*variable*⟩ |⟨*constant*⟩ |(⟨*expression*⟩) |**not** ⟨*factor*⟩
⟨*relational operator*⟩ :: = = |<> |< |< = | > = | >
⟨*sign*⟩ :: = + | − |⟨*empty*⟩
⟨*adding operator*⟩ :: = + | − |**or**
⟨*multiplying operator*⟩ :: = * |**div** |**and**

⟨*variable*⟩ :: = ⟨*entire variable*⟩ |⟨*indexed variable*⟩
⟨*indexed variable*⟩ :: = ⟨*array variable*⟩ [⟨*expression*⟩]
⟨*array variable*⟩ :: = ⟨*entire variable*⟩
⟨*entire variable*⟩ :: = ⟨*variable identifier*⟩
⟨*variable identifier*⟩ :: = ⟨*identifier*⟩

⟨*constant*⟩ :: = ⟨*integer constant*⟩ |⟨*character constant*⟩ |⟨*constant identifier*⟩
⟨*constant identifier*⟩ :: = ⟨*identifier*⟩

The procedures already devised for program and block analysis follow directly from application of rules 1–3 to the first two syntax rules. The next syntax rule, viz.

⟨*variable declaration part*⟩ ::= ⟨*empty*⟩ |
　　　　　　var ⟨*variable declaration*⟩;
　　　　　　{⟨*variable declaration*⟩;}

presents a more significant translation task. Its allowable form involves
alternatives, one of which is ⟨*empty*⟩. We must therefore check that condition (b) is met in this case. The only symbols which can follow a variable
declaration part are **procedure** and **begin**, while the only symbol with which
a non-empty variable declaration part can begin is **var**, so condition (b) is
clearly met. Similarly we find that the possible repetition {⟨*variable declaration*⟩;} creates no problems, so using rules 4 and 5 in their simplified forms
we obtain

```
        procedure variable declaration part ;
          begin
            if scan.symbol = varsy then
          begin
            accept (varsy) ;
          repeat
            variable declaration ;
            accept (semicolon)
            until scan.symbol ≠ identifier
          end
        end ;
```

The remaining syntax rules can be checked and transformed in a similar
manner. Listing 3 shows the complete syntax analyzer which results. This
analyzer is exactly that dictated by the syntax rules except that

(a)　the procedures are nested within each other as tightly as their use
　　　permits;
(b)　certain redundant procedures are eliminated;
(c)　procedure names are shortened to meet the limits put on the significant
　　　length of identifiers by Pascal compilers;
(d)　four conflicts with conditions (a) and (b) arise which are resolved as
　　　follows.

An obvious conflict with condition (a) arises in the syntax rule for the
⟨*if statement*⟩

⟨*if statement*⟩ ::= **if** ⟨*expression*⟩ **then** ⟨*statement*⟩ |
　　　　　　if ⟨*expression*⟩ **then** ⟨*statement*⟩ **else** ⟨*statement*⟩

since the two alternatives begin with the same symbols. This is resolved by *factorizing* out the common symbols as follows:

⟨*if statement*⟩ ::= **if** ⟨*expression*⟩ **then** ⟨*statement*⟩⟨*if tail*⟩
⟨*if tail*⟩ ::= ⟨*empty*⟩ | **else** ⟨*statement*⟩

Condition (a) is thus fulfilled but we now find that condition (b) is violated by ⟨*if tail*⟩ since an ⟨*if tail*⟩ can be followed by the **else** symbol (of an enclosing **if** statement). This well-known problem is fortunately resolved for us by a rider in the language definition which states that the correct interpretation of the sequence **if** .. **then if** .. **then** .. **else** .. is that which will result by transformation of the syntax rules above to give the procedure

> **procedure** *if statement* ;
> **begin**
>   *accept* (*ifsy*) ;
>   *expression* ;
>   *accept* (*thensy*) ;
>   *statement* ;
>   **if** *scan.symbol* = *elsesy* **then**
>   **begin**
>   *accept* (*elsesy*) ;
>   *statement*
>   **end**
> **end** ;

A similar problem with the syntax rule for ⟨*expression*⟩ is also resolved by factorization to give a procedure

> **procedure** *expression* ;
> **begin**
>   *simple expression* ;
>   **if** *scan.symbol* **in** [*eqop, neop,* ..] **then**
>   **begin**
>   *accept* (*scan.symbol*) ;
>   *simple expression*
>   **end**
> **end**

Notice we avoid the need for six distinct syntax paths for the acceptance of the particular relational operator involved by the coding *accept* (*scan.symbol*) . Since this cannot produce an error it might be further reduced to *scan.next-symbol* .

A more difficult problem arises in ⟨*simple statement*⟩ whose syntax rule is

⟨*simple statement*⟩ ::= ⟨*assignment statement*⟩ |
⟨*procedure statement*⟩ |
⟨*read statement*⟩ |
⟨*write statement*⟩

Symbol sequences allowed by the alternatives ⟨*assignment statement*⟩ and ⟨*procedure statement*⟩ both start with an identifier, so the choice between them cannot be made on the basis of the (first) symbol under scan. A similar problem arises in ⟨*factor*⟩

⟨*factor*⟩ ::= ⟨*variable*⟩ | ⟨*constant*⟩ | . . .

since both ⟨*variable*⟩ and ⟨*constant*⟩ may begin with an identifier.

These problems are due to the fact that the syntax constructs ⟨*variable identifier*⟩, ⟨*procedure identifier*⟩ and ⟨*constant identifier*⟩ are lexically indistinguishable. A purely syntactic solution can be found by eliminating their distinction from the syntax rules, and then factorizing and transforming the revised syntax. However, the distinction can and must be made during *semantic analysis*. Anticipating that syntax and semantic analyses are to take place in parallel we may assume that a semantic check can be used to resolve the syntactic choice, and so retain the general form of syntax given by the language definition.

Adding Syntax Error Recovery

The syntax analyzer constructed so far will function satisfactorily on syntactically correct programs, i.e. it will verify that the programs obey the syntax rules of the language, and in doing so determine their syntactic structures. For an incorrect program, however, the analyzer's behavior is acceptable only up to the detection of the *first* syntax error. Thereafter the analysis process is liable to get out of step with the sequence of symbols under scan, and so either loop or produce a welter of syntax-error messages irrelevant to these symbols. In short the analyzer lacks the quality of *error recovery* identified as a project objective.

To achieve syntax-error recovery we must maintain a reasonable synchronization between the analyzer and the symbol sequence under scan. The analyzer functions as a set of syntax procedures. If we could enforce synchronization at entry to and exit from each procedure, then the effects of desynchronization would be limited to the range of symbols accepted between any two successive calls or exits. This range is dependent on the number of

Listing 3

```
ENVELOPE MODULE ANALYZE ;

  CONST ALFALENGTH = 8 ;

  TYPE  ALFA = PACKED ARRAY [1..ALFALENGTH] OF CHAR ;

        SYMBOLTYPE = ( IDENT,INTCONST,CHARCONST,
                       NOTOP,ANDOP,OROP,
                       TIMES,DIVOP,PLUS,MINUS,
                       LTOP,LEOP,GEOP,GTOP,NEOP,EQOP,
                       RIGHTPARENT,LEFTPARENT,LEFTBRACKET,RIGHTBRACKET,
                       COMMA,SEMICOLON,PERIOD,COLON,BECOMES,THRU,
                       PROGRAMSY,VARSY,PROCSY,ARRAYSY,OFSY,
                       BEGINSY,ENDSY,IFSY,THENSY,ELSESY,WHILESY,DOSY,
                       READSY,WRITESY,
                       OTHERSY ) ;


  ENVELOPE MODULE SCAN = LISTING2 IN LIBRARY ;


  (* (A) SYNTAX ANALYSIS                                              *)
  (*                                                                  *)
  (*    SYNTAX ANALYSIS OF MINI-PASCAL PROGRAMS IS IMPLEMENTED        *)
  (*    AS A SET OF RECURSIVE DESCENT PROCEDURES. THESE PROCEDURES    *)
  (*    ARE BASED ON THE SYNTAX RULES GIVEN IN THE LANGUAGE DEFN      *)
  (*    AND ARE NESTED AS TIGHTLY AS THE MUTUAL INTERACTION PERMITS.  *)
  (*    THE ORDER, NAMES, AND NESTING OF THE PROCEDURES IS AS FOLLOWS *)
  (*                                                                  *)
  (*       PROGRAMME                                                  *)
  (*          BLOCK                                                   *)
  (*             VARPART                                              *)
  (*                VARDECLARATION                                    *)
  (*                   TYP                                            *)
  (*                      SIMPLETYPE                                  *)
  (*                      INDEXRANGE                                  *)
  (*             PROCPART                                             *)
  (*                PROCDECLARATION                                   *)
  (*             STATPART                                             *)
  (*                COMPOUNDSTATEMENT                                 *)
  (*                   STATEMENT                                      *)
  (*                      VARIABLE                                    *)
  (*                      EXPRESSION                                  *)
  (*                         SIMPLEEXPRESSION                         *)
  (*                            TERM                                  *)
  (*                               FACTOR                             *)
  (*                      ASSIGNMENT                                  *)
  (*                      READSTATEMENT                               *)
  (*                         INPUTVARIABLE                            *)
  (*                      WRITESTATEMENT                              *)
  (*                         OUTPUTVALUE                              *)
  (*                      IFSTATEMENT                                 *)
  (*                      WHILESTATEMENT                              *)
  (*                                                                  *)
  (*                                                                  *)
```

```
(*    THE SYNTAX ANALYZERS ARE WRITTEN ON THE ASSUMPTION THAT THE    *)
(*    NEXT SYNTACTIC GOAL CAN ALWAYS BE SELECTED BY INSPECTION OF    *)
(*    (AT MOST) THE NEXT INCOMING SYMBOL ( I.E. THAT THE UNDERLYING  *)
(*    GRAMMAR IS LL(1) ). THIS IS NOT SO AT THE FOLLOWING POINTS     *)
(*    IN THE SYNTAX RULES ACTUALLY USED                             *)
(*                                                                   *)
(*       1. A STATEMENT BEGINNING WITH AN IDENTIFIER MAY BE          *)
(*          EITHER AN ASSIGNMENT OR A PROCEDURE CALL                 *)
(*       2. A FACTOR BEGINNING WITH AN IDENTIFIER MAY BE EITHER      *)
(*          A VARIABLE OR A CONSTANT                                 *)
(*                                                                   *)
(*    IN  CASE 1 TO RESOLVE THE CHOICE ON A PURELY SYNTACTIC         *)
(*    BASIS WOULD REQUIRE A DISTORTION OF THE SYNTAX RULES           *)
(*    CHOICE 2 CANNOT BE SYNTACTICALLY RESOLVED IN SOME CASES .      *)
(*    HOWEVER IF PARALLEL SEMANTIC ANALYSIS IS ASSUMED (AS IN        *)
(*    THE CASE OF THIS COMPILER) THESE CHOICES CAN BE RESOLVED       *)
(*    WITHOUT SYNTAX DISTORTION, BY INSPECTION OF THE CURRENT        *)
(*    SEMANTIC ATTRIBUTES OF THE IDENTIFIER INVOLVED. FOR THIS       *)
(*    REASON SYNTACTIC RESOLUTION OF THESE CHOICES IS NOT USED.      *)
(*                                                                   *)
(*    THE ANALYSER GENERATES SYNTAX ERROR CODES WITH THE             *)
(*    FOLLOWING MEANINGS:                                            *)
(*                                                                   *)
(*    10 ...... SYMBOL EXPECTED WAS IDENTIFIER                       *)
(*    11 ...... SYMBOL EXPECTED WAS INTEGER CONSTANT                 *)
(*    12 ...... SYMBOL EXPECTED WAS CHARACTER CONSTANT               *)
(*    13 ...... .......                                              *)
(*                                                                   *)
(*    I.E. ONE VALUE FOR EACH OF THE VALUES OF SYMBOLTYPE.           *)
(*    THE FINAL VALUE ORD(OTHERSY)+10 IS USED TO MEAN                *)
(*                                                                   *)
(*    NN ...... UNEXPECTED SYMBOL                                    *)


TYPE

    SETOFSYMBOLS = SET OF SYMBOLTYPE ;


VAR

    STATSTARTERS,FACTORSTARTERS,MULOPS,SIGNS,ADDOPS,RELOPS : SETOFSYMBOLS ;


PROCEDURE SYNTAXERROR ( EXPECTEDSYMBOL : SYMBOLTYPE ) ;

    BEGIN
      SOURCE.ERROR(ORD(EXPECTEDSYMBOL)+10,SCAN.SYMBOLPOSITION)
    END (* SYNTAXERROR *) ;


PROCEDURE ACCEPT ( SYMBOLEXPECTED : SYMBOLTYPE ) ;

    BEGIN
      IF SCAN.SYMBOL = SYMBOLEXPECTED
      THEN SCAN.NEXTSYMBOL
      ELSE SYNTAXERROR(SYMBOLEXPECTED)
    END (* ACCEPT *) ;
```

```
PROCEDURE *PROGRAMME ;



   PROCEDURE BLOCK ;



      PROCEDURE VARPART ;


         PROCEDURE VARDECLARATION ;


            PROCEDURE TYP ;

               PROCEDURE SIMPLETYPE ;

                  BEGIN
                     ACCEPT(IDENT) ;
                  END (* SIMPLETYPE *) ;

               PROCEDURE INDEXRANGE  ;

                  BEGIN
                     ACCEPT(INTCONST) ;
                     ACCEPT(THRU) ;
                     ACCEPT(INTCONST) ;
                  END (* INDEXRANGE *) ;


               BEGIN (* TYP *)
                  IF SCAN.SYMBOL = IDENT
                  THEN SIMPLETYPE
                  ELSE
                  BEGIN
                     ACCEPT(ARRAYSY) ;
                     ACCEPT(LEFTBRACKET) ;
                     INDEXRANGE ;
                     ACCEPT(RIGHTBRACKET) ;
                     ACCEPT(OFSY) ;
                     SIMPLETYPE ;
                  END
               END (* TYP *) ;


            BEGIN (* VARDECLARATION *)
               ACCEPT(IDENT) ;
               WHILE SCAN.SYMBOL = COMMA DO
               BEGIN
                  ACCEPT(COMMA) ;
                  ACCEPT(IDENT)
               END ;
               ACCEPT(COLON) ;
               TYP
            END (* VARDECLARATION *) ;
```

```
    BEGIN (* VARPART *)
      IF SCAN.SYMBOL = VARSY THEN
      BEGIN
        ACCEPT(VARSY) ;
        REPEAT
          VARDECLARATION ;
          ACCEPT(SEMICOLON)
        UNTIL SCAN.SYMBOL <> IDENT
      END
    END (* VARPART *) ;



PROCEDURE PROCPART ;

  PROCEDURE PROCDECLARATION ;

    BEGIN (* PROCDECLARATION *)
      ACCEPT(PROCSY) ;
      ACCEPT(IDENT) ;
      ACCEPT(SEMICOLON) ;
      BLOCK ;
    END (* PROCDECLARATION *) ;

  BEGIN (* PROCPART *)
    WHILE SCAN.SYMBOL = PROCSY DO
    BEGIN
      PROCDECLARATION ;
      ACCEPT(SEMICOLON)
    END·
  END (* PROCPART *) ;



PROCEDURE STATPART ;

  PROCEDURE COMPOUNDSTATEMENT ;

    PROCEDURE STATEMENT ;

      PROCEDURE EXPRESSION ; FORWARD ;

      PROCEDURE VARIABLE ;

        BEGIN (* VARIABLE *)
          ACCEPT(IDENT) ;
          IF SCAN.SYMBOL = LEFTBRACKET THEN
          BEGIN
            ACCEPT(LEFTBRACKET) ;
            EXPRESSION ;
            ACCEPT(RIGHTBRACKET)
          END ;
        END (* VARIABLE *) ;
```

```
PROCEDURE EXPRESSION ;

  PROCEDURE SIMPLEEXPRESSION ;

    PROCEDURE TERM ;

      PROCEDURE FACTOR ;

        BEGIN
          IF SCAN.SYMBOL IN FACTORSTARTERS
          THEN
          BEGIN
            CASE SCAN.SYMBOL OF
            IDENT :
            (* IF VARIABLE IDENTIFIER  *)
            (* THEN                    *)
                VARIABLE
            (* ELSE ACCEPT AS CONSTANT *) ;
            INTCONST :
              ACCEPT(INTCONST) ;
            CHARCONST :
              ACCEPT(CHARCONST) ;
            LEFTPARENT :
              BEGIN
                ACCEPT(LEFTPARENT) ;
                EXPRESSION ;
                ACCEPT(RIGHTPARENT)
              END ;
            NOTOP :
              BEGIN
                ACCEPT(NOTOP) ;
                FACTOR
              END ;
            END ;
          END
          ELSE SYNTAXERROR(OTHERSY)
        END (* FACTOR *) ;

      BEGIN (* TERM *)
        FACTOR ;
        WHILE SCAN.SYMBOL IN MULOPS DO
        BEGIN
          SCAN.NEXTSYMBOL ;
          FACTOR ;
        END
      END (* TERM *) ;

    BEGIN (* SIMPLE EXPRESSION *)
      IF SCAN.SYMBOL IN SIGNS THEN
        SCAN.NEXTSYMBOL ;
      TERM ;
      WHILE SCAN.SYMBOL IN ADDOPS DO
      BEGIN
        SCAN.NEXTSYMBOL ;
        TERM ;
      END
    END (* SIMPLE EXPRESSION *) ;
```

```
   BEGIN (* EXPRESSION *)
      SIMPLEEXPRESSION ;
      IF SCAN.SYMBOL IN RELOPS THEN
      BEGIN
         SCAN.NEXTSYMBOL ;
         SIMPLEEXPRESSION ;
      END
   END (* EXPRESSION *) ;


PROCEDURE ASSIGNMENT ;

   BEGIN (* ASSIGNMENT *)
      VARIABLE ;
      ACCEPT(BECOMES) ;
      EXPRESSION
   END (* ASSIGNMENT *) ;


PROCEDURE READSTATEMENT ;

   PROCEDURE INPUTVARIABLE ;
      BEGIN
         VARIABLE
      END (* INPUTVARIABLE *);

   BEGIN
      ACCEPT(READSY) ;
      ACCEPT(LEFTPARENT) ;
      INPUTVARIABLE ;
      WHILE SCAN.SYMBOL = COMMA DO
      BEGIN
         ACCEPT(COMMA) ;
         INPUTVARIABLE
      END ;
      ACCEPT(RIGHTPARENT)
   END (* READSTATEMENT *) ;


PROCEDURE WRITESTATEMENT ;

   PROCEDURE OUTPUTVALUE ;
      BEGIN
         EXPRESSION
      END (* OUTPUTVALUE *) ;

   BEGIN
      ACCEPT(WRITESY) ;
      ACCEPT(LEFTPARENT) ;
      OUTPUTVALUE ;
      WHILE SCAN.SYMBOL = COMMA DO
      BEGIN
         ACCEPT(COMMA) ;
         OUTPUTVALUE
      END ;
      ACCEPT(RIGHTPARENT)
   END (* WRITESTATEMENT *) ;
```

```
PROCEDURE IFSTATEMENT ;

    BEGIN (* IFSTATEMENT *)
       ACCEPT(IFSY) ;
       EXPRESSION ;
       ACCEPT(THENSY) ;
       STATEMENT ;
       IF SCAN.SYMBOL = ELSESY
       THEN
       BEGIN
          ACCEPT(ELSESY) ;
          STATEMENT ;
       END
    END (* IFSTATEMENT *) ;


PROCEDURE WHILESTATEMENT ;

    BEGIN (* WHILESTATEMENT *)
       ACCEPT(WHILESY) ;
       EXPRESSION ;
       ACCEPT(DOSY) ;
       STATEMENT
    END (* WHILESTATEMENT *) ;


BEGIN (* STATEMENT *)
    IF SCAN.SYMBOL IN STATSTARTERS
    THEN
       CASE SCAN.SYMBOL OF
       IDENT :
       (* IF PROCEDURE IDENTIFIER            *)
       (* THEN ACCEPT AS PROCEDURE STATEMENT *)
       (* ELSE                               *)
          ASSIGNMENT ;
       BEGINSY :
          COMPOUNDSTATEMENT ;
       IFSY :
          IFSTATEMENT ;
       WHILESY :
          WHILESTATEMENT ;
       READSY :
          READSTATEMENT ;
       WRITESY :
          WRITESTATEMENT
       END (* CASE *)
    ELSE SYNTAXERROR(OTHERSY)
END (* STATEMENT *) ;


BEGIN (*COMPOUNDSTATEMENT *)
   ACCEPT(BEGINSY) ;
   STATEMENT ;
   WHILE SCAN.SYMBOL = SEMICOLON DO
   BEGIN
      ACCEPT(SEMICOLON) ;
      STATEMENT
   END ;
   ACCEPT(ENDSY)
END (* COMPOUND STATEMENT *) ;
```

```
      BEGIN (* STATPART *)
         COMPOUNDSTATEMENT
      END (* STATPART *) ;


      BEGIN (* BLOCK *)
         VARPART ;
         PROCPART ;
         STATPART
      END (* BLOCK *) ;


    BEGIN (* PROGRAMME *)
       ACCEPT(PROGRAMSY) ;
       ACCEPT(IDENT) ;
       ACCEPT(SEMICOLON) ;
       BLOCK
    END (* PROGRAMME *) ;


BEGIN
    STATSTARTERS := [IDENT,BEGINSY,READSY,WRITESY,IFSY,WHILESY] ;
    FACTORSTARTERS := [IDENT,INTCONST,CHARCONST,NOTOP,LEFTPARENT] ;
    MULOPS := [TIMES,DIVOP,ANDOP] ;
    SIGNS := [PLUS,MINUS] ;
    ADDOPS := [PLUS,MINUS,OROP] ;
    RELOPS := [EQOP,NEOP,LTOP,LEOP,GEOP,GTOP] ;

    ***

END (* ANALYZER MODULE *) ;
```

procedures used within the analyzer, but for the analyzer already constructed is rarely more than one or two symbols.

It is easy to enforce this synchronization at the start of the procedure S corresponding to a syntax rule $\langle S \rangle$. The set of symbols which are legitimate starters for a sequence of form $\langle S \rangle$ is known so a preliminary statement of the form

> **if not** (*scan.symbol* **in** *starters*) **then**
> **begin**
>   *error* ... ;
>   *skipto* (*starters*)
> **end** ;

can be added to the procedure body of S, where *skipto* is an operation which accepts symbols from the input stream until one of the set of symbols specified is found.

The obvious danger is that if the intended starter has been omitted the *skipto* operation may skip over symbols which should have been processed by the procedures which called *S*.

What do we mean by synchronization at procedure exit? In practice it implies that the symbol under scan when execution of *S* is complete is one which the procedure which called *S* is prepared to deal with next. The procedure *S* has no intrinsic knowledge of which symbols these are, but it can be passed this information as a parameter at the point of call. We therefore add a parameter to the syntax procedure corresponding to the syntax rule $\langle S \rangle$:

procedure *S* (*followers* : *set of symbols*) ;

where followers are those symbols which the calling procedure is prepared to deal with after the call to *S* is completed. Now we can readily add to the body of *S* a trailing statement of the form

> **if not** (*scan.symbol* **in** *followers*) **then**
> **begin**
>   *error* . . . ;
>   *skipto* (*followers*)
> **end**

Introduction of *followers* also enables us to avoid the dangers inherent in the statement to enforce synchronization at procedure entry, by re-writing it in the rather more complex form

> **if not** (*scan.symbol* **in** *starters*) **then**
> **begin**
>   *error* . . . ;
>   *skipto* (*starters* + *followers*)
> **end** ;
> **if** *scan.symbol* **in** *starters* **then** . . .

With this prelude, if a follower of *S* is met before a starter an immediate exit from *S* will occur without execution of the body proper.

What actual parameter is used in making a call to procedure *S*? Clearly it must include the set of symbols which may legitimately occur *immediately* after the sequence scanned by *S*. However, since the legitimate immediate follower may itself be missing in an incorrect program the actual set used is strengthened by the addition of

(a) subsequent symbols which the calling procedure expects to deal with after the call to *S*, and

(b) the follower symbols which the calling procedure has itself received as parameter.

The inclusion of (b) guarantees that within any nest of active syntax procedures a lower-level procedure cannot inadvertently skip over a symbol which a higher-level procedure expects to deal with.

So our revised picture of the syntax procedure corresponding to a syntax rule $\langle S \rangle$ is

> **procedure** S (*followers* : *set of symbols*) ;
> **begin**
> **if not** (*scan.symbol* **in** *starters*) **then**
> **begin**
> *error* ... ;
> *skipto* (*starters* + *followers*)
> **end** ;
> **if** *scan.symbol* **in** *starters* **then**
> **begin**
>
>
> **if not** (*scan.symbol* **in** *followers*) **then**
> **begin**
> *error* ... ;
> *skipto* (*followers*)
> **end**
> **end**
> **end** ;

where the dotted lines represent the analyzer body constructed as before, except that each call to any other syntax procedure T takes the form

$$T([\quad] + followers)$$

where [ ] is the set of symbols which S, or a procedure which S calls, expects to deal with after the call to T.

Modification of each syntax procedure of the analyzer in this way would achieve a reasonable level of syntax-error recovery, but at a considerable expansion of the code length of the analyzer as a whole. However, the same effect can be achieved much more economically by abstracting the synchronization code in the form of an *envelope*. The code structure bracketing each procedure body differs only in the starters and followers sets which are manipulated, so we may define an envelope in the form

      envelope *check* (*starters, followers* : *set of symbols*) ;
      begin
        if not (*scan.symbol* **in** *starters*) **then**
        begin
          source.error (, *scan.symbol position*) ;
          skipto (*starters* + *followers*)
        end
        if *scan.symbol* **in** *starters* **then**
        begin
          *** ;
          if not (*scan.symbol* **in** *followers*) **then**
          begin
            source.error (, *scan.symbol position*) ;
            skipto (*followers*)
          end
        end
      end ;

and declare each syntax procedure in the form

      procedure *S* (*followers* : *set of symbols*) ;
      instance *context* : *check* (*starters of S, followers*) ;
      begin

```
┌─────────┐
│ . . . . . . │
│ . . . . . . │
│ . . . . . . │
└─────────┘
```

      end ;

where the dotted lines are again the procedure body with parameterized syntax procedure calls as before. The result is an analyzer with the desired syntax-error recovery at the cost of a modest code increase on the analyzer previously constructed.

    Listing 4 shows a syntax analyzer derived from that in Listing 3 in this way. It corresponds to a purely mechanical introduction of the followers parameters and context envelopes for each syntax procedure, with the following exceptions:

(a)   The procedures *assignment, readstatement, writestatement, ifstatement* and *whilestatement* serve only as alternative paths through the enclosing procedure *statement* and do not require followers parameters, or context envelopes of their own.

(b) The syntax form $S\{aS\}$ consisting of a sequence of one or more sub forms S separated by separators a, translates to analyzer code of the form

$$S \; ;$$
while *scan.symbol* $= a$ **do**
begin
　　accept (a) ;
　　S
end

In adding syntax recovery it is logical to guard against a missing separator a by including the starters of S in the actual followers parameter used for each call of S in this code. However, if this is to be effective, the **while** loop condition must also be relaxed to continue looping when a starter of S actually occurs, thus:

$$S \, ([a] + \textit{startersof } S + \textit{followers}) \; ;$$
while *scan.symbol* **in** $[a]$ $+$ *startersof S* **do**
begin
　　accept (a) ;
　　$S \, ([a] + \textit{startersof } S + \textit{followers})$
end

This technique is used in the procedure *compoundstatement* to handle missing semicolons, and in the procedure *term* to handle missing operators in an expression.

Test 4, which follows Listing 4, shows a suitable driver program to test the syntax analyzer, and the output produced for one test input. In practice a carefully chosen sequence of such test programs is necessary to test the analyzer's behavior over the range of possible syntax errors and recovery.

Listing 4

```
ENVELOPE MODULE ANALYZE ;


   CONST ALFALENGTH = 8 ;

   TYPE  ALFA = PACKED ARRAY [1..ALFALENGTH] OF CHAR ;

         SYMBOLTYPE = ( IDENT,INTCONST,CHARCONST,
                        NOTOP,ANDOP,OROP,
                        TIMES,DIVOP,PLUS,MINUS,
                        LTOP,LEOP,GEOP,GTOP,NEOP,EQOP,
                        RIGHTPARENT,LEFTPARENT,LEFTBRACKET,RIGHTBRACKET,
                        COMMA,SEMICOLON,PERIOD,COLON,BECOMES,THRU,
                        PROGRAMSY,VARSY,PROCSY,ARRAYSY,OFSY,
                        BEGINSY,ENDSY,IFSY,THENSY,ELSESY,WHILESY,DOSY,
                        READSY,WRITESY,
                        OTHERSY ) ;


   ENVELOPE MODULE SCAN = LISTING2 IN LIBRARY  ;

   (* (A) SYNTAX ANALYSIS                                              *)
   (*                                                                  *)
   (*    SYNTAX ANALYSIS OF MINI-PASCAL PROGRAMS IS IMPLEMENTED        *)
   (*    AS A SET OF RECURSIVE DESCENT PROCEDURES. THESE PROCEDURES    *)
   (*    ARE BASED ON THE SYNTAX RULES GIVEN IN THE LANGUAGE DEFN      *)
   (*    AND ARE NESTED AS TIGHTLY AS THE MUTUAL INTERACTION PERMITS.  *)
   (*    THE ORDER, NAMES, AND NESTING OF THE PROCEDURES IS AS FOLLOWS *)
   (*                                                                  *)
   (*        PROGRAMME                                                 *)
   (*          BLOCK                                                   *)
   (*            VARPART                                               *)
   (*              VARDECLARATION                                      *)
   (*                TYP                                               *)
   (*                  SIMPLETYPE                                      *)
   (*                  INDEXRANGE                                      *)
   (*            PROCPART                                              *)
   (*              PROCDECLARATION                                     *)
   (*            STATPART                                              *)
   (*              COMPOUNDSTATEMENT                                   *)
   (*                STATEMENT                                         *)
   (*                  VARIABLE                                        *)
   (*                  EXPRESSION                                      *)
   (*                    SIMPLEEXPRESSION                              *)
   (*                      TERM                                        *)
   (*                        FACTOR                                    *)
   (*                  ASSIGNMENT                                      *)
   (*                  READSTATEMENT                                   *)
   (*                    INPUTVARIABLE                                 *)
   (*                  WRITESTATEMENT                                  *)
   (*                    OUTPUTVALUE                                   *)
   (*                  IFSTATEMENT                                     *)
   (*                  WHILESTATEMENT                                  *)
   (*                                                                  *)
   (*                                                                  *)
```

```
(*   THE SYNTAX ANALYZERS ARE WRITTEN ON THE ASSUMPTION THAT THE        *)
(*   NEXT SYNTACTIC GOAL CAN ALWAYS BE SELECTED BY INSPECTION OF        *)
(*   (AT MOST) THE NEXT INCOMING SYMBOL ( I.E. THAT THE UNDERLYING      *)
(*   GRAMMAR IS LL(1) ). THIS IS NOT SO AT THE FOLLOWING POINTS         *)
(*   IN THE SYNTAX RULES ACTUALLY USED                                 *)
(*                                                                     *)
(*      1. A STATEMENT BEGINNING WITH AN IDENTIFIER MAY BE             *)
(*         EITHER AN ASSIGNMENT OR A PROCEDURE CALL                    *)
(*      2. A FACTOR BEGINNING WITH AN IDENTIFIER MAY BE EITHER         *)
(*         A VARIABLE OR A CONSTANT                                    *)
(*                                                                     *)
(*   IN  CASE 1 TO RESOLVE THE CHOICE ON A PURELY SYNTACTIC            *)
(*   BASIS WOULD REQUIRE A DISTORTION OF THE SYNTAX RULES              *)
(*   CHOICE 2 CANNOT BE SYNTACTICALLY RESOLVED IN SOME CASES .         *)
(*   HOWEVER IF PARALLEL SEMANTIC ANALYSIS IS ASSUMED (AS IN           *)
(*   THE CASE OF THIS COMPILER) THESE CHOICES CAN BE RESOLVED          *)
(*   WITHOUT SYNTAX DISTORTION, BY INSPECTION OF THE CURRENT           *)
(*   SEMANTIC ATTRIBUTES OF THE IDENTIFIER INVOLVED. FOR THIS          *)
(*   REASON SYNTACTIC RESOLUTION OF THESE CHOICES IS NOT USED.         *)
(*                                                                     *)
(*   THE ANALYZER GENERATES SYNTAX ERROR CODES WITH THE                *)
(*   FOLLOWING MEANINGS:                                               *)
(*                                                                     *)
(*   10 ...... SYMBOL EXPECTED WAS IDENTIFIER                          *)
(*   11 ...... SYMBOL EXPECTED WAS INTEGER CONSTANT                    *)
(*   12 ...... SYMBOL EXPECTED WAS CHARACTER CONSTANT                  *)
(*   13 ...... .......                                                 *)
(*                                                                     *)
(*   I.E. ONE VALUE FOR EACH OF THE VALUES OF SYMBOLTYPE.              *)
(*   THE FINAL VALUE ORD(OTHERSY)+10 IS USED TO MEAN                   *)
(*                                                                     *)
(*   NN ...... UNEXPECTED SYMBOL                                       *)


TYPE

    SETOFSYMBOLS = SET OF SYMBOLTYPE ;


VAR

    STATSTARTERS,FACTORSTARTERS,MULOPS,SIGNS,ADDOPS,RELOPS : SETOFSYMBOLS ;

PROCEDURE SYNTAXERROR ( EXPECTEDSYMBOL : SYMBOLTYPE ) ;

    BEGIN
      SOURCE.ERROR(ORD(EXPECTEDSYMBOL)+10,SCAN.SYMBOLPOSITION)
    END (* SYNTAXERROR *) ;


PROCEDURE ACCEPT ( SYMBOLEXPECTED : SYMBOLTYPE ) ;

    BEGIN
      IF SCAN.SYMBOL = SYMBOLEXPECTED
      THEN SCAN.NEXTSYMBOL
      ELSE SYNTAXERROR(SYMBOLEXPECTED)
    END (* ACCEPT *) ;
```

```
(*  (B) SYNTACTIC ERROR RECOVERY                                      *)
(*                                                                    *)
(*   RECOVERY IN THE SYNTAX ANALYSIS PROCESS FOLLOWING THE            *)
(*   DISCOVERY OF A SYNTAX ERROR IS INCORPORATED INTO THE             *)
(*   SYNTAX PROCEDURES ON THE FOLLOWING BASIS                         *)
(*                                                                    *)
(*      1. EACH PROCEDURE WHEN CALLED IS PASSED AN ACTUAL             *)
(*         PARAMETER WHICH IS A SET OF SYMBOLS WHICH ARE              *)
(*         POSSIBLE FOLLOWERS OF THE STRING WHICH IT SHOULD           *)
(*         SCAN. THESE FOLLOWERS NORMALLY INCLUDE                     *)
(*            (A) ALL SYMBOLS WHICH MAY LEGITIMATELY FOLLOW           *)
(*                THE STRING TO BE SCANNED                            *)
(*            (B) SUCH ADDITIONAL SYMBOLS AS A SUPERIOR               *)
(*                (CALLING) PROCEDURE MAY WISH TO HANDLE IN           *)
(*                THE EVENT OF ERROR RECOVERY                         *)
(*                                                                    *)
(*      2. WHEN ENTERED THE PROCEDURE MAY ENSURE THAT THE             *)
(*         CURRENT SYMBOL IS AN ACCEPTABLE STARTER FOR THE            *)
(*         STRING TO BE SCANNED, AND IF NOT SCAN FORWARD              *)
(*         UNTIL SUCH A SYMBOL IS FOUND (SUBJECT TO 4. BELOW)         *)
(*                                                                    *)
(*      3. WHEN CALLING A SUBSIDIARY SYNTAX PROCEDURE THE             *)
(*         PROCEDURE PASSES ON AS FOLLOWERS ITS OWN FOLLOWERS PLUS    *)
(*         THOSE SYMBOLS IF ANY WHICH IT MAY DETERMINE AS             *)
(*         FOLLOWERS FOR THE SUBSTRING TO BE SCANNED                  *)
(*                                                                    *)
(*      4. TO RECOVER FROM A SYNTAX ERROR THE PROCEDURE MAY           *)
(*         SCAN OVER (SKIP) ANY SYMBOL PROVIDED IT IS NOT             *)
(*         CONTAINED IN THE FOLLOWERS PASSED TO IT                    *)
(*                                                                    *)
(*      5. ON EXIT THE SYNTAX PROCEDURE ENSURES THAT THE CURRENT      *)
(*         SYMBOL IS CONTAINED IN THE FOLLOWERS PASSED TO IT,         *)
(*         FLAGGING A TERMINAL ERROR AND SKIPPING IF THIS IS NOT      *)
(*         INITIALLY THE CASE.                                        *)
(*                                                                    *)
(*   TESTS 2 AND 5 ARE IMPLEMENTED BY THE DECLARATION OF AN           *)
(*   INSTANCE OF A CONTEXT CHECKING ENVELOPE WITHIN EACH              *)
(*   SYNTAX PROCEDURE                                                 *)


ENVELOPE CHECK ( STARTERS,FOLLOWERS : SETOFSYMBOLS ) ;

    PROCEDURE SKIPTO ( RELEVANTSYMBOLS : SETOFSYMBOLS ) ;
      BEGIN
        WHILE NOT (SCAN.SYMBOL IN RELEVANTSYMBOLS)
        DO SCAN.NEXTSYMBOL
      END (* SKIPTO *) ;

    BEGIN
      IF NOT (SCAN.SYMBOL IN STARTERS) THEN
      BEGIN SYNTAXERROR(OTHERSY);  SKIPTO(STARTERS+FOLLOWERS) END ;
      IF SCAN.SYMBOL IN STARTERS THEN
      BEGIN
        *** (* EXECUTE ENVELOPED BLOCK *) ;
        IF NOT (SCAN.SYMBOL IN FOLLOWERS) THEN
        BEGIN SYNTAXERROR(OTHERSY); SKIPTO(FOLLOWERS) END
      END
    END (* CHECK ENVELOPE *) ;
```

```
PROCEDURE *PROGRAMME ;



   PROCEDURE BLOCK ( FOLLOWERS : SETOFSYMBOLS ) ;

   INSTANCE CONTEXT:CHECK([VARSY,PROCSY,BEGINSY],FOLLOWERS) ;



      PROCEDURE VARPART ( FOLLOWERS : SETOFSYMBOLS ) ;

        INSTANCE CONTEXT:CHECK([VARSY]+FOLLOWERS,FOLLOWERS) ;


        PROCEDURE VARDECLARATION ( FOLLOWERS : SETOFSYMBOLS ) ;

          INSTANCE CONTEXT:CHECK([IDENT,COMMA,COLON],FOLLOWERS) ;


          PROCEDURE TYP ( FOLLOWERS : SETOFSYMBOLS ) ;

            INSTANCE CONTEXT:CHECK([IDENT,ARRAYSY],FOLLOWERS) ;

            PROCEDURE SIMPLETYPE ( FOLLOWERS : SETOFSYMBOLS ) ;

              INSTANCE CONTEXT:CHECK([IDENT],FOLLOWERS) ;

              BEGIN
                 ACCEPT(IDENT) ;
              END (* SIMPLETYPE *) ;

            PROCEDURE INDEXRANGE  ( FOLLOWERS : SETOFSYMBOLS ) ;

              INSTANCE CONTEXT:CHECK([INTCONST,THRU],FOLLOWERS) ;

              BEGIN
                 ACCEPT(INTCONST) ;
                 ACCEPT(THRU) ;
                 ACCEPT(INTCONST) ;
              END (* INDEXRANGE *) ;


            BEGIN (* TYP *)
               IF SCAN.SYMBOL = IDENT
               THEN SIMPLETYPE(FOLLOWERS)
               ELSE
               BEGIN
                  ACCEPT(ARRAYSY) ;
                  ACCEPT(LEFTBRACKET) ;
                  INDEXRANGE([RIGHTBRACKET,OFSY]+FOLLOWERS) ;
                  ACCEPT(RIGHTBRACKET) ;
                  ACCEPT(OFSY) ;
                  SIMPLETYPE(FOLLOWERS) ;
               END
            END (* TYP *) ;
```

```
      BEGIN (* VARDECLARATION *)
         ACCEPT(IDENT) ;
         WHILE SCAN.SYMBOL = COMMA DO
         BEGIN
            ACCEPT(COMMA) ;
            ACCEPT(IDENT)
         END ;
         ACCEPT(COLON) ;
         TYP(FOLLOWERS)
      END (* VARDECLARATION *) ;


   BEGIN (* VARPART *)
      IF SCAN.SYMBOL = VARSY THEN
      BEGIN
         ACCEPT(VARSY) ;
         REPEAT
            VARDECLARATION([SEMICOLON]+FOLLOWERS) ;
            ACCEPT(SEMICOLON)
         UNTIL SCAN.SYMBOL <> IDENT
      END
   END (* VARPART *) ;


PROCEDURE PROCPART ( FOLLOWERS : SETOFSYMBOLS ) ;

   INSTANCE CONTEXT:CHECK([PROCSY]+FOLLOWERS,FOLLOWERS) ;

   PROCEDURE PROCDECLARATION ( FOLLOWERS : SETOFSYMBOLS ) ;

      INSTANCE CONTEXT:CHECK([PROCSY],FOLLOWERS) ;

      BEGIN (* PROCDECLARATION *)
         ACCEPT(PROCSY) ;
         ACCEPT(IDENT) ;
         ACCEPT(SEMICOLON) ;
         BLOCK(FOLLOWERS) ;
      END (* PROCDECLARATION *) ;

   BEGIN (* PROCPART *)
      WHILE SCAN.SYMBOL = PROCSY DO
      BEGIN
         PROCDECLARATION([SEMICOLON,PROCSY]+FOLLOWERS) ;
         ACCEPT(SEMICOLON)
      END
   END (* PROCPART *) ;

PROCEDURE STATPART ( FOLLOWERS : SETOFSYMBOLS ) ;

   INSTANCE CONTEXT:CHECK([BEGINSY],FOLLOWERS) ;


   PROCEDURE COMPOUNDSTATEMENT ( FOLLOWERS : SETOFSYMBOLS ) ;

      INSTANCE CONTEXT:CHECK([BEGINSY],FOLLOWERS) ;


      PROCEDURE STATEMENT ( FOLLOWERS : SETOFSYMBOLS ) ;

         INSTANCE CONTEXT:CHECK(STATSTARTERS,FOLLOWERS) ;
```

```
PROCEDURE EXPRESSION ( FOLLOWERS : SETOFSYMBOLS ) ; FORWARD ;

PROCEDURE VARIABLE ( FOLLOWERS : SETOFSYMBOLS ) ;

   INSTANCE CONTEXT:CHECK([IDENT],FOLLOWERS) ;

   BEGIN (* VARIABLE *)
      ACCEPT(IDENT) ;
      IF SCAN.SYMBOL = LEFTBRACKET THEN
      BEGIN
         ACCEPT(LEFTBRACKET) ;
         EXPRESSION([RIGHTBRACKET]+FOLLOWERS) ;
         ACCEPT(RIGHTBRACKET)
      END ;
   END (* VARIABLE *) ;


PROCEDURE EXPRESSION :

   PROCEDURE SIMPLEEXPRESSION ( FOLLOWERS : SETOFSYMBOLS ) ;

      INSTANCE CONTEXT:CHECK(FACTORSTARTERS+SIGNS,FOLLOWERS) ;

      PROCEDURE TERM ( FOLLOWERS : SETOFSYMBOLS ) ;

         PROCEDURE FACTOR ( FOLLOWERS : SETOFSYMBOLS ) ;

            INSTANCE CONTEXT:CHECK(FACTORSTARTERS,FOLLOWERS) ;

            BEGIN
               BEGIN
                  CASE SCAN.SYMBOL OF
                  IDENT :
                  (* IF VARIABLE IDENTIFIER *)
                  (* THEN                   *)
                         VARIABLE(FOLLOWERS)
                  (* ELSE ACCEPT AS CONSTANT *) ;
                  INTCONST :
                     ACCEPT(INTCONST) ;
                  CHARCONST :
                     ACCEPT(CHARCONST) ;
                  LEFTPARENT :
                     BEGIN
                        ACCEPT(LEFTPARENT) ;
                        EXPRESSION([RIGHTPARENT]+FOLLOWERS) ;
                        ACCEPT(RIGHTPARENT)
                     END ;
                  NOTOP :
                     BEGIN
                        ACCEPT(NOTOP) ;
                        FACTOR(FOLLOWERS)
                     END ;
                  END ;
               END
            END (* FACTOR *) ;
```

```
        BEGIN (* TERM *)
        FACTOR(MULOPS+FACTORSTARTERS+FOLLOWERS) ;
        WHILE SCAN.SYMBOL IN MULOPS+FACTORSTARTERS DO
        BEGIN
            IF SCAN.SYMBOL IN MULOPS
            THEN SCAN.NEXTSYMBOL
            ELSE SYNTAXERROR(TIMES) ;
            FACTOR(MULOPS+FACTORSTARTERS+FOLLOWERS) ;
        END
        END (* TERM *) ;

    BEGIN (* SIMPLE EXPRESSION *)
        IF SCAN.SYMBOL IN SIGNS THEN
            SCAN.NEXTSYMBOL ;
        TERM(ADDOPS+FOLLOWERS) ;
        WHILE SCAN.SYMBOL IN ADDOPS DO
        BEGIN
            SCAN.NEXTSYMBOL ;
            TERM(ADDOPS+FOLLOWERS) ;
        END
        END (* SIMPLE EXPRESSION *) ;

    BEGIN (* EXPRESSION *)
        SIMPLEEXPRESSION(RELOPS+FOLLOWERS) ;
        IF SCAN.SYMBOL IN RELOPS THEN
        BEGIN
            SCAN.NEXTSYMBOL ;
            SIMPLEEXPRESSION(FOLLOWERS) ;
        END
        END (* EXPRESSION *) ;
PROCEDURE ASSIGNMENT ;

    BEGIN (* ASSIGNMENT *)
        VARIABLE([BECOMES]+FOLLOWERS) ;
        ACCEPT(BECOMES) ;
        EXPRESSION(FOLLOWERS)
        END (* ASSIGNMENT *) ;


PROCEDURE READSTATEMENT ;

    PROCEDURE INPUTVARIABLE ;
        BEGIN
            VARIABLE([COMMA,RIGHTPARENT]+FOLLOWERS)
            END (* INPUTVARIABLE *);

    BEGIN
        ACCEPT(READSY) ;
        ACCEPT(LEFTPARENT) ;
        INPUTVARIABLE ;
        WHILE SCAN.SYMBOL = COMMA DO
        BEGIN
            ACCEPT(COMMA) ;
            INPUTVARIABLE
        END ;
        ACCEPT(RIGHTPARENT)
        END (* READSTATEMENT *) ;
```

```
PROCEDURE WRITESTATEMENT ;

   PROCEDURE OUTPUTVALUE ;
      BEGIN
         EXPRESSION([COMMA,RIGHTPARENT]+FOLLOWERS)
      END (* OUTPUTVALUE *) ;

   BEGIN
      ACCEPT(WRITESY) ;
      ACCEPT(LEFTPARENT) ;
      OUTPUTVALUE ;
      WHILE SCAN.SYMBOL = COMMA DO
      BEGIN
         ACCEPT(COMMA) ;
         OUTPUTVALUE
      END ;
      ACCEPT(RIGHTPARENT)
   END (* WRITESTATEMENT *) ;
PROCEDURE IFSTATEMENT ;

   BEGIN (* IFSTATEMENT *)
      ACCEPT(IFSY) ;
      EXPRESSION([THENSY,ELSESY]+FOLLOWERS) ;
      ACCEPT(THENSY) ;
      STATEMENT([ELSESY]+FOLLOWERS) ;
      IF SCAN.SYMBOL = ELSESY
      THEN
      BEGIN
         ACCEPT(ELSESY) ;
         STATEMENT(FOLLOWERS) ;
      END
   END (* IFSTATEMENT *) ;

PROCEDURE WHILESTATEMENT ;

   BEGIN (* WHILESTATEMENT *)
      ACCEPT(WHILESY) ;
      EXPRESSION([DOSY]+FOLLOWERS) ;
      ACCEPT(DOSY) ;
      STATEMENT(FOLLOWERS)
   END (* WHILESTATEMENT *) ;

BEGIN (* STATEMENT *)
      CASE SCAN.SYMBOL OF
      IDENT :
      (* IF PROCEDURE IDENTIFIER         *)
      (* THEN ACCEPT AS PROCEDURE STATEMENT *)
      (* ELSE                            *)
         ASSIGNMENT ;
      BEGINSY :
         COMPOUNDSTATEMENT(FOLLOWERS) ;
      IFSY :
         IFSTATEMENT ;
      WHILESY :
         WHILESTATEMENT ;
      READSY :
         READSTATEMENT ;
      WRITESY :
         WRITESTATEMENT
      END (* CASE *)
END (* STATEMENT *) ;
```

```
      BEGIN (*COMPOUNDSTATEMENT *)
        ACCEPT(BEGINSY) ;
        STATEMENT([SEMICOLON,ENDSY]+STATSTARTERS
                              -[IDENT]+FOLLOWERS) ;
        WHILE SCAN.SYMBOL IN [SEMICOLON]+STATSTARTERS-[IDENT] DO
        BEGIN
          ACCEPT(SEMICOLON) ;
          STATEMENT([SEMICOLON,ENDSY]+STATSTARTERS
                            -[IDENT]+FOLLOWERS)
        END ;
        ACCEPT(ENDSY)
      END (* COMPOUND STATEMENT *) ;

    BEGIN (* STATPART *)
      COMPOUNDSTATEMENT(FOLLOWERS)
    END (* STATPART *) ;


  BEGIN (* BLOCK *)
    VARPART([PROCSY,BEGINSY]) ;
    PROCPART([BEGINSY]) ;
    STATPART(FOLLOWERS)
  END (* BLOCK *) ;


  BEGIN (* PROGRAMME *)
    ACCEPT(PROGRAMSY) ;
    ACCEPT(IDENT) ;
    ACCEPT(SEMICOLON) ;
    BLOCK([PERIOD])
  END (* PROGRAMME *) ;


BEGIN
  STATSTARTERS := [IDENT,BEGINSY,READSY,WRITESY,IFSY,WHILESY] ;
  FACTORSTARTERS := [IDENT,INTCONST,CHARCONST,NOTOP,LEFTPARENT] ;
  MULOPS := [TIMES,DIVOP,ANDOP] ;
  SIGNS := [PLUS,MINUS] ;
  ADDOPS := [PLUS,MINUS,OROP] ;
  RELOPS := [EQOP,NEOP,LTOP,LEOP,GEOP,GTOP] ;

  ***

END (* ANALYZER MODULE *) ;
```

Test 4

PASCAL PLUS COMPILER

```
0    3300   PROGRAM TESTANALYZER (INPUT,OUTPUT) ;
1
2             ENVELOPE MODULE SOURCE = LISTING1 IN LIBRARY ;
3
4    3644   ENVELOPE MODULE ANALYZE = LISTING4 IN LIBRARY ;
5
6    5512   BEGIN
7    5512      ANALYZE.PROGRAMME
8    5512   END.
```

```
COMPILATION COMPLETE :        NO ERRORS REPORTED
COMPILATION TIME      =    2680 MILLISECONDS
SOURCE PROGRAM        =    1027 LINES
OBJECT PROGRAM        =    5635 WORDS
```

LISTING PRODUCED BY MINI-PASCAL COMPILER MK 1

```
   0   PROGRAM SYNTAX ;
   1   VAR I,J : INTEGER ;
   2       A : ARRAY [1..10] OF CHAR
   3   PROCEDURE P ;
*****     ^ERROR  31

   4      VAR J : INTEGER ;
   5      BEGIN
   6         READ J ;
*****              ^ERROR  27
*****                ^ERROR  26

   7         I := I I-I I DIV I ;
*****              ^ERROR  16
*****                  ^ERROR  16

   8         IF((J=I) OR NOT (J<>I) THEN A[I]:=' ' ELSE A[ ]:='''' ;
*****                     ^ERROR  26
*****                                                ^ERROR  50

   9         IF (J=I) OR NOT (J<>I))THEN A[I]:=' ' ELSE A[ ]:='''' ;
*****                     ^ERROR  50
*****                                                ^ERROR  50

  10         WRITE(A[I]) ;
  11         I := I+1
  12      END ;
  13   BEGIN
  14      I:= 1 ; J := 1000000 ;
  15      WHILE (I>0)AND(I<11)OR(I>=1)AND(I<=10) DO I := I+1
  16      WRITE J)
*****     ^ERROR  31
*****          ^ERROR  27

  17   END.
```

COMPILATION COMPLETED :   11 ERRORS REPORTED

Exercise 3   Modify the syntax of Mini-Pascal, and then the syntax analyzer given in Listing 4, to allow a multiple assignment statement of the form

$$v_1, v_2, \ldots, v_n := e$$

SEMANTIC ANALYSIS

Attributes and their Representation

Syntax analysis applies the formally expressed syntax rules of the language definition to the program under analysis. Semantic analysis is concerned with the informal semantic rules which accompany this formal syntax. Their application involves the collection and examination of the *attributes* associated with the identifiers, constants and expressions which appear in the program. For the time being we confine our attention to those attributes necessary for *semantic checking*, i.e. verifying that the semantic rules of the language are obeyed. The construction of attributes which reflect the object program to be produced will be considered with the generator interface in the next chapter.

Clearly semantic analysis requires some means of representing the attributes associated with identifiers, constants and expressions. For identifiers the attributes necessary to semantic checking are

(a)   the declared class of usage of the identifier—in Mini-Pascal identifiers may denote types, constants, variables and procedures, so class of usage may be represented by an enumerated type:

$$idclass = (types, consts, vars, procs) ;$$

(b)   for type, constant and variable identifiers, the associated *type* itself (Mini-Pascal's parameterless procedures require no further attributes for semantic checking).

The association of each identifier with its attributes must involve the maintenance of some record of the form

$$idrec = \textbf{record}$$
$$name : alfa ;$$
$$class : idclass ;$$
$$idtype : \qquad ?$$
$$\textbf{end} ;$$

(where the field *idtype* is redundant in the case when *class* = *procs*).

The number of such records required is determined by the program being compiled, and varies greatly from one program to another. In the interests of compile-time storage economy, therefore, the representation of the records in dynamically allocated storage is preferable to any statically allocated structure, a decision which we reflect in Pascal by introduction of the pointer type

$$identry = \uparrow \ idrec \ ;$$

The creation and access of all *idrecs* required will be made through pointers of type *identry*.

How should we represent types? Each type in a program is shared by, and must be associated with, a number of data objects. For storage economy each association with a given type should be represented by some reference to a single descriptor of the type, rather than by duplication of the descriptor at each point of association. Where the number of types to be represented is not predetermined, the pointer is again the natural means of denoting such references in Pascal, so we introduce a type

$$typentry = \uparrow \ typerec \ ;$$

In Mini-Pascal a type is either one of the built-in scalar types (*integer*, *char*, *Boolean*) or an array type whose index range and element type is determined by the type definition within a variable declaration. A suitable form for the type descriptors is thus defined by

>   *typeform* = (*scalars, arrays*) ;
>   *typerec* = **record**
>   **case** *form* : *typeform* **of**
>   *arrays* : (*indexmin, indexmax* : *integer* ;
>   *elementtype* : *typentry*)
>   **end** ;

Notice that no explicit discrimination between the individual scalar types is necessary within the descriptors. The descriptor for type *integer* is that pointed to by the entry for the identifier *"integer"*. Any type represented by the same pointer value must be *integer*.

The Semantic Table

The semantic analysis of identifiers involves

(a) creating a new identifier record for each identifier on encountering its declaration, and recording its attributes therein;
(b) locating the entry for a particular identifier on each of its subsequent occurrences, and inspecting its attributes.

For block-structured languages such as Mini-Pascal, the process is complicated by the fact that more than one entry for an identifier may exist and the appropriate entry, as determined by the scope rules of the language, must always be selected.

Clearly some form of table is required to hold the identifier records. Since its organization seems independent of the actual analysis applied to the attributes stored there, it is logical to isolate this organization from the semantic analyzer proper. This separation might be achieved by the introduction of a module of the following form:

```
envelope module Table ;
    envelope *Newscope ;
        procedure *Newid (spelling : alfa ;
                          var entry : identry) ;
            . . .
        procedure *Searchid (spelling : alfa ;
                             var entry : identry) ;
            . . .
        begin
            {initialize new scope};
            *** ;
            {finalize scope}
        end ;
    begin
        {initialize table of scopes} ;
        ***
    end ;
```

The semantic analyzer must signal the beginning and end of each scope range, as determined by the syntactic block structure of the program, by creating an instance of the scope envelope. Within this envelope the analyzer may create a new identifier entry in the current scope by a call to *Newid*, or locate the appropriate entry for an identifier, in the current or any enclosing scope, by a call to *Searchid*.

Context-error detection and recovery

This interface reflects the basic functions of the identifier table in the semantic-analysis process. However, its precise behavior may be further refined in relation to the errors of identifier context which semantic analysis must detect and recover from.

Consider, for example, the handling of an identifier encountered as the first symbol of a statement. The analyzer actions must take the general form:

> Locate identifier in table ;
> **if** none exists
> **then** error—undeclared identifier
> **else**
> > **if not** class **in** [vars,procs]
> > **then** error—identifier out of context
> > **else** . . .

It turns out that the screening tests for:

(a) undeclared identifiers, and
(b) identifiers of inappropriate class

are common to every context in which Searchid is required. It is more logical therefore to incorporate them within Searchid. To do so, however, requires a further parameter in the parameter list—to specify the acceptable classes of identifier at that moment—thus:

> **procedure** Searchid (spelling : alfa ;
> > > allowableclasses : set of idclass ;
> > > **var** entry : identry) ;

When an undeclared identifier is detected, semantic error recovery demands that a new entry for the identifier be created at that point. This will prevent repeated flagging of the same undeclared identifier at its every occurrence in the program being compiled. This too can be incorporated within the specification of Searchid.

With these refinements the procedure Searchid is guaranteed to return a pointer to an identifier entry of appropriate class at every call. This guarantee considerably simplifies the semantic analysis code around the point of call. For example the statement analysis outlined above becomes:

> Table.Searchid (scan.spelling, [vars, procs], idfound) ;
> > **case** idfound ↑ .class **of**
> > vars : assignment ;
> > procs : . . .
> > **end**

The procedure Newid can deal with duplicate declaration errors in a similar manner. When a second declaration of some identifier occurs in a given scope, whose attributes differ from the first, semantic-error recovery suggests that both entries should be retained and the more appropriate one chosen at any subsequent occurrence of the identifier. Provided Newid makes the duplicate entries, *Searchid* will sometimes be able to choose between them —on the basis of appropriate class.

Storage control and recovery

Newid is responsible for the creation of the dynamically allocated records used to hold the identifier attributes. While our concept of these attributes so far is simple, in general they, and the storage required for their representation, may vary considerably from one class of identifier to another. To achieve storage economy *Newid* must therefore be aware of the required class of identifier and hence of its storage requirement. We therefore extend the parameter list to accommodate this information, thus:

> **procedure** *Newid* (*spelling* : *alfa* ;
> *classneeded* : *idclass* ;
> **var** *entry* : *identry*) ;

This new parameter also enables *Newid* to fill each new identifier record with a set of default attributes, an action which again simplifies coding in the analyzer proper.

In a one-pass compiler all usage of the identifier entries takes place between the opening and closing of the scope in which they are created. It is possible therefore to reclaim the storage occupied by the local identifier entries when closing any scope, and storage economy dictates that this should be done. This storage recovery can be programmed into the finalization sequence of the scope envelope, according to the organization chosen for identifier records within the table module.

A similar lifetime is sufficient for the type records created within any scope. To enable these to be dealt with in the same way a final extension is made to the scope envelope interface—to put the creation of type records, and hence their collection and disposal, under its control. This we do by a further interface procedure:

> **procedure** *Newtype* (**var** *entry* : *typentry* ;
> *formneeded* : *typeform*) ;

Programming the Table Module

With these refinements of its interface settled, the internal organization of the table module can now be considered. To reflect the block structure and corresponding identifier scopes in the program being compiled the table must clearly be held as a stack of sub-tables, one for each scope currently in existence, with the topmost sub-table holding the identifier records for the current local scope. As we saw in Section 1, this organization can be represented in Pascal by introducing types

```
scope  =  ↑  scoperec ;
scoperec = record
              local identifiers . . . ;
              enclosing scope : scope
           end ;
```

and a pointer variable which always points to the *scoperec* representing the current local scope:

```
localscope : scope ;
```

The initial action required on creating a new instance of a scope envelope is readily expressed as

```
procedure Openscope ;
  var newscope : scope ;
  begin
    new(newscope) ;
    with newscope ↑ do
    begin
      local identifiers := none ;
      enclosing scope := localscope
    end ;
    localscope := newscope
  end ;
```

The hierarchical search which block structure demands of *Searchid* will have the form

```
procedure Searchid (. . .) ;
  var thisscope : scope ;
  begin
    thisscope := localscope ;
    repeat
      search for identifier required
      in subtable thisscope ↑ .local identifiers
      and exit if found ;
      thisscope := thisscope ↑ .enclosingscope
    until thisscope = nil ;
    identifier not found
  end ;
```

How do we organize and search the sub-tables holding the identifiers local to each scope? After character handling, table searching is the second most time-consuming activity in most compilers, so it is important that an organization allowing fast searching be chosen. Simple linear lists are too slow when programs containing a large number of identifiers are compiled. Hash tables are undoubtedly the fastest organization for simple table look-up, but their advantage is blunted when used in a block-structured environment. As a simpler compromise we will adopt a *binary-tree* organization for each sub-table, which gives a reasonably fast search without excessive storage overheads.

The identifier records created in each scope can be organized as nodes in a binary tree by the addition of two pointer fields to each record, which point to the root node of the left and right sub-trees, thus

$$idrec = \textbf{record}$$
$$name : alfa \ ;$$
$$leftlink, rightlink : identry \ ;$$
$$class : \ldots$$
$$\ldots$$
$$\textbf{end} \ ;$$

Trees are maintained such that the identifier at any node is alphabetically greater than any identifier in its left sub-tree, but less than any identifier in its right sub-tree. This allows searching by the binary-split technique.

Each sub-table within a scope record is now representable by a pointer to the root node of the corresponding binary tree, thus:

$$scoperec = \textbf{record}$$
$$firstlocal \ ; identry \ ;$$
$$enclosingscope : scope$$
$$\textbf{end}$$

and the process of searching the sub-tables within *Searchid* is expressible as follows

```
thisentry := thisscope ↑ .firstlocal ;
while thisentry ≠ nil do
    if thisentry ↑ .name > spelling
    then thisentry := thisentry ↑ . leftlink
    else
    if thisentry ↑ .name < spelling
    then thisentry := thisentry ↑ .rightlink
    else entry found ;
entry not found
```

The logic for inserting a new entry within *Newid* is similar except that the occurrence of a **nil** pointer denotes the appropriate point for insertion. Listing 5 shows the detailed realization of this logic for both *Newid* and *Searchid*.

Listing 5

```
ENVELOPE MODULE TABLE ;

  (* THE TABLE MODULE ORGANISES THE CREATION OF, LOCATION OF, AND      *)
  (* STORAGE RECOVERY FROM, THE IDENTIFIER AND TYPE RECORDS WHICH      *)
  (* SUPPORT SEMANTIC ANALYSIS                                         *)
  (*                                                                   *)
  (* THE TABLE IS ORGANISED AS A SET OF BINARY TREES, ONE FOR         *)
  (* EACH IDENTIFIER SCOPE CURRENTLY OPEN, THE NESTING OF THESE       *)
  (* SCOPES BEING REPRESENTED BY A STACK OF SCOPE RECORDS             *)
  (*                                                                   *)
  (* SCOPE HOUSEKEEPING IS CARRIED OUT BY AN INSTANCE OF THE SCOPE    *)
  (* ENVELOPE CREATED FOR EACH BLOCK. WITHIN THIS ENVELOPE           *)
  (* INSERTION AND LOOKUP OF IDENTIFIERS WITHIN THE TABLE IS         *)
  (* PROVIDED BY THE TWO PROCEDURES "NEWID" AND "SEARCHID".          *)
  (*                                                                   *)
  (* RECOVERY FROM SEMANTIC ERRORS IS ACCOMODATED WITHIN THESE DATA  *)
  (* STRUCTURES AND PROCEDURES AS FOLLOWS                            *)
  (*                                                                   *)
  (*    (1) IF NEWID FINDS AN ENTRY FOR THE IDENTIFIER ALREADY IN    *)
  (*        THE CURRENT SCOPE, AN ERROR IS FLAGGED BUT A SECOND ENTRY*)
  (*        IS STILL MADE(FOR POSSIBLE SELECTION BY SEARCHID AS      *)
  (*        BELOW)                                                   *)
  (*                                                                   *)
  (*    (2) SEARCHID WHEN CALLED IS PASSED A PARAMETER SPECIFYING    *)
  (*        THE ACCEPTABLE CLASSES OF ENTRY TO BE FOUND . IF THE     *)
  (*        FIRST ENTRY ENCOUNTERED FOR THE IDENTIFIER IS NOT OF AN  *)
  (*        ACCEPTABLE CLASS SEARCHING CONTINUES WITHIN THE CURRENT  *)
  (*        SCOPE FOR A POSSIBLE DUPLICATE ENTRY. IF NO ACCEPTABLE   *)
  (*        DUPLICATE IS FOUND IN THE SCOPE A MISUSE ERROR IS        *)
  (*        REPORTED AND AN ANONYMOUS DEFAULT ENTRY OF ACCEPTABLE    *)
  (*        CLASS IS RETURNED.                                       *)
  (*                                                                   *)
  (*    (3) IF SEARCHID FAILS TO FIND AN ENTRY IN ANY SCOPE FOR THE  *)
  (*        IDENTIFIER SOUGHT,AN UNDECLARED ERROR IS REPORTED AND    *)
  (*        AN ENTRY OF ACCEPTABLE CLASS IS CREATED FOR THE IDENT-   *)
  (*        IFIER, WITH OTHERWISE DEFAULT ATTRIBUTES.                *)
  (*                                                                   *)
  (* TO FACILITATE STORAGE RECOVERY THE CREATION OF TYPE ENTRIES     *)
  (* IS HANDLED BY THE TABLE MODULE. EACH TYPE ENTRY CREATED BY      *)
  (* "NEWTYPE" IS APPENDED IN A LINEAR CHAIN TO THE CURRENT BLOCK    *)
  (* SCOPE ENTRY IN THE DISPLAY. ALL STORAGE ALLOCATED TO TABLE      *)
  (* ENTRIES IS RECOVERED AT FINAL CLOSURE OF A BLOCK SCOPE          *)
  (*                                                                   *)
  (* THE TABLE MODULE REPORTS ERRORS WITH THE FOLLOWING CODES        *)
  (*                                                                   *)
  (* 51 .... IDENTIFIER DECLARED TWICE                               *)
  (* 52 .... IDENTIFIER NOT DECLARED                                 *)
  (* 53 .... IDENTIFIER OF WRONG CLASS FOR THIS CONTEXT              *)

TYPE SCOPE = ^SCOPEREC ;
     SCOPEREC = RECORD
                    FIRSTLOCAL : IDENTRY ;
                    TYPECHAIN : TYPENTRY ;
                    ENCLOSINGSCOPE : SCOPE
                END ;

VAR LOCALSCOPE : SCOPE ;
    DEFAULTENTRY : ARRAY[IDCLASS] OF IDENTRY ;
    C : IDCLASS ;
```

```
PROCEDURE OPENSCOPE ;

  VAR NEWSCOPE : SCOPE ;

  BEGIN
    NEW(NEWSCOPE) ;
    WITH NEWSCOPE^ DO
    BEGIN
      FIRSTLOCAL := NIL ;
      TYPECHAIN := NIL ;
      ENCLOSINGSCOPE := LOCALSCOPE
    END ;
    LOCALSCOPE := NEWSCOPE
  END (* OPENSCOPE *) ;


PROCEDURE CLOSESCOPE ;

  VAR OLDSCOPE : SCOPE ;

  PROCEDURE DISPOSEIDS  ( ROOT : IDENTRY ) ;

    BEGIN
      IF ROOT <> NIL THEN
      WITH ROOT^ DO
      BEGIN
        DISPOSEIDS (LEFTLINK) ;
        DISPOSEIDS (RIGHTLINK) ;
        DISPOSE(ROOT)
      END
    END (* DISPOSEIDS  *) ;

  PROCEDURE DISPOSETYPES ( FIRSTTYPE : TYPENTRY ) ;

    VAR THISTYPE,NEXTTYPE : TYPENTRY ;

    BEGIN
      NEXTTYPE := FIRSTTYPE ;
      WHILE NEXTTYPE <> NIL DO
      BEGIN
        THISTYPE := NEXTTYPE ; NEXTTYPE := THISTYPE^.NEXT ;
        CASE THISTYPE^.FORM OF
        SCALARS : DISPOSE(THISTYPE,SCALARS) ;
        ARRAYS    : DISPOSE(THISTYPE,ARRAYS)
        END
      END
    END (* DISPOSETYPES *) ;

  BEGIN (*CLOSESCOPE *)
    OLDSCOPE := LOCALSCOPE ;
    LOCALSCOPE := LOCALSCOPE^.ENCLOSINGSCOPE ;
    WITH OLDSCOPE^ DO
    BEGIN
      DISPOSEIDS(FIRSTLOCAL) ;
      DISPOSETYPES(TYPECHAIN)
    END ;
    DISPOSE(OLDSCOPE)
  END (* CLOSESCOPE *) ;
```

```
ENVELOPE *NEWSCOPE ;

   PROCEDURE *NEWID ( SPELLING : ALFA ;
                      VAR ENTRY : IDENTRY ;
                      CLASSNEEDED : IDCLASS ) ;

       VAR
          THISSCOPE : SCOPE ;
          NEWENTRY,THISENTRY,LASTENTRY : IDENTRY ;
          LEFTTAKEN : BOOLEAN ;

       BEGIN

          NEW(NEWENTRY) ;

          (* SET NAME, CLASS, AND DEFAULT ATTRIBUTES *)
          WITH NEWENTRY^ DO
          BEGIN
             NAME := SPELLING ; IDTYPE := NIL ;
             LEFTLINK := NIL ; RIGHTLINK := NIL ;
             CLASS := CLASSNEEDED ;
          END ;

          (* ENTER IN CURRENT SCOPE *)
          THISSCOPE := LOCALSCOPE ;
          THISENTRY := THISSCOPE^.FIRSTLOCAL ;
          IF THISENTRY = NIL
          THEN THISSCOPE^.FIRSTLOCAL := NEWENTRY
          ELSE
          BEGIN
             REPEAT
                LASTENTRY := THISENTRY ;
                IF THISENTRY^.NAME > SPELLING
                THEN
                BEGIN
                   THISENTRY := THISENTRY^.LEFTLINK ;
                   LEFTTAKEN := TRUE
                END
                ELSE
                   IF THISENTRY^.NAME < SPELLING
                   THEN
                   BEGIN
                      THISENTRY := THISENTRY^.RIGHTLINK ;
                      LEFTTAKEN := FALSE
                   END
                   ELSE
                   BEGIN
                      SEMANTICERROR(51) ;
                      THISENTRY := THISENTRY^.RIGHTLINK ;
                      LEFTTAKEN := FALSE
                   END
             UNTIL THISENTRY = NIL ;
             IF LEFTTAKEN
             THEN LASTENTRY^.LEFTLINK := NEWENTRY
             ELSE LASTENTRY^.RIGHTLINK := NEWENTRY
          END ;

          ENTRY := NEWENTRY

       END (* NEWID *) ;
```

```
PROCEDURE *SEARCHID ( SPELLING : ALFA ;
                      VAR ENTRY : IDENTRY ;
                      ALLOWABLECLASSES : SETOFIDCLASS ) ;

   LABEL 1 ;

   VAR THISENTRY,LASTENTRY : IDENTRY ;
       MISUSED,LEFTTAKEN : BOOLEAN ;
       THISSCOPE : SCOPE ;

   FUNCTION MOSTLIKELYOF ( CLASSES : SETOFIDCLASS ) : IDCLASS ;
      BEGIN
         IF VARS IN CLASSES
         THEN MOSTLIKELYOF := VARS
         ELSE IF PROCS IN CLASSES
              THEN MOSTLIKELYOF := PROCS
              ELSE IF TYPES IN CLASSES
                   THEN MOSTLIKELYOF := TYPES
                   ELSE MOSTLIKELYOF := CONSTS
      END (* MOSTLIKELYOF *) ;

   BEGIN (* SEARCHID *)

      MISUSED := FALSE ;

      THISSCOPE := LOCALSCOPE ;
      REPEAT
         THISENTRY := THISSCOPE^.FIRSTLOCAL ;

         WHILE THISENTRY <> NIL DO
            IF THISENTRY^.NAME > SPELLING
            THEN THISENTRY := THISENTRY^.LEFTLINK
            ELSE
               IF THISENTRY^.NAME < SPELLING
               THEN THISENTRY := THISENTRY^.RIGHTLINK
               ELSE
                  IF THISENTRY^.CLASS IN ALLOWABLECLASSES
                  THEN GOTO 1
                  ELSE
                  BEGIN
                     MISUSED := TRUE ;
                     THISENTRY := THISENTRY^.RIGHTLINK
                  END ;

         IF MISUSED THEN
         BEGIN
            SEMANTICERROR(53) ;
            THISENTRY := DEFAULTENTRY[MOSTLIKELYOF(ALLOWABLECLASSES)] ;
            GOTO 1
         END ;

         THISSCOPE := THISSCOPE^.ENCLOSINGSCOPE
      UNTIL THISSCOPE = NIL ;

      SEMANTICERROR(52) ;
      NEWID(SPELLING,THISENTRY,MOSTLIKELYOF(ALLOWABLECLASSES)) ;

   1: ENTRY := THISENTRY

   END (* SEARCHID *) ;
```

```
PROCEDURE *NEWTYPE ( VAR ENTRY : TYPENTRY ; FORMNEEDED : TYPEFORM ) ;

    VAR THISSCOPE : SCOPE ;
        NEWENTRY : TYPENTRY ;

    BEGIN
      CASE FORMNEEDED OF
        SCALARS :
            BEGIN
              NEW(NEWENTRY,SCALARS) ;
              NEWENTRY^.FORM := SCALARS
            END ;
        ARRAYS :
            BEGIN
              NEW(NEWENTRY,ARRAYS) ;
              WITH NEWENTRY^ DO
              BEGIN
                FORM := ARRAYS ;
                INDEXMIN := 0 ; INDEXMAX := 1 ;
                ELEMENTTYPE := NIL
              END
            END
      END ;
      THISSCOPE := LOCALSCOPE ;
      WITH THISSCOPE^ DO
      BEGIN
        NEWENTRY^.NEXT := TYPECHAIN ;
        TYPECHAIN := NEWENTRY
      END ;
      ENTRY := NEWENTRY
    END (* NEWTYPE *) ;



  BEGIN (* NEWSCOPE INITIALIZATION *)
    OPENSCOPE ;
    *** ;
    CLOSESCOPE
  END (* NEWSCOPE FINALIZATION *);


BEGIN (* TABLE MODULE INITIALIZATION *)

  LOCALSCOPE := NIL ;

  FOR C := TYPES TO PROCS DO
  BEGIN
    NEW(DEFAULTENTRY[C]) ;
    WITH DEFAULTENTRY[C]^ DO
    BEGIN
      NAME := '        ' ;
      IDTYPE := NIL ;
      CLASS := C
    END
  END ;

  ***

END (*TABLE MODULE *) ;
```

Programming the Semantic Analyzer

Having chosen a representation for identifiers and their attributes and defined a table module to maintain them, we may easily add to the existing syntax analyzer framework the additional coding necessary to carry out semantic analysis.

Scope housekeeping is achieved simply by declaring an instance of the *Newscope* envelope in the head of the block analysis procedure *Block*. The built-in identifiers and types which are provided for every Mini-Pascal program are implemented by a further scope instance created in the program analysis procedure, in which appropriate entries for the built-in identifiers and types are created before program analysis begins, thus:

```
procedure Programme ;
  instance Builtin : table.newscope ;
  procedure Block ;
    instance Scope : table.newscope ;
    :
```

Within the procedure *Statementpart* the attributes of identifiers denoting variables, constants or procedures are obtained by calls to *Searchid*. Thereafter semantic analysis involves a copying and comparison of *typentry* pointer values which represent the types of the variables, operands and expressions occurring within statements. By extending each syntax procedure which scans a typed construct (*Variable*, *Expression*, etc.) by an additional parameter through which it returns the type pointer for the construct scanned, the transmission of type information between procedures is neatly and securely programmed.

For example the procedure *Assignment* now becomes:

```
procedure Assignment ;
  var vartype, extype : typentry ;
  begin
    Variable (. . . , vartype) ;
    Accept (becomes) ;
    Expression (. . . , extype) ;
    if not compatible (vartype, extype)
    then semanticerror (   )
  end ;
```

The predicate *compatible* is one needed throughout the semantic-analysis code. How should it be defined? Clearly the types denoted by two pointer values are compatible:

(a)   if they point to the same type record (i.e. the pointers are equal), or

(b) if they point to distinct type records of form arrays, with equal bounds and element types.

Situations may arise, however, due to some preceding error in the program, in which the type of some data item is in doubt or unknown. Error recovery requires that an unknown type should be regarded as compatible with any other type, to avoid unnecessary semantic error messages. By including this tolerance of unknown types within the function *compatible*, repeated screening against the effects of previous errors can be avoided in the semantic-analysis code.

In the Mini-Pascal analyzer unknown types are denoted by the pointer value **nil**, so the appropriate definition for the function *compatible* is as follows:

```
function compatible (type1, type2 : typentry) : Boolean ;
  begin
    if type1 = type2
    then compatible := true
    else
      if (type1 = nil) or (type2 = nil)
      then compatible := true
      else
        if (type1 ↑ .form = arrays) and (type2 ↑ .form = arrays)
        then compatible :=
          (type1 ↑ .indexmin = type2 ↑ .indexmin) and
          (type1 ↑ .indexmax = type2 ↑ .indexmax) and
          compatible (type1 ↑ .elementtype,
                      type2 ↑ . elementtype)
        else compatible := false
  end ;
```

With this function the semantic analysis required in the remainder of the analyzer is easily programmed. Listing 6 gives a complete listing of the augmented syntax/semantic analyzer which results, and Test 6 shows its output for an appropriate test program.

Listing 6

```
ENVELOPE MODULE ANALYZE ;


   CONST ALFALENGTH = 8 ;

   TYPE  ALFA = PACKED ARRAY [1..ALFALENGTH] OF CHAR ;

         SYMBOLTYPE = ( IDENT,INTCONST,CHARCONST,
                        NOTOP,ANDOP,OROP,
                        TIMES,DIVOP,PLUS,MINUS,
                        LTOP,LEOP,GEOP,GTOP,NEOP,EQOP,
                        RIGHTPARENT,LEFTPARENT,LEFTBRACKET,RIGHTBRACKET,
                        COMMA,SEMICOLON,PERIOD,COLON,BECOMES,THRU,
                        PROGRAMSY,VARSY,PROCSY,ARRAYSY,OFSY,
                        BEGINSY,ENDSY,IFSY,THENSY,ELSESY,WHILESY,DOSY,
                        READSY,WRITESY,
                        OTHERSY ) ;


   ENVELOPE MODULE SCAN = LISTING2 IN LIBRARY ;


   (* (A) SYNTAX ANALYSIS                                               *)
   (*                                                                   *)
   (*    SYNTAX ANALYSIS OF MINI-PASCAL PROGRAMS IS IMPLEMENTED         *)
   (*    AS A SET OF RECURSIVE DESCENT PROCEDURES. THESE PROCEDURES     *)
   (*    ARE BASED ON THE SYNTAX RULES GIVEN IN THE LANGUAGE DEFN       *)
   (*    AND ARE NESTED AS TIGHTLY AS THE MUTUAL INTERACTION PERMITS.   *)
   (*    THE ORDER, NAMES, AND NESTING OF THE PROCEDURES IS AS FOLLOWS  *)
   (*                                                                   *)
   (*        PROGRAMME                                                  *)
   (*          BLOCK                                                    *)
   (*            VARPART                                                *)
   (*              VARDECLARATION                                       *)
   (*                TYP                                                *)
   (*                  SIMPLETYPE                                       *)
   (*                  INDEXRANGE                                       *)
   (*            PROCPART                                               *)
   (*              PROCDECLARATION                                      *)
   (*            STATPART                                               *)
   (*              COMPOUNDSTATEMENT                                    *)
   (*                STATEMENT                                          *)
   (*                  VARIABLE                                         *)
   (*                  EXPRESSION                                       *)
   (*                    SIMPLEEXPRESSION                               *)
   (*                      TERM                                         *)
   (*                        FACTOR                                     *)
   (*                  ASSIGNMENT                                       *)
   (*                  READSTATEMENT                                    *)
   (*                    INPUTVARIABLE                                  *)
   (*                  WRITESTATEMENT                                   *)
   (*                    OUTPUTVALUE                                    *)
   (*                  IFSTATEMENT                                      *)
   (*                  WHILESTATEMENT                                   *)
   (*                                                                   *)
   (*                                                                   *)
```

```
(*    THE SYNTAX ANALYZERS ARE WRITTEN ON THE ASSUMPTION THAT THE      *)
(*    NEXT SYNTACTIC GOAL CAN ALWAYS BE SELECTED BY INSPECTION OF      *)
(*    (AT MOST) THE NEXT INCOMING SYMBOL ( I.E. THAT THE UNDERLYING    *)
(*    GRAMMAR IS LL(1) ). THIS IS NOT SO AT THE FOLLOWING POINTS       *)
(*    IN THE SYNTAX RULES ACTUALLY USED                               *)
(*                                                                     *)
(*    1. A STATEMENT BEGINNING WITH AN IDENTIFIER MAY BE               *)
(*       EITHER AN ASSIGNMENT OR A PROCEDURE CALL                      *)
(*    2. A FACTOR BEGINNING WITH AN IDENTIFIER MAY BE EITHER           *)
(*       A VARIABLE OR A CONSTANT                                      *)
(*                                                                     *)
(*    IN  CASE 1 TO RESOLVE THE CHOICE ON A PURELY SYNTACTIC           *)
(*    BASIS WOULD REQUIRE A DISTORTION OF THE SYNTAX RULES             *)
(*    CHOICE 2 CANNOT BE SYNTACTICALLY RESOLVED IN SOME CASES .        *)
(*    HOWEVER IF PARALLEL SEMANTIC ANALYSIS IS ASSUMED (AS IN          *)
(*    THE CASE OF THIS COMPILER) THESE CHOICES CAN BE RESOLVED         *)
(*    WITHOUT SYNTAX DISTORTION, BY INSPECTION OF THE CURRENT          *)
(*    SEMANTIC ATTRIBUTES OF THE IDENTIFIER INVOLVED. FOR THIS         *)
(*    REASON SYNTACTIC RESOLUTION OF THESE CHOICES IS NOT USED.        *)
(*                                                                     *)
(*    THE ANALYZER GENERATES SYNTAX ERROR CODES WITH THE               *)
(*    FOLLOWING MEANINGS:                                              *)
(*                                                                     *)
(*    10 ...... SYMBOL EXPECTED WAS IDENTIFIER                         *)
(*    11 ...... SYMBOL EXPECTED WAS INTEGER CONSTANT                   *)
(*    12 ...... SYMBOL EXPECTED WAS CHARACTER CONSTANT                 *)
(*    13 ...... .......                                                *)
(*                                                                     *)
(*    I.E. ONE VALUE FOR EACH OF THE VALUES OF SYMBOLTYPE.             *)
(*    THE FINAL VALUE ORD(OTHERSY)+10 IS USED TO MEAN                  *)
(*                                                                     *)
(*    NN ...... UNEXPECTED SYMBOL                                      *)

TYPE

    SETOFSYMBOLS = SET OF SYMBOLTYPE ;

VAR

    STATSTARTERS,FACTORSTARTERS,MULOPS,SIGNS,ADDOPS,RELOPS : SETOFSYMBOLS ;


PROCEDURE SYNTAXERROR ( EXPECTEDSYMBOL : SYMBOLTYPE ) ;

    BEGIN
        SOURCE.ERROR(ORD(EXPECTEDSYMBOL)+10,SCAN.SYMBOLPOSITION)
    END (* SYNTAXERROR *) ;


PROCEDURE ACCEPT ( SYMBOLEXPECTED : SYMBOLTYPE ) ;

    BEGIN
        IF SCAN.SYMBOL = SYMBOLEXPECTED
        THEN SCAN.NEXTSYMBOL
        ELSE SYNTAXERROR(SYMBOLEXPECTED)
    END (* ACCEPT *) ;
```

```
(* (B) SYNTACTIC ERROR RECOVERY                                    *)
(*                                                                 *)
(*    RECOVERY IN THE SYNTAX ANALYSIS PROCESS FOLLOWING THE        *)
(*    DISCOVERY OF A SYNTAX ERROR IS INCORPORATED INTO THE         *)
(*    SYNTAX PROCEDURES ON THE FOLLOWING BASIS                     *)
(*                                                                 *)
(*    1. EACH PROCEDURE WHEN CALLED IS PASSED AN ACTUAL            *)
(*       PARAMETER WHICH IS A SET OF SYMBOLS WHICH ARE             *)
(*       POSSIBLE FOLLOWERS OF THE STRING WHICH IT SHOULD          *)
(*       SCAN. THESE FOLLOWERS NORMALLY INCLUDE                    *)
(*          (A) ALL SYMBOLS WHICH MAY LEGITIMATELY FOLLOW          *)
(*              THE STRING TO BE SCANNED                           *)
(*          (B) SUCH ADDITIONAL SYMBOLS AS A SUPERIOR              *)
(*              (CALLING) PROCEDURE MAY WISH TO HANDLE IN          *)
(*              THE EVENT OF ERROR RECOVERY                        *)
(*                                                                 *)
(*    2. WHEN ENTERED THE PROCEDURE MAY ENSURE THAT THE            *)
(*       CURRENT SYMBOL IS AN ACCEPTABLE STARTER FOR THE           *)
(*       STRING TO BE SCANNED, AND IF NOT SCAN FORWARD             *)
(*       UNTIL SUCH A SYMBOL IS FOUND (SUBJECT TO 4. BELOW)        *)
(*                                                                 *)
(*    3. WHEN CALLING A SUBSIDIARY SYNTAX PROCEDURE THE            *)
(*       PROCEDURE PASSES ON AS FOLLOWERS ITS OWN FOLLOWERS PLUS   *)
(*       THOSE SYMBOLS IF ANY WHICH IT MAY DETERMINE AS            *)
(*       FOLLOWERS FOR THE SUBSTRING TO BE SCANNED                 *)
(*                                                                 *)
(*    4. TO RECOVER FROM A SYNTAX ERROR THE PROCEDURE MAY          *)
(*       SCAN OVER (SKIP) ANY SYMBOL PROVIDED IT IS NOT            *)
(*       CONTAINED IN THE FOLLOWERS PASSED TO IT                   *)
(*                                                                 *)
(*    5. ON EXIT THE SYNTAX PROCEDURE ENSURES THAT THE CURRENT     *)
(*       SYMBOL IS CONTAINED IN THE FOLLOWERS PASSED TO IT,        *)
(*       FLAGGING A TERMINAL ERROR AND SKIPPING IF THIS IS NOT     *)
(*       INITIALLY THE CASE.                                       *)
(*                                                                 *)
(*    TESTS 2 AND 5 ARE IMPLEMENTED BY THE DECLARATION OF AN       *)
(*    INSTANCE OF A CONTEXT CHECKING ENVELOPE WITHIN EACH          *)
(*    SYNTAX PROCEDURE                                             *)


ENVELOPE CHECK ( STARTERS,FOLLOWERS : SETOFSYMBOLS ) ;

    PROCEDURE SKIPTO ( RELEVANTSYMBOLS : SETOFSYMBOLS ) ;
        BEGIN
            WHILE NOT (SCAN.SYMBOL IN RELEVANTSYMBOLS)
            DO SCAN.NEXTSYMBOL
        END (* SKIPTO *) ;

    BEGIN
        IF NOT (SCAN.SYMBOL IN STARTERS) THEN
        BEGIN SYNTAXERROR(OTHERSY);  SKIPTO(STARTERS+FOLLOWERS) END ;
        IF SCAN.SYMBOL IN STARTERS THEN
        BEGIN
            *** (* EXECUTE ENVELOPED BLOCK *) ;
            IF NOT (SCAN.SYMBOL IN FOLLOWERS) THEN
            BEGIN SYNTAXERROR(OTHERSY);  SKIPTO(FOLLOWERS) END
        END
    END (* CHECK ENVELOPE *) ;
```

```
(* (C) SEMANTIC ANALYSIS AND SEMANTIC ERROR RECOVERY                *)
(*                                                                  *)
(*                                                                  *)
(*    SEMANTIC ANALYSIS AND SEMANTIC ERROR RECOVERY ARE IMPLEMENTED *)
(*    BY "ENRICHMENT" OF THE SYNTAX ANALYZER  WITH                  *)
(*    SEMANTIC INTERLUDES. THE SEMANTIC ANALYSIS DEPENDS ON THE     *)
(*    FOLLOWING DATA STRUCTURES AND MANIPULATIVE                    *)
(*    PROCEDURES                                                    *)
(*                                                                  *)
(*                                                                  *)
(* (1) IDENTIFIER ENTRIES                                           *)
(*                                                                  *)
(*    AN ENTRY IS RECORDED FOR EACH IDENTIFIER,EITHER STANDARD OR   *)
(*    PROGRAM DEFINED, WHICH MAY APPEAR IN THE PROGRAM BEING        *)
(*    COMPILED. THE FORM OF ENTRY USED DEPENDS ON THE "CLASS" OF    *)
(*    USAGE OF THE IDENTIFIER AND IS REPRESENTED BY THE             *)
(*    RECORD TYPE "IDREC". CREATION, LOCATION AND DESTRUCTION OF    *)
(*    THESE RECORDS IS HANDLED BY THE SUB-MODULE "TABLE".           *)
(*                                                                  *)
(*    STANDARD IDENTIFIERS SUPPORTED BY THE LANGUAGE ARE HELD       *)
(*    WITHIN THE TABLE AS IF DECLARED IN A PSEUDO-BLOCK             *)
(*    ENCLOSING THE MAIN PROGRAM . THESE ENTRIES ARE CREATED ON     *)
(*    INITIAL ENTRY TO THE ANALYZER MODULE                         *)
(*                                                                  *)
(*                                                                  *)
(* (2) TYPE ENTRIES                                                 *)
(*                                                                  *)
(*    ALL TYPES UNDERLYING THE DATA DEFINED BY THE PROGRAM BEING    *)
(*    COMPILED ARE REPRESENTED BY TYPE ENTRIES WHOSE FORM IS        *)
(*    DETERMINED BY THE "FORM" OF THE TYPE SO REPRESENTED (I.E.     *)
(*    SCALARS,ARRAYS,ETC.). ENTRIES ARE CONSTRUCTED USING A         *)
(*    CORRESPONDING VARIANT RECORD TYPE "TYPEREC".                  *)
(*                                                                  *)
(*    THESE TYPE ENTRIES ARE ACCESSED ONLY VIA THE IDENTIFIER       *)
(*    TABLE ENTRIES FOR TYPE IDENTIFIERS, OR VIA THE REPRESENTATION *)
(*    OF THE DATA OBJECTS (VARIABLES,CONSTANTS,EXPRESSIONS)         *)
(*    WHOSE TYPE THEY DESCRIBE. THUS FOR EXAMPLE ALL IDENTIFIER     *)
(*    TABLE ENTRIES HAVE A COMMON FIELD "IDTYPE" WHICH POINTS TO    *)
(*    AN UNDERLYING TYPE ENTRY (WITH AN OBVIOUS INTERPRETATION FOR  *)
(*    ALL CLASSES OF IDENTIFIER OTHER THAN "PROC")                  *)
(*                                                                  *)
(*    THE TYPE ENTRIES REPRESENTING THE STANDARD TYPES SUPPORTED    *)
(*    BY THE LANGUAGE (INTEGER,CHAR,ETC.) ARE CREATED ON INITIAL    *)
(*    ENTRY TO THE ANALYZER. THESE ENTRIES ARE DIRECTLY ACCESSIBLE  *)
(*    VIA POINTER VARIABLES "INTYPE","CHARTYPE",ETC., AS            *)
(*    WELL AS VIA THE IDENTIFIER ENTRIES FOR "INTEGER","CHAR",ETC.  *)
(*                                                                  *)
(*                                                                  *)
(* (3) THE FUNCTION COMPATIBLE                                      *)
(*                                                                  *)
(*    TO FACILITATE TYPE ANALYSIS WITHIN THE SEMANTIC ANALYZER      *)
(*    A GENERAL-PURPOSE BOOLEAN FUNCTION "COMPATIBLE" IS PROVIDED   *)
(*    TO TEST THE COMPATIBILITY OF TWO TYPES AS REPRESENTED BY      *)
(*    POINTERS TO THE CORRESPONDING TYPE ENTRIES. A RESULT TRUE IS  *)
(*    RETURNED IF THE TYPES ARE IDENTICAL (I.E. THE POINTERS POINT  *)
(*    TO THE SAME TYPE ENTRY), OR STRICTLY EQUIVALENT (I.E. TWO     *)
(*    DISTINCT TYPE ENTRIES OF IDENTICAL FORM AND CONTENT)          *)
(*                                                                  *)
```

```
(*                                                                    *)
(*    IN ALL SITUATIONS WHERE THE TYPE OF A DATA OBJECT IS NOT        *)
(*    DETERMINED IT IS REPRESENTED BY A POINTER VALUE 'NIL'.          *)
(*    THE TYPE-CHECKING FUNCTION "COMPATIBLE" IS DEFINED TO RETURN    *)
(*    'TRUE' IF EITHER OF ITS PARAMETERS HAS THIS VALUE. IN THIS      *)
(*    WAY NORMAL TYPE ANALYSIS CAN PROCEED WITHOUT A PRELIMINARY      *)
(*    SCREENING FOR INDETERMINATE TYPES AT EVERY POINT AT WHICH       *)
(*    THEY MIGHT ARISE.                                               *)
(*                                                                    *)
(*    SEMANTIC ERRORS ARE REPORTED WITH THE FOLLOWING CODES           *)
(*                                                                    *)
(*    61 .... INDEXED VARIABLE MUST BE OF ARRAY TYPE                  *)
(*    62 .... INDEX EXPRESSION MUST BE OF TYPE INTEGER                *)
(*    63 .... OPERAND MUST BE OF TYPE BOOLEAN                         *)
(*    64 .... OPERAND MUST BE OF TYPE INTEGER                         *)
(*    65 .... OPERANDS MUST BOTH BE INTEGER, OR BOTH CHAR             *)
(*    66 .... EXPRESSION MUST BE OF SAME TYPE AS VARIABLE             *)
(*    67 .... INPUT VARIABLE MUST BE OF TYPE INTEGER OR CHAR          *)
(*    68 .... OUTPUT VALUE MUST BE OF TYPE INTEGER OR CHAR            *)
(*    69 .... EXPRESSION MUST BE OF TYPE BOOLEAN                      *)


TYPE

    TYPENTRY = ^TYPEREC ; IDENTRY = ^IDREC ;

    TYPEFORM = (SCALARS,ARRAYS) ;

    TYPEREC = RECORD
                 NEXT : TYPENTRY ;
                 CASE FORM : TYPEFORM OF
                    ARRAYS :
                         (INDEXMIN,INDEXMAX : INTEGER :
                          ELEMENTTYPE : TYPENTRY )
              END ;


    IDCLASS = (TYPES,CONSTS,VARS,PROCS) ;

    SETOFIDCLASS = SET OF IDCLASS ;

    IDREC = RECORD
                 NAME : ALFA ;
                 LEFTLINK,RIGHTLINK : IDENTRY ;
                 IDTYPE : TYPENTRY ;
                 CLASS : IDCLASS
             END ;

VAR

    INTTYPE,BOOLTYPE,CHARTYPE : TYPENTRY ;


PROCEDURE SEMANTICERROR ( CODE : INTEGER ) ;

   BEGIN
      SOURCE.ERROR(CODE,SCAN.SYMBOLPOSITION)
   END (* SEMANTICERROR *) ;
```

```
ENVELOPE MODULE TABLE = LISTING5 IN LIBRARY ;



FUNCTION COMPATIBLE (TYPE1,TYPE2 : TYPENTRY) : BOOLEAN ;

  (* DECIDES WHETHER TYPES POINTED AT BY
     TYPE1-AND TYPE2 ARE COMPATIBLE      *)


  BEGIN (* COMPATIBLE *) ;
    IF TYPE1 = TYPE2
    THEN COMPATIBLE := TRUE
    ELSE
        IF (TYPE1=NIL) OR (TYPE2=NIL)
        THEN COMPATIBLE := TRUE
        ELSE
            IF (TYPE1^.FORM=ARRAYS) AND (TYPE2^.FORM=ARRAYS)
            THEN COMPATIBLE :=
                    (TYPE1^.INDEXMIN = TYPE2^.INDEXMIN) AND
                    (TYPE1^.INDEXMAX = TYPE2^.INDEXMAX) AND
                    COMPATIBLE(TYPE1^.ELEMENTTYPE,TYPE2^.ELEMENTTYPE)
            ELSE COMPATIBLE := FALSE
  END (* COMPATIBLE *) ;




PROCEDURE *PROGRAMME ;

  INSTANCE BUILTIN : TABLE.NEWSCOPE ;

  VAR ENTRY : IDENTRY ;

  PROCEDURE BLOCK ( FOLLOWERS : SETOFSYMBOLS ; BLOCKID : IDENTRY ) ;

      INSTANCE CONTEXT:CHECK([VARSY,PROCSY,BEGINSY],FOLLOWERS) ;

                  SCOPE : TABLE.NEWSCOPE ;


      PROCEDURE VARPART ( FOLLOWERS : SETOFSYMBOLS ) ;

          INSTANCE CONTEXT:CHECK([VARSY]+FOLLOWERS,FOLLOWERS) ;


          PROCEDURE VARDECLARATION ( FOLLOWERS : SETOFSYMBOLS ) ;

              INSTANCE CONTEXT:CHECK([IDENT,COMMA,COLON],FOLLOWERS) ;
```

```
TYPE
   IDLIST = ^LISTREC ;
   LISTREC = RECORD
                 ID : IDENTRY ;
                 NEXTONLIST : IDLIST
             END ;

VAR
   VARIABLELIST : RECORD
                      HEAD,TAIL : IDLIST
                  END ;
   VARTYPE : TYPENTRY ;

PROCEDURE NEWVARIABLE ;
   VAR
      VARENTRY : IDENTRY ;
      LISTENTRY : IDLIST ;
   BEGIN
      IF SCAN.SYMBOL = IDENT THEN
      BEGIN
         SCOPE.NEWID(SCAN.SPELLING,VARENTRY,VARS) ;
         NEW(LISTENTRY) ;
         WITH LISTENTRY^ DO
         BEGIN
            ID := VARENTRY ;
            NEXTONLIST := NIL
         END ;
         WITH VARIABLELIST DO
          BEGIN
            IF HEAD = NIL
            THEN HEAD := LISTENTRY
            ELSE TAIL^.NEXTONLIST := LISTENTRY ;
            TAIL := LISTENTRY
          END
      END
   END (* NEW VARIABLE *) ;

PROCEDURE ADDATTRIBUTES ;
   VAR
      LISTENTRY,OLDENTRY : IDLIST ;
   BEGIN
      LISTENTRY := VARIABLELIST.HEAD ;
      WHILE LISTENTRY <> NIL DO
         WITH LISTENTRY^ DO
         BEGIN
            ID^.IDTYPE := VARTYPE ;
            OLDENTRY := LISTENTRY ;
            LISTENTRY := NEXTONLIST ;
            DISPOSE(OLDENTRY)
         END
   END (* ADD ATTRIBUTES *) ;
```

```
PROCEDURE TYP ( FOLLOWERS : SETOFSYMBOLS ;
                VAR TYPEFOUND : TYPENTRY ) ;

   INSTANCE CONTEXT:CHECK([IDENT,ARRAYSY],FOLLOWERS) ;

   PROCEDURE SIMPLETYPE ( FOLLOWERS : SETOFSYMBOLS ;
                          VAR TYPENAMED : TYPENTRY ) ;

      INSTANCE CONTEXT:CHECK([IDENT],FOLLOWERS) ;

      VAR
         TYPEID : IDENTRY ;
      BEGIN
         SCOPE.SEARCHID(SCAN.SPELLING,TYPEID,[TYPES]);
         TYPENAMED := TYPEID^.IDTYPE ;
         ACCEPT(IDENT) ;
      END (* SIMPLETYPE *) ;

   PROCEDURE INDEXRANGE  ( FOLLOWERS : SETOFSYMBOLS ) ;

      INSTANCE CONTEXT:CHECK([INTCONST,THRU],FOLLOWERS) ;

      BEGIN
         TYPEFOUND^.INDEXMIN := SCAN.CONSTANT ;
         ACCEPT(INTCONST) ;
         ACCEPT(THRU) ;
         TYPEFOUND^.INDEXMAX := SCAN.CONSTANT ;
         ACCEPT(INTCONST) ;
      END (* INDEXRANGE *) ;


   BEGIN (* TYP *)
      IF SCAN.SYMBOL = IDENT
      THEN SIMPLETYPE(FOLLOWERS,TYPEFOUND)
      ELSE
      BEGIN
         SCOPE.NEWTYPE(TYPEFOUND,ARRAYS) ;
         ACCEPT(ARRAYSY) ;
         ACCEPT(LEFTBRACKET) ;
         INDEXRANGE([RIGHTBRACKET,OFSY]+FOLLOWERS) ;
         ACCEPT(RIGHTBRACKET) ;
         ACCEPT(OFSY) ;
         SIMPLETYPE(FOLLOWERS,TYPEFOUND^.ELEMENTTYPE) ;
      END
   END (* TYP *) ;
```

```
        BEGIN (* VARDECLARATION *)
           VARIABLELIST.HEAD := NIL ;
           NEWVARIABLE ;
           ACCEPT(IDENT) ;
           WHILE SCAN.SYMBOL = COMMA DO
           BEGIN
              ACCEPT(COMMA) ;
              NEWVARIABLE ;
              ACCEPT(IDENT)
           END ;
           ACCEPT(COLON) ;
           TYP(FOLLOWERS,VARTYPE) ;
           ADDATTRIBUTES
        END (* VARDECLARATION *) ;


     BEGIN (* VARPART *)
        IF SCAN.SYMBOL = VARSY THEN
        BEGIN
           ACCEPT(VARSY) ;
           REPEAT
              VARDECLARATION([SEMICOLON]+FOLLOWERS) ;
              ACCEPT(SEMICOLON)
           UNTIL SCAN.SYMBOL <> IDENT
        END
     END (* VARPART *) ;



  PROCEDURE PROCPART ( FOLLOWERS : SETOFSYMBOLS ) ;

     INSTANCE CONTEXT:CHECK([PROCSY]+FOLLOWERS,FOLLOWERS) ;

     PROCEDURE PROCDECLARATION ( FOLLOWERS : SETOFSYMBOLS ) ;

        INSTANCE CONTEXT:CHECK([PROCSY],FOLLOWERS) ;

        VAR
           PROCID : IDENTRY ; PROCNAME : ALFA ;

        BEGIN (* PROCDECLARATION *)
           ACCEPT(PROCSY) ;
           IF SCAN.SYMBOL = IDENT
           THEN PROCNAME := SCAN.SPELLING
           ELSE PROCNAME := '????????' ;
           SCOPE.NEWID(PROCNAME,PROCID,PROCS) ;
           ACCEPT(IDENT) ;
           ACCEPT(SEMICOLON) ;
           BLOCK(FOLLOWERS,PROCID) ;
        END (* PROCDECLARATION *) ;

     BEGIN (* PROCPART *)
        WHILE SCAN.SYMBOL = PROCSY DO
        BEGIN
           PROCDECLARATION([SEMICOLON,PROCSY]+FOLLOWERS) ;
           ACCEPT(SEMICOLON)
        END
     END (* PROCPART *) ;
```

```
PROCEDURE STATPART ( FOLLOWERS : SETOFSYMBOLS ) ;

  INSTANCE CONTEXT:CHECK([BEGINSY],FOLLOWERS) ;


  PROCEDURE COMPOUNDSTATEMENT ( FOLLOWERS : SETOFSYMBOLS ) ;

    INSTANCE CONTEXT:CHECK([BEGINSY],FOLLOWERS) ;


    PROCEDURE STATEMENT ( FOLLOWERS : SETOFSYMBOLS ) ;

      INSTANCE CONTEXT:CHECK(STATSTARTERS,FOLLOWERS) ;

      VAR
         FIRSTID : IDENTRY ;


      PROCEDURE EXPRESSION ( FOLLOWERS : SETOFSYMBOLS ;
                             VAR EXPTYPE : TYPENTRY ) ; FORWARD ;

      PROCEDURE VARIABLE ( FOLLOWERS : SETOFSYMBOLS ;
                           VAR VARTYPE : TYPENTRY ) ;

        INSTANCE CONTEXT:CHECK([IDENT],FOLLOWERS) ;

        VAR
           VARID : IDENTRY ;
           INDEXTYPE : TYPENTRY ;

        BEGIN (* VARIABLE *)
           SCOPE.SEARCHID(SCAN.SPELLING,VARID,[VARS]) ;
           VARTYPE := VARID^.IDTYPE ;
           ACCEPT(IDENT) ;
           IF SCAN.SYMBOL = LEFTBRACKET THEN
           BEGIN
              IF VARTYPE <> NIL THEN
                 IF VARTYPE^.FORM <> ARRAYS THEN
                 BEGIN
                    SEMANTICERROR(61) ;
                    VARTYPE := NIL
                 END ;
              ACCEPT(LEFTBRACKET) ;
              EXPRESSION([RIGHTBRACKET]+FOLLOWERS,INDEXTYPE) ;
              IF NOT COMPATIBLE(INDEXTYPE,INTTYPE)
              THEN SEMANTICERROR(62) ;
              IF VARTYPE <> NIL THEN
              VARTYPE := VARTYPE^.ELEMENTTYPE ;
              ACCEPT(RIGHTBRACKET)
           END ;
        END (* VARIABLE *) ;
```

```
PROCEDURE EXPRESSION ;

   VAR
      FIRSTTYPE : TYPENTRY ;
      OPERATOR  : SYMBOLTYPE ;

   PROCEDURE SIMPLEEXPRESSION ( FOLLOWERS : SETOFSYMBOLS ) ;

      INSTANCE CONTEXT:CHECK(FACTORSTARTERS+SIGNS,FOLLOWERS) ;

      VAR
         SIGNED : BOOLEAN ;
         FIRSTTYPE : TYPENTRY ;
         OPERATOR : SYMBOLTYPE ;

      PROCEDURE TERM ( FOLLOWERS : SETOFSYMBOLS ) ;

         VAR
            FIRSTTYPE : TYPENTRY ;
            OPERATOR  : SYMBOLTYPE ;

         PROCEDURE FACTOR ( FOLLOWERS : SETOFSYMBOLS ) ;

            INSTANCE CONTEXT:CHECK(FACTORSTARTERS,FOLLOWERS) ;

            VAR
               FIRSTID : IDENTRY ;

            BEGIN
               BEGIN
                  CASE SCAN.SYMBOL OF
                  IDENT :
                     BEGIN
                        SCOPE.SEARCHID(SCAN.SPELLING,
                                       FIRSTID,
                                       [VARS,CONSTS]) ;
                        CASE FIRSTID^.CLASS OF
                        CONSTS :
                           BEGIN
                              EXPTYPE := FIRSTID^.IDTYPE ;
                              ACCEPT(IDENT)
                           END ;
                        VARS :
                           VARIABLE(FOLLOWERS,EXPTYPE)
                        END
                     END ;
                  INTCONST :
                     BEGIN
                        EXPTYPE := INTTYPE ;
                        ACCEPT(INTCONST)
                     END ;
                  CHARCONST :
                     BEGIN
                        EXPTYPE := CHARTYPE ;
                        ACCEPT(CHARCONST)
                     END ;
```

```
           LEFTPARENT :
              BEGIN
                 ACCEPT(LEFTPARENT) ;
                 EXPRESSION([RIGHTPARENT]+FOLLOWERS,
                             EXPTYPE) ;
                 ACCEPT(RIGHTPARENT)
              END ;
           NOTOP :
              BEGIN
                 ACCEPT(NOTOP) ;
                 FACTOR(FOLLOWERS) ;
                 IF NOT COMPATIBLE(EXPTYPE,BOOLTYPE)
                 THEN SEMANTICERROR(63) ;
                 EXPTYPE := BOOLTYPE
              END ;
           END ;
        END
     END (* FACTOR *) ;

  BEGIN (* TERM *)
     FACTOR(MULOPS+FACTORSTARTERS+FOLLOWERS) ;
     WHILE SCAN.SYMBOL IN MULOPS+FACTORSTARTERS DO
     BEGIN
        FIRSTTYPE := EXPTYPE ;
        OPERATOR := SCAN.SYMBOL ;
        IF SCAN.SYMBOL IN MULOPS
        THEN SCAN.NEXTSYMBOL
        ELSE SYNTAXERROR(TIMES) ;
        FACTOR(MULOPS+FACTORSTARTERS+FOLLOWERS) ;
        IF OPERATOR IN MULOPS
        THEN
           CASE OPERATOR OF
           TIMES,DIVOP :
              BEGIN
                 IF NOT
                 (COMPATIBLE(FIRSTTYPE,INTTYPE)
                  AND COMPATIBLE(EXPTYPE,INTTYPE))
                 THEN SEMANTICERROR(64) ;
                 EXPTYPE := INTTYPE
              END ;
           ANDOP :
              BEGIN
                 IF NOT
                 (COMPATIBLE(FIRSTTYPE,BOOLTYPE)
                  AND COMPATIBLE(EXPTYPE,BOOLTYPE))
                 THEN SEMANTICERROR(63) ;
                 EXPTYPE := BOOLTYPE
              END
           END
        ELSE EXPTYPE := NIL
     END
  END (* TERM *) ;

BEGIN (* SIMPLE EXPRESSION *)
   IF SCAN.SYMBOL IN SIGNS THEN
   BEGIN
      SIGNED := TRUE ;
      SCAN.NEXTSYMBOL ;
   END
   ELSE SIGNED := FALSE ;
```

```
                    TERM(ADDOPS+FOLLOWERS) ;
                    IF SIGNED THEN
                        IF NOT COMPATIBLE(EXPTYPE,INTTYPE)
                        THEN SEMANTICERROR(64) ;
                    WHILE SCAN.SYMBOL IN ADDOPS DO
                    BEGIN
                        FIRSTTYPE := EXPTYPE ;
                        OPERATOR := SCAN.SYMBOL ;
                        SCAN.NEXTSYMBOL ;
                        TERM(ADDOPS+FOLLOWERS) ;
                        CASE OPERATOR OF
                        PLUS,MINUS :
                            BEGIN
                                IF NOT (COMPATIBLE(FIRSTTYPE,INTTYPE)
                                        AND COMPATIBLE(EXPTYPE,INTTYPE))
                                THEN SEMANTICERROR(64) ;
                                EXPTYPE := INTTYPE
                            END ;
                        OROP :
                            BEGIN
                                IF NOT (COMPATIBLE(FIRSTTYPE,BOOLTYPE)
                                        AND COMPATIBLE(EXPTYPE,BOOLTYPE))
                                THEN SEMANTICERROR(63) ;
                                EXPTYPE := BOOLTYPE
                            END
                        END
                    END
            END (* SIMPLE EXPRESSION *) ;

    BEGIN (* EXPRESSION *)
        SIMPLEEXPRESSION(RELOPS+FOLLOWERS) ;
        IF SCAN.SYMBOL IN RELOPS THEN
        BEGIN
            FIRSTTYPE := EXPTYPE ;
            OPERATOR := SCAN.SYMBOL ;
            SCAN.NEXTSYMBOL ;
            SIMPLEEXPRESSION(FOLLOWERS) ;
            IF NOT ( COMPATIBLE(FIRSTTYPE,INTTYPE) AND
                    COMPATIBLE(EXPTYPE,INTTYPE)     OR
                    COMPATIBLE(FIRSTTYPE,CHARTYPE) AND
                    COMPATIBLE(EXPTYPE,CHARTYPE))
            THEN SEMANTICERROR(65) ;
            EXPTYPE := BOOLTYPE
        END
    END (* EXPRESSION *) ;


PROCEDURE ASSIGNMENT ;

    VAR
        VARTYPE,EXPTYPE : TYPENTRY ;

    BEGIN (* ASSIGNMENT *)
        VARIABLE([BECOMES]+FOLLOWERS,VARTYPE) ;
        ACCEPT(BECOMES) ;
        EXPRESSION(FOLLOWERS,EXPTYPE) ;
        IF NOT COMPATIBLE(VARTYPE,EXPTYPE)
        THEN SEMANTICERROR(66)
    END (* ASSIGNMENT *) ;
```

```
PROCEDURE READSTATEMENT ;

  PROCEDURE INPUTVARIABLE ;

    VAR
      VARTYPE : TYPENTRY ;
    BEGIN
      VARIABLE([COMMA,RIGHTPARENT]+FOLLOWERS,VARTYPE) ;
      IF NOT COMPATIBLE(VARTYPE,CHARTYPE)
      AND NOT COMPATIBLE(VARTYPE,INTTYPE)
      THEN SEMANTICERROR(67)
    END (* INPUTVARIABLE *);

  BEGIN
    ACCEPT(READSY) ;
    ACCEPT(LEFTPARENT) ;
    INPUTVARIABLE ;
    WHILE SCAN.SYMBOL = COMMA DO
    BEGIN
      ACCEPT(COMMA) ;
      INPUTVARIABLE
    END ;
    ACCEPT(RIGHTPARENT)
  END (* READSTATEMENT *) ;


PROCEDURE WRITESTATEMENT ;

  PROCEDURE OUTPUTVALUE ;

    VAR
      EXPTYPE : TYPENTRY ;
    BEGIN
      EXPRESSION([COMMA,RIGHTPARENT]+FOLLOWERS,EXPTYPE) ;
      IF NOT COMPATIBLE(EXPTYPE,CHARTYPE)
      AND NOT COMPATIBLE(EXPTYPE,INTTYPE)
      THEN SEMANTICERROR(68)
    END (* OUTPUTVALUE *) ;

  BEGIN
    ACCEPT(WRITESY) ;
    ACCEPT(LEFTPARENT) ;
    OUTPUTVALUE ;
    WHILE SCAN.SYMBOL = COMMA DO
    BEGIN
      ACCEPT(COMMA) ;
      OUTPUTVALUE
    END ;
    ACCEPT(RIGHTPARENT)
  END (* WRITESTATEMENT *) ;
```

```
PROCEDURE IFSTATEMENT ;

    VAR
        EXPTYPE : TYPENTRY ;

    BEGIN (* IFSTATEMENT *)
        ACCEPT(IFSY) ;
        EXPRESSION([THENSY,ELSESY]+FOLLOWERS,EXPTYPE) ;
        IF NOT COMPATIBLE(EXPTYPE,BOOLTYPE)
        THEN SEMANTICERROR(69) ;
        ACCEPT(THENSY) ;
        STATEMENT([ELSESY]+FOLLOWERS) ;
        IF SCAN.SYMBOL = ELSESY
        THEN
        BEGIN
            ACCEPT(ELSESY) ;
            STATEMENT(FOLLOWERS) ;
        END
    END (* IFSTATEMENT *) ;


PROCEDURE WHILESTATEMENT ;

    VAR
        EXPTYPE : TYPENTRY ;

    BEGIN (* WHILESTATEMENT *)
        ACCEPT(WHILESY) ;
        EXPRESSION([DOSY]+FOLLOWERS,EXPTYPE) ;
        IF NOT COMPATIBLE(EXPTYPE,BOOLTYPE)
        THEN SEMANTICERROR(69) ;
        ACCEPT(DOSY) ;
        STATEMENT(FOLLOWERS)
    END (* WHILESTATEMENT *) ;


BEGIN (* STATEMENT *)
    CASE SCAN.SYMBOL OF
    IDENT :
        BEGIN
            SCOPE.SEARCHID(SCAN.SPELLING,FIRSTID,
                           [PROCS,VARS]) ;
            IF FIRSTID^.CLASS = VARS
            THEN ASSIGNMENT
            ELSE ACCEPT(IDENT)
          END ;
    BEGINSY :
        COMPOUNDSTATEMENT(FOLLOWERS) ;
    IFSY :
        IFSTATEMENT ;
    WHILESY :
        WHILESTATEMENT ;
    READSY :
        READSTATEMENT ;
    WRITESY :
        WRITESTATEMENT
    END (* CASE *)
END (* STATEMENT *) ;
```

```
          BEGIN (*COMPOUNDSTATEMENT *)
            ACCEPT(BEGINSY) ;
            STATEMENT([SEMICOLON,ENDSY]+STATSTARTERS
                              -[IDENT]+FOLLOWERS) ;
            WHILE SCAN.SYMBOL IN [SEMICOLON]+STATSTARTERS-[IDENT] DO
            BEGIN
                ACCEPT(SEMICOLON) ;
                STATEMENT([SEMICOLON,ENDSY]+STATSTARTERS
                              -[IDENT]+FOLLOWERS)
            END ;
            ACCEPT(ENDSY)
          END (* COMPOUND STATEMENT *) ;


        BEGIN (* STATPART *)
          COMPOUNDSTATEMENT(FOLLOWERS)
        END (* STATPART *) ;


      BEGIN (* BLOCK *)
        VARPART([PROCSY,BEGINSY]) ;
        PROCPART([BEGINSY]) ;
        STATPART(FOLLOWERS)
      END (* BLOCK *) ;


    BEGIN (* PROGRAMME *)

      BUILTIN.NEWTYPE(INTTYPE,SCALARS) ;
      BUILTIN.NEWTYPE(CHARTYPE,SCALARS) ;
      BUILTIN.NEWTYPE(BOOLTYPE,SCALARS) ;
      BUILTIN.NEWID( 'INTEGER ',ENTRY,TYPES) ;
      ENTRY^.IDTYPE := INTTYPE ;
      BUILTIN.NEWID( 'CHAR    ',ENTRY,TYPES) ;
      ENTRY^.IDTYPE := CHARTYPE ;
      BUILTIN.NEWID( 'BOOLEAN ',ENTRY,TYPES) ;
      ENTRY^.IDTYPE   := BOOLTYPE ;
      BUILTIN.NEWID( 'FALSE   ',ENTRY,CONSTS) ;
      ENTRY^.IDTYPE := BOOLTYPE ;
      BUILTIN.NEWID( 'TRUE    ',ENTRY,CONSTS) ;
      ENTRY^.IDTYPE := BOOLTYPE ;

      ACCEPT(PROGRAMSY) ;
      ACCEPT(IDENT) ;
      ACCEPT(SEMICOLON) ;
      BLOCK([PERIOD],NIL)
    END (* PROGRAMME *) ;


BEGIN
  STATSTARTERS := [IDENT,BEGINSY,READSY,WRITESY,IFSY,WHILESY] ;
  FACTORSTARTERS := [IDENT,INTCONST,CHARCONST,NOTOP,LEFTPARENT] ;
  MULOPS := [TIMES,DIVOP,ANDOP] ;
  SIGNS := [PLUS,MINUS] ;
  ADDOPS := [PLUS,MINUS,OROP] ;
  RELOPS := [EQOP,NEOP,LTOP,LEOP,GEOP,GTOP] ;

  ***

END (* ANALYZER MODULE *) ;
```

Test 6

PASCAL PLUS COMPILER

```
   0   3300   PROGRAM TESTANALYZER (INPUT,OUTPUT) ;              I := I+J-I*I DIV J ;
   1                                                        *****                  ^ERROR 64
   2          ENVELOPE MODULE SOURCE = LISTING1 IN LIBRARY ;  *****                ^ERROR 64
   3
   4   3644   ENVELOPE MODULE ANALYZE = LISTING6 IN LIBRARY ;   IF (J=I) OR NOT (J<>I) THEN A[J]:=' ' ELSE A[J]:='''''' ;
   5                                                        *****                         ^ERROR 65
   6   6744   BEGIN                                          *****                                          ^ERROR 62
   7   6744       ANALYZE.PROGRAMME
   8   6744   END.                                              WRITE (I[I],J) ;
   9                                                        *****     ^ERROR 61
                                                                ^ERROR 68
COMPILATION COMPLETE :     NO ERRORS REPORTED           *****
COMPILATION TIME     =    4523 MILLISECONDS               10          I := I+1
SOURCE PROGRAM       =    1745 LINES                       11       END ;
OBJECT PROGRAM       =    6879 WORDS                       12    BEGIN
                                                           13    I:='1'; J := 1000000 ;
                                                        *****   ^ERROR 66
LISTING PRODUCED BY MINI-PASCAL COMPILER                *****          ^ERROR 52

   0   PROGRAM SEMANTICS ;                                   14    WHILE I-10 DO P ;
   1   VAR I,I : INTEGER ;                               *****            ^ERROR 69
*****          ^ERROR 51
                                                           15    WHILE I*'1'-10 DO P ;
   2      A : ARRAY [1..10] OF CHAR ;                    *****           ^ERROR 64
   3   PROCEDURE P ;                                     *****                ^ERROR 69
   4      VAR J : BOOLEAN ;
   5   BEGIN                                                16    WRITE(J)
   6      READ(J) ;                                         17    END.
*****          ^ERROR 67

COMPILATION COMPLETED :    14 ERRORS REPORTED
```

Exercise 4 Modify the syntax/semantic analyzer in Listing 6 to handle the multiple assignment statement suggested in Exercise 3.

THE CODE-GENERATION INTERFACE

A Hypothetical Machine

We split the compilation process between analyzer and generator modules thus:

> *analyzer* (*character stream*)(*errors, analyzed program*)
> *generator* (*analyzed program*)(*object code*)

where *analyzed program* is some representation of the program analyzed which enables the generator to produce equivalent object code. Our motive in rigidly enforcing this split was to isolate the machine- and object code-dependent aspects of compilation, and so facilitate adaptation of the compiler to a variety of object codes and/or machines. It follows that the interface, the *analyzed program*, must be such that

(a) no features peculiar to any particular object code or machine are implied, and
(b) generation of any particular object code can be achieved without additional knowledge of, or access to the internal functioning and data of the analyzer.

A commonly used technique in such situations is to define a *hypothetical machine* whose features are those convenient for the execution of programs of the source language, but which can be readily realized in whatever object code/hardware environment is actually selected. The action of the analyzer is to translate the source program into an equivalent sequence of operations, or program, for the hypothetical machine. The generator's task is then to translate this sequence of operations into whatever object-code form is required.

In principle analysis and generation may take place either in sequence or in parallel. In sequential mode the analyzer must create and "output" the entire sequence of hypothetical operations for subsequent input to the generator. In parallel mode the analyzer need only signal each hypothetical operation; the generator acts immediately to translate this operation into equivalent object code. In practice, however, the analyzer need not be aware of which mode is in use, since it may in either case transmit the hypothetical operation by a procedure call, whose effect may either be to file the operation for subsequent translation, or to translate it immediately.

The generation interface is thus a series of procedure calls, each of which corresponds to a hypothetical machine operation. Our next task is to determine the range of hypothetical operations, and hence procedure calls, required. We note, however, that the term "operation" must be interpreted loosely, since the interface must cover all aspects of program generation— such static operations as determining data representations and storage as well as the dynamic operations required in program execution.

Defining the Hypothetical Machine Interface

Data representation and storage

On any machine which is to execute a program, a means of representing the data items which the program manipulates must first be determined. For a simple typed language such as Mini-Pascal, all items of a given type share a common form of representation. Our generator must determine, therefore, a *representation* within the object program for each *type* in the source program. To represent these representations we introduce a type within the generator

$$typerepresentation = \ldots\ldots ;$$

whose form will depend on the particular object machine involved. A value of this type is created by the generator for each Mini-Pascal type encountered in the program being compiled. This value describes how items of the type are to be represented on the object machine. Although the analyzer should not have any understanding of type representations as such, it can be used to maintain the association between types and their representations—by requesting from the generator some indication of the representation for a type when the type is created, and supplying this each time an item of the type is to be manipulated. If the analyzer and generator run in parallel, the representation details themselves may be passed to and fro in this way. If they run in sequence, then the "representation" given to the analyzer may be just an index to the actual details to be created at generation time.

The generator makes representations available in two ways. For the built-in types *integer, char, Boolean* we assume corresponding built-in representations in the generator, thus

$$integerrepresentation, charrepresentation,$$
$$Booleanrepresentation : typerepresentation ;$$

For array types the generator will construct a representation on request, given the index range and element representation, through a call to the procedure:

procedure *arrayrepresentation* (*numberofelements* : *integer* ;
                               elementrepresentation : *typerepresentation* ;
                               var *representation* : *typerepresentation*) ;

The generator must also determine the storage locations which individual data items occupy in the object program during execution. We will assume that these locations are specified within the generator as values of a type

$$runtimeaddress = \ldots \ldots ;$$

whose details again depend on the storage structure and organization of the particular object machine.

The analyzer must maintain the association between variables and run-time addresses. At variable declaration time it must request a run-time address for each variable through a call to the procedure

procedure *addressfor* (*representation* : *typerepresentation* ;
                        var *address***:** *runtimeaddress*) ;

To enable the generator to exploit the store sharing which block structure permits, and to implement recursion correctly, the analyzer must also signal this block structure to the generator. Since the storage organization chosen is normally a stack of storage "frames", one frame for each variable space currently in existence, the signaling is carried out by calls to procedures:

procedure *Openstackframe* ;
procedure *Closestackframe* ;

Within each matching pair of calls all storage addresses will be allocated in the storage frame associated with the bracketed code body.

Variables, expressions and assignment

For variable access and expression evaluation the hypothetical machine is assumed to use an evaluation stack, the operands on which are either *references* (to storage locations) or *values*. The hypothetical code transmitted by the analyzer is then a sequence of stack manipulating post-fix operations, represented by calls to the following procedures:

procedure *Stackreference* (*address* : *runtimeaddress*) ;
         {*push reference or address given onto the*
            evaluation stack}

procedure *Indexedreference* (*boundmin,boundmax* : *integer* ;
                              elementrepresentation : *typerepresentation*) ;
{*pop an index value and an array reference from the
evaluation stack and push a reference to the
corresponding array element*}

procedure *Dereference* (*representation* : *typerepresentation*) ;
{*pop a reference from the evaluation stack and
push the value referenced*}

procedure *Stackconstant* (*constantvalue* : *integer*) ;
{*push a constant value onto the evaluation stack*}

The range of possible arithmetic operations is representable as the corresponding subrange of the language symbols as denoted by *symboltype*, thus

$$optype = notop .. eqop$$

The corresponding postfix operations on the hypothetical machine are then representable as calls to the procedures:

procedure *Negateinteger* ;
{*pop integer value a from stack* ;
push integer value ($-a$) *onto stack*}

procedure *Binaryintegeroperation* (*operator* : *optype*) ;
{*pop integer values a, b from stack* ;
push integer value (*a operator b*) ,
where operator denotes $+ - *$ *or* **div**}

procedure *Negateboolean* ;
{*pop Boolean value a from stack* ;
push Boolean value (**not** *a*) *onto stack*}

procedure *Binarybooleanoperation* (*operator* : *optype*) ;
{*pop Boolean values a,b from stack* ;
push Boolean value (*a operator b*) ,
where operator denotes **and** *or* **or**}

procedure *Comparison* (*operator* : *optype*) ;
{*pop scalar values a,b from stack* ;
push Boolean value (*a operator b*),
where operator denotes $=$, $<>$, $<$, $<=$, $>=$, $>$}

Finally the operation of assigning the topmost value on the evaluation stack to the location referenced immediately below is representable as a call to the procedure

procedure *Assign* ;

Thus the sequence of hypothetical operations, or procedure calls, resulting from the Mini-Pascal assignment statement

$$A := B + 4$$

would be as follows:

> *Stackreference (address of A)*
> *Stackreference (address of B)*
> *Dereference (integer representation)*
> *Stackconstant (4)*
> *Binaryintegeroperation (plus)*
> *Assign*

Input/Output

For the input/output the hypothetical machine is assumed to have an input and an output channel which may be operated in either character or integer mode

> *iomode* = (*charmode, integermode*) ;

I/O operations to and from the evaluation stack are then represented by calls to the procedures:

> **procedure** *Readoperation* (*mode : iomode*) ;
> **procedure** *Writeoperation* (*mode : iomode*) ;

Control statements

The object code generated, whatever its form, is assumed to be executed in the order of its generation except where explicit control operations intervene. The code can therefore be modeled as a series of code sequences, each of which can be entered either sequentially from its predecessor, or by an explicit transfer of control to a label at its head. To represent each label the generator provides a type

> *codelabel* = ... ;

Variables of this type can be used by the analyzer to identify labeled points in the code sequence under generation. Binding of these variables to the appropriate points in the actual sequence under generation is allowed by three generator procedures:

> **procedure** *Newcodelabel* (**var** *sequence* : *codelabel*) ;
> **procedure** *Futurecodelabel* (**var** *sequence* : *codelabel*) ;
> **procedure** *Expectedcodelabel* (**var** *sequence* : *codelabel*) ;

The first is used for labels not previously referenced. The second is used to announce a codelabel which is referenced (by some control operation) before the code which it labels is generated, and the third to bind such a label when this code eventually is generated.

With this codelabel facility the control operations necessary to Mini-Pascal's **if** and **while** statements can be expressed as calls to two procedures:

> **procedure** *Jump* (**var** *sequence* : *codelabel*) ;
> **procedure** *Jumponfalse* (**var** *sequence* : *codelabel*) ;

The first represents an unconditional jump, the second a jump conditional on the (Boolean) value on the top of the evaluation stack.

Procedures

Besides a simple transfer of control, procedure calls in a block-structured language involve housekeeping activity to maintain variable access. To represent the information necessary to support a procedure call, the generator provides a type

> *proclinkage* = ... ;

a value of which must be associated with each procedure in the program. The analyzer must request this linkage at procedure-declaration time, by a call to the procedure

> **procedure** *Newlinkage* (**var** *linkage* : *proclinkage*) ;

and must supply this linkage in translating a procedure call into the hypothetical operation

> **procedure** *Callproc* (*linkage* : *proclinkage*) ;

Besides the calling sequence procedure activation requires some prelude and postlude code located at the beginning and end of the procedure's code body. These can be represented as additional hypothetical operations

> **procedure** *Enterbody* (*linkage* : *proclinkage*);
> **procedure** *Leavebody* ;

The corresponding prelude and postlude code required for the main program body itself can be similarly represented as

> **procedure** *Enterprogram* ;
> **procedure** *Leaveprogram* ;

These two complete the range of hypothetical operations necessary for the execution of Mini-Pascal programs. A summary of the complete generation interface which they define is given in Listing 7.

Using the Interface

After definition of the code-generation interface, the incorporation of its use within the existing analyzer is easily accomplished.

The additional code-generating attributes which the analyzer must associate with types, variables, and procedures are readily accommodated by the extension of the type and identifier records as follows:

```
typerec = record
               representation : typerepresentation ;
               case form : . . .
               . . .
          end ;
idrec = record
             name : alfa ;
             leftlink, rightlink : identry ;
             idtype : typentry ;
             case class : idclass of
             vars : (varaddress : runtimeaddress) ;
             consts : (constvalue : integer) ;
             procs : (linkage : proclinkage)
        end ;
```

The generation and assignment of values to these additional attributes is then coded as generator calls in the analyzer sequences which create the type and identifier records themselves.

Listing 7

```
ENVELOPE MODULE GENERATE ;

    (*    THE GENERATOR PROVIDES A PROGRAM GENERATION INTERFACE FOR THE      *)
    (*    SYNTACTIC/SEMANTIC ANALYZER AS A SET OF PROCEDURE CALLS.           *)
    (*    THESE CALLS, AND THE TYPES UNDERLYING THEIR PARAMETER LISTS,       *)
    (*    PROVIDE A GENERATION INTERFACE WHICH IS INDEPENDENT OF THE         *)
    (*    PRECISE OBJECT CODE TO BE GENERATED. BETWEEN CALLS THE             *)
    (*    ANALYZER STORES AND TRANSMITS DATA OF THESE TYPES BUT WITHOUT      *)
    (*    ANY NECESSARY KNOWLEDGE OF THEIR INTERNAL NATURE.                  *)
    (*                                                                       *)
    (*                                                                       *)
    (*      (1) REPRESENTATION AND STORAGE OF DATA                           *)
    (*                                                                       *)
    (*         THE REPRESENTATION AND STORAGE OF DATA WITHIN THE OBJECT      *)
    (*         PROGRAM IS DESCRIBED BY THE GENERATOR AS FOLLOWS              *)
    (*                                                                       *)
    (*            1.  FOR EACH TYPE THE GENERATOR CREATES A REPRESENTATION*)
    (*                OF TYPE 'TYPEREPRESENTATION' WHICH DESCRIBES HOW       *)
    (*                SUCH DATA ARE TO BE REPRESENTED IN THE OBJECT          *)
    (*                PROGRAM.                                               *)
    (*                                                                       *)
    (*            2. FOR EACH VARIABLE THE GENERATOR CREATES AN ADDRESS      *)
    (*                'RUNTIMEADDRESS' WHICH HOLDS THE NECESSARY ADDRESS     *)
    (*                CO-ORDINATES FOR THE RUN-TIME ACCESS OF THOSE DATA.    *)
    (*                                                                       *)
    (*         THESE DESCRIPTORS ARE GENERATED AS FOLLOWS                    *)
    (*                                                                       *)
    (*            3. REPRESENTATION FOR THE BUILT-IN TYPES ARE MADE          *)
    (*                AVAILABLE AS ACCESSIBLE VALUES INTEGERREPRESENTATION *)
    (*                ETC. THE PROCEDURE ARRAYREPRESENTATION GENERATES A     *)
    (*                REPRESENTATION FOR EACH PROGRAM-DEFINED ARRAY TYPE.    *)
    (*                                                                       *)
    (*            4. THE PROCEDURE ADDRESSFOR DETERMINES THE RUN-TIME        *)
    (*                ADDRESS CO-ORDINATES FOR A VARIABLE.  SINCE THESE      *)
    (*                RUN-TIME ADDRESSES ARE ASSUMED TO LIE WITHIN A         *)
    (*                CONVENTIONAL RUN-TIME STORAGE STACK, PROCEDURE         *)
    (*                CALLS 'OPENSTACKFRAME' AND 'CLOSESTACKFRAME' ARE       *)
    (*                USED TO DELIMIT THE STATIC NESTING OF STACK FRAMES     *)
    (*                FOR THE ADDRESS ALLOCATOR.                             *)
    (*                                                                       *)
    (*      (2) PROCEDURE AND PROGRAM CONTROL                                *)
    (*                                                                       *)
    (*         THE NECESSARY COMPILE- AND RUNTIME HOUSEKEEPING               *)
    (*         OPERATIONS ASSOCIATED WITH THE OBJECT PROGRAM ARE            *)
    (*         REALIZED AS FOLLOWS                                           *)
    (*                                                                       *)
    (*            1. A LINKAGE RECORD IS GENERATED FOR EACH PROCEDURE        *)
    (*                BY THE PROCEDURE NEWLINKAGE                            *)
    (*                                                                       *)
    (*            2. TRANSFER OF CONTROL TO A PROCEDURE                      *)
    (*                IS REALIZED BY THE OPERATION CALLPROC                  *)
    (*                                                                       *)
    (*            3. THE NECESSARY PRELUDE AND POSTLUDE CODE FOR EACH        *)
    (*                PROCEDURE OR PROGRAM BLOCK IS REALIZED BY THE          *)
    (*                OPERATIONS                                             *)
    (*                                                                       *)
    (*                   ENTERBODY                                          *)
    (*                   LEAVEBODY                                          *)
    (*                   ENTERPROGRAM                                       *)
    (*                   LEAVEPROGRAM                                       *)
```

```
(*                                                                    * )
(*                                                                    * )
(*     (3) VARIABLES, EXPRESSIONS AND ASSIGNMENT                      * )
(*                                                                    * )
(*         THE CODE GENERATION INTERFACE FOR VARIABLE ACCESS,         * )
(*         EXPRESSION EVALUATION AND ASSIGNMENT ASSUMES A POSTFIX     * )
(*         CODE FORM (THOUGH THE GENERATING PROCEDURES CALLED MAY     * )
(*         TRANSFORM THIS CODE THEREAFTER). THE GENERATING CALLS      * )
(*         REPRESENT OPERATIONS ON A HYPOTHETICAL RUN-TIME STACK      * )
(*         OF OPERAND REFERENCES AND VALUES, AS FOLLOWS               * )
(*                                                                    * )
(*              1. VARIABLE ACCESS IS REALIZED BY THE FOLLOWING       * )
(*                 HYPOTHETICAL OPERATIONS                            * )
(*                                                                    * )
(*                     STACKREFERENCE                                 * )
(*                     INDEXEDREFERENCE                               * )
(*                                                                    * )
(*              2. EXPRESSION EVALUATION IS REALIZED BY THE FOLLOWING * )
(*                 ADDITIONAL STACK OPERATIONS                        * )
(*                                                                    * )
(*                     DEREFERENCE                                    * )
(*                     STACKCONSTANT                                  * )
(*                                                                    * )
(*                     NEGATEINTEGER                                  * )
(*                     BINARYINTEGEROPERATION                         * )
(*                                                                    * )
(*                     COMPARISON                                     * )
(*                                                                    * )
(*                     NEGATEBOOLEAN                                  * )
(*                     BINARYBOOLEANOPERATION                         * )
(*                                                                    * )
(*                 THE OPERATION BINARYBOOLEANOPERATION IS DEFINED    * )
(*                 AND USED IN A WAY WHICH PERMITS EITHER INFIX OR    * )
(*                 POSTFIX EVALUATION OF AND/OR OPERATIONS            * )
(*                                                                    * )
(*              3. FINALLY ASSIGNMENT IS REALIZED BY THE SINGLE       * )
(*                 HYPOTHETICAL STACK OPERATION - ASSIGN.             * )
(*                                                                    * )
(*                                                                    * )
(*     (4) I-O OPERATIONS                                             * )
(*                                                                    * )
(*         THE I-O OPERATIONS ARE REALIZED BY THE FOLLOWING           * )
(*         GENERATIVE OPERATIONS                                      * )
(*                                                                    * )
(*                     READOPERATION                                  * )
(*                     WRITEOPERATION                                 * )
(*                                                                    * )
(*                                                                    * )
(*     (5) CONTROL STATEMENTS AND                                     * )
(*         SEQUENTIAL CODE GENERATION                                 * )
(*                                                                    * )
(*         THE CODE GENERATED, WHATEVER ITS FORM, IS ASSUMED TO BE    * )
(*         FOR SEQUENTIAL EXECUTION. EACH CODE SEQUENCE WHICH CAN     * )
(*         BE ENTERED OTHER THAN SEQUENTIALLY IS REPRESENTED AT       * )
(*         COMPILE TIME BY A RECORD OF TYPE 'CODELABEL'. THESE        * )
(*         RECORDS ARE BOUND TO POINTS IN THE CODE BY THE PROCEDURES  * )
```

```
(*                                                             *)
(*           NEWLABEL  -  FOR A PREVIOUSLY UNREFERENCED        *)
(*                        LABEL                                *)
(*                                                             *)
(*           FUTURELABEL -  FOR A LABEL WHICH MAY BE           *)
(*                          REFERENCED BEFORE IT IS            *)
(*                          GENERATED                          *)
(*                                                             *)
(*           EXPECTEDLABEL -  FOR A LABEL PREVIOUSLY           *)
(*                            'EXPECTED'                       *)
(*                                                             *)
(*       ALL REFERENCES(JUMPS ETC.) ARE GENERATED BY THE CONTROL *)
(*       GENERATING PROCEDURES MANIPULATING THESE LABEL RECORDS  *)
(*                                                             *)
(*       CONTROL STATEMENT CODE IS REALIZED BY THE FOLLOWING   *)
(*       HYPOTHETICAL OPERATIONS                               *)
(*                                                             *)
(*           JUMPONFALSE                                       *)
(*           JUMP                                              *)
(*                                                             *)
(*    THE ANALYZER MAY SUPPRESS FURTHER GENERATOR ACTIVITY AT ANY *)
(*    TIME BY CALLING THE PROCEDURE NOFURTHERCODE . ALL SUBSEQUENT *)
(*    GENERATOR CALLS ARE IGNORED. THIS IS NECESSARY IF  ANALYSIS OF *)
(*    (ANY PART OF) AN INCORRECT PROGRAM CAUSES INCONSISTENT   *)
(*    SEQUENCES OF INTERFACE CALLS                             *)


PROCEDURE *NOFURTHERCODE ;



TYPE *TYPEREPRESENTATION = ...... ;

CONST

   *BOOLEANREPRESENTATION = ...... ;
   *CHARREPRESENTATION    = ...... ;
   *INTEGERREPRESENTATION = ...... ;

PROCEDURE *ARRAYREPRESENTATION ( BOUNDMIN,BOUNDMAX : INTEGER ;
                                 ELEMENTREPRESENTATION : TYPEREPRESENTATION ;
                                 VAR REPRESENTATION : TYPEREPRESENTATION ) ;


TYPE *RUNTIMEADDRESS = ..... ;

PROCEDURE *OPENSTACKFRAME ;

PROCEDURE *ADDRESSFOR ( REPRESENTATION : TYPEREPRESENTATION ;
                        VAR ADDRESS : RUNTIMEADDRESS ) ;

PROCEDURE *CLOSESTACKFRAME ;
```

```
TYPE *PROCLINKAGE = ...... ;

PROCEDURE *NEWLINKAGE ( VAR LINKAGE : PROCLINKAGE ) ;

PROCEDURE *CALLPROC ( VAR LINKAGE : PROCLINKAGE ) ;

PROCEDURE *ENTERBODY ( VAR LINKAGE : PROCLINKAGE ) ;

PROCEDURE *LEAVEBODY ;

PROCEDURE *ENTERPROGRAM ;

PROCEDURE *LEAVEPROGRAM ;


PROCEDURE *STACKREFERENCE ( LOCATION : RUNTIMEADDRESS ) ;

PROCEDURE *INDEXEDREFERENCE ( BOUNDMIN,BOUNDMAX : INTEGER ;
                              ELEMENTREPRESENTATION:TYPEREPRESENTATION) :

PROCEDURE *DEREFERENCE ( REPRESENTATION : TYPEREPRESENTATION ) ;

PROCEDURE *STACKCONSTANT ( CVALUE : INTEGER ;
                           REPRESENTATION : TYPEREPRESENTATION ) ;


PROCEDURE *NEGATEINTEGER ;

PROCEDURE *BINARYINTEGEROPERATION ( OPERATOR : OPTYPE ) ;

PROCEDURE *COMPARISON ( OPERATOR : OPTYPE ) ;

PROCEDURE *NEGATEBOOLEAN ;

PROCEDURE *BINARYBOOLEANOPERATOR ( OPERATOR : OPTYPE ;
                                   FIRSTSUCHOPERATOR : BOOLEAN ) ;


PROCEDURE *ASSIGN ;

PROCEDURE *READOPERATION ( READMODE : IOMODE ) ;

PROCEDURE *WRITEOPERATION ( WRITEMODE : IOMODE ) ;


TYPE *CODELABEL = ...... ;

PROCEDURE *NEWCODELABEL ( VAR SEQUENCE : CODELABEL ) ;

PROCEDURE *FUTURECODELABEL ( VAR SEQUENCE : CODELABEL ) ;

PROCEDURE *EXPECTEDCODELABEL ( VAR SEQUENCE : CODELABEL ) ;


PROCEDURE *JUMPONFALSE ( VAR DESTINATION : CODELABEL ) ;

PROCEDURE *JUMP ( VAR DESTINATION : CODELABEL ) ;
```

Thereafter, generation of object code for the statement parts of the program being analyzed is easily added at appropriate points in the analyzer code. The use of code labels to generate the necessary control structure in the object code is illustrated by the **while** statement analyzer, which in its final form is as follows:

```
procedure whilestatement ;
    var extype : typentry ;
        totestcondition, afterloop : Generate.codelabel ;
    begin
        accept (whilesy) ;
        Generate.newcodelabel (totestcondition) ;
        Expression ([dosy] + followers, extype) ;
        if not compatible (extype, booltype) then semanticerror ;
        Generate.futurecodelabel (afterloop) ;
        Generate.jumponfalse (afterloop) ;
        accept (dosy) ;
        statement (followers) ;
        Generate.jump (totestcondition) ;
        Generate.expectedcodelabel (after loop)
    end ;
```

This coding illustrates one remaining problem with the interface. Can an error during the call to *Expression* sabotage the subsequent generator call *jumponfalse*? More generally can analysis of an erroneous program produce a malformed sequence of hypothetical operations with which the generator cannot cope? Clearly it can, and possible solutions to the problem are

(a) to guard against the generation of malformed sequences within the analyzer, or

(b) to detect and ignore malformed sequences within the generator.

Various complicated ways of achieving either of these can be conceived, but a simpler expedient adopted in many compilers is to suppress code generation permanently at the occurrence of the first error. With the form of interface chosen it is easier to make this suppression test within the generator, so we extend the interface by one further procedure:

```
procedure nofurthercode ;
```

which the analyzer will call on detecting any syntax or semantic error.

A complete listing of the final augmented analyzer with all its generator calls is given in Listing 8.

Listing 8

```
ENVELOPE MODULE ANALYZE ;


CONST ALFALENGTH = 8 ;

TYPE  ALFA = PACKED ARRAY [1..ALFALENGTH] OF CHAR ;


ENVELOPE MODULE SCAN = LISTING2 IN LIBRARY  ;



(* (A) SYNTAX ANALYSIS                                              *)
(*                                                                  *)
(*    SYNTAX ANALYSIS OF MINI-PASCAL PROGRAMS IS IMPLEMENTED        *)
(*    AS A SET OF RECURSIVE DESCENT PROCEDURES. THESE PROCEDURES    *)
(*    ARE BASED ON THE SYNTAX RULES GIVEN IN THE LANGUAGE DEFN      *)
(*    AND ARE NESTED AS TIGHTLY AS THE MUTUAL INTERACTION PERMITS.  *)
(*    THE ORDER, NAMES, AND NESTING OF THE PROCEDURES IS AS FOLLOWS *)
(*                                                                  *)
(*        PROGRAMME                                                 *)
(*          BLOCK                                                   *)
(*            VARPART                                               *)
(*              VARDECLARATION                                      *)
(*                TYP                                               *)
(*                  SIMPLETYPE                                      *)
(*                  INDEXRANGE                                      *)
(*            PROCPART                                              *)
(*              PROCDECLARATION                                     *)
(*            STATPART                                              *)
(*              COMPOUNDSTATEMENT                                   *)
(*                STATEMENT                                         *)
(*                  VARIABLE                                        *)
(*                  EXPRESSION                                      *)
(*                    SIMPLEEXPRESSION                              *)
(*                      TERM                                        *)
(*                        FACTOR                                    *)
(*                  ASSIGNMENT                                      *)
(*                  READSTATEMENT                                   *)
(*                    INPUTVARIABLE                                 *)
(*                  WRITESTATEMENT                                  *)
(*                    OUTPUTVALUE                                   *)
(*                  IFSTATEMENT                                     *)
(*                  WHILESTATEMENT                                  *)
(*                                                                  *)
(*                                                                  *)
```

```
(*    THE SYNTAX ANALYZERS ARE WRITTEN ON THE ASSUMPTION THAT THE        *)
(*    NEXT SYNTACTIC GOAL CAN ALWAYS BE SELECTED BY INSPECTION OF        *)
(*    (AT MOST) THE NEXT INCOMING SYMBOL ( I.E. THAT THE UNDERLYING      *)
(*    GRAMMAR IS LL(1) ). THIS IS NOT SO AT THE FOLLOWING POINTS         *)
(*    IN THE SYNTAX RULES ACTUALLY USED                                  *)
(*                                                                       *)
(*       1. A STATEMENT BEGINNING WITH AN IDENTIFIER MAY BE              *)
(*          EITHER AN ASSIGNMENT OR A PROCEDURE CALL                     *)
(*       2. A FACTOR BEGINNING WITH AN IDENTIFIER MAY BE EITHER          *)
(*          A VARIABLE OR A CONSTANT                                     *)
(*                                                                       *)
(*    IN  CASE 1 TO RESOLVE THE CHOICE ON A PURELY SYNTACTIC             *)
(*    BASIS WOULD REQUIRE A DISTORTION OF THE SYNTAX RULES               *)
(*    CHOICE 2 CANNOT BE SYNTACTICALLY RESOLVED IN SOME CASES .          *)
(*    HOWEVER IF PARALLEL SEMANTIC ANALYSIS IS ASSUMED (AS IN            *)
(*    THE CASE OF THIS COMPILER) THESE CHOICES CAN BE RESOLVED           *)
(*    WITHOUT SYNTAX DISTORTION, BY INSPECTION OF THE CURRENT            *)
(*    SEMANTIC ATTRIBUTES OF THE IDENTIFIER INVOLVED. FOR THIS           *)
(*    REASON SYNTACTIC RESOLUTION OF THESE CHOICES IS NOT USED.          *)
(*                                                                       *)
(*    THE ANALYZER GENERATES SYNTAX ERROR CODES WITH THE                 *)
(*    FOLLOWING MEANINGS:                                                *)
(*                                                                       *)
(*    10 ...... SYMBOL EXPECTED WAS IDENTIFIER                           *)
(*    11 ...... SYMBOL EXPECTED WAS INTEGER CONSTANT                     *)
(*    12 ...... SYMBOL EXPECTED WAS CHARACTER CONSTANT                   *)
(*    13 ...... ........                                                 *)
(*                                                                       *)
(*    I.E. ONE VALUE FOR EACH OF THE VALUES OF SYMBOLTYPE.               *)
(*    THE FINAL VALUE ORD(OTHERSY)+10 IS USED TO MEAN                    *)
(*                                                                       *)
(*    NN ...... UNEXPECTED SYMBOL                                        *)


TYPE

    SETOFSYMBOLS = SET OF SYMBOLTYPE ;


VAR

    STATSTARTERS,FACTORSTARTERS,MULOPS,SIGNS,ADDOPS,RELOPS : SETOFSYMBOLS ;


PROCEDURE SYNTAXERROR ( EXPECTEDSYMBOL : SYMBOLTYPE ) ;

  BEGIN
     SOURCE.ERROR(ORD(EXPECTEDSYMBOL)+10,SCAN.SYMBOLPOSITION) ;
     GENERATE.NOFURTHERCODE
  END (* SYNTAXERROR *) ;


PROCEDURE ACCEPT ( SYMBOLEXPECTED : SYMBOLTYPE ) ;

  BEGIN
     IF SCAN.SYMBOL = SYMBOLEXPECTED
     THEN SCAN.NEXTSYMBOL
     ELSE SYNTAXERROR(SYMBOLEXPECTED)
  END (* ACCEPT *) ;
```

```
(* (B) SYNTACTIC ERROR RECOVERY                                    *)
(*                                                                 *)
(*   RECOVERY IN THE SYNTAX ANALYSIS PROCESS FOLLOWING THE         *)
(*   DISCOVERY OF A SYNTAX ERROR IS INCORPORATED INTO THE          *)
(*   SYNTAX PROCEDURES ON THE FOLLOWING BASIS                      *)
(*                                                                 *)
(*     1. EACH PROCEDURE WHEN CALLED IS PASSED AN ACTUAL           *)
(*        PARAMETER WHICH IS A SET OF SYMBOLS WHICH ARE            *)
(*        POSSIBLE FOLLOWERS OF THE STRING WHICH IT SHOULD         *)
(*        SCAN. THESE FOLLOWERS NORMALLY INCLUDE                   *)
(*           (A) ALL SYMBOLS WHICH MAY LEGITIMATELY FOLLOW         *)
(*               THE STRING TO BE SCANNED                          *)
(*           (B) SUCH ADDITIONAL SYMBOLS AS A SUPERIOR             *)
(*               (CALLING) PROCEDURE MAY WISH TO HANDLE IN         *)
(*               THE EVENT OF ERROR RECOVERY                       *)
(*                                                                 *)
(*     2. WHEN ENTERED THE PROCEDURE MAY ENSURE THAT THE           *)
(*        CURRENT SYMBOL IS AN ACCEPTABLE STARTER FOR THE          *)
(*        STRING TO BE SCANNED, AND IF NOT SCAN FORWARD            *)
(*        UNTIL SUCH A SYMBOL IS FOUND (SUBJECT TO 4. BELOW)       *)
(*                                                                 *)
(*     3. WHEN CALLING A SUBSIDIARY SYNTAX PROCEDURE THE           *)
(*        PROCEDURE PASSES ON AS FOLLOWERS ITS OWN FOLLOWERS PLUS  *)
(*        THOSE SYMBOLS IF ANY WHICH IT MAY DETERMINE AS           *)
(*        FOLLOWERS FOR THE SUBSTRING TO BE SCANNED                *)
(*                                                                 *)
(*     4. TO RECOVER FROM A SYNTAX ERROR THE PROCEDURE MAY         *)
(*        SCAN OVER (SKIP) ANY SYMBOL PROVIDED IT IS NOT           *)
(*        CONTAINED IN THE FOLLOWERS PASSED TO IT                  *)
(*                                                                 *)
(*     5. ON EXIT THE SYNTAX PROCEDURE ENSURES THAT THE CURRENT    *)
(*        SYMBOL IS CONTAINED IN THE FOLLOWERS PASSED TO IT,       *)
(*        FLAGGING A TERMINAL ERROR AND SKIPPING IF THIS IS NOT    *)
(*        INITIALLY THE CASE.                                      *)
(*                                                                 *)
(*   TESTS 2 AND 5 ARE IMPLEMENTED BY THE DECLARATION OF AN        *)
(*   INSTANCE OF A CONTEXT CHECKING ENVELOPE WITHIN EACH           *)
(*   SYNTAX PROCEDURE                                              *)


ENVELOPE CHECK ( STARTERS,FOLLOWERS : SETOFSYMBOLS ) ;

    PROCEDURE SKIPTO ( RELEVANTSYMBOLS : SETOFSYMBOLS ) ;
       BEGIN
           WHILE NOT (SCAN.SYMBOL IN RELEVANTSYMBOLS)
           DO SCAN.NEXTSYMBOL
       END (* SKIPTO *) ;

    BEGIN
        IF NOT (SCAN.SYMBOL IN STARTERS) THEN
        BEGIN SYNTAXERROR(OTHERSY);  SKIPTO(STARTERS+FOLLOWERS) END ;
        IF SCAN.SYMBOL IN STARTERS THEN
        BEGIN
            *** (* EXECUTE ENVELOPED BLOCK *) ;
            IF NOT (SCAN.SYMBOL IN FOLLOWERS) THEN
            BEGIN SYNTAXERROR(OTHERSY);  SKIPTO(FOLLOWERS) END
        END
    END (* CHECK ENVELOPE *) ;
```

```
(* (C) SEMANTIC ANALYSIS AND SEMANTIC ERROR RECOVERY              *)
(*                                                                *)
(*                                                                *)
(*    SEMANTIC ANALYSIS AND SEMANTIC ERROR RECOVERY ARE IMPLEMENTED *)
(*    BY "ENRICHMENT" OF THE SYNTAX ANALYZER  WITH                *)
(*    SEMANTIC INTERLUDES. THE SEMANTIC ANALYSIS DEPENDS ON THE   *)
(*    FOLLOWING DATA STRUCTURES AND MANIPULATIVE                  *)
(*    PROCEDURES                                                  *)
(*                                                                *)
(*                                                                *)
(* (1) IDENTIFIER ENTRIES                                         *)
(*                                                                *)
(*    AN ENTRY IS RECORDED FOR EACH IDENTIFIER,EITHER STANDARD OR *)
(*    PROGRAM DEFINED, WHICH MAY APPEAR IN THE PROGRAM BEING      *)
(*    COMPILED. THE FORM OF ENTRY USED DEPENDS ON THE "CLASS" OF  *)
(*    USAGE OF THE IDENTIFIER AND IS REPRESENTED BY THE           *)
(*    RECORD TYPE "IDREC". CREATION, LOCATION AND DESTRUCTION OF  *)
(*    THESE RECORDS IS HANDLED BY THE SUB-MODULE "TABLE".         *)
(*                                                                *)
(*    STANDARD IDENTIFIERS SUPPORTED BY THE LANGUAGE ARE HELD     *)
(*    WITHIN THE TABLE AS IF DECLARED IN A PSEUDO-BLOCK           *)
(*    ENCLOSING THE MAIN PROGRAM . THESE ENTRIES ARE CREATED ON   *)
(*    INITIAL ENTRY TO THE ANALYZER MODULE                        *)
(*                                                                *)
(*                                                                *)
(* (2) TYPE ENTRIES                                               *)
(*                                                                *)
(*    ALL TYPES UNDERLYING THE DATA DEFINED BY THE PROGRAM BEING  *)
(*    COMPILED ARE REPRESENTED BY TYPE ENTRIES WHOSE FORM IS      *)
(*    DETERMINED BY THE "FORM" OF THE TYPE SO REPRESENTED (I.E.   *)
(*    SCALARS,ARRAYS,ETC.). ENTRIES ARE CONSTRUCTED USING A       *)
(*    CORRESPONDING VARIANT RECORD TYPE "TYPEREC".                *)
(*                                                                *)
(*    THESE TYPE ENTRIES ARE ACCESSED ONLY VIA THE IDENTIFIER     *)
(*    TABLE ENTRIES FOR TYPE IDENTIFIERS, OR VIA THE REPRESENTATION *)
(*    OF THE DATA OBJECTS (VARIABLES,CONSTANTS,EXPRESSIONS)       *)
(*    WHOSE TYPE THEY DESCRIBE. THUS FOR EXAMPLE ALL IDENTIFIER   *)
(*    TABLE ENTRIES HAVE A COMMON FIELD "IDTYPE" WHICH POINTS TO  *)
(*    AN UNDERLYING TYPE ENTRY (WITH AN OBVIOUS INTERPRETATION FOR *)
(*    ALL CLASSES OF IDENTIFIER OTHER THAN "PROC")                *)
(*                                                                *)
(*    THE TYPE ENTRIES REPRESENTING THE STANDARD TYPES SUPPORTED  *)
(*    BY THE LANGUAGE (INTEGER,CHAR,ETC.) ARE CREATED ON INITIAL  *)
(*    ENTRY TO THE ANALYZER. THESE ENTRIES ARE DIRECTLY ACCESSIBLE *)
(*    VIA POINTER VARIABLES "INTYPE","CHARTYPE",ETC., AS          *)
(*    WELL AS VIA THE IDENTIFIER ENTRIES FOR "INTEGER","CHAR",ETC. *)
(*                                                                *)
(*                                                                *)
(* (3) THE FUNCTION COMPATIBLE                                    *)
(*                                                                *)
(*    TO FACILITATE TYPE ANALYSIS WITHIN THE SEMANTIC ANALYZER    *)
(*    A GENERAL-PURPOSE BOOLEAN FUNCTION "COMPATIBLE" IS PROVIDED  *)
(*    TO TEST THE COMPATIBILITY OF TWO TYPES AS REPRESENTED BY    *)
(*    POINTERS TO THE CORRESPONDING TYPE ENTRIES. A RESULT TRUE IS *)
(*    RETURNED IF THE TYPES ARE IDENTICAL (I.E. THE POINTERS POINT *)
(*    TO THE SAME TYPE ENTRY), OR STRICTLY EQUIVALENT (I.E. TWO   *)
(*    DISTINCT TYPE ENTRIES OF IDENTICAL FORM AND CONTENT)        *)
(*                                                                *)
```

```
(*                                                                *)
(*     IN ALL SITUATIONS WHERE THE TYPE OF A DATA OBJECT IS NOT    *)
(*     DETERMINED IT IS REPRESENTED BY A POINTER VALUE 'NIL'.      *)
(*     THE TYPE-CHECKING FUNCTION "COMPATIBLE" IS DEFINED TO RETURN *)
(*     'TRUE' IF EITHER OF ITS PARAMETERS HAS THIS VALUE. IN THIS  *)
(*     WAY NORMAL TYPE ANALYSIS CAN PROCEED WITHOUT A PRELIMINARY  *)
(*     SCREENING FOR INDETERMINATE TYPES AT EVERY POINT AT WHICH   *)
(*     THEY MIGHT ARISE.                                           *)
(*                                                                *)
(*     SEMANTIC ERRORS ARE REPORTED WITH THE FOLLOWING CODES       *)
(*                                                                *)
(*     61 .... INDEXED VARIABLE MUST BE OF ARRAY TYPE              *)
(*     62 .... INDEX EXPRESSION MUST BE OF TYPE INTEGER            *)
(*     63 .... OPERAND MUST BE OF TYPE BOOLEAN                     *)
(*     64 .... OPERAND MUST BE OF TYPE INTEGER                     *)
(*     65 .... OPERANDS MUST BOTH BE INTEGER, OR BOTH CHAR         *)
(*     66 .... EXPRESSION MUST BE OF SAME TYPE AS VARIABLE         *)
(*     67 .... INPUT VARIABLE MUST BE OF TYPE INTEGER OR CHAR      *)
(*     68 .... OUTPUT VALUE MUST BE OF TYPE INTEGER OR CHAR        *)
(*     69 .... EXPRESSION MUST BE OF TYPE BOOLEAN                  *)


TYPE

    TYPENTRY = ^TYPEREC ; IDENTRY = ^IDREC ;

    TYPEFORM = (SCALARS,ARRAYS) ;

    TYPEREC = RECORD
                NEXT : TYPENTRY ;
                REPRESENTATION : GENERATE.TYPEREPRESENTATION ;
                CASE FORM : TYPEFORM OF
                    ARRAYS :
                        (INDEXMIN,INDEXMAX : INTEGER ;
                        ELEMENTTYPE : TYPENTRY )
              END ;


    IDCLASS = (TYPES,CONSTS,VARS,PROCS) ;

    SETOFIDCLASS = SET OF IDCLASS ;

    IDREC = RECORD
                NAME : ALFA ;
                LEFTLINK,RIGHTLINK : IDENTRY ;
                IDTYPE : TYPENTRY ;
                CASE CLASS : IDCLASS OF
                    CONSTS : ( CONSTVALUE : INTEGER ) ;
                    VARS   : ( VARADDRESS : GENERATE.RUNTIMEADDRESS ) ;
                    PROCS  : ( LINKAGE : GENERATE.PROCLINKAGE )
              END ;

VAR

    INTTYPE,BOOLTYPE,CHARTYPE : TYPENTRY ;
```

```
PROCEDURE SEMANTICERROR ( CODE : INTEGER ) ;

   BEGIN
      SOURCE.ERROR(CODE,SCAN.SYMBOLPOSITION) ;
      GENERATE.NOFURTHERCODE
   END (* SEMANTICERROR *) ;


ENVELOPE MODULE TABLE  = LISTING5 IN LIBRARY ;


FUNCTION COMPATIBLE (TYPE1,TYPE2 : TYPENTRY) : BOOLEAN ;

   (* DECIDES WHETHER TYPES POINTED AT BY
      TYPE1 AND TYPE2 ARE COMPATIBLE       *)

   BEGIN (* COMPATIBLE *) ;
      IF TYPE1 = TYPE2
      THEN COMPATIBLE := TRUE
      ELSE
         IF (TYPE1=NIL) OR (TYPE2=NIL)
         THEN COMPATIBLE := TRUE
         ELSE
            IF (TYPE1^.FORM=ARRAYS) AND (TYPE2^.FORM=ARRAYS)
            THEN COMPATIBLE :=
                 (TYPE1^.INDEXMIN = TYPE2^.INDEXMIN) AND
                 (TYPE1^.INDEXMAX = TYPE2^.INDEXMAX) AND
                 COMPATIBLE(TYPE1^.ELEMENTTYPE,TYPE2^.ELEMENTTYPE)
            ELSE COMPATIBLE := FALSE
   END (* COMPATIBLE *) ;



(* (D) OBJECT PROGRAM GENERATION                                     *)
(*                                                                   *)
(*     OBJECT PROGRAM GENERATION IS IMPLEMENTED BY INTERFACING THE   *)
(*     ANALYZER MODULE TO AN OBJECT-CODE-DEPENDENT GENERATOR MODULE  *)
(*     THE INTERFACE ITSELF HOWEVER IS INDEPENDENT OF THE OBJECT     *)
(*     CODE TO BE PRODUCED. THE INTERFACE SPECIFICATION IS GIVEN IN  *)
(*     THE GENERATOR MODULE                                          *)



PROCEDURE *PROGRAMME ;

   INSTANCE BUILTIN : TABLE.NEWSCOPE ;

   VAR ENTRY : IDENTRY ;


   PROCEDURE BLOCK ( FOLLOWERS : SETOFSYMBOLS ; BLOCKID : IDENTRY ) ;

      INSTANCE CONTEXT:CHECK([VARSY,PROCSY,BEGINSY],FOLLOWERS) ;

               SCOPE : TABLE.NEWSCOPE ;


      PROCEDURE VARPART ( FOLLOWERS : SETOFSYMBOLS ) ;

         INSTANCE CONTEXT:CHECK([VARSY]+FOLLOWERS,FOLLOWERS) ;
```

```
PROCEDURE VARDECLARATION ( FOLLOWERS : SETOFSYMBOLS ) ;

  INSTANCE CONTEXT:CHECK([IDENT,COMMA,COLON],FOLLOWERS) ;

  TYPE
     IDLIST = ^LISTREC ;
     LISTREC = RECORD
                     ID : IDENTRY ;
                     NEXTONLIST : IDLIST
                 END ;

  VAR
     VARIABLELIST : RECORD
                        HEAD,TAIL : IDLIST
                    END ;
     VARTYPE : TYPENTRY ;

  PROCEDURE NEWVARIABLE ;
     VAR
        VARENTRY : IDENTRY ;
        LISTENTRY : IDLIST ;
     BEGIN
        IF SCAN.SYMBOL = IDENT THEN
        BEGIN
           SCOPE.NEWID(SCAN.SPELLING,VARENTRY,VARS) ;
           NEW(LISTENTRY) ;
           WITH LISTENTRY^ DO
           BEGIN
              ID := VARENTRY ;
              NEXTONLIST := NIL
           END ;
           WITH VARIABLELIST DO
            BEGIN
              IF HEAD = NIL
              THEN HEAD := LISTENTRY
              ELSE TAIL^.NEXTONLIST := LISTENTRY ;
              TAIL := LISTENTRY
            END
        END
     END (* NEW VARIABLE *) ;

  PROCEDURE ADDATTRIBUTES ;
     VAR
        LISTENTRY,OLDENTRY : IDLIST ;
     BEGIN
        LISTENTRY := VARIABLELIST.HEAD ;
        WHILE LISTENTRY <> NIL DO
           WITH LISTENTRY^ DO
           BEGIN
              ID^.IDTYPE := VARTYPE ;
              IF VARTYPE <> NIL
              THEN GENERATE.ADDRESSFOR(VARTYPE^.REPRESENTATION,
                                       ID^.VARADDRESS) ;
              OLDENTRY := LISTENTRY ;
              LISTENTRY := NEXTONLIST ;
              DISPOSE(OLDENTRY)
           END
     END (* ADD ATTRIBUTES *) ;
```

```
PROCEDURE TYP ( FOLLOWERS : SETOFSYMBOLS ;
               VAR TYPEFOUND : TYPENTRY ) ;

   INSTANCE CONTEXT:CHECK([IDENT,ARRAYSY],FOLLOWERS) ;

   PROCEDURE SIMPLETYPE ( FOLLOWERS : SETOFSYMBOLS ;
                          VAR TYPENAMED : TYPENTRY ) ;

      INSTANCE CONTEXT:CHECK([IDENT],FOLLOWERS) ;

      VAR
         TYPEID : IDENTRY ;
      BEGIN
         SCOPE.SEARCHID(SCAN.SPELLING,TYPEID,[TYPES]);
         TYPENAMED := TYPEID^.IDTYPE ;
         ACCEPT(IDENT) ;
      END (* SIMPLETYPE *) ;

   PROCEDURE INDEXRANGE  ( FOLLOWERS : SETOFSYMBOLS ) ;

      INSTANCE CONTEXT:CHECK([INTCONST,THRU],FOLLOWERS) ;

      BEGIN
         TYPEFOUND^.INDEXMIN := SCAN.CONSTANT ;
         ACCEPT(INTCONST) ;
         ACCEPT(THRU) ;
         TYPEFOUND^.INDEXMAX := SCAN.CONSTANT ;
         ACCEPT(INTCONST) ;
      END (* INDEXRANGE *) ;


   BEGIN (* TYP *)
      IF SCAN.SYMBOL = IDENT
      THEN SIMPLETYPE(FOLLOWERS,TYPEFOUND)
      ELSE
      BEGIN
         SCOPE.NEWTYPE(TYPEFOUND,ARRAYS) ;
         ACCEPT(ARRAYSY) ;
         ACCEPT(LEFTBRACKET) ;
         INDEXRANGE([RIGHTBRACKET,OFSY]+FOLLOWERS) ;
         ACCEPT(RIGHTBRACKET) ;
         ACCEPT(OFSY) ;
         SIMPLETYPE(FOLLOWERS,TYPEFOUND^.ELEMENTTYPE) ;
         WITH TYPEFOUND^ DO
            IF ELEMENTTYPE <> NIL
            THEN GENERATE.ARRAYREPRESENTATION
                 (INDEXMIN,INDEXMAX,
                  ELEMENTTYPE^.REPRESENTATION,REPRESENTATION)
      END
   END (* TYP *) ;
```

```
      BEGIN (* VARDECLARATION *)
         VARIABLELIST.HEAD := NIL ;
         NEWVARIABLE ;
         ACCEPT(IDENT) ;
         WHILE SCAN.SYMBOL = COMMA DO
         BEGIN
            ACCEPT(COMMA) ;
            NEWVARIABLE ;
            ACCEPT(IDENT)
         END ;
         ACCEPT(COLON) ;
         TYP(FOLLOWERS,VARTYPE) ;
         ADDATTRIBUTES
      END (* VARDECLARATION *) ;


   BEGIN (* VARPART *)
      IF SCAN.SYMBOL = VARSY THEN
      BEGIN
         ACCEPT(VARSY) ;
         REPEAT
            VARDECLARATION([SEMICOLON]+FOLLOWERS) ;
            ACCEPT(SEMICOLON)
         UNTIL SCAN.SYMBOL <> IDENT
      END
   END (* VARPART *) ;



PROCEDURE PROCPART ( FOLLOWERS : SETOFSYMBOLS ) ;

   INSTANCE CONTEXT:CHECK([PROCSY]+FOLLOWERS,FOLLOWERS) ;

   PROCEDURE PROCDECLARATION ( FOLLOWERS : SETOFSYMBOLS ) ;

      INSTANCE CONTEXT:CHECK([PROCSY],FOLLOWERS) ;

      VAR
         PROCID : IDENTRY ; PROCNAME : ALFA ;

      BEGIN (* PROCDECLARATION *)
         ACCEPT(PROCSY) ;
         IF SCAN.SYMBOL = IDENT
         THEN PROCNAME := SCAN.SPELLING
         ELSE PROCNAME := '????????' ;
         SCOPE.NEWID(PROCNAME,PROCID,PROCS) ;
         GENERATE.NEWLINKAGE(PROCID^.LINKAGE) ;
         ACCEPT(IDENT) ;
         ACCEPT(SEMICOLON) ;
         BLOCK(FOLLOWERS,PROCID) ;
      END (* PROCDECLARATION *) ;

   BEGIN (* PROCPART *)
      WHILE SCAN.SYMBOL = PROCSY DO
      BEGIN
         PROCDECLARATION([SEMICOLON,PROCSY]+FOLLOWERS) ;
         ACCEPT(SEMICOLON)
      END
   END (* PROCPART *) ;
```

```
PROCEDURE STATPART ( FOLLOWERS : SETOFSYMBOLS ) ;

  INSTANCE CONTEXT:CHECK([BEGINSY],FOLLOWERS) ;


  PROCEDURE COMPOUNDSTATEMENT ( FOLLOWERS : SETOFSYMBOLS ) ;

    INSTANCE CONTEXT:CHECK([BEGINSY],FOLLOWERS) ;


    PROCEDURE STATEMENT ( FOLLOWERS : SETOFSYMBOLS ) ;

      INSTANCE CONTEXT:CHECK(STATSTARTERS,FOLLOWERS) ;

      VAR
         FIRSTID : IDENTRY ;


      PROCEDURE EXPRESSION ( FOLLOWERS : SETOFSYMBOLS ;
                             VAR EXPTYPE : TYPENTRY ) ; FORWARD ;

      PROCEDURE VARIABLE ( FOLLOWERS : SETOFSYMBOLS ;
                           VAR VARTYPE : TYPENTRY ) ;

        INSTANCE CONTEXT:CHECK([IDENT],FOLLOWERS) ;

        VAR
           VARID : IDENTRY ;
           INDEXTYPE : TYPENTRY ;

        BEGIN (* VARIABLE *)
           SCOPE.SEARCHID(SCAN.SPELLING,VARID,[VARS]) ;
           VARTYPE := VARID^.IDTYPE ;
           GENERATE.STACKREFERENCE(VARID^.VARADDRESS) ;
           ACCEPT(IDENT) ;
           IF SCAN.SYMBOL = LEFTBRACKET THEN
           BEGIN
              IF VARTYPE <> NIL THEN
                 IF VARTYPE^.FORM <> ARRAYS THEN
                 BEGIN
                    SEMANTICERROR(61) ;
                    VARTYPE := NIL
                 END ;
              ACCEPT(LEFTBRACKET) ;
              EXPRESSION([RIGHTBRACKET]+FOLLOWERS,INDEXTYPE) ;
              IF NOT COMPATIBLE(INDEXTYPE,INTTYPE)
              THEN SEMANTICERROR(62) ;
              IF VARTYPE <> NIL THEN
              BEGIN
                 WITH VARTYPE^ DO
                 GENERATE.INDEXEDREFERENCE(INDEXMIN,INDEXMAX,
                               ELEMENTTYPE^.REPRESENTATION) ;
                 VARTYPE := VARTYPE^.ELEMENTTYPE ;
              END ;
              ACCEPT(RIGHTBRACKET)
           END ;
        END (* VARIABLE *) ;
```

```
PROCEDURE EXPRESSION ;

   VAR
      FIRSTTYPE : TYPENTRY ;
      OPERATOR  : SYMBOLTYPE ;

   PROCEDURE SIMPLEEXPRESSION ( FOLLOWERS : SETOFSYMBOLS ) ;

      INSTANCE CONTEXT:CHECK(FACTORSTARTERS+SIGNS,FOLLOWERS) ;

      VAR
         SIGNED,NEGATED : BOOLEAN ;
         FIRSTTYPE : TYPENTRY ;
         OPERATOR : SYMBOLTYPE ;

      PROCEDURE TERM ( FOLLOWERS : SETOFSYMBOLS ) ;

         VAR
            FIRSTTYPE : TYPENTRY ;
            OPERATOR  : SYMBOLTYPE ;

         PROCEDURE FACTOR ( FOLLOWERS : SETOFSYMBOLS ) ;

            INSTANCE CONTEXT:CHECK(FACTORSTARTERS,FOLLOWERS) ;

            VAR
               FIRSTID : IDENTRY ;

            BEGIN
               BEGIN
                  CASE SCAN.SYMBOL OF
                  IDENT :
                     BEGIN
                        SCOPE.SEARCHID(SCAN.SPELLING,
                                       FIRSTID,
                                       [VARS,CONSTS]) ;
                        CASE FIRSTID^.CLASS OF
                        CONSTS :
                           BEGIN
                              EXPTYPE := FIRSTID^.IDTYPE ;
                              GENERATE.STACKCONSTANT
                                   (FIRSTID^.CONSTVALUE,
                                    EXPTYPE^.REPRESENTATION) ;
                              ACCEPT(IDENT)
                           END ;
                        VARS :
                           BEGIN
                              VARIABLE(FOLLOWERS,EXPTYPE) ;
                              IF EXPTYPE <> NIL THEN
                                 GENERATE.DEREFERENCE
                                    (EXPTYPE^.REPRESENTATION) ;
                           END
                        END
                     END ;
```

```
            INTCONST :
            BEGIN
                EXPTYPE := INTTYPE ;
                GENERATE.STACKCONSTANT
                    (SCAN.CONSTANT,
                     INTTYPE^.REPRESENTATION) ;
                ACCEPT(INTCONST)
            END ;
            CHARCONST :
            BEGIN
                EXPTYPE := CHARTYPE ;
                GENERATE.STACKCONSTANT
                    (SCAN.CONSTANT,
                     CHARTYPE^.REPRESENTATION);
                ACCEPT(CHARCONST)
            END ;
            LEFTPARENT :
            BEGIN
                ACCEPT(LEFTPARENT) ;
                EXPRESSION([RIGHTPARENT]+FOLLOWERS,
                           EXPTYPE) ;
                ACCEPT(RIGHTPARENT)
            END ;
            NOTOP :
            BEGIN
                ACCEPT(NOTOP) ;
                FACTOR(FOLLOWERS) ;
                IF NOT COMPATIBLE(EXPTYPE,BOOLTYPE)
                THEN SEMANTICERROR(63) ;
                GENERATE.NEGATEBOOLEAN ;
                EXPTYPE := BOOLTYPE
            END ;
        END ;
    END
END (* FACTOR *) ;

    BEGIN (* TERM *)
        FACTOR(MULOPS+FACTORSTARTERS+FOLLOWERS) ;
        IF SCAN.SYMBOL = ANDOP THEN
            GENERATE.BINARYBOOLEANOPERATION(ANDOP,TRUE);
        WHILE SCAN.SYMBOL IN MULOPS+FACTORSTARTERS DO
        BEGIN
            FIRSTTYPE := EXPTYPE ;
            OPERATOR := SCAN.SYMBOL ;
            IF SCAN.SYMBOL IN MULOPS
            THEN SCAN.NEXTSYMBOL
            ELSE SYNTAXERROR(TIMES) ;
            FACTOR(MULOPS+FACTORSTARTERS+FOLLOWERS) ;
            IF OPERATOR IN MULOPS
            THEN
                CASE OPERATOR OF
                TIMES,DIVOP :
                    BEGIN
                        IF NOT
                        (COMPATIBLE(FIRSTTYPE,INTTYPE)
                         AND COMPATIBLE(EXPTYPE,INTTYPE))
                        THEN SEMANTICERROR(64) ;
                        GENERATE.BINARYINTEGEROPERATION
                                        (OPERATOR) ;
                        EXPTYPE := INTTYPE
                    END ;
```

```
              ANDOP :
                  BEGIN
                     IF NOT
                     (COMPATIBLE(FIRSTTYPE,BOOLTYPE)
                      AND COMPATIBLE(EXPTYPE,BOOLTYPE))
                     THEN SEMANTICERROR(63) ;
                     GENERATE.BINARYBOOLEANOPERATION
                                         (ANDOP,FALSE) ;
                     EXPTYPE := BOOLTYPE
                  END
              END
            ELSE EXPTYPE := NIL
        END
    END (* TERM *) ;

BEGIN (* SIMPLE EXPRESSION *)
    IF SCAN.SYMBOL IN SIGNS THEN
    BEGIN
        SIGNED := TRUE ;
        NEGATED := (SCAN.SYMBOL = MINUS) ;
        SCAN.NEXTSYMBOL ;
    END
    ELSE SIGNED := FALSE ;
    TERM(ADDOPS+FOLLOWERS) ;
    IF SIGNED THEN
        IF NOT COMPATIBLE(EXPTYPE,INTTYPE)
        THEN SEMANTICERROR(64)
        ELSE
            IF NEGATED THEN GENERATE.NEGATEINTEGER ;
    IF SCAN.SYMBOL = OROP THEN
        GENERATE.BINARYBOOLEANOPERATION(OROP,TRUE) ;
    WHILE SCAN.SYMBOL IN ADDOPS DO
    BEGIN
        FIRSTTYPE := EXPTYPE ;
        OPERATOR := SCAN.SYMBOL ;
        SCAN.NEXTSYMBOL ;
        TERM(ADDOPS+FOLLOWERS) ;
        CASE OPERATOR OF
        PLUS,MINUS :
            BEGIN
                IF NOT (COMPATIBLE(FIRSTTYPE,INTTYPE)
                        AND COMPATIBLE(EXPTYPE,INTTYPE))
                THEN SEMANTICERROR(64) ;
                GENERATE.BINARYINTEGEROPERATION
                                        (OPERATOR) ;
                EXPTYPE := INTTYPE
            END ;
        OROP :
            BEGIN
                IF NOT (COMPATIBLE(FIRSTTYPE,BOOLTYPE)
                        AND COMPATIBLE(EXPTYPE,BOOLTYPE))
                THEN SEMANTICERROR(63) ;
                GENERATE.BINARYBOOLEANOPERATION
                                        (OROP,FALSE) ;
                EXPTYPE := BOOLTYPE
            END
        END
    END
END (* SIMPLE EXPRESSION *) ;
```

```
        BEGIN (* EXPRESSION *)
           SIMPLEEXPRESSION(RELOPS+FOLLOWERS) ;
           IF SCAN.SYMBOL IN RELOPS THEN
           BEGIN
              FIRSTTYPE := EXPTYPE ;
              OPERATOR := SCAN.SYMBOL ;
              SCAN.NEXTSYMBOL ;
              SIMPLEEXPRESSION(FOLLOWERS) ;
              IF NOT ( COMPATIBLE(FIRSTTYPE,INTTYPE) AND
                       COMPATIBLE(EXPTYPE,INTTYPE)    OR
                       COMPATIBLE(FIRSTTYPE,CHARTYPE) AND
                       COMPATIBLE(EXPTYPE,CHARTYPE))
              THEN SEMANTICERROR(65) ;
              GENERATE.COMPARISON(OPERATOR) ;
              EXPTYPE := BOOLTYPE
           END
        END (* EXPRESSION *) ;


   PROCEDURE ASSIGNMENT ;

      VAR
         VARTYPE,EXPTYPE : TYPENTRY ;

      BEGIN (* ASSIGNMENT *)
         VARIABLE([BECOMES]+FOLLOWERS,VARTYPE) ;
         ACCEPT(BECOMES) ;
         EXPRESSION(FOLLOWERS,EXPTYPE) ;
         IF NOT COMPATIBLE(VARTYPE,EXPTYPE)
         THEN SEMANTICERROR(66) ;
         GENERATE.ASSIGN
      END (* ASSIGNMENT *) ;

   PROCEDURE READSTATEMENT ;

      PROCEDURE INPUTVARIABLE ;

         VAR
            VARTYPE : TYPENTRY ;
         BEGIN
            VARIABLE([COMMA,RIGHTPARENT]+FOLLOWERS,VARTYPE) ;
            IF COMPATIBLE(VARTYPE,CHARTYPE)
            THEN GENERATE.READOPERATION(CHARMODE)
            ELSE
               IF COMPATIBLE(VARTYPE,INTTYPE)
               THEN GENERATE.READOPERATION(INTEGERMODE)
               ELSE SEMANTICERROR(67)
         END (* INPUTVARIABLE *);

      BEGIN
         ACCEPT(READSY) ;
         ACCEPT(LEFTPARENT) ;
         INPUTVARIABLE ;
         WHILE SCAN.SYMBOL = COMMA DO
         BEGIN
            ACCEPT(COMMA) ;
            INPUTVARIABLE
         END ;
         ACCEPT(RIGHTPARENT)
      END (* READSTATEMENT *) ;
```

```
PROCEDURE WRITESTATEMENT ;

   PROCEDURE OUTPUTVALUE ;

      VAR
         EXPTYPE : TYPENTRY ;
      BEGIN
         EXPRESSION([COMMA,RIGHTPARENT]+FOLLOWERS,EXPTYPE) ;
         IF COMPATIBLE(EXPTYPE,CHARTYPE)
         THEN GENERATE.WRITEOPERATION(CHARMODE)
         ELSE
            IF COMPATIBLE(EXPTYPE,INTTYPE)
            THEN GENERATE.WRITEOPERATION(INTEGERMODE)
            ELSE SEMANTICERROR(68)
      END (* OUTPUTVALUE *) ;

   BEGIN
      ACCEPT(WRITESY) ;
      ACCEPT(LEFTPARENT) ;
      OUTPUTVALUE ;
      WHILE SCAN.SYMBOL = COMMA DO
      BEGIN
         ACCEPT(COMMA) ;
         OUTPUTVALUE
      END ;
      ACCEPT(RIGHTPARENT)
   END (* WRITESTATEMENT *) ;


PROCEDURE IFSTATEMENT ;

   VAR
      EXPTYPE : TYPENTRY ;
      AFTERTRUEACTION,
      AFTERFALSEACTION : GENERATE.CODELABEL ;

   BEGIN (* IFSTATEMENT *)
      ACCEPT(IFSY) ;
      EXPRESSION([THENSY,ELSESY]+FOLLOWERS,EXPTYPE) ;
      IF NOT COMPATIBLE(EXPTYPE,BOOLTYPE)
      THEN SEMANTICERROR(69) ;
      GENERATE.FUTURECODELABEL(AFTERTRUEACTION) ;
      GENERATE.JUMPONFALSE(AFTERTRUEACTION) ;
      ACCEPT(THENSY) ;
      STATEMENT([ELSESY]+FOLLOWERS) ;
      IF SCAN.SYMBOL = ELSESY
      THEN
      BEGIN
         GENERATE.FUTURECODELABEL(AFTERFALSEACTION) ;
         GENERATE.JUMP(AFTERFALSEACTION) ;
         GENERATE.EXPECTEDSEQUENCE(AFTERTRUEACTION) ;
         ACCEPT(ELSESY) ;
         STATEMENT(FOLLOWERS) ;
         GENERATE.EXPECTEDCODELABEL(AFTERFALSEACTION)
      END
      ELSE GENERATE.EXPECTEDCODELABEL(AFTERTRUEACTION)
   END (* IFSTATEMENT *) ;
```

```
PROCEDURE WHILESTATEMENT ;

    VAR
        EXPTYPE : TYPENTRY ;
        TOTESTCONDITION,
        AFTERSTATEMENT : GENERATE.CODELABEL ;

    BEGIN (* WHILESTATEMENT *)
        GENERATE.NEWCODELABEL(TOTESTCONDITION) ;
        GENERATE.FUTURECODELABEL(AFTERSTATEMENT) ;
        ACCEPT(WHILESY) ;
        EXPRESSION([DOSY]+FOLLOWERS,EXPTYPE) ;
        IF NOT COMPATIBLE(EXPTYPE,BOOLTYPE)
        THEN SEMANTICERROR(69) ;
        GENERATE.JUMPONFALSE(AFTERSTATEMENT) ;
        ACCEPT(DOSY) ;
        STATEMENT(FOLLOWERS) ;
        GENERATE.JUMP(TOTESTCONDITION) ;
        GENERATE.EXPECTEDCODELABEL(AFTERSTATEMENT)
    END (* WHILESTATEMENT *) ;

BEGIN (* STATEMENT *)
    CASE SCAN.SYMBOL OF
    IDENT :
        BEGIN
            SCOPE.SEARCHID(SCAN.SPELLING,FIRSTID,
                           [PROCS,VARS]) ;
            IF FIRSTID^.CLASS = VARS
            THEN ASSIGNMENT
            ELSE
            BEGIN
                GENERATE.CALLPROC(FIRSTID^.LINKAGE) ;
                ACCEPT(IDENT)
            END
        END ;
    BEGINSY :
        COMPOUNDSTATEMENT(FOLLOWERS) ;
    IFSY :
        IFSTATEMENT ;
    WHILESY :
        WHILESTATEMENT ;
    READSY :
        READSTATEMENT ;
    WRITESY :
        WRITESTATEMENT
    END (* CASE *)
END (* STATEMENT *) ;


BEGIN (*COMPOUNDSTATEMENT *)
  ACCEPT(BEGINSY) ;
  STATEMENT([SEMICOLON,ENDSY]+STATSTARTERS
                          -[IDENT]+FOLLOWERS) ;
  WHILE SCAN.SYMBOL IN [SEMICOLON]+STATSTARTERS-[IDENT] DO
  BEGIN
     ACCEPT(SEMICOLON) ;
     STATEMENT([SEMICOLON,ENDSY]+STATSTARTERS
                          -[IDENT]+FOLLOWERS)
  END ;
  ACCEPT(ENDSY)
END (* COMPOUND STATEMENT *) ;
```

```
    BEGIN (* STATPART *)
      IF BLOCKID = NIL
      THEN GENERATE.ENTERPROGRAM
      ELSE GENERATE.ENTERBODY(BLOCKID^.LINKAGE) ;
      COMPOUNDSTATEMENT(FOLLOWERS) ;
      IF BLOCKID = NIL
      THEN GENERATE.LEAVEPROGRAM
      ELSE GENERATE.LEAVEBODY
    END (* STATPART *) ;

  BEGIN (* BLOCK *)
    GENERATE.OPENSTACKFRAME ;
    VARPART([PROCSY,BEGINSY]) ;
    PROCPART([BEGINSY]) ;
    STATPART(FOLLOWERS) ;
    GENERATE.CLOSESTACKFRAME
  END (* BLOCK *) ;


BEGIN (* PROGRAMME *)

  BUILTIN.NEWTYPE(INTTYPE,SCALARS) ;
  BUILTIN.NEWTYPE(CHARTYPE,SCALARS) ;
  BUILTIN.NEWTYPE(BOOLTYPE,SCALARS) ;
  INTTYPE^.REPRESENTATION :=  GENERATE.INTEGERREPRESENTATION ;
  CHARTYPE^.REPRESENTATION := GENERATE.CHARREPRESENTATION ;
  BOOLTYPE^.REPRESENTATION := GENERATE.BOOLEANREPRESENTATION ;
  BUILTIN.NEWID( 'INTEGER ',ENTRY,TYPES) ;
  ENTRY^.IDTYPE := INTTYPE ;
  BUILTIN.NEWID( 'CHAR    ',ENTRY,TYPES) ;
  ENTRY^.IDTYPE := CHARTYPE ;
  BUILTIN.NEWID( 'BOOLEAN ',ENTRY,TYPES) ;
  ENTRY^.IDTYPE := BOOLTYPE ;
  BUILTIN.NEWID( 'FALSE   ',ENTRY,CONSTS) ;
  ENTRY^.IDTYPE := BOOLTYPE ;
  ENTRY^.CONSTVALUE := 0 ;
  BUILTIN.NEWID( 'TRUE    ',ENTRY,CONSTS) ;
  ENTRY^.IDTYPE := BOOLTYPE ;
  ENTRY^.CONSTVALUE := 1 ;

  ACCEPT(PROGRAMSY) ;
  ACCEPT(IDENT) ;
  ACCEPT(SEMICOLON) ;
  BLOCK([PERIOD],NIL)
END (* PROGRAMME *) ;


BEGIN
  STATSTARTERS := [IDENT,BEGINSY,READSY,WRITESY,IFSY,WHILESY] ;
  FACTORSTARTERS := [IDENT,INTCONST,CHARCONST,NOTOP,LEFTPARENT] ;
  MULOPS := [TIMES,DIVOP,ANDOP] ;
  SIGNS := [PLUS,MINUS] ;
  ADDOPS := [PLUS,MINUS,OROP] ;
  RELOPS := [EQOP,NEOP,LTOP,LEOP,GEOP,GTOP] ;

  ***

END (* ANALYZER MODULE *) ;
```

Exercise 5   Modify the code-generation interface given in Listing 7 to allow generation of the code for the multiple assignment statement, and make the necessary
corresponding changes to the analyzer given in Listing 8.

CODE GENERATION

Beyond the code-generation interface all design decisions reflect the particular
object-code form to be generated. In this project our aim is to generate
directly executable machine code for a machine which we will call the REAL
computer. In fact the REAL computer is not an actual existing machine,
but it is modeled very closely on the simpler features of ICL 1900 series
computers, and is typical of many available computers. In the space available
we cannot cover all aspects of the generation of such code, but we will
examine some of the areas to see how the machine and object-code characteristics influence the generation process and how they can be handled in the
generator module.

Representation of Object Program Data

The generator interface introduced a type *typerepresentation* to describe how
values of each type in a Mini-Pascal program are represented. The REAL is a
strictly word-oriented machine with a wordlength of 24 bits. For the range
of types which Mini-Pascal permits, the obvious representation is one REAL
word for each of the built-in scalar types *integer*, *char*, and *Boolean*, and *n*
contiguous words for each array of *n* elements. The only information required on the representation of each type is its size in words, which may in
principle be any size within the available address space of the REAL computer. We therefore define typerepresentation as follows:

$$typerepresentation \ = \ addressrange \ ;$$

where *addressrange* is a subrange representing the available address space for
the object program, say

$$addressrange \ = \ 0 \ . \ . \ addressmax \ ;$$

The built-in representations can then be expressed as constants

$$\textbf{const} \ integerrepresentation \ = \ 1 \ ;$$
$$charrepresentation \ = \ 1 \ ;$$
$$Booleanrepresentation \ = \ 1 \ ;$$

and the array representation procedure becomes

procedure *arrayrepresentation* (*boundmin, boundmax* : *integer* ;
                                elementrepresentation : *typerepresentation* ;
                                var *representation* : *typerepresentation*) ;
begin
   representation := *boundmax* − *boundmin* + 1
end ;

Storage Allocation and Control

The normal run-time storage organization used for block-structured languages is a dynamically allocated *stack* of storage *frames*, one for each procedure currently under execution. The topmost frame holds the variables local to the procedure being executed, the one below holds those of the procedure which called it, and so on.

On entering a block, a new frame can be allocated on top of the stack to accommodate the administrative data and local variables of the block, and on exit from the block this frame can be retrieved. The administrative data include the address to which control must return on exit from the block, and information describing the contexts in which the block was defined and invoked: this information is provided by two pointers to the stack frames of the appropriate blocks. These pointers thus form links in two chains called the *static chain* and the *dynamic chain* respectively; the former enables a block to access variables declared outside or *global* to it, while the latter is used for collapsing the top frame of the stack on exit from the block.

Suppose a procedure *A* encloses procedures *B* and *C*, and that *A* calls *C* which calls *B*, as shown:

            procedure *A* ;
               procedure *B* ;
                  begin . . . . . . **end** ;
               procedure *C* ;
                  begin . . . . ; *B* ; . . . **end** ;
               begin . . . ; *C* ; . . . **end** ;

During the resultant execution of *B* the topmost frames on the storage stack would be as shown in Fig. 2.1. Within this stack of frames at any moment there is exactly one accessible for each level of nesting in the corresponding source program—the accessible frames being held on the *static chain*. To address any variable the information needed is the *static level* of its declaration, which identifies the stack frame's position on the static chain, and its *relative address* within this frame.

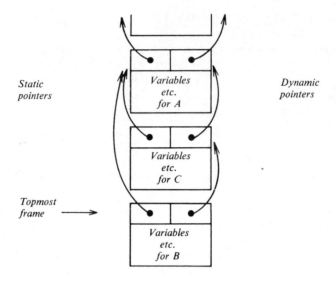

Fig. 2.1

$$runtimeaddress = \textbf{record}$$
$$staticlevel : integer \ ;$$
$$relativeaddress : addressrange$$
$$\textbf{end} \ ;$$

The code generated to access the variable must convert the static level into the corresponding stack-frame address, by stepping down the static chain.

The practical efficiency of the scheme can be guaranteed by

(a)   Dedicating one address register to address the topmost stack frame at all times. Local variables are thus accessible without any frame location code.

(b)   Allocating *absolute* addresses to the global (main program) variables.

The stack overheads of variable access are thus confined to the (relatively infrequent) access of non-local non-global variables.

In a one-pass compiler for Mini-Pascal, allocation of addresses for global variables will take place before any code generation for the procedure or program bodies. It is thus both possible and convenient to allocate the global variables to object-program locations which precede those allocated to the object code. On some machines this has the additional advantage of locating as many as possible, perhaps all, of the global variables within low-address locations which are more efficiently accessible than those beyond.

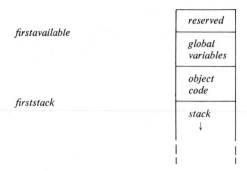

Fig. 2.2

The overall picture of the object program to be generated is thus as shown in Fig. 2.2, with the generator sequentially allocating those locations from *firstavailable* to *firststack*. To represent the progress of this allocation we introduce a module *Store* as follows:

> **envelope module** *Store* ;
>   **var** *∗address* : *addressrange* ; {*next available address*}
>   • • •
>   **procedure** *∗allocate* (*area* : *addressrange* ; **var** *startaddress* :
>   *addressrange*)
>   {*sets startaddress to next available address*
>   *and advances next available address by area*}
>   • • •
>   **procedure** *∗copy* (*contents* : *integer*) ;
>   {*copies contents to current available address*
>   *and advances address by one*}
>   • • •
>   **begin**
>   *address* := *firstavailable* ;
>   ∗∗∗
>   **end**

To allocate addresses correctly the generator must maintain a record of the level of nesting of the stack frames and the number of locations allocated within each. This it can do with a variable

$$level : integer ;$$

and a stack of frame records of the form

$$framerec = \textbf{record}$$
$$nextlocal : addressrange \; ;$$
$$nextframe : framentry$$
$$\textbf{end}$$

where $\quad framentry = \uparrow framerec \; ;$

The top of this stack can be located by a variable

$$localframe : framentry \; ;$$

The appropriate initialization for the frame stack is

$$localframe := nil \; ; \; level := globallevel - 1 \; ;$$

and the operations *openstackframe* and *closestackframe* are then readily programmed as straightforward pushing and popping operations on this stack.

The address allocation procedure is programmable as follows:

procedure *addressfor* (*representation* : *typerepresentation* ,
$\qquad\qquad\qquad\qquad$ **var** *address* : *runtimeaddress*) ;
$\quad$ **begin**
$\qquad$ *address.staticlevel* := *level* ;
$\qquad$ **if** *level* = *globallevel*
$\qquad$ **then** *Store.allocate* (*representation, address.relativeaddress*)
$\qquad$ **else**
$\qquad$ **with** *localframe* $\uparrow$ **do**
$\qquad$ **begin**
$\qquad\qquad$ *address.relativeaddress* := *nextlocal* ;
$\qquad\qquad$ *nextlocal* := *nextlocal* + *representation*
$\qquad$ **end**
$\quad$ **end** ;

Generating Code

Before considering the problems of object-code generation we must introduce some details of the object REAL computer. The REAL has a set of eight general purpose 24-bit registers $X0$–$X7$, but three of these $X1$–$X3$ double as index or modifier registers.

Each REAL instruction is held as one 24-bit word comprising

$\qquad$ a 7-bit function field F
$\qquad$ a 3-bit register field X
$\qquad$ a 2-bit index or modifier field M
$\qquad$ a 12-bit operand field N

In store-addressing instructions the operand field N is added to the contents of the modifier register M to determine the store location addressed, usually written $N(M)$; $M=0$ means no modification i.e. the address used is N.

The range of functions relevant to our code-generation problem and their effect is shown in Table 2.1, where x and n are used to denote the contents of register X and store location $N(M)$ respectively.

Table 2.1

LDX	*X*	*N(M)*	$\{x := n$
NGX	*X*	*N(M)*	$\{x := -n$
ADX	*X*	*N(M)*	$\{x := x + n$
SBX	*X*	*N(M)*	$\{x := x - n$
MPX	*X*	*N(M)*	$\{x := x * n$
DVX	*X*	*N(M)*	$\{x := x \text{ div } n$
STO	*X*	*N(M)*	$\{n := x$
STOZ		*N(M)*	$\{n := O$
MOVE	*X*	*N*	$\{move\ N\ words\ from\ address\ in\ X$ $to\ address\ in\ X + 1$
BRN		*N*	$\{jump\ to\ instruction\ N$
BZE	*X*	*N*	$\{jump\ to\ instruction\ N\ if\ x = 0$
BNZ	*X*	*N*	$\{jump\ to\ instruction\ N\ if\ x = 0$
BNG	*X*	*N*	$\{jump\ to\ instruction\ N\ if\ x < 0$
BPZ	*X*	*N*	$\{jump\ to\ instruction\ N\ if\ x \geqslant 0$
CALL	*X*	*N*	$\{x := address\ of\ next\ instruction;$ $jump\ to\ instruction\ N$
EXIT	*X*	*O*	$\{jump\ to\ instruction\ x$
HALT			$\{stop\ execution$
LDN	*X*	*N*	$\{x := N$
NGN	*X*	*N*	$\{x := -N$
ADN	*X*	*N*	$\{x := x + N$
SBN	*X*	*N*	$\{x := x - N$
MPN	*X*	*N*	$\{x := x * N$
DVN	*X*	*N*	$\{x := x \text{ div } N$

The final group of functions, which use the 12-bit operand field N itself as an "immediate" operand, rather than the contents of the store location which it addresses, can be exploited in many contexts where constant values are manipulated by the program being compiled.

The major problem in generating object code for the statement parts of a Mini-Pascal program is that the REAL architecture and instruction set do not directly mirror the architecture and operations of our hypothetical stack machine, in two significant aspects:

(a) Given that registers $X1-X3$ have to be reserved for addressing purposes, the remaining four $X4-X7$ do not provide an adequate stack for expression evaluation.

(b) The arithmetic instructions all operate on one operand in store and their efficient usage precludes prior loading of both operands into registers.

The difference is well illustrated by the code sequences on either machine for the Mini-Pascal assignment

$$A := B + 4 * C$$

which are as shown in Table 2.2. This basic mismatch between the hypothetical and actual object machines is overcome in the generator by simulating the state of both at any point in the execution of the program being compiled, and using this simulation to choose the most efficient sequence of REAL instructions which keeps the latter in a state equivalent to the former.

Table 2.2

Hypothetical machine	REAL		
Stackreference (A)	*LDN*	4	4
Stackreference (B)	*MPX*	4	*C*
Dereference ( )	*ADX*	4	*B*
Stackconstant (4)	*STO*	4	*A*
Stackreference (C)			
Dereference ( )			
Binaryintegerop (*)			
Binaryintegerop (+)			
Assign			

To carry out this simulation the generator must keep track of operands held by the hypothetical stack at any moment, of the corresponding contents of the registers and work locations used on the REAL machine, and of the sequence of REAL instructions required to maintain their equivalence. To look after these housekeeping operations we will introduce four corresponding modules as follows:

envelope module *Stack* ;

. . .

envelope module *Registers* ;

. . .

envelope module *Worklocations* ;

. . .

envelope module *Code* ;

. . .

The precise range of facilities which these modules must provide will emerge as we consider the various aspects of code generation which the generator interface procedures imply.

The primary strategy in achieving efficient object code is *delay*—no object code is ever generated until it is essential in maintaining the equivalence of the hypothetical and actual machine states. This delaying strategy is illustrated by considering generator actions in handling a few of the basic stack-manipulation operations of the hypothetical machine.

Programming basic stack operations

Simulation of the hypothetical stack contents involves maintaining within the generator operand descriptions of the general form:

$$operandkind = (reference, \ldots) \ ;$$
$$operand = \uparrow oprec \ ;$$
$$oprec = \mathbf{record}$$

     case *kind* : *operandkind* **of**

     reference : (. . . . . .) ;

     . . .

   end ;

When a new reference has to be added to the stack by the procedure *Stackreference*, no addressing code is generated at that stage. The address co-ordinates are simply copied across into a new operand description, for which a suitable form is thus

  oprec = **record**

     case *kind* : *operandkind* **of**

     reference : (*address* : *runtimeaddress* ;

        indexed : *Boolean* ;

       . . . . . .

   end

The procedure *Stackreference* is then expressible as

  procedure *Stackreference* (*location* : *runtimeaddress*) ;

  var *refentry* : *operand* ;

  begin

   New (*refentry*) ;

   with *refentry* ↑ **do**

   begin

    kind := *reference* ;

    address := *location* ;

    indexed := *false*

   end ;

   Stack.push(*refentry*)

  end ;

Since operand descriptions sometimes exist outside the simulated hypothetical stack, we separate their creation and disposal from the *Stack* module's housekeeping procedures *push* and *pop*.

The field *indexed* anticipates that indexed references will in some way form an extension of this simple case.

In practice the *Indexedreference* operation also avoids the generation of any code. It removes the description of the index value from the stack and appends it to the array reference beneath together with sufficient information to enable the subscripting code to be generated when it becomes necessary to do so.

A suitable extension of the stack-record variant concerned is thus

$$reference \ : \ (address \ : \ runtimeaddress \ ;$$
$$\textbf{case} \ indexed \ : \ Boolean \ \textbf{of}$$
$$true \ : \ (index \ : \ operand \ ;$$
$$indexmin, \ indexmax \ : \ integer \ ))$$

and the procedure *Indexedreference* takes the form

```
procedure Indexedreference (boundmin, boundmax : integer ;
                            elementrepresentation : typerepresentation) ;
  var indexentry,arrayentry : operand ;
  begin
    Stack.pop(indexentry) ;
    Stack.pop(arrayentry) ;
    with arrayentry ↑ do
    begin
      indexed := true ;
      index := indexentry ;
      indexmin := boundmin ;
      indexmax := boundmax
    end ;
    Stack.push(arrayentry)
  end ;
```

The dereferencing of a reference in principle implies the replacement of the reference by the value to which it refers. In practice no code need be generated at that stage and the only action required is to add to the reference the representation details necessary when the value does have to be accessed. Since this representation information is common to other forms of operand we add it thus:

> $oprec =$ **record**
>> rep : $typerepresentation$;
>> **case** $kind$: $operandkind$ **of**
>> . . .
>
> **end** ;

and the *Dereference* operation requires only the following

> **procedure** *Dereference* (*representation* : *typerepresentation*) ;
>> **var** *reference* : *operand* ;
>> **begin**
>>> *Stack.pop*(*reference*) ;
>>> *reference* ↑ *.rep* := *representation* ;
>>> *Stack.push*(*reference*)
>> **end** ;

Constant operands are also processed without any immediate generation of code. To accommodate them a second form of operand record is added, thus

> $operandkind = (reference, constant, \ldots)$;
> $oprec =$ **record**
>> rep : $typerepresentation$;
>> **case** $kind$: $operandkind$ **of**
>> $reference$: (. . . . .) ;
>> $constant$: ($constvalue$: $integer$) ;
>> . . .
>
> **end** ;

and the procedure *Stackconstant* is written

```
procedure Stackconstant (value:integer;representation:typerepresentation) ;
  var constentry : operand ;
  begin
    New (constentry) ;
    with constentry ↑ do
    begin
      rep := representation ;
      kind := constant ;
      constvalue := value
    end ;
    Stack.push (constentry)
  end ;
```

In this way all primary operands are handled by the generator without any immediate code generation. How the code is ultimately generated by the application of arithmetic or other operations to them is well illustrated by the assignment operation, which we consider next.

A general strategy for Mini-Pascal assignments on the REAL computer is

> **if** *more than one word is being assigned*
> **then** *generate code to use store-to-store* **MOVE** *instruction*
> **else if** *assigning zero*
> > **then** *generate code using* **STOZ** *instruction*
> > **else** *generate code to load and store value*

Using the stack refinements so far, and introducing some basic procedures for code generation, we can program this strategy as follows

```
procedure Assign ;
   var size : addressrange ;
       value,variable : operand ;
   begin
   Stack.pop(value) ;
   Stack.pop(variable) ;
   size := value ↑ .rep ;
   if size > 1
   then begin
           Loadaddress (6, value) ;
           Loadaddress (7, variable) ;
           Code.ins (MOVE,6,size,0)
        end
   else if (value ↑ .kind = constant) and (value ↑ .constvalue = 0)
   then begin
           address (variable) ;
           with addressed do Code.ins (STOZ,O,N,M,)
        end
   else begin
           load (value) ;
           address (variable) ;
           with addressed do Code.ins (STO,loadreg,N,M)
        end ;
   Dispose (value) ;
   Dispose (variable)
   end ;
```

Here we have introduced

(a) A *Code* module procedure *ins* which assembles a REAL instruction from its component fields and appends it to the current code sequence.

(b) A procedure *Loadaddress* which generates code to load the register specified with the address of the operand specified.

(c) A procedure *Load* which generates code, if necessary, to load some convenient register with the value of the operand specified, leaving the register chosen in the variable *loadedreg*.

(d) A procedure *address* which generates code, if necessary, to enable a subsequent instruction to address the location occupied by the operand specified. The addressing co-ordinates to be used in the subsequent instruction are left as the components of a record variable

> *addressed* : **record**
>
> $N : 0 .. 4095$;
>
> M : *modifier register*
>
> **end** ;

These last two procedures are the basic work-horses of all the code-generation logic associated with the manipulation of hypothetical stack operands, e.g. integer arithmetic. It is interesting to carry their development a stage further. This we do in the next section.

Loading and addressing operands

Besides references and constants, stacked operands may be the result of some previous stack operation. Such a result will be left in a computation register of the actual machine. Since the number of registers is limited it is possible that the register may have to be re-used before its contents have been consumed. In this case the result has to be saved in a temporary work location until it is required. These possibilities are reflected by extending our operand records as follows:

> *operandkind* = *(reference, constant, result . . .)*
>
> *oprec* = **record**
>
> > *rep* : *typerepresentation* ;
> >
> > **case** *kind* : *operandkind* **of**
> >
> > *reference* : (. . . . .) ;
> >
> > *constant* : (. . . . .) ;
> >
> > *result* :   (**case** *inregister* : *Boolean* **of**
> >
> > > *true* : (*reg* : *register*) ;
> > >
> > > *false* : (*tempresult* : *worklocation*))
>
> > . . .
>
> **end** ;

The *reg* field provides an *operand* → *register* association. Register protection requires that some reverse association, i.e. *register* → *operand*, also be maintained. To maintain this binding between registers and operands we will assume that the *Registers* module provides procedures

>**procedure** *Bindto* (*entry* : *operand*) ;
>**procedure** *Freefrom* (*entry* : *operand*) ;

The procedure *Load* might now be written as

>**procedure** *Load* (*entry* : *operand*) ;
>   **var** *chosenregister* : *register* ;
>   **begin**
>   **if** (*entry* ↑ .*kind*=*result*) **and** *entry* ↑ .*inregister*
>   **then begin**
>   *chosenregister* := *entry* ↑ .*reg* ;
>   *Registers.freefrom* (*entry*)
>   **end**
>   **else begin**
>   *chosenregister* := *Registers.bestfor* (*entry*) ;
>   *LoadX* (*chosenregister*, *entry*)
>   **end** ;
>   *loaded reg* := *chosenregister*
>   **end** ;

The operation *LoadX*, which generates code to load an operand value into a *specified* register, is required elsewhere in the code-generation logic, and is therefore isolated as a separate procedure. In coding *LoadX* we must remember that the register specified may already be occupied by some other operand which must first be moved to a temporary location and its operand description adjusted accordingly. *LoadX* therefore takes the form

>**procedure** *LoadX* (*X* : *register* ; *entry* : *operand*) ;
>   **begin**
>   **if not** (*X* **in** *Registers.usedby* (*entry*)) **then** *Registers.save* (*X*) ;
>   **with** *entry* ↑ **do**
>   **case** *kind* **of**
>   *reference* : **begin**
>   *address* (*entry*) ;
>   **with** *addressed* **do** *Code.ins* (*LDX,X,N,M*)
>   **end** ;
>   *constant* :   *constins* (*LDX,X,constvalue*) ;

```
result :    if inregister
            then begin
                    if reg ≠ X then Code.ins (LDX,X,reg,0) ;
                        Registers.freefrom (entry)
                    end
            else begin
                    Code.ins (LDX,X,tempresult,0) ;
                        worklocations.free (tempresult)
                    end
        end
end ;
```

The procedure *Registers.save*(X) is assumed to test whether register X is free and if not generate an instruction to save its contents in an available work location, resetting the corresponding stack record accordingly.

The procedure *constins* generates an instruction with the literal operand specified, making use of the REAL's "immediate operand" instructions LDN, ADN, etc. whenever possible.

Addressing operands require some decisions on the use of the REAL's address or modifier registers $X1-3$. We have already decided to dedicate one of these to the topmost frame of the run-time storage stack. It is immaterial which is chosen: let us denote it by *Xlocal*. A second, *Xref*, we will always use in constructing addresses which require a modifier other than *Xlocal*. The third, which we denote by *Xmod*, we will leave free for other purposes for the time being.

With these decisions we can proceed to code the address procedure as follows:

```
procedure address (entry : operand) ;
    var Xrefset : Boolean ;
        adjustment, finalN : integer ;
        finalM : modifier ;
    begin
        with entry ↑ do
        case kind of
        reference :
            begin
                if indexed
                then begin
                        if index ↑ .kind = constant
                        then begin
                                adjustment: = index ↑ .constvalue − indexmin ;
```

$$Xrefset := false$$
end
else begin
$$LoadX (Xref, index) ;$$
$$adjustment := -indexmin ;$$
$$Xrefset := true$$
end ;
Dispose (*index*)
end
else begin
$$adjustment := 0 ;$$
$$Xrefset := false$$
end ;

At this stage any compile-time adjustment of the address due to an index has been calculated, and any run-time adjustment loaded into *Xref.* Incorporation of these in an address-co-ordinates pair (*finalN,finalM*) then proceeds:

with *refaddress* **do**
begin
finalN := *relativeaddress* + *adjustment* ;
if *staticlevel* = *globallevel*
then if *Xrefset* **then** *finalM* := *Xref*
            else *finalM* := 0
else
if *staticlevel* = *level*
then if *Xrefset* **then begin**
             Code.ins (*ADX,Xref,Xlocal,*0) ;
             finalM := *Xref*
         end
        else *finalM* := *Xlocal*
else begin
  if *Xrefset*
  then if *staticlevel* = *level*–1
     then *Code.ins* (*ADX,Xref,static,Xlocal*)
     else begin
         SetXtolevel (*Xmod,staticlevel*+1) ;
         Code.ins (*ADX,Xref,static,Xmod*)
      end
  else *SetXtolevel* (*Xref,staticlevel*) ;
  finalM := *Xref*

end
end
end ;

where the procedure *SetXtolevel* generates code to load the specified register with the address of the stack frame for the specified level—by stepping down the static pointer chain the necessary number of levels.

The resulting address co-ordinates (*finalN* , *finalM*) may be unusable in one case—for an indexed variable *finalN* will be negative if the lower bound of the index exceeds the relative address of the array. To avoid this we add the following code:

if *finalN* < 0 **then**
begin
    constins (*ADX, Xref, finalN*) ;
    finalN := 0
end

—since *finalM* must equal *Xref* in this case.

The procedure *address* may also be used for operands with *kind* = *constant* or *result*, but the coding needed is straightforward in these cases.

Other code generation

We have considered only the code generation for Mini-Pascal assignments, and the underlying operand loading and addressing involved. Other areas unexamined are integer and Boolean arithmetic, control operations, procedure calls and input/output. Thereafter the supporting modules for register and work location housekeeping, stack maintenance, and code assembly have to be programmed. However, all of these can be tackled in the same basic manner. Listing 9 shows a complete code generator and the local modules on which it depends. As a measure of the effectiveness of the programming style used, the reader might consider the ease with which those parts of the generator not discussed in the text can be followed by a first-time reader.

Listing 9

```
ENVELOPE MODULE GENERATE ;

    (*   THE GENERATOR PROVIDES A PROGRAM GENERATION INTERFACE FOR THE      *)
    (*   SYNTACTIC/SEMANTIC ANALYZER AS A SET OF PROCEDURE CALLS.           *)
    (*   THESE CALLS, AND THE TYPES UNDERLYING THEIR PARAMETER LISTS,       *)
    (*   PROVIDE A GENERATION INTERFACE WHICH IS INDEPENDENT OF THE         *)
    (*   PRECISE OBJECT CODE TO BE GENERATED.  BETWEEN CALLS THE            *)
    (*   ANALYZER STORES AND TRANSMITS DATA OF THESE TYPES BUT WITHOUT      *)
    (*   ANY NECESSARY KNOWLEDGE OF THEIR INTERNAL NATURE.                  *)
    (*                                                                      *)
    (*                                                                      *)
    (*      (1) REPRESENTATION AND STORAGE OF DATA                          *)
    (*                                                                      *)
    (*         THE REPRESENTATION AND STORAGE OF DATA WITHIN THE OBJECT     *)
    (*         PROGRAM IS DESCRIBED BY THE GENERATOR AS FOLLOWS             *)
    (*                                                                      *)
    (*            1.  FOR EACH TYPE THE GENERATOR CREATES A REPRESENTATION*)
    (*                OF TYPE 'TYPEREPRESENTATION' WHICH DESCRIBES HOW      *)
    (*                SUCH DATA ARE TO BE REPRESENTED IN THE OBJECT         *)
    (*                PROGRAM.                                              *)
    (*                                                                      *)
    (*            2. FOR EACH VARIABLE THE GENERATOR CREATES AN ADDRESS     *)
    (*                'RUNTIMEADDRESS' WHICH HOLDS THE NECESSARY ADDRESS    *)
    (*                CO-ORDINATES FOR THE RUN-TIME ACCESS OF THOSE DATA.   *)
    (*                                                                      *)
    (*         THESE DESCRIPTORS ARE GENERATED AS FOLLOWS                   *)
    (*                                                                      *)
    (*            3. REPRESENTATION FOR THE BUILT-IN TYPES ARE MADE         *)
    (*                AVAILABLE AS ACCESSIBLE VALUES INTEGERREPRESENTATION *)
    (*                ETC. THE PROCEDURE ARRAYREPRESENTATION GENERATES A    *)
    (*                REPRESENTATION FOR EACH PROGRAM-DEFINED ARRAY TYPE.   *)
    (*                                                                      *)
    (*            4. THE PROCEDURE ADDRESSFOR DETERMINES THE RUN-TIME       *)
    (*                ADDRESS CO-ORDINATES FOR A VARIABLE.  SINCE THESE     *)
    (*                RUN-TIME ADDRESSES ARE ASSUMED TO LIE WITHIN A        *)
    (*                CONVENTIONAL RUN-TIME STORAGE STACK, PROCEDURE        *)
    (*                CALLS 'OPENSTACKFRAME' AND 'CLOSESTACKFRAME' ARE      *)
    (*                USED TO DELIMIT THE STATIC NESTING OF STACK FRAMES    *)
    (*                FOR THE ADDRESS ALLOCATOR.                            *)
    (*                                                                      *)
    (*      (2) PROCEDURE AND PROGRAM CONTROL                               *)
    (*                                                                      *)
    (*         THE NECESSARY COMPILE- AND RUNTIME HOUSEKEEPING              *)
    (*         OPERATIONS ASSOCIATED WITH THE OBJECT PROGRAM ARE            *)
    (*         REALIZED AS FOLLOWS                                          *)
    (*                                                                      *)
    (*            1. A LINKAGE RECORD IS GENERATED FOR EACH PROCEDURE       *)
    (*                BY THE PROCEDURE NEWLINKAGE                           *)
    (*                                                                      *)
    (*            2. TRANSFER OF CONTROL TO A PROCEDURE                     *)
    (*                IS REALIZED BY THE OPERATION CALLPROC                 *)
    (*                                                                      *)
    (*            3. THE NECESSARY PRELUDE AND POSTLUDE CODE FOR EACH       *)
    (*                PROCEDURE OR PROGRAM BLOCK IS REALIZED BY THE         *)
    (*                OPERATIONS                                            *)
    (*                                                                      *)
    (*                    ENTERBODY                                         *)
    (*                    LEAVEBODY                                         *)
    (*                    ENTERPROGRAM                                      *)
    (*                    LEAVEPROGRAM                                      *)
```

```
(*                                                                    *)
(*                                                                    *)
(*   (3) VARIABLES, EXPRESSIONS AND ASSIGNMENT                        *)
(*                                                                    *)
(*     THE CODE GENERATION INTERFACE FOR VARIABLE ACCESS,            *)
(*     EXPRESSION EVALUATION AND ASSIGNMENT ASSUMES A POSTFIX        *)
(*     CODE FORM (THOUGH THE GENERATING PROCEDURES CALLED MAY        *)
(*     TRANSFORM THIS CODE THEREAFTER). THE GENERATING CALLS         *)
(*     REPRESENT OPERATIONS ON A HYPOTHETICAL RUN-TIME STACK         *)
(*     OF OPERAND REFERENCES AND VALUES, AS FOLLOWS                  *)
(*                                                                    *)
(*       1. VARIABLE ACCESS IS REALIZED BY THE FOLLOWING            *)
(*          HYPOTHETICAL OPERATIONS                                  *)
(*                                                                    *)
(*            STACKREFERENCE                                         *)
(*            INDEXEDREFERENCE                                       *)
(*                                                                    *)
(*       2. EXPRESSION EVALUATION IS REALIZED BY THE FOLLOWING      *)
(*          ADDITIONAL STACK OPERATIONS                             *)
(*                                                                    *)
(*            DEREFERENCE                                            *)
(*            STACKCONSTANT                                          *)
(*                                                                    *)
(*            NEGATEINTEGER                                          *)
(*            BINARYINTEGEROPERATION                                *)
(*                                                                    *)
(*            COMPARISON                                             *)
(*                                                                    *)
(*            NEGATEBOOLEAN                                          *)
(*            BINARYBOOLEANOPERATION                               *)
(*                                                                    *)
(*       THE OPERATION BINARYBOOLEANOPERATION IS DEFINED           *)
(*       AND USED IN A WAY WHICH PERMITS EITHER INFIX OR           *)
(*       POSTFIX EVALUATION OF AND/OR OPERATIONS                   *)
(*                                                                    *)
(*       3. FINALLY ASSIGNMENT IS REALIZED BY THE SINGLE           *)
(*          HYPOTHETICAL STACK OPERATION - ASSIGN.                  *)
(*                                                                    *)
(*                                                                    *)
(*   (4) I-O OPERATIONS                                              *)
(*                                                                    *)
(*     THE I-O OPERATIONS ARE REALIZED BY THE FOLLOWING            *)
(*     GENERATIVE OPERATIONS                                        *)
(*                                                                    *)
(*            READOPERATION                                         *)
(*            WRITEOPERATION                                        *)
(*                                                                    *)
(*                                                                    *)
(*   (5) CONTROL STATEMENTS AND                                      *)
(*       SEQUENTIAL CODE GENERATION                                 *)
(*                                                                    *)
(*     THE CODE GENERATED, WHATEVER ITS FORM, IS ASSUMED TO BE     *)
(*     FOR SEQUENTIAL EXECUTION. EACH CODE SEQUENCE WHICH CAN      *)
(*     BE ENTERED OTHER THAN SEQUENTIALLY IS REPRESENTED AT        *)
(*     COMPILE TIME BY A RECORD OF TYPE 'CODELABEL'. THESE         *)
(*     RECORDS ARE BOUND TO POINTS IN THE CODE BY THE PROCEDURES   *)
```

```
(*                                                              *)
(*          NEWLABEL  -  FOR A PREVIOUSLY UNREFERENCED          *)
(*                         LABEL                                *)
(*                                                              *)
(*          FUTURELABEL -  FOR A LABEL WHICH MAY BE             *)
(*                         REFERENCED BEFORE IT IS              *)
(*                         GENERATED                            *)
(*                                                              *)
(*          EXPECTEDLABEL -  FOR A LABEL PREVIOUSLY             *)
(*                         'EXPECTED'                           *)
(*                                                              *)
(*       ALL REFERENCES(JUMPS ETC.) ARE GENERATED BY THE CONTROL *)
(*       GENERATING PROCEDURES MANIPULATING THESE LABEL RECORDS *)
(*                                                              *)
(*       CONTROL STATEMENT CODE IS REALIZED BY THE FOLLOWING    *)
(*       HYPOTHETICAL OPERATIONS                                *)
(*                                                              *)
(*          JUMPONFALSE                                         *)
(*          JUMP                                                *)
(*                                                              *)
(*    THE ANALYZER MAY SUPPRESS FURTHER GENERATOR ACTIVITY AT ANY *)
(*    TIME BY CALLING THE PROCEDURE NOFURTHERCODE . ALL SUBSEQUENT *)
(*    GENERATOR CALLS ARE IGNORED. THIS IS NECESSARY IF   ANALYSIS OF *)
(*    (ANY PART OF) AN INCORRECT PROGRAM CAUSES INCONSISTENT    *)
(*    SEQUENCES OF INTERFACE CALLS                              *)


VAR

    CODEISTOBEGENERATED : BOOLEAN ;



PROCEDURE *NOFURTHERCODE ;
    BEGIN
        CODEISTOBEGENERATED := FALSE
    END ;




(*    THE GENERATOR REPORTS  ERRORS OR VIOLATIONS OF           *)
(*    IMPLEMENTATION RESTRICTIONS WITH THE FOLLOWING CODES      *)
(*                                                              *)
(*    91 .... BLOCK TOO LONG                                   *)
(*    92 .... TOO MUCH NON-LOCAL RECURSION                     *)
(*    93 .... EXPRESSION TOO COMPLICATED                       *)
(*    94 .... DIVISION BY ZERO                                 *)



PROCEDURE GENERROR ( CODE : INTEGER ) ;
    BEGIN
        SOURCE.ERROR(CODE,SOURCE.POSITIONNOW)
    END ;
```

```
(*******************************************************)
(*********** REAL MACHINE CHARACTERISTICS ***********)
(*******************************************************)


CONST

   ADDRESSMAX = 4095 ;

   SCR = 8 ; (* WORD 8 IS SEQUENCE CONTROL REGISTER *)

TYPE

   ADDRRANGE = 0..ADDRESSMAX ;
   REGISTER = 0..7 ;
   MODIFIER = 0..3 ;
   ORDERCODE = 0..127 ;

   SYSTEMROUTINES = (INITIALIO,FINALIO,
                     READCHAR,READINTEGER,
                     WRITECHAR,WRITEINTEGER) ;


CONST

   (********** ORDER CODE MNEMONICS **********)

   LDX = 000B; ADX = 001B; NGX = 002B; SBX = 003B;
   STO = 010B;
   STOZ = 033B;
   MPX = 040B; DVX = 046B;
   BZE = 050B; BNZ = 052B; BPZ = 054B; BNG = 56B;
   CALL = 070B; EXIT = 072B;  BRN = 074B;
   LDN = 100B; ADN = 101B; NGN = 102B; SBN = 103B;
   MPN = 140B; DVN = 146B; ERN = 122B; MOVE = 126B;
   HALT = 161B ;
```

```
ENVELOPE MODULE STORE ;

   (* SEQUENTIALLY ALLOCATES OBJECT PROGRAM LOCATIONS FROM  *)
   (* FIRSTAVAILABLE ONWARDS. AT RUNTIME THE FIRST UNALLOC- *)
   (* ATED LOCATION MAY BE ADDRESSED VIA LOCATION STACKBASE *)


   CONST

      FIRSTAVAILABLE = 500 ;

   VAR

      *ADDRESS : ADDRRANGE ;

      *STACKBASE : ADDRRANGE ;

      (* ADDRESSES OF PRESET STORE LOCATIONS *)

      *ADDRESSFOR : ARRAY [SYSTEMROUTINES] OF ADDRRANGE ;

   PROCEDURE *COPY ( WORD : INTEGER ) ;

      BEGIN
         CODEFILE.LOCATE(ADDRESS,WORD) ;
         ADDRESS := ADDRESS+1
      END ;

   PROCEDURE *ALLOCATE ( AREA : ADDRRANGE ; VAR STARTADDRESS : ADDRRANGE ) ;

      BEGIN
         STARTADDRESS := ADDRESS ;
         ADDRESS := ADDRESS+AREA
      END ;


   BEGIN
      (* INITIALIZE PRESET STORE ADDRESSES *)

      ADDRESSFOR[INITIALIO    ] := 100 ;
      ADDRESSFOR[FINALIO      ] := 150 ;
      ADDRESSFOR[READCHAR     ] := 200 ;
      ADDRESSFOR[WRITECHAR    ] := 250 ;
      ADDRESSFOR[READINTEGER ] := 300 ;
      ADDRESSFOR[WRITEINTEGER] := 400 ;

      STACKBASE := FIRSTAVAILABLE ;
      ADDRESS := FIRSTAVAILABLE+1 ;
      *** ;
      CODEFILE.LOCATE(STACKBASE,ADDRESS)
   END (* STORE MODULE *) ;
```

```
(*****************************************************)
(***** DATA REPRESENTATION AND STORAGE ALLOCATION *****)
(*****************************************************)


TYPE


   *TYPEREPRESENTATION = ADDRRANGE ;


CONST


   *BOOLEANREPRESENTATION = 1 ;
   *CHARREPRESENTATION = 1 ;
   *INTEGERREPRESENTATION = 1 ;



PROCEDURE *ARRAYREPRESENTATION ( BOUNDMIN,BOUNDMAX : INTEGER ;
                                 ELEMENTREPRESENTATION : TYPEREPRESENTATION ;
                                 VAR REPRESENTATION : TYPEREPRESENTATION ) ;
   BEGIN
      IF CODEISTOBEGENERATED THEN
         REPRESENTATION := BOUNDMAX - BOUNDMIN + 1
   END ;



CONST

   GLOBALLEVEL = 1 ;

   (* STACKFRAME OFFSETS *)

   DYNAMIC = 0 ;
   STATIC = 1;
   LINK = 2 ;
   NEXTFRAME = 3 ;
   FIRSTLOCAL = 4 ;

TYPE

   FRAMENTRY = ^FRAMEREC ;

   FRAMEREC = RECORD
                 NEXTLOCAL : ADDRRANGE ;
                 NEXTFRAME : FRAMENTRY
              END ;

   *RUNTIMEADDRESS = RECORD
                        STATICLEVEL : INTEGER ;
                        RELATIVEADDRESS : ADDRRANGE
                     END ;
```

```
VAR

   LEVEL : INTEGER ;

   LOCALFRAME : FRAMENTRY ;

PROCEDURE *OPENSTACKFRAME ;
   VAR
      NEWFRAME : FRAMENTRY ;
   BEGIN
      IF CODEISTOBEGENERATED THEN
      BEGIN
         NEW(NEWFRAME) ;
         WITH NEWFRAME^ DO
         BEGIN
            NEXTLOCAL := FIRSTLOCAL ;
            NEXTFRAME := LOCALFRAME
         END ;
         LOCALFRAME := NEWFRAME ; LEVEL := LEVEL+1
      END
   END (* OPENSTACKFRAME *) ;

PROCEDURE *ADDRESSFOR ( REPRESENTATION : TYPEREPRESENTATION ;
                        VAR ADDRESS : RUNTIMEADDRESS ) ;
   BEGIN
      IF CODEISTOBEGENERATED THEN
      BEGIN
         ADDRESS.STATICLEVEL := LEVEL ;
         IF LEVEL = GLOBALLEVEL
         THEN
         STORE.ALLOCATE(REPRESENTATION,ADDRESS.RELATIVEADDRESS)
         ELSE
            WITH LOCALFRAME^ DO
            BEGIN
               ADDRESS.RELATIVEADDRESS := NEXTLOCAL ;
               NEXTLOCAL := NEXTLOCAL + REPRESENTATION
            END
      END
   END (* ADDRESSFOR *) ;

PROCEDURE *CLOSESTACKFRAME ;
   VAR
      OLDFRAME : FRAMENTRY ;
   BEGIN
      IF CODEISTOBEGENERATED THEN
      BEGIN
         OLDFRAME := LOCALFRAME ;
         LOCALFRAME := LOCALFRAME^.NEXTFRAME ; LEVEL := LEVEL-1 ;
         DISPOSE(OLDFRAME)
      END
   END (* CLOSESTACKFRAME *) ;
```

```
ENVELOPE MODULE CODE ;

    (* ASSEMBLES AND FILES REAL MACHINE INSTRUCTIONS VIA      *)
    (* THE PROCEDURES INS , JUMPINS ,AND LINKEDJUMPINS         *)
    (* LABELED POINTS IN THE CODE MAY BE REPRESENTED BY        *)
    (* VARIABLES OF TYPE CODELABEL, WHICH ARE BOUND TO THE     *)
    (* CODE ITSELF BY THE PROCEDURES NEWLABEL, FUTURELABEL,    *)
    (* AND EXPECTEDLABEL. TWO LABELS MAY BE EQUIVALENCED BY    *)
    (* THE PROCEDURE LINKLABEL                                 *)


    CONST

        CODEMAX = 1000 ;
        LINKMAX = 50 ;

    TYPE

        CODERANGE = 0..CODEMAX ;
        LINKRANGE = 0..LINKMAX ;

      *CODELABEL = RECORD
                            CASE EXPECTED : BOOLEAN OF
                                FALSE :
                                    ( STARTADDRESS : ADDRRANGE ) ;
                                TRUE  :
                                    ( LASTCODEREFERENCE : CODERANGE ;
                                      CASE LINKED : BOOLEAN OF
                                          TRUE :
                                              ( LINKINDEX : LINKRANGE ))

                    END ;

        DIRECTOPERAND = 0..4095 ;

        REALINSTRUCTION = PACKED RECORD
                                    N : DIRECTOPERAND ;
                                    M : MODIFIER ;
                                    F : ORDERCODE ;
                                    X : REGISTER
                                END ;

    VAR

        ADDRESS : ADDRRANGE ;

        CODE : ARRAY[CODERANGE] OF REALINSTRUCTION ;
        NEXTINS,FIXUPSNEEDED : CODERANGE ;
        NOCODEOVERFLOW : BOOLEAN ;

        LINKTABLE : ARRAY[LINKRANGE] OF INTEGER ;
        FIRSTLINKADDRESS : ADDRRANGE ;
        NEXTLINK,I : LINKRANGE ;
        NOLINKOVERFLOW : BOOLEAN ;
```

```
PROCEDURE *ALIGNINSTORE;

   BEGIN
      ADDRESS := STORE.ADDRESS
   END ;

PROCEDURE COPYCODE ( CODEVALUE : REALINSTRUCTION ) ;

   (* COPIES CODEVALUE  AS NEXT INSTRUCTION OF OBJECT PROGRAM
      EITHER BY PASSING IT DIRECTLY TO THE STORE MODULE,
      OR BY HOLDING IT IN THE CODE ARRAY PENDING FIXUPS     *)

   VAR
      CODEBASE : ADDRRANGE ;
      CODEOFFSET : CODERANGE ;
   BEGIN
      IF FIXUPSNEEDED = 0
      THEN
      BEGIN
         IF NEXTINS <> 1 THEN
         BEGIN
            CODEBASE := ADDRESS - NEXTINS ;
            FOR CODEOFFSET := 1 TO NEXTINS-1 DO
               STORE.COPY(ORD(CODE[CODEOFFSET])) ;
            NEXTINS := 1 ; NOCODEOVERFLOW := TRUE
         END ;
         STORE.COPY(ORD(CODEVALUE))
      END
      ELSE
      BEGIN
         IF NEXTINS > CODEMAX THEN
         BEGIN
            IF NOCODEOVERFLOW THEN
            BEGIN
               GENERROR(91) ;
               NOCODEOVERFLOW := FALSE
            END ;
            NEXTINS := 1
         END ;
         CODE[NEXTINS] := CODEVALUE ;
         NEXTINS := NEXTINS + 1 ;
      END ;
      ADDRESS := ADDRESS + 1
   END (* COPYCODE *) ;


PROCEDURE *INS ( F : ORDERCODE ; X : REGISTER ;
                 N : DIRECTOPERAND ; M : MODIFIER ) ;

   (* GENERATES REAL INSTRUCTION  F X N(M)   *)

   VAR
      INSTRUCTION : REALINSTRUCTION ;
   BEGIN
      INSTRUCTION.F := F ;
      INSTRUCTION.X := X ;
      INSTRUCTION.N := N ;
      INSTRUCTION.M := M ;
      COPYCODE(INSTRUCTION)
   END (* INS *) ;
```

```
PROCEDURE *JUMPINS ( F : ORDERCODE ; X : REGISTER ;
                     VAR SEQUENCE : CODELABEL ) ;

   (* GENERATES REAL JUMP INSTRUCTION   F X ..
      TO THE CODELABEL DESCRIBED BY SEQUENCE       *)

   VAR
      N : DIRECTOPERAND ;
   BEGIN
      WITH SEQUENCE DO
         IF EXPECTED
         THEN
         BEGIN
            FIXUPSNEEDED := FIXUPSNEEDED+1 ;
            N := LASTCODEREFERENCE ;
            LASTCODEREFERENCE := NEXTINS
         END
         ELSE N := STARTADDRESS ;
      INS(F,X,N,0)
   END (* JUMPINS *) ;

PROCEDURE *LINKEDJUMPINS ( F : ORDERCODE ; X : REGISTER ;
                           VAR SEQUENCE : CODELABEL ) ;

   (* AS JUMPINS, BUT AVOIDS FIXUPS BY USE OF LINKTABLE *)

   VAR
      N : DIRECTOPERAND ;
   BEGIN
      WITH SEQUENCE DO
         IF EXPECTED
         THEN
         BEGIN
            IF NOT LINKED THEN
            BEGIN
               IF NEXTLINK > LINKMAX THEN
               BEGIN
                  IF NOLINKOVERFLOW THEN
                  BEGIN
                     GENERROR(92) ;
                     NOLINKOVERFLOW := FALSE
                  END ;
                  NEXTLINK := 0
               END ;
               LINKED := TRUE ;
               LINKINDEX := NEXTLINK ;
               NEXTLINK := NEXTLINK + 1
            END ;
            N := FIRSTLINKADDRESS + LINKINDEX ;
            F := F+1
         END
         ELSE N := STARTADDRESS ;
      INS(F,X,N,0)
   END (* LINKEDJUMPINS *) ;
```

```
PROCEDURE *SYSTEMCALL ( ROUTINENEEDED : SYSTEMROUTINE ) ;

   (* GENERATES CALL TO SYSTEM ROUTINE SPECIFIED *)

   BEGIN
      INS(CALL,0,STORE.ADDRESSFOR[ROUTINENEEDED],0)
   END ;

   PROCEDURE *NEWLABEL ( VAR SEQUENCE : CODELABEL ) ;
      BEGIN
         WITH SEQUENCE DO
         BEGIN
            EXPECTED := FALSE ;
            STARTADDRESS := ADDRESS
         END
      END (* NEWLABEL *) ;

   PROCEDURE *FUTURELABEL ( VAR SEQUENCE : CODELABEL ) ;
      BEGIN
         WITH SEQUENCE DO
         BEGIN
            EXPECTED := TRUE ;
            LASTCODEREFERENCE := 0 ;
            LINKED := FALSE
         END
      END (* FUTURELABEL *) ;

   PROCEDURE *EXPECTEDLABEL ( VAR SEQUENCE : CODELABEL ) ;
      VAR
         THISFIXUP,NEXTFIXUP : CODERANGE ;
      BEGIN
         WITH SEQUENCE DO
         BEGIN
            IF LINKED
            THEN LINKTABLE[LINKINDEX] := ADDRESS ;
            NEXTFIXUP:= LASTCODEREFERENCE ;
            WHILE NEXTFIXUP <> 0 DO
            BEGIN
               FIXUPSNEEDED := FIXUPSNEEDED-1 ;
               THISFIXUP := NEXTFIXUP ;
               NEXTFIXUP := CODE[THISFIXUP].N ;
               CODE[THISFIXUP].N := ADDRESS
            END ;
            EXPECTED := FALSE ;
            STARTADDRESS := ADDRESS
         END
      END (* EXPECTEDLABEL *) ;
```

```
PROCEDURE *LINKLABEL ( EXPECTEDSEQUENCE : CODELABEL ;
                           VAR DESTINATION : CODELABEL ) ;

   (* REDIRECTS ANY BRANCH INSTRUCTIONS FOR EXPECTEDLABEL
      TO THE SEQUENCE DESCRIBED BY DESTINATION              *)

   VAR
      THISREFERENCE,NEXTREFERENCE : CODERANGE ;
      CODEADDRESS : INTEGER ;
   BEGIN
      IF(EXPECTEDSEQUENCE.LASTCODEREFERENCE <> 0) AND NOCODEOVERFLOW
      THEN
         IF DESTINATION.EXPECTED
         THEN
         BEGIN
            NEXTREFERENCE := EXPECTEDSEQUENCE.LASTCODEREFERENCE ;
            REPEAT
               THISREFERENCE := NEXTREFERENCE ;
               NEXTREFERENCE := CODE[THISREFERENCE].N
            UNTIL NEXTREFERENCE = 0 ;
            CODE[THISREFERENCE].N := DESTINATION.LASTCODEREFERENCE ;
            DESTINATION.LASTCODEREFERENCE :=
                              EXPECTEDSEQUENCE.LASTCODEREFERENCE
         END
         ELSE
         BEGIN
            NEXTREFERENCE := EXPECTEDSEQUENCE.LASTCODEREFERENCE ;
            REPEAT
               FIXUPSNEEDED := FIXUPSNEEDED-1 ;
               THISREFERENCE := NEXTREFERENCE ;
               NEXTREFERENCE := CODE[THISREFERENCE].N ;
               CODE[THISREFERENCE].N :=DESTINATION.STARTADDRESS
            UNTIL NEXTREFERENCE = 0
         END
   END (* LINKLABEL *) ;

PROCEDURE *ENTERHERE ;

   (* SETS OBJECT PROGRAM SCR TO NEXT INSTRUCTION *)

   BEGIN
      CODEFILE.LOCATE(SCR,ADDRESS)
   END ;


BEGIN (* CODE MODULE INITIALIZATION *)
   NEXTINS := 1 ; FIXUPSNEEDED := 0 ; NOCODEOVERFLOW := TRUE ;
   NEXTLINK := 0 ; NOLINKOVERFLOW := TRUE ;
   STORE.ALLOCATE(LINKMAX+1,FIRSTLINKADDRESS) ;

   *** ;

   IF CODEISTOBEGENERATED THEN
   BEGIN
      FOR I := 0 TO NEXTLINK-1 DO
         CODEFILE.LOCATE(FIRSTLINKADDRESS+I,LINKTABLE[I])
   END
END (*CODE MODULE *) ;
```

```
ENVELOPE MODULE CONSTNTS ;

   (* COLLATES A TABLE OF CONSTANTS DURING CODE GENERATION   *)
   (* WHICH IS LOCATED AT THE END OF THE PROGRAM GENERATED   *)
   (* CONSTANTS WITHIN IT ARE ADDRESSES BY AN OFFSET FROM    *)
   (* A BASE ADDRESS AVAILABLE AT RUNTIME IN 'BASEADDRESS'   *)

   TYPE
      WORDPTR = ^WORDREC ;
      WORDREC = RECORD
                      CONTENTS : INTEGER ;
                      NEXTWORD : WORDPTR
                  END ;

VAR
     *BASEADDRESS : ADDRRANGE ;

     FIRSTWORD,THISWORD,LASTWORD : WORDPTR ;

   PROCEDURE *LOCATE ( CONSTANT :INTEGER ;
                       VAR OFFSET : ADDRRANGE ) ;

      VAR
          THISWORD,LASTWORD : WORDPTR ;

      BEGIN
          THISWORD := FIRSTWORD ; OFFSET := 0 ;
          WHILE (THISWORD<>NIL) AND (THISWORD^.CONTENTS<>CONSTANT) DO
          BEGIN
             LASTWORD := THISWORD ;
             THISWORD := THISWORD^.NEXTWORD ;
             OFFSET := OFFSET+1
          END ;
          IF THISWORD=NIL THEN
          BEGIN
             NEW(THISWORD) ;
             THISWORD^.CONTENTS := CONSTANT ;
             THISWORD^.NEXTWORD := NIL ;
             IF FIRSTWORD=NIL
             THEN FIRSTWORD := THISWORD
             ELSE LASTWORD^.NEXTWORD := THISWORD
          END
      END ;

BEGIN
   STORE.ALLOCATE(1,BASEADDRESS) ;
   FIRSTWORD := NIL ;
   *** ;
   CODEFILE.LOCATE(BASEADDRESS,STORE.ADDRESS) ;
   THISWORD := FIRSTWORD ;
   WHILE THISWORD<>NIL DO
   BEGIN
      STORE.COPY(THISWORD^.CONTENTS) ;
      LASTWORD := THISWORD ;
      THISWORD := THISWORD^.NEXTWORD ;
      DISPOSE(LASTWORD)
   END
END (* CONSTNTS MODULE *) ;
```

```
ENVELOPE MODULE WORKLOCATIONS ;

   (* ALLOCATES AND MAKES AVAILABLE A SET OF TEMPORARY       *)
   (* WORK LOCATIONS                                          *)



   CONST

      WORKMAX = 9 ;


   TYPE

      WORKRANGE = 0..WORKMAX ;

      WORKSET = SET OF WORKRANGE ;

   VAR

      WORKSPACE : WORKSET ;

   FIRSTWORKADDRESS : ADDRRANGE ;



   PROCEDURE *GET ( VAR WORKADDRESS : ADDRRANGE ) ;
      LABEL 1 ;
      VAR
         WORKINDEX : WORKRANGE ;
      BEGIN
         FOR WORKINDEX := 0 TO WORKMAX DO
           IF WORKINDEX IN WORKSPACE THEN
           BEGIN
              WORKSPACE := WORKSPACE - [WORKINDEX] ;
              WORKADDRESS := FIRSTWORKADDRESS + WORKINDEX ;
              GOTO 1
           END ;
         GENERROR(93) ;
         WORKADDRESS := FIRSTWORKADDRESS ;
      1:
      END ;

   PROCEDURE *FREE ( WORKADDRESS : ADDRRANGE ) ;
      BEGIN
         WORKSPACE := WORKSPACE + [WORKADDRESS-FIRSTWORKADDRESS]
      END ;


   BEGIN (* WORKLOCATIONS MODULE INITIALIZATION *)
      STORE.ALLOCATE(WORKMAX+1,FIRSTWORKADDRESS) ;
      WORKSPACE := [0..WORKMAX] ;
      ***
   END (* WORKLOCATIONS MODULE *) ;
```

```
(*******************************************************)
(* *** STACK OPERAND DESCRIPTION ********************* *)
(*******************************************************)


TYPE OPERAND = ^ OPREC ;
     OPKIND = (REFERENCE,CONSTANT,RESULT,CONDITION) ;
     CONDKIND = (XCONDITION,MULTIJUMPCONDITION) ;
     OPREC = RECORD
                   NEXTENTRY : OPERAND ;
                   REP : TYPEREPRESENTATION ;
                   CASE KIND : OPKIND OF
                   REFERENCE :
                      ( REFADDRESS : RUNTIMEADDRESS ;
                        CASE INDEXED : BOOLEAN OF
                           TRUE :
                              ( INDEX : OPERAND ;
                                INDEXMIN,INDEXMAX : INTEGER )) ;
                   CONSTANT :
                      ( CONSTVALUE : INTEGER ) ;
                   RESULT :
                      ( CASE INREGISTER : BOOLEAN OF
                        FALSE :
                           ( TEMPRESULT : ADDRRANGE ) ;
                        TRUE :
                           ( REG : REGISTER )) ;
                   CONDITION :
                      ( CASE KINDOFCONDITION : CONDKIND OF
                        XCONDITION :
                           ( FALSEJUMPINS : BZE..BNG ;
                             CASE INCONDITIONREGISTER: BOOLEAN OF
                             FALSE :
                                ( TEMPCONDITION : ADDRRANGE ) ;
                             TRUE :
                                ( CONDREGISTER : REGISTER )) ;
                        MULTIJUMPCONDITION :
                           ( JUMPCONDITION : BOOLEAN ;
                             JUMPDESTINATION : CODE.CODELABEL ))
               END ;

ENVELOPE MODULE STACK ;

   (* MAINTAINS SIMULATION OF HYPOTHETICAL EVALUATION STACK *)

   VAR
      TOP : OPERAND ;

   PROCEDURE *PUSH ( ENTRY : OPERAND ) ;
      BEGIN
         ENTRY^.NEXTENTRY := TOP ;
         TOP := ENTRY
      END ;
```

```
    PROCEDURE * POP ( VAR ENTRY : OPERAND ) ;
       BEGIN
          ENTRY := TOP ;
          TOP := TOP^.NEXTENTRY
       END ;

    BEGIN (* STACK INITIALIZATION *)
       TOP := NIL ;
       ***
    END (* STACK MODULE *) ;

ENVELOPE MODULE REGISTRS ;

    (* MAINTAINS BINDINGS BETWEEN THE REAL MACHINE REGISTERS *)
    (* AND HYPOTHETICAL STACK OPERANDS                        *)

    TYPE SETOFREGISTERS = SET OF REGISTER ;

    VAR THOSEFREE : SETOFREGISTERS ;
        OPERANDUSING : ARRAY[REGISTER] OF OPERAND ;


    PROCEDURE *BINDTO ( ENTRY : OPERAND ) ;

       (* RECORDS ANY REGISTERS ASSOCIATED WITH THE VALUE DESCRIBED BY
          ENTRY AS BEING BOUND TO THE ENTRY, SO THAT ANY ATTEMPT TO
          USE THE REGISTERS FOR ANY OTHER PURPOSE MAY FIRST GENERATE
          CODE TO SAVE THEIR CONTENTS, AND ADJUST ENTRY ACCORDINGLY *)

       BEGIN
          WITH ENTRY^ DO
             CASE KIND OF
             REFERENCE ,
             CONSTANT :
                ;
             RESULT :
                IF INREGISTER THEN
                BEGIN
                   THOSEFREE := THOSEFREE - [REG] ;
                   OPERANDUSING[REG] := ENTRY ;
                END ;
             CONDITION :
                IF (KINDOFCONDITION = XCONDITION) AND
                    INCONDITIONREGISTER THEN
                BEGIN
                   THOSEFREE := THOSEFREE - [CONDREGISTER] ;
                   OPERANDUSING[CONDREGISTER] := ENTRY
                END
             END
       END (* BINDTO *) ;
```

```
PROCEDURE *FREEFROM ( ENTRY : OPERAND ) ;

   (* REVERSES EFFECT OF BINDTO *)

   VAR
      THOSEUSED : SETOFREGISTERS ;
   BEGIN
      THOSEUSED := [ ] ;
      WITH ENTRY^ DO
         CASE KIND OF
         REFERENCE ,
         CONSTANT :
            ;
         RESULT :
            IF INREGISTER THEN THOSEUSED := [REG] ;
         CONDITION :
            IF (KINDOFCONDITION = XCONDITION) AND INCONDITIONREGISTER
            THEN THOSEUSED := [CONDREGISTER]
         END ;
      THOSEFREE := THOSEFREE + THOSEUSED
   END (* FREEFROM *) ;

PROCEDURE *SAVE ( X : REGISTER ) ;
   VAR N : ADDRRANGE ;
   BEGIN
      IF NOT (X IN THOSEFREE) THEN
      BEGIN
         WORKLOCATIONS.GET(N) ; CODE.INS(STO,X,N,0) ;
         WITH OPERANDUSING[X]^ DO
            CASE KIND OF
            RESULT :
               BEGIN
                  INREGISTER := FALSE ; TEMPRESULT := N
               END ;
            CONDITION :
               BEGIN
                  INCONDITIONREGISTER := FALSE ;
                  TEMPCONDITION := N
               END
            END ;
         THOSEFREE := THOSEFREE + [X]
      END
   END (* SAVE *) ;
```

```
FUNCTION *USEDBY ( ENTRY : OPERAND ) : SETOFREGISTERS ;
   BEGIN
      WITH ENTRY^ DO
         CASE KIND OF
         REFERENCE :
            IF INDEXED
            THEN USEDBY := USEDBY(INDEX)
            ELSE USEDBY := [ ] ;
         CONSTANT :
            USEDBY := [ ] ;
         RESULT :
            IF INREGISTER
            THEN USEDBY := [REG]
            ELSE USEDBY := [ ] ;
         CONDITION :
            IF (KINDOFCONDITION = XCONDITION) AND INCONDITIONREGISTER
            THEN USEDBY := [CONDREGISTER]
            ELSE USEDBY := [ ]
         END
   END (* USEDBY *) ;

FUNCTION *BESTFOR ( ENTRY : OPERAND ) : REGISTER ;
   VAR THOSEAVAILABLE : SETOFREGISTERS ;
       X : 4..7 ;
   BEGIN
      THOSEAVAILABLE := (USEDBY(ENTRY)÷THOSEFREE)*[4..7] ;
      IF THOSEAVAILABLE <> [ ]
      THEN
      BEGIN
         X := 4 ;
         WHILE NOT (X IN THOSEAVAILABLE) DO X := X+1
      END
      ELSE X := 4 ;
      BESTFOR := X
   END (* BESTFOR *) ;

BEGIN (* REGISTERS MODULE *)
   THOSEFREE := [0..7] ;
   ***
END (* REGISTERS MODULE *) ;
```

```
(*********************************************************)
(***** PROCEDURE, PROGRAM AND STORAGE HOUSEKEEPING *****)
(*********************************************************)


CONST

    (*** ADDRESS REGISTER USAGE ***)

    XLOCAL = 1 ; (* ALWAYS ADDRESSES LOCAL STACKFRAME *)
    XREF   = 3 ; (* USED FOR REFERENCE EVALUATION     *)
    XMOD   = 2 ; (* UTILITY ADDRESS REGISTER          *)


TYPE
    *PROCLINKAGE = RECORD
                        STATICLEVEL : INTEGER ;
                        CODEBODY : CODE.CODELABEL
                   END ;

PROCEDURE *NEWLINKAGE ( VAR LINKAGE : PROCLINKAGE ) ;
    BEGIN
        IF CODEISTOBEGENERATED THEN
        WITH LINKAGE DO
        BEGIN
            STATICLEVEL := LEVEL ;
            CODE.FUTURELABEL(CODEBODY)
        END
    END (* NEWLINKAGE *) ;

PROCEDURE SETXTOLEVEL ( X : REGISTER ; REQUIREDLEVEL : INTEGER ) ;

    (* GENERATES CODE TO SET THE REGISTER X EQUAL TO THE ADDRESS
       OF THE CURRENT STACKFRAME FOR STATIC LEVEL REQUIREDLEVEL *)

    VAR
        NEXTLEVEL : INTEGER ;
    BEGIN
        IF REQUIREDLEVEL = LEVEL
        THEN CODE.INS(LDX,X,XLOCAL,0)
        ELSE
            IF REQUIREDLEVEL = LEVEL-1
            THEN CODE.INS(LDX,X,STATIC,XLOCAL)
            ELSE
            BEGIN
                CODE.INS(LDX,XMOD,STATIC,XLOCAL) ;
                NEXTLEVEL := LEVEL-2 ;
                WHILE NEXTLEVEL <> REQUIREDLEVEL DO
                BEGIN
                    CODE.INS(LDX,XMOD,STATIC,XMOD) ;
                    NEXTLEVEL := NEXTLEVEL-1
                END ;
                CODE.INS(LDX,X,STATIC,XMOD)
            END
    END (* SETXTOLEVEL *) ;
```

```
PROCEDURE *CALLPROC ( VAR LINKAGE : PROCLINKAGE ) ;
   BEGIN
      IF CODEISTOBEGENERATED THEN
      WITH LINKAGE DO
      BEGIN
         IF STATICLEVEL <> GLOBALLEVEL THEN SETXTOLEVEL(4,STATICLEVEL) ;
         CODE.LINKEDJUMPINS(CALL,5,CODEBODY)
      END
   END (* CALLPROC *) ;

PROCEDURE *ENTERBODY ( VAR LINKAGE : PROCLINKAGE ) ;
   BEGIN
      IF CODEISTOBEGENERATED THEN
      WITH LINKAGE DO
      BEGIN
         CODE.ALIGNINSTORE ;
         CODE.EXPECTEDLABEL(CODEBODY) ;
         CODE.INS(LDX,XREF,NEXTFRAME,XLOCAL) ;
         CODE.INS(STO,XLOCAL,DYNAMIC,XREF) ;
         IF STATICLEVEL <> GLOBALLEVEL THEN CODE.INS(STO,4,STATIC,XREF) ;
         CODE.INS(STO,5,LINK,XREF) ;
         CODE.INS(LDX,XLOCAL,XREF,0) ;
         CODE.INS(ADN,XREF,LOCALFRAME^.NEXTLOCAL,0) ;
         CODE.INS(STO,XREF,NEXTFRAME,XLOCAL)
      END
   END (* ENTERBODY *) ;

PROCEDURE *LEAVEBODY ;
   BEGIN
      IF CODEISTOBEGENERATED THEN
      BEGIN
         CODE.INS(LDX,5,LINK,XLOCAL) ;
         CODE.INS(LDX,XLOCAL,DYNAMIC,XLOCAL) ;
         CODE.INS(EXIT,5,0,0)
      END
   END (* LEAVEBODY *) ;

PROCEDURE *ENTERPROGRAM ;
   BEGIN
      IF CODEISTOBEGENERATED THEN
      BEGIN
         CODE.ALIGNINSTORE ;
         CODE.ENTERHERE ;
         CODE.INS(LDX,XLOCAL,STORE.STACKBASE,0) ;
         CODE.INS(LDN,XREF,FIRSTLOCAL,XLOCAL) ;
         CODE.INS(STO,XREF,NEXTFRAME,XLOCAL) ;
         CODE.SYSTEMCALL(INITIALIO) ;
      END
   END (* ENTERPROGRAM *) ;

PROCEDURE *LEAVEPROGRAM ;
   BEGIN
      IF CODEISTOBEGENERATED THEN
      BEGIN
         CODE.SYSTEMCALL(FINALIO) ;
         CODE.INS(HALT,0,0,0)
      END
   END (* LEAVEPROGRAM *) ;
```

```
(*********************************************************)
(********* OPERAND ADDRESSING AND LOADING **************)
(*********************************************************)




PROCEDURE CONSTINS ( F:ORDERCODE ; X:REGISTER ; N:INTEGER ) ;

    (* GENERATES CODE EQUIVALENT TO INSTRUCTION F X 'N'
       WHERE F IS ONE OF LDX,ADX,NGX,SBX,MPX,DVX          *)

    VAR OFFSET : ADDRRANGE ;

    BEGIN
        IF (N<0) AND (N>=-4095) AND (F IN [LDX,ADX,NGX,SBX]) THEN
        BEGIN
            N := -N ;
            CASE F OF
            LDX : F:=NGX ;
            NGX : F:=LDX ;
            ADX : F:=SBX ;
            SBX : F:=ADX
            END
        END ;
        IF (N>=0) AND (N<=4095)
        THEN CODE.INS(F+100B,X,N,0)
        ELSE WITH CONSTNTS DO
                BEGIN
                    LOCATE(N,OFFSET) ;
                    CODE.INS(LDX,XMOD,BASEADDRESS,0) ;
                    CODE.INS(F,X,OFFSET,XMOD)
                END
    END (* CONSTINS *) ;



VAR

    ADDRESSED : RECORD
                    N : 0..4095 ;
                    M : MODIFIER
                END ;

    LOADEDREG  : REGISTER ;



PROCEDURE LOADX ( X : REGISTER ; ENTRY : OPERAND ) ; FORWARD ;
```

```
PROCEDURE ADDRESS ( ENTRY : OPERAND ) ;

   (* GENERATES CODE (IF NECESSARY) TO ENABLE THE VALUE DESCRIBED
      BY ENTRY TO BE ADDRESSED, AND LEAVES ADDRESSING CO-ORDINATES
      IN THE GLOBAL RECORD ADDRESSED. ANY REGISTERS BOUND TO ENTRY,
      OR STACK ENTRIES OCCUPIED BY ITS INDICES ARE FREED IN THE
      PROCESS                                                        *)

VAR
   XREFSET : BOOLEAN ;
   ADJUSTMENT,FINALN : INTEGER ;
   FINALM : MODIFIER ;
BEGIN
   WITH ENTRY^ DO
      CASE KIND OF
      REFERENCE :
         BEGIN
            IF INDEXED
            THEN
            BEGIN
               IF INDEX^.KIND = CONSTANT
               THEN
               BEGIN
                  ADJUSTMENT := INDEX^.CONSTVALUE-INDEXMIN ;
                  XREFSET := FALSE
               END
               ELSE
               BEGIN
                  LOADX(XREF,INDEX) ;
                  ADJUSTMENT := - INDEXMIN ;
                  XREFSET := TRUE
               END ;
               DISPOSE(INDEX)
            END
            ELSE
            BEGIN
               ADJUSTMENT := 0 ;
               XREFSET := FALSE
            END ;
            WITH REFADDRESS DO
            BEGIN
               FINALN := RELATIVEADDRESS + ADJUSTMENT ;
               IF STATICLEVEL = GLOBALLEVEL
               THEN
               BEGIN
                  IF XREFSET
                  THEN FINALM := XREF
                  ELSE FINALM := 0 ;
               END
               ELSE
                  IF STATICLEVEL = LEVEL
                  THEN
                     IF XREFSET
                     THEN
                     BEGIN
                        CODE.INS(ADX,XREF,XLOCAL,0) ;
                        FINALM := XREF
                     END
                     ELSE FINALM := XLOCAL
                  ELSE
```

```
                    BEGIN
                        IF XREFSET
                        THEN
                            IF STATICLEVEL = LEVEL-1
                            THEN CODE.INS(ADX,XREF,STATIC,XLOCAL)
                            ELSE
                            BEGIN
                                SETXTOLEVEL(XMOD,STATICLEVEL+1) ;
                                CODE.INS(ADX,XREF,STATIC,XMOD)
                            END
                        ELSE SETXTOLEVEL(XREF,STATICLEVEL) ;
                        FINALM := XREF
                    END
                END ;
                IF FINALM < 0 THEN
                BEGIN
                    CONSTINS(ADX,XREF,FINALM) ;
                    FINALM := 0
                END
            END ;
        CONSTANT :
            BEGIN
                CONSTNTS.LOCATE(CONSTVALUE,FINALM) ;
                CODE.INS(LDX,XMOD,CONSTNTS.BASEADDRESS,0) ;
                FINALM := XMOD
            END ;
        RESULT :
            BEGIN
                IF INREGISTER
                THEN FINALN := REG
                ELSE FINALN := TEMPRESULT ;
                FINALM := 0
            END ;
        CONDITION :
            BEGIN
                LOADX(0,ENTRY) ;
                FINALN := 0 ; FINALM := 0
            END
        END ;
    WITH ADDRESSED DO
    BEGIN
        N := FINALN ;
        M := FINALM
    END ;
    REGISTRS.FREEFROM(ENTRY)
  END (* ADDRESS *) ;

PROCEDURE LOADADDRESS ( X : REGISTER ; ENTRY : OPERAND ) ;

  (* GENERATES CODE TO LOAD ADDRESS OF VALUE DESCRIBED BY
     ENTRY INTO REGISTER X, SAVING PREVIOUS CONTENTS OF X
     IF NECESSARY                                          *)
  BEGIN
    IF NOT (X IN REGISTRS.USEDBY(ENTRY)) THEN REGISTRS.SAVE(X) ;
    ADDRESS(ENTRY) ;
    WITH ADDRESSED DO CODE.INS(LDN,X,N,M)
  END (* LOADADDRESS *) ;

PROCEDURE JUMPIF ( ENTRY : OPERAND ; JUMPONTRUE : BOOLEAN ;
                   VAR DESTINATION : CODE.CODELABEL ) ; FORWARD ;
```

```
PROCEDURE LOADX ;

    (* GENERATES CODE TO LOAD VALUE DESCRIBED BY ENTRY INTO
       REGISTER X ( IF NECESSARY ) . REGISTERS BOUND TO ENTRY
       ARE FREED IN THE PROCESS, BUT ENTRY ITSELF IS RESET TO
       DESCRIBE THE LOADED VALUE (FOR POSSIBLE REBINDING)       *)
    VAR
        TOBEJUMPEDON : BOOLEAN ;
        TOLOADCONDITIONJUMPEDON,AFTERCONDITIONLOADED : CODE.CODELABEL ;

    PROCEDURE LOADBOOLEANVALUE ( CONDITION : BOOLEAN ) ;
        BEGIN
            IF CONDITION
            THEN CODE.INS(LDN,X,1,0)
            ELSE CODE.INS(LDN,X,0,0)
        END ;

    BEGIN
        IF NOT(X IN REGISTRS.USEDBY(ENTRY)) THEN REGISTRS.SAVE(X) ;
        WITH ENTRY^ DO
        BEGIN
            CASE KIND OF
            REFERENCE :
                BEGIN
                    ADDRESS(ENTRY) ;
                    WITH ADDRESSED DO CODE.INS(LDX,X,N,M)
                END ;
            CONSTANT :
                CONSTINS(LDX,X,CONSTVALUE) ;
            RESULT :
                IF INREGISTER
                THEN
                BEGIN
                    REGISTRS.FREEFROM(ENTRY) ;
                    IF REG <> X THEN CODE.INS(LDX,X,REG,0)
                END
                ELSE
                BEGIN
                    ADDRESS(ENTRY) ;
                    WITH ADDRESSED DO CODE.INS(LDX,X,N,M)
                END ;
            CONDITION :
                BEGIN
                    TOBEJUMPEDON := (KINDOFCONDITION = MULTIJUMPCONDITION)
                                     AND JUMPCONDITION ;
                    CODE.FUTURELABEL(TOLOADCONDITIONJUMPEDON) ;
                    CODE.FUTURELABEL(AFTERCONDITIONLOADED) ;
                    JUMPIF(ENTRY,TOBEJUMPEDON,TOLOADCONDITIONJUMPEDON) ;
                    LOADBOOLEANVALUE(NOT TOBEJUMPEDON) ;
                    CODE.JUMPINS(BRN,0,AFTERCONDITIONLOADED) ;
                    CODE.EXPECTEDLABEL(TOLOADCONDITIONJUMPEDON) ;
                    LOADBOOLEANVALUE(TOBEJUMPEDON) ;
                    CODE.EXPECTEDLABEL(AFTERCONDITIONLOADED)
                END
            END ;
            KIND := RESULT ;
            INREGISTER := TRUE ;
            REG := X
        END
    END (* LOADX *) ;
```

```
PROCEDURE LOAD ( ENTRY : OPERAND ) ;

   (* GENERATES CODE TO LOAD VALUE DESCRIBED BY ENTRY INTO AN
      APPROPRIATE REGISTER (IF NOT ALREADY LOADED) AND SETS THE
      GLOBAL VARIABLE LOADEDREG TO DESCRIBE THE LOADED VALUE.
      ANY REGISTERS BOUND TO THE ENTRY ARE FREED IN THE PROCESS
      BUT ENTRY IS UPDATED TO DESCRIBE THE LOADED VALUE
      (FOR POSSIBLE REBINDING)                               *)


   VAR
      CHOSENREGISTER : REGISTER ;

   BEGIN
      IF (ENTRY^.KIND = RESULT) AND ENTRY^.INREGISTER
      THEN
      BEGIN
         CHOSENREGISTER := ENTRY^.REG ;
         REGISTRS.FREEFROM(ENTRY)
      END
      ELSE
      BEGIN
         CHOSENREGISTER := REGISTRS.BESTFOR(ENTRY) ;
         LOADX(CHOSENREGISTER,ENTRY)
      END ;
      LOADEDREG := CHOSENREGISTER
   END (* LOAD *) ;


PROCEDURE LOADNEGATIVE ( ENTRY : OPERAND ) ;

   (* SAME AS LOAD, EXCEPT VALUE IS NEGATED *)

   VAR
      CHOSENREGISTER : REGISTER ;
   BEGIN
      CHOSENREGISTER := REGISTRS.BESTFOR(ENTRY) ;
      IF NOT (CHOSENREGISTER IN REGISTRS.USEDBY(ENTRY))
      THEN REGISTRS.SAVE(CHOSENREGISTER) ;
      ADDRESS(ENTRY) ;
      WITH ADDRESSED DO CODE.INS(NGX,CHOSENREGISTER,N,M) ;
      WITH ENTRY^ DO
      BEGIN
         KIND := RESULT ;
         INREGISTER := TRUE ;
         REG := CHOSENREGISTER
      END ;
      LOADEDREG := CHOSENREGISTER
   END (* LOADNEGATIVE *) ;
```

```
PROCEDURE JUMPIF (* ENTRY : OPERAND ; JUMPONTRUE : BOOLEAN ;
                   VAR DESTINATION : CODE.CODELABEL *) ;
   (* GENERATES CODE TO EXAMINE THE BOOLEAN VALUE DESCRIBED
      BY ENTRY AND JUMP TO THE LABEL DESTINATION IF
      ITS VALUE IS EQUAL TO JUMPONTRUE. ANY REGISTERS BOUND
      TO ENTRY ARE FREED IN THE PROCESS                    *)
   VAR
      BRINS : BZE .. BNG ;
      X : REGISTER ;
   BEGIN
      WITH ENTRY^ DO
         CASE KIND OF
         REFERENCE ,
         RESULT :
            BEGIN
               LOAD(ENTRY) ;
               IF JUMPONTRUE THEN BRINS := BNZ ELSE BRINS := BZE ;
               CODE.JUMPINS(BRINS,LOADEDREG,DESTINATION)
            END ;
         CONSTANT :
            IF CONSTVALUE = ORD(JUMPONTRUE)
            THEN CODE.JUMPINS(BRN,0,DESTINATION) ;
         CONDITION :
            CASE KINDOFCONDITION OF
            XCONDITION :
               BEGIN
                  IF INCONDITIONREGISTER
                  THEN
                  BEGIN
                     X := CONDREGISTER ;
                     REGISTRS.FREEFROM(ENTRY)
                  END
                  ELSE
                  BEGIN
                     CODE.INS(LDX,0,TEMPCONDITION,0) ;
                     WORKLOCATIONS.FREE(TEMPCONDITION) ;
                     X := 0
                  END ;
                  IF JUMPONTRUE
                  THEN
                  CASE FALSEJUMPINS OF
                  BZE : BRINS := BNZ ;
                  BNZ : BRINS := BZE ;
                  BPZ : BRINS := BNG ;
                  BNG : BRINS := BPZ
                  END
                  ELSE BRINS := FALSEJUMPINS ;
                  CODE.JUMPINS(BRINS,X,DESTINATION)
               END ;
            MULTIJUMPCONDITION :
               IF JUMPCONDITION = JUMPONTRUE
               THEN CODE.LINKLABEL(JUMPDESTINATION,DESTINATION)
               ELSE
               BEGIN
                  CODE.JUMPINS(BRN,0,DESTINATION) ;
                  CODE.EXPECTEDLABEL(JUMPDESTINATION)
               END
            END (* CASE KINDOFCONDITION *)
         END
   END (* JUMPIF *) ;
```

```
(*********************************************************)
(******* VARIABLES, EXPRESSIONS, AND ASSIGNMENT *********)
(*********************************************************)



PROCEDURE *STACKREFERENCE ( LOCATION : RUNTIMEADDRESS ) ;
   VAR
      REFENTRY : OPERAND ;
   BEGIN
      IF CODEISTOBEGENERATED
      THEN
      BEGIN
         NEW(REFENTRY) ;
         WITH REFENTRY^ DO
         BEGIN
            KIND := REFERENCE ;
            REFADDRESS := LOCATION ;
            INDEXED := FALSE
         END ;
         STACK.PUSH(REFENTRY)
      END
   END (* STACKREFERENCE *) ;

PROCEDURE *INDEXEDREFERENCE ( BOUNDMIN,BOUNDMAX : INTEGER ;
                             ELEMENTREPRESENTATION:TYPEREPRESENTATION) ;
   VAR
      VARIABLE,INDEXENTRY : OPERAND ;
   BEGIN
      IF CODEISTOBEGENERATED THEN
      BEGIN
         STACK.POP(INDEXENTRY) ;
         STACK.POP(VARIABLE) ;
         WITH VARIABLE^ DO
         BEGIN
            INDEXED := TRUE ;
            INDEX := INDEXENTRY ;
            INDEXMIN := BOUNDMIN ;
            INDEXMAX := BOUNDMAX ;
         END ;
         STACK.PUSH(VARIABLE)
      END
   END (* INDEXEDREFERENCE *) ;
```

```
PROCEDURE *DEREFERENCE ( REPRESENTATION : TYPEREPRESENTATION ) ;
   VAR REFERENCE : OPERAND ;
   BEGIN
      IF CODEISTOBEGENERATED THEN
      BEGIN
         STACK.POP(REFERENCE) ;
         REFERENCE^.REP := REPRESENTATION ;
         STACK.PUSH(REFERENCE)
      END
   END (* DEREFERENCE *) ;


PROCEDURE *STACKCONSTANT ( CVALUE : INTEGER ;
                           REPRESENTATION : TYPEREPRESENTATION ) ;
   VAR
      CONSTENTRY : OPERAND ;
   BEGIN
      IF CODEISTOBEGENERATED THEN
      BEGIN
         NEW(CONSTENTRY) ;
         WITH CONSTENTRY^ DO
         BEGIN
            REP := REPRESENTATION ;
            KIND := CONSTANT ;
            CONSTVALUE := CVALUE
         END ;
         STACK.PUSH(CONSTENTRY)
      END
   END (* STACKCONSTANT *) ;

PROCEDURE *NEGATEINTEGER ;
   VAR INTEGERVALUE : OPERAND ;
   BEGIN
      IF CODEISTOBEGENERATED THEN
      BEGIN
         STACK.POP(INTEGERVALUE) ;
         WITH INTEGERVALUE^ DO
            IF KIND = CONSTANT
            THEN CONSTVALUE := -CONSTVALUE
            ELSE
            BEGIN
               LOADNEGATIVE(INTEGERVALUE) ;
               REGISTRS.BINDTO(INTEGERVALUE)
            END ;
         STACK.PUSH(INTEGERVALUE)
      END
   END (* NEGATEINTEGER *) ;
```

```
PROCEDURE *BINARYINTEGEROPERATION ( OPERATOR : OPTYPE ) ;

   TYPE
      OPERANDDESCRIPTION = RECORD
                              ENTRY : OPERAND ;
                              ISCONSTANT,ISZERO,ISINREGISTER : BOOLEAN ;
                              CVALUE : INTEGER
                           END ;
   VAR
      LEFTOPERAND,RIGHTOPERAND,
      INCREMENT : OPERANDDESCRIPTION ;
      RESLT : INTEGER ;
      RESULTENTRY : OPERAND ;
      OPINS : ORDERCODE ;

   PROCEDURE ANALYZE ( VAR OPERAND : OPERANDDESCRIPTION ) ;
      BEGIN
         WITH OPERAND,ENTRY^ DO
            IF KIND = CONSTANT
            THEN
            BEGIN
               ISINREGISTER := FALSE ;
               ISCONSTANT := TRUE ;
               CVALUE := CONSTVALUE ;
               ISZERO := (CVALUE = 0)
            END
            ELSE
            BEGIN
               ISCONSTANT := FALSE ;
               ISZERO := FALSE :
               ISINREGISTER := (KIND = RESULT) AND INREGISTER
            END
      END (* ANALYZE *) ;

   BEGIN
      IF CODEISTOBEGENERATED THEN
      BEGIN
         STACK.POP(RIGHTOPERAND.ENTRY) ;
         STACK.POP(LEFTOPERAND.ENTRY) ;
         NEW(RESULTENTRY) ;
         RESULTENTRY^.REP := INTEGERREPRESENTATION ;
         ANALYZE(LEFTOPERAND) ;
         ANALYZE(RIGHTOPERAND);
         IF LEFTOPERAND.ISCONSTANT AND RIGHTOPERAND.ISCONSTANT
         THEN
         BEGIN
            CASE OPERATOR OF
            PLUS : RESLT := LEFTOPERAND.CVALUE  +  RIGHTOPERAND.CVALUE ;
            MINUS: RESLT := LEFTOPERAND.CVALUE  -  RIGHTOPERAND.CVALUE ;
            TIMES: RESLT := LEFTOPERAND.CVALUE  *  RIGHTOPERAND.CVALUE ;
            DIVOP: RESLT := LEFTOPERAND.CVALUE DIV RIGHTOPERAND.CVALUE
            END ;
            WITH RESULTENTRY^ DO
            BEGIN
               KIND := CONSTANT ;
               CONSTVALUE := RESLT
            END
         END
         ELSE
```

```
IF LEFTOPERAND.ISZERO
THEN
   CASE OPERATOR OF
   PLUS :
      RESULTENTRY^ := RIGHTOPERAND.ENTRY^ ;
   MINUS :
      BEGIN
         LOADNEGATIVE(RIGHTOPERAND.ENTRY) ;
         RESULTENTRY^ := RIGHTOPERAND.ENTRY^ ;
         REGISTRS.BINDTO(RESULTENTRY)
      END ;
   TIMES ,
   DIVOP :
      RESULTENTRY^ := LEFTOPERAND.ENTRY^
   END (* CASE *)
ELSE
   IF RIGHTOPERAND.ISZERO
   THEN
      CASE OPERATOR OF
      PLUS ,
      MINUS :
         RESULTENTRY^ := LEFTOPERAND.ENTRY^ ;
      TIMES :
         RESULTENTRY^ := RIGHTOPERAND.ENTRY^ ;
      DIVOP :
         GENERROR(94)
      END (* CASE *)
   ELSE
   BEGIN
      CASE OPERATOR OF
      PLUS ,
      TIMES :
         BEGIN
            IF OPERATOR = PLUS THEN OPINS:=ADX ELSE OPINS:=MPX ;
            IF RIGHTOPERAND.ISINREGISTER
            THEN
            BEGIN
               LOAD(RIGHTOPERAND.ENTRY) ;
               INCREMENT := LEFTOPERAND
            END
            ELSE
            BEGIN
               LOAD(LEFTOPERAND.ENTRY) ;
               INCREMENT := RIGHTOPERAND
            END ;
            IF INCREMENT.ISCONSTANT
            THEN CONSTINS(OPINS,LOADEDREG,INCREMENT.CVALUE)
            ELSE
            BEGIN
               ADDRESS(INCREMENT.ENTRY) ;
               WITH ADDRESSED DO CODE.INS(OPINS,LOADEDREG,N,M)
            END
         END ;
      MINUS ,
      DIVOP :
```

```
                    BEGIN
                        IF OPERATOR = MINUS THEN OPINS:=SBX ELSE OPINS:= DVX ;
                        LOAD(LEFTOPERAND.ENTRY) ;
                        IF RIGHTOPERAND.ISCONSTANT
                        THEN
                            CONSTINS(OPINS,LOADEDREG,RIGHTOPERAND.CVALUE)
                        ELSE
                        BEGIN
                            ADDRESS(RIGHTOPERAND.ENTRY) ;
                            WITH ADDRESSED DO CODE.INS(OPINS,LOADEDREG,N,M)
                        END
                    END
                END (* CASE *) ;
                WITH RESULTENTRY^ DO
                BEGIN
                    KIND := RESULT ;
                    INREGISTER := TRUE ;
                    REG := LOADEDREG
                END ;
                REGISTRS.BINDTO(RESULTENTRY)
            END ;
        STACK.PUSH(RESULTENTRY) ;
        DISPOSE(LEFTOPERAND.ENTRY) ;
        DISPOSE(RIGHTOPERAND.ENTRY)
    END
END (* BINARYINTEGEROPERATION *) ;

PROCEDURE *COMPARISON ( OPERATOR : OPTYPE ) ;
    VAR
        LEFTOPERAND,RIGHTOPERAND,RESULTENTRY : OPERAND ;
        DIFFERENCE : INTEGER ;
        RESULTVALUE : BOOLEAN ;
    BEGIN
        IF CODEISTOBEGENERATED THEN
        BEGIN
            IF OPERATOR IN [LEOP,GTOP] THEN
            BEGIN
                STACK.POP(RIGHTOPERAND) ; STACK.POP(LEFTOPERAND) ;
                STACK.PUSH(RIGHTOPERAND) ; STACK.PUSH(LEFTOPERAND)
            END ;
            BINARYINTEGEROPERATION(MINUS) ;
            STACK.POP(RESULTENTRY) ;
            WITH RESULTENTRY^ DO
            BEGIN
                IF KIND = CONSTANT
                THEN
                BEGIN
                    DIFFERENCE := CONSTVALUE ;
                    CASE OPERATOR OF
                        LTOP ,
                        GTOP : RESULTVALUE := (DIFFERENCE < 0) ;
                        LEOP ,
                        GEOP : RESULTVALUE := (DIFFERENCE >=0) ;
                        EQOP : RESULTVALUE := (DIFFERENCE = 0) ;
                        NEOP : RESULTVALUE := (DIFFERENCE <> 0)
                    END ;
                    IF RESULTVALUE THEN CONSTVALUE := 1 ELSE CONSTVALUE := 0
                END
                ELSE
```

```
        BEGIN
            LOAD(RESULTENTRY) ;
            KIND := CONDITION ;
            KINDOFCONDITION := XCONDITION ;
            CASE OPERATOR OF
            LTOP,GTOP : FALSEJUMPINS := BPZ ;
            LEOP,GEOP : FALSEJUMPINS := BNG ;
            EQOP      : FALSEJUMPINS := BNZ ;
            NEOP      : FALSEJUMPINS := BZE
            END ;
            INCONDITIONREGISTER := TRUE ;
            CONDREGISTER := LOADEDREG ;
            REGISTRS.BINDTO(RESULTENTRY)
        END ;
        REP := BOOLEANREPRESENTATION
      END ;
      STACK.PUSH(RESULTENTRY)
    END
  END (* COMPARISON *) ;

PROCEDURE *NEGATEBOOLEAN ;
  VAR BOOLEANVALUE : OPERAND ;
  BEGIN
    IF CODEISTOBEGENERATED THEN
    BEGIN
      STACK.POP(BOOLEANVALUE) ;
      WITH BOOLEANVALUE^ DO
        CASE KIND OF
        CONSTANT :
          CONSTVALUE := ABS(CONSTVALUE-1) ;
        CONDITION :
          CASE KINDOFCONDITION OF
          XCONDITION :
            CASE FALSEJUMPINS OF
            BZE : FALSEJUMPINS := BNZ ;
            BNZ : FALSEJUMPINS := BZE ;
            BPZ : FALSEJUMPINS := BNG ;
            BNG : FALSEJUMPINS := BPZ
            END ;
          MULTIJUMPCONDITION :
            JUMPCONDITION := NOT JUMPCONDITION
          END ;
        REFERENCE ,
        RESULT :
          BEGIN
            LOAD(BOOLEANVALUE) ;
            CODE.INS(ERN,LOADEDREG,1,0) ;
            REGISTRS.BINDTO(BOOLEANVALUE)
          END
        END (* CASE *) ;
      STACK.PUSH(BOOLEANVALUE)
    END
  END (* NEGATEBOOLEAN *) ;
```

```
PROCEDURE *BINARYBOOLEANOPERATOR ( OPERATOR : OPTYPE ;
                                   FIRSTSUCHOPERATOR : BOOLEAN ) ;
   VAR BOOLEANOPERAND,CONDENTRY : OPERAND ;
   BEGIN
      IF CODEISTOBEGENERATED THEN
      BEGIN
         STACK.POP(BOOLEANOPERAND) ;
         IF FIRSTSUCHOPERATOR THEN
         BEGIN
            NEW(CONDENTRY) ;
            WITH CONDENTRY^ DO
            BEGIN
               REP := BOOLEANREPRESENTATION ;
               KIND := CONDITION ;
               KINDOFCONDITION := MULTIJUMPCONDITION ;
               JUMPCONDITION := (OPERATOR = OROP) ;
               CODE.FUTURELABEL(JUMPDESTINATION)
            END
         END
            ELSE STACK.POP(CONDENTRY) ;
         WITH CONDENTRY^ DO
            JUMPIF(BOOLEANOPERAND,JUMPCONDITION,JUMPDESTINATION) ;
         STACK.PUSH(CONDENTRY) ;
         DISPOSE(BOOLEANOPERAND)
      END
   END (* BINARYBOOLEANOPERATOR *) ;

PROCEDURE *ASSIGN ;
   VAR
      EXPRESSION,VARIABLE : OPERAND ;
      SIZE : ADDRRANGE ;
   BEGIN
      IF CODEISTOBEGENERATED THEN
      BEGIN
         STACK.POP(EXPRESSION) ;
         STACK.POP(VARIABLE) ;
         SIZE := EXPRESSION^.REP ;
         IF SIZE > 1
         THEN
         BEGIN
            LOADADDRESS(6,EXPRESSION) ;
            LOADADDRESS(7,VARIABLE) ;
            CODE.INS(MOVE,6,SIZE ,0)
         END
         ELSE
            IF (EXPRESSION^.KIND = CONSTANT)
            AND (EXPRESSION^.CONSTVALUE = 0)
            THEN
            BEGIN
               ADDRESS(VARIABLE) ;
               WITH ADDRESSED DO CODE.INS(STOZ,0,N,M)
            END
            ELSE
            BEGIN
               LOAD(EXPRESSION) ;
               ADDRESS(VARIABLE) ;
               WITH ADDRESSED DO CODE.INS(STO,LOADEDREG,N,M)
            END ;
         DISPOSE(EXPRESSION) ;
         DISPOSE(VARIABLE)
      END
   END (* ASSIGN *) ;
```

```
(*******************************************************)
(************** INPUT/OUTPUT OPERATIONS *****************)
(*******************************************************)

PROCEDURE *READOPERATION ( READMODE : IOMODE ) ;

   VAR
      VALUEREAD : OPERAND ;

   BEGIN
      IF CODEISTOBEGENERATED THEN
      BEGIN
         NEW(VALUEREAD) ;
         WITH VALUEREAD^ DO
         BEGIN
            KIND := RESULT ;
            INREGISTER := TRUE ;
            REG := 6 ;
            CASE READMODE OF
            INTEGERMODE :
               BEGIN
                  CODE.SYSTEMCALL(READINTEGER) ;
                  REP := INTEGERREPRESENTATION
               END ;
            CHARMODE :
               BEGIN
                  CODE.SYSTEMCALL(READCHAR) ;
                  REP := CHARREPRESENTATION
               END
            END
         END ;
         REGISTRS.BINDTO(VALUEREAD) ;
         STACK.PUSH(VALUEREAD) ;
         ASSIGN
      END
   END (* READOPERATION *) ;

PROCEDURE *WRITEOPERATION ( WRITEMODE : IOMODE ) ;

   VAR
      SCALARVALUE : OPERAND ;

   BEGIN
      IF CODEISTOBEGENERATED THEN
      BEGIN
         STACK.POP(SCALARVALUE) ;
         LOADX(6,SCALARVALUE) ;
         CASE WRITEMODE OF
         CHARMODE : CODE.SYSTEMCALL(WRITECHAR) ;
         INTEGERMODE  : CODE.SYSTEMCALL(WRITEINTEGER)
         END ;
         DISPOSE(SCALARVALUE)
      END
   END (* WRITEOPERATION *) ;
```

```
(*******************************************************************)
(************** CONTROL STATEMENTS **********************)
(*******************************************************************)


(****MAKE CODE MODULE'S LABEL FACILITIES AVAILABLE *****)
(****TO ANALYZER                                  *****)


TYPE
   *CODELABEL = CODE.CODELABEL ;

PROCEDURE *NEWCODELABEL ( VAR SEQUENCE : CODELABEL ) ;

   BEGIN
      CODE.NEWLABEL(SEQUENCE)
   END ;

PROCEDURE *FUTURECODELABEL ( VAR SEQUENCE : CODELABEL ) ;

   BEGIN
      CODE.FUTURELABEL(SEQUENCE)
   END ;

PROCEDURE *EXPECTEDCODELABEL ( VAR SEQUENCE : CODELABEL ) ;

   BEGIN
      CODE.EXPECTEDLABEL(SEQUENCE)
   END ;


PROCEDURE *JUMPONFALSE ( VAR DESTINATION : CODELABEL ) ;
   VAR
      BOOLEANENTRY : OPERAND ;
   BEGIN
      IF CODEISTOBEGENERATED THEN
      BEGIN
        STACK.POP(BOOLEANENTRY) ;
        JUMPIF(BOOLEANENTRY,FALSE,DESTINATION) ;
        DISPOSE(BOOLEANENTRY)
      END
   END (* JUMPONFALSE *) ;

PROCEDURE *JUMP ( VAR DESTINATION : CODELABEL ) ;
   BEGIN
      IF CODEISTOBEGENERATED THEN
         CODE.JUMPINS(BRN,0,DESTINATION)
   END (* JUMP *) ;




BEGIN (* GENERATOR INITIALIZATION *)
   LEVEL := GLOBALLEVEL-1 ; LOCALFRAME := NIL ;
   CODEISTOBEGENERATED := TRUE ;

   *** ;

END (*GENERATOR MODULE *) ;
```

With the generator module complete it remains only to provide a suitable codefile module which files the object code produced, and then to assemble the various modules which we have constructed, to produce a complete compiler for Mini-Pascal as we set out to do.

The codefile module used in the final version of the compiler will depend on the conventions for storing object programs in the environment of its use. However, during compiler development and testing, the compiler writer might use a substitute codefile module which collects the object code generated and prints it out at the end of compilation in a form suitable for inspection.

Test 9 shows the complete compiler and a sample of the output which it produces using a code-printing codefile module such as that suggested above.

Test 9

PASCAL PLUS COMPILER

```
 0    3300   PROGRAM MINIPASCALCOMPILER   (INPUT,OUTPUT) ;
 1
 2           ENVELOPE MODULE CODEFILE IN LIBRARY ;
 3
 4    4294   ENVELOPE MODULE SOURCE = LISTING1 IN LIBRARY ;
 5
 6    4636   ENVELOPE MODULE COMPILER ;
 7
 8
 9           TYPE
10             SYMBOLTYPE = (IDENT,INTCONST,CHARCONST,
11                          NOTOP,ANDOP,OROP,
12                          TIMES,DIVOP,PLUS,MINUS,
13                          LTOP,LEOP,GEOP,GTOP,NEOP,EQOP,
14                          RIGHTPARENT,LEFTPARENT,LEFTBRACKET,RIGHTBRACKET,
15                          COMMA,SEMICOLON,PERIOD,COLON,BECOMES,THRU,
16                          PROGRAMSY,VARSY,PROCSY,ARRAYSY,OFSY,
17                          BEGINSY,ENDSY,IFSY,THENSY,ELSESY,WHILESY,DOSY,
18                          READSY,WRITESY,
19                          OTHERSY) ;
20
21               OPTYPE = NOTOP .. EQOP ;
22               IOMODE = (INTEGERMODE,CHARMODE) ;
23
24
25           ENVELOPE MODULE GENERATE = LISTING9 IN LIBRARY ;
26
27    9048   ENVELOPE MODULE ANALYZE = LISTING8 IN LIBRARY ;
28
29
30   12583   BEGIN
31   12583     ANALYZE.PROGRAMME ;
32   12584     ***
33   12587   END  (* COMPILER MODULE *) ;
```

```
34
35
36  12613  BEGIN  END .
```

```
COMPILATION COMPLETE :       NO ERRORS REPORTED
COMPILATION TIME      =   11829 MILLISECONDS
SOURCE PROGRAM        =    4242 LINES
OBJECT PROGRAM        =   12775 WORDS
```

LISTING PRODUCED BY MINI-PASCAL COMPILER MK 1

```
 0   PROGRAM CODE ;
 1   VAR I,J : INTEGER ;
 2       A : ARRAY [1..10] OF CHAR ;
 3   PROCEDURE P ;
 4      VAR J : INTEGER ;
 5      BEGIN
 6         READ(J) ;
 7         I := I+I-I*I DIV I ;
 8         IF J=I THEN A[I]:=' ' ELSE A[I]:='''' ;
 9         WRITE(A[I]) ;
10         I := I+1
11      END ;
12   BEGIN
13      I:= 1 ; J := 1000000 ;
14      WHILE (I>0) AND (I<11) DO P ;
15      WRITE(J)
16   END.
```

COMPILATION COMPLETED : NO ERRORS REPORTED

*** OBJECT CODE GENERATED ***

8	609	LDX	0	609	600	6292019	LDX	3	563
					601	-4181452	LDX	6	564(3)
552	629	LDX	0	629	602	917754	CALL	0	250
					603	-8388045	LDX	4	563
500	630	LDX	0	630	604	-7323647	ADN	4	1
					605	-8256973	STO	4	563
575	6295555	LDX	3	3(1)	606	-6287358	LDX	5	2(1)
576	2240512	STO	1	0(3)	607	2101248	LDX	1	0(1)
577	-6148094	STO	5	2(3)	608	-5341184	EXIT	5	0
578	2097155	LDX	1	3	609	2097652	LDX	1	500
579	7356421	ADN	3	5	610	7344132	LDN	3	4(1)
580	6426627	STO	3	3(1)	611	6426627	STO	3	3(1)
581	917804	CALL	0	300	612	917604	CALL	0	100
582	-4059132	STO	6	4(1)	613	-7340031	LDN	4	1
583	-8388045	LDX	4	563	614	-8256973	STO	4	563
584	-8371661	ADX	4	563	615	4194856	LDX	2	552
585	-6290893	LDX	5	563	616	-8380416	LDX	4	0(2)
586	-5766605	MPX	5	563	617	-8256972	STO	4	564
587	-5668301	DVX	5	563	618	-8355277	NGX	4	563
588	-8339451	SBX	4	5	619	-7667087	BPZ	4	625
589	-8256973	STO	4	563	620	-8388045	LDX	4	563
590	-8384508	LDX	4	4(1)	621	-7290869	SBN	4	11
591	-8338893	SBX	4	563	622	-7667087	BPZ	4	625
592	-7699883	BNZ	4	597	623	-5373377	CALL	5	575
593	-7340016	LDN	4	16	624	983658	BRN		618
594	6292019	LDX	3	563	625	-4193740	LDX	6	564
595	-8244684	STO	4	564(3)	626	917904	CALL	0	400
596	983640	BRN		600	627	917654	CALL	0	150
597	-7340009	LDN	4	23	628	1851392	HALT		0
598	6292019	LDX	3	563	629	1000000	BRN	0	16960
599	-8244684	STO	4	564(3)					

************ END ************

The final compiler is a program of some 4000 lines. It has been developed as a set of modules, each of which deals with a particular aspect of the overall compilation process. Each module has been programmed in isolation from the other modules, so simplifying the programming task at each stage. Whenever possible each module has been tested in isolation, or by its addition to a set of modules already tested, thus simplifying the identification of errors within and between the modules concerned.

Within each module a similar structured approach has been used to simplify the programming task. The stepwise refinement of the code and data structures required leads to a final program which is easy to understand, to debug and to maintain.

The modular structure of the compiler and the logical structure of the code and data within each module are significantly reinforced by the notations of Pascal Plus. However, it is the perception of this structure which is the vital factor in achieving a clear reliable program, not the precise notation used to express it. If the Mini-Pascal compiler demonstrates to its readers that the same approach can be used on other comparable programming projects, then the objective of this text has been achieved.

Exercise 6   (a) Extend the code generator in Listing 9 to produce REAL code for multiple assignment statements, according to the extended interface defined in Exercise 5.

(b) Using only the repertoire of REAL instructions defined in the text, devise a means of checking the array subscripts occurring in Mini-Pascal programs, and modify the generator to produce the code you have chosen.

Section 3

A STRUCTURED OPERATING SYSTEM

In this section structured programming techniques are applied to the construction of an operating system.

The users' view of the operating system and the configuration on which the system is to run are specified in the first chapter, and then the principal components and their interfaces are identified. These components are the processes that run users' jobs and the resources that those processes need. In the second chapter the user processes are programmed and each of the remaining chapters treats the administration of one type of resource: the main store, the processor, the cardreaders, the lineprinters, the typewriters and the file store.

On the whole, simple operating system techniques have been chosen in order to avoid distracting attention from the structural aspects of the design, but the two final chapters show how more complicated algorithms can be incorporated within the structure adopted. Each chapter concludes with a program listing and, taken together, these listings comprise the complete operating system. Several adaptations or extensions of the system have been suggested as exercises.

THE OPERATING SYSTEM SPECIFICATION

Introduction

Purpose

Following Hoare (in Hoare and Perrott (1972), pp. 11–19), we define the purpose of an operating system as being to share the resources of a computer among a number of programs which make unpredictable demands upon those resources.

In a general purpose operating system the resources may include processors, main store, file store, input and output devices—such as cardreaders, lineprinters and typewriters—and "artificial" resources such as a limitation on the number of user programs that may be active at any moment. The users may perhaps be running Fortran programs to solve differential equations, or Cobol programs to process transactions and update master files, or statistical packages to analyze survey results.

A special purpose operating system might be running programs to enable travel agents to book airline seats, or programs to process and display radar signals, or programs to monitor and control the operation of a chemical plant. The resources might be large files of data or radar displays or analog control devices. Such operating systems for computers dedicated to a particular task are called *command and control systems* or, because they have to respond to external events in some limited time, typically of the order of seconds or milliseconds, *real-time systems*.

Objectives

Hoare *(op. cit.)* lists the following objectives that the constructor of an operating system should bear in mind. One important reason for sharing the use of a computer is to make efficient use of its resources, and this should therefore be a primary objective of the operating systems; a corollary of this is that the operating system must not use too much of those resources itself. Another objective of an operating system is reliability, mainly because the effects of a hardware failure or a user-program failure on a shared computer could be many times more serious than on an unshared computer; in addition, the correctness of the operating system is crucial. A further objective of an operating system must be to provide the users with a reasonably predictable service, despite the unpredictability of the demands which they make.

To this list one must add simplicity: without simplicity—of concept, of specification, of design, of implementation and of use—one cannot have a complete understanding of one's system, nor can one exercise complete control over it. To a certain degree these objectives are mutually incompatible and it is more important that none is neglected than that one is fully met at the expense of the others; however, the compulsory and pervasive nature of the use of an operating system imposes upon its constructor the obligation to fulfil each objective to a high degree.

Specification

The specification of an operating system is intimately concerned with the specification of the computer configuration on which it is implemented. With other programs portability or device independence is often deemed a desirable objective and so such programs make as few suppositions as possible about their environment. With an operating system this is not always the case. It is true that sometimes an operating system is designed for use on a number of different configurations, but these configurations must be the same in essentials, and the differences in details can be but limited. For example, one configuration may have an extra cardreader or faster lineprinters or more store, but even here one has to be careful that the balance of the system is not upset. Major differences in configuration, such as whether or not there is a file store, affect the design of the operating system very considerably; the speed of the backing store can dictate whether an interactive system is feasible or whether only batch jobs can be processed. If the operating system provides the user with a "virtual machine" that differs considerably from the "real machine" then this must be the result of a deliberate decision by the system's designer to make some features provided by the hardware unavailable to the user. There is a variety of reasons for taking such a decision: for simplicity, for cheapness, for range compatibility, or to enable jobs to be run on configurations from a variety of manufacturers.

A top-down specification would entail defining the users' views of the system, quantifying the use they will make of the resources and then deducing what hardware is needed to support the system. Often, though, one has to start with the hardware and design in a bottom-up manner. In practice several iterations up and down may be required before one eventually achieves a specification for an operating system that is useful and a configuration that one can afford.

The users' jobs

For the purpose of this book we shall construct a batch-processing system and we shall begin by considering the user's view. Each job is submitted as a deck of cards (or we could equally well use paper tape). The first card of the deck, the title card, not only contains administrative information such as the title of the job and the user's name but also states which library program (either a compiler or a package) is to be invoked. This card is followed by the data, including any program to be compiled, and the deck is terminated by a card beginning with four asterisks.

The system holds a library of programs (compilers and packages) and, on reading a user's job, loads the specified program from the library into main store and begins execution. This program, if part of a multi-pass suite, will generally finish by calling for the next program in the suite to be loaded and run; if the program is a compiler its final act is to call for the newly compiled program to be loaded and run, if no errors have been encountered during compilation. To pass data (or the code of a compiled program) from one program of a suite to the next, an intermediate file is used.

The output from the job is printed on a lineprinter, or we might use a typewriter or even a paper tape or card punch if we chose to abstract away the differences between these peripheral devices.

As an example suppose that we wish to compile a program using a one-pass Mini-Pascal compiler and then run it to process some data; the job would be submitted as the deck of cards shown in Fig. 3.1.

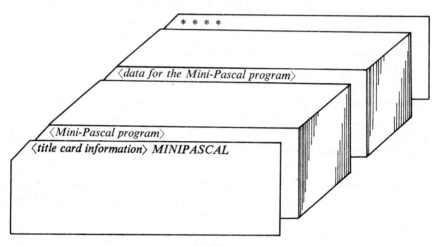

Fig. 3.1

The title card is read and the Mini-Pascal compiler is loaded from the program library into main store and then executed, reading the Mini-Pascal program from the input, translating it, writing the compiled code to the intermediate file, directing the listing and any error reports to the output and, finally, if no errors have been detected, calling for the program in the intermediate file to be loaded. When the compiled Mini-Pascal program has been loaded, it is then run, getting its data from the input and sending its results to the output for printing. When the job has finished execution the intermediate file is deleted.

Another example of a job is that of a user who wishes to call a two-pass package to process some data: the first program of the suite is called PACKAGE99, the second PACKAGE99A. The job would be submitted as shown in Fig. 3.2. The title card is read, PACKAGE99 is loaded into main store and execution commences. Data are read from the input and partially processed, the intermediate results are written to the intermediate file and PACKAGE99 calls for the loading of PACKAGE99A. That program is loaded and runs, taking the partial results from the intermediate file and writing the final results to the output.

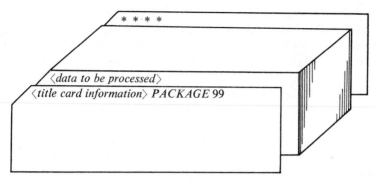

Fig. 3.2

A more complicated use of the intermediate file occurs when it is used by, say, the second program of a three-pass suite to transmit data to the third program while reading data from the first program. If the first program has written blocks b_1 to b_n to the intermediate file, the second program may read these while appending blocks b_{n+1} to b_{n+m} to the file. We shall define the file in such a way that when a block is read from the file that block is deleted and so, when the third program runs, the first block remaining in the file will be block b_{n+1}, blocks b_1 to b_n having been read and deleted by the second program. It is, of course, necessary for the first two programs to agree upon some convention, for example a terminator in block b_n, to ensure that the second program does not try to consume data that it had intended to transmit to the third program!

It is possible for one program to write data to the intermediate file and, later, to read it back, although the principal use of this file is to pass data through a sequence of programs. Usually this sequence is limited either to a single or multi-pass compile-and-run sequence or to a single or multi-pass package: in each case each program in the suite explicitly names its successor if it has one; it is, of course, possible for the user's own program to name as its successor some library program, say a report writer, for which it has generated data in the intermediate file.

The configuration

In order to specify a suitable configuration we must know something of the use that jobs will make of the various resources of the system. For our purposes we shall assume the average job has 500 cards of input, generates 1000 lines of output and occupies 100 000 characters of main store for about a minute, slightly over half that time being used for data transfers (program loading, and input and output of data) and rather less than half a minute being spent in processing.

To keep a single processor busy we should have sufficient main store to hold two programs simultaneously, thereby processing an average of two jobs a minute. We must therefore have sufficient capacity to process 1000 lines of input and 2000 lines of output each minute. A configuration of one processor, 256K characters of main store (to hold two 100K-character programs and a 56K-character operating system), two 500 cards-per-minute cardreaders and two 1000 lines-per-minute lineprinters should be reasonably well balanced. This balance may be upset if too many jobs depart significantly from the average, but we shall assume here that this happens sufficiently infrequently to be acceptable and to make it unnecessary to spend more on a larger configuration to iron out fluctuations in the characteristics of jobs. Similarly, we shall assume that a rate of two jobs a minute is sufficient to prevent large queues building up during normal peaks.

We shall, however, need further equipment. To enable operators and operating system to communicate we shall provide a typewriter or, better still, two, as the typewriter is necessary but slow and not altogether reliable. To store a library of compilers and packages we shall provide some sort of file store; this will also be used for holding the intermediate file of each job being run. We shall also use the file store for spooling each job's input and output. This entails running each job in three stages: first the input is copied from the reader to a *spooled input file*; then the programs that constitute the job are executed, obtaining their input from this file and directing their output to a *spooled output file*; and finally this output is copied from file to printer. Spooling is used to decouple the job's input, execution and output from one another, thereby avoiding the expensive delays that would otherwise result from the differences in speed of these three operations. Spooling enables each peripheral device to run at full speed, thereby contributing not only to its efficiency but also to its reliability. Spooling also makes the system less susceptible to peripheral failure and avoids processing being delayed while the cardreaders' hoppers and the lineprinters' supplies of paper are being replenished.

Let us suppose that, for the system we are postulating, we shall have perhaps twenty library files, each of 100K characters, two intermediate files of say 100K characters, and some number of users' jobs, each with an input file of about 40K characters (or 20K characters if packed to suppress leading and trailing spaces) and an output file of 120K characters (or 60K characters if packed), although if, as with intermediate files, we delete records as they are read we shall not need both a full input file and a full output file simultaneously.

The number of users' jobs in the system at any moment must exceed six if we are to keep both readers and both printers busy as well as execute two programs and also iron out fluctuations in the demand for those resources—

twelve should be adequate; we may thus expect a turnround time of about five minutes per job. A standard exchangeable disk pack with 200 cylinders of 10 tracks of 3K characters would thus be half used. Many files, of course, will be much smaller than those we have postulated but we should also cater for larger data files of up to, say, 500K characters. Since the disk store is unlikely to be fully used we shall not pack the data since such an operation is expensive.

We shall update the library off-line and, because the users have no permanent files, we do not need to cater for the dumping and restoration of files to guard against corruption. In the case of a breakdown we shall simply restart the system, reloading the library first if necessary, and accept the loss of all the jobs that were in the system at the time of failure.

Although we have a specific configuration we shall design the operating system in such a way that it will be easily adaptable to slightly different configurations. For instance it should be able to accommodate three slower printers instead of two fast ones, or to support just one typewriter, or to run three programs simultaneously rather than two, or to work with paper-tape readers rather than cardreaders. However, some other changes would entail more drastic alterations: the introduction of permanent files that a user could keep from one job to another, the introduction of a multiple-access service with several users running their programs interactively from typewriter or display terminals, or the introduction of a dynamic storage allocation scheme such as paging.

Structure

The user processes

The principal component of the operating system is a Pascal Plus **process**, of which we shall declare twelve instances, to run a succession of users' jobs. Running a job entails reading the job's title card from the spooled input, loading the appropriate library program into main store and executing that program. Execution involves supplying the program with data from the spooled input, directing results to the spooled output, supplying blocks from and directing blocks to the intermediate file, and loading further programs from the library or the intermediate file. The skeletal form of the process is as follows.

```
process userprocess ;
  procedure runuserjob ;
    begin
      {read title card from spooled cardreader} ;
      repeat
```

```
        {load program} ;
        {run program ; i.e. execute the instructions in sequence,
        with the supervisor calls (i.e. calls upon the operating
        system), such as 'read a card', 'print a line', 'input a
        block' and 'output a block', being translated into corresponding
        operations on the spooled input file, the spooled output file
        and the intermediate file ; this continues until the supervisor
        call 'finish' or 'load and run next program' is
        encountered or until the program fails}
      until { job finished}
    end ;
    begin while {system switched on} do runuserjob end ;
    instance user : array [1 .. 12] of userprocess
```

The resources

To run a user's job the process requires the use of various resources. Each of these resources we shall represent by a Pascal Plus **envelope**, each instance of which provides its user with a "virtual resource" and maps that virtual resource onto the corresponding real resource. The real resources have to be shared among many users and so we shall represent each type of real resource by a **monitor module** in Pascal Plus. For example to administer a pool of fifty buffers we might declare a monitor module called *pool* containing:

(a) a scheduler to keep track of which of the fifty buffers are available for use;
(b) fifty controllers, one to control the use of each buffer; and
(c) an envelope, called *buffer*, each instance of which would provide its user with a virtual buffer on which operations such as *read* and *write* would be defined.

The outline of the *pool* monitor is given below.

```
    monitor module pool ;
      monitor module buffer scheduler ;
        {records availability of buffers and provides two
         procedures, 'acquire' and 'release'} ;
      monitor controller ;
        {owns a buffer and provides procedures
         to 'read' and 'write' data} ;
      instance buffercontroller : array [1 .. 50] of controller ;
      envelope *buffer ;
        {records which buffer is being used} ;
```

```
      procedure *read (. . .) ;
        {calls 'read' procedure of appropriate controller} ;
      procedure *write (. . .) ;
        {calls 'write' procedure of appropriate controller} ;
      begin
        {call 'acquire' procedure of scheduler} ;
        *** ;
        {call 'release' procedure of scheduler}
      end ;
   begin
      ***
   end
```

When an instance of the *buffer* envelope is declared, as in the example below, the body of the envelope is executed: it begins by invoking the scheduler to acquire permission to use one of the fifty buffers and, when this is granted, it records which buffer it is to use. The user of the virtual buffer then continues (to execute the body of the procedure *P*) and from time to time carries out *read* and *write* operations on the virtual buffer: these the envelope transforms into corresponding operations on the real buffer that it has been allocated. Eventually, when the virtual buffer is no longer required (on exit from the procedure *P*), the envelope returns the real buffer to the scheduler.

```
   procedure P ;
     instance B : pool.buffer ;
     begin
       B.write (. . .)
       :
       B.read (. . .)
     end
```

The system

Before considering the details of the resource administration monitors we shall outline the structure of the entire operating system. This consists not only of the several instances of *userprocess* but also one monitor module to administer each type of resource and, in general, each will have much the same structure as the *pool* monitor, namely a scheduler, one controller per resource of that type, and an envelope presenting the user with a virtual resource. Two points should be made about the structure. Firstly, each controller is represented by a monitor despite the fact that usually (but not always) the scheduler will have ensured that only one process at a time has permission to use that controller—the Pascal Plus compiler cannot tell that the controller is being used in such a disciplined manner, although an implementation in some other language might take advantage of such knowledge. Secondly, although the *mainstore* monitor and all the other resource administration monitors are *designed* in this way, the *mainstore* monitor in particular will be *implemented* very differently: the frequency with which main store is accessed dictates that the mapping of an operation on a virtual address into an operation on a real address must be very fast and must be accomplished by special-purpose hardware—this matter is dealt with more fully in a later chapter.

The outline structure of the complete system is as follows.

```
program operating system ;
  monitor module processor ;
    . . . . . . ;
  monitor module mainstore ;
    . . . . . . ;
  monitor module typewriter ;
    . . . . . . ;
  monitor module filestore ;
    . . . . . . ;
  monitor module cardreader ;
    . . . . . . ;
  monitor module lineprinter ;
    . . . . . . ;
  process userprocess ;
    procedure runuserjob ;
      {declare instances of the virtual resource envelopes needed—
       these, together, constitute the virtual machine in which
       the user's job is run} ;
      begin
        {read title card} ;
        repeat
          {load program} ;
          {run program}
        until {job finished}
      end ;
    begin
      while {system switched on} do runuserjob
    end ;
  instance user : array [1 . . maxuser] of userprocess ;
  begin
    ***
  end.
```

Interfaces

The main store

In order to consider the detailed design of the user process and of each resource administration monitor it is necessary to define the exact interface between the process and each monitor. The main store is essentially a pool of two partitions and its interface is thus similar to that of the buffer pool that we have already outlined: the monitor *mainstore* provides the user with an envelope called *store* which makes available a partition of some agreed size and also makes available procedures to *read* data from and *write* data to the store in some agreed units. We shall assume that the store is to be considered as a linear array of some agreed number of characters (100K in our case), each identified by an address ranging from zero upwards. So the *mainstore* monitor provides the user with a constant, *maxchar* = 102399, and a type, *address* = 0 .. *maxchar*. The complete interface is summarized below.

> **monitor module** *mainstore*
> **const** *maxchar = 102399 {100*K characters per virtual store*}
> **type** *address = 0 .. *maxchar*
> **envelope** *store
>   **procedure** *read (*address* ; **var** *char*)
>   **procedure** *write (*address* ; *char*)

If we made three partitions of store available to users there would be no need to change this interface, but if we were to allow each user to specify the size of his partition we should have to add a parameter to *store* and so such a change would affect the user as well as this monitor.

The processor

Processor time is a resource that has to be shared: we must ensure that no process monopolizes the use of a processor to the exclusion of others for an unduly long time. We shall assume that while a process is performing supervisory functions (in other words it is not executing some user's program) it uses the processor for only a short time before relinquishing it: this is a reasonable assumption since such supervisory functions are almost exclusively concerned with initiating or servicing input and output operations. Furthermore we shall assume that the time thus spent processing is small compared with the time spent waiting for data transfers to be completed and so the processing load will be small. These assumptions enable us to exclude "supervisory processing" from the scheduling of the processor (or processors) and so we concern ourselves with just the "user processing".

Some user programs will do little processing and will be "peripheral bound" while others will do much processing and can be said to be "processor bound"; still others will fall between these two categories or their characteristics will fluctuate. As a general rule a peripheral bound program should be given the use of a processor when it wants one in order to keep its peripheral devices busy and because it will not monopolize the processor for long. Processor bound jobs, though, must not in consequence be starved of processor time. As the characteristics of user programs are not known in advance, and may change, it is necessary to detect their characteristics at run time and adjust the scheduling of the processor accordingly.

Thus each user process that has acquired a partition of main store, and is ready to begin running a user's program, declares an instance of the *cpu* envelope of the processor administration monitor. This envelope keeps an account of the program's use of the processor and provides a procedure, *timeslice*, which the user invokes before embarking on each "slice" of, say, 100 ms of processing. The effect of this procedure is to update the account and, possibly, to delay the program if some other program with a better claim is waiting for the processor. In this way no program can monopolize a processor for more than 100 ms, and a program that has been progressing slowly is given the chance to catch up. The interface with the *processor* monitor is as follows:

> **monitor module** *processor*
> **const** **slice* = 100 *{milliseconds}*
> **envelope** **cpu*
> **procedure** **timeslice*

Increasing the number of processors would not alter this interface, but each program would more speedily be granted permission to embark on its next timeslice. Changing the scheduling algorithm would, likewise, alter the relative speeds at which programs are run but would not alter the logical interface. Allowing different programs to have timeslices of differing lengths would entail adding a parameter to *cpu* or to *timeslice* and would therefore necessitate a change to the user process.

The lineprinters

A virtual lineprinter should provide its user with procedures to print a line and to throw to a new line or a new page; depending on the type of printer used other control operations such as vertical tabulation may also be available but we shall not provide these. The interface is quite a simple one, complicated only by the need to cater for the failure of a data transfer: we introduce a type, *status*, with two values, *success* and *failure*.

```
monitor module lineprinter
  const *maxchar = 120 {characters per line}
  type
    *line = packed array [1 . . maxchar] of char
    *status = (*success, *failure)
  envelope *printer
    var *result : status
    procedure *print (line)
    procedure *newline
    procedure *newpage
```

The cardreaders

The cardreader envelope is similar in form to that of the lineprinter but here the type *status* has three values, *success, failure* and also *endoffile* to indicate that the four-star terminator has been read.

```
monitor module cardreader
  const *maxchar = 80 {characters per card}
  type
    *card = packed array [1 . . maxchar] of char
    *status = (*success, *failure, *endoffile)
  envelope *reader
    var *result : status
    procedure *read (var card )
```

The typewriters

A typewriter, or alternatively a keyboard with a character display, is necessary to enable an operator to converse with some process in the computer. Each typewriter may be used for a variety of conversations and so the printed (or displayed) record of each conversation should be prefaced by a name to enable the operator to distinguish easily between one conversation and the next and to know for sure with which process he is conversing.

More often than not a conversation will be "outgoing" in that it will be initiated by some process to inform the operator of, say, a fault on a peripheral device. Occasionally "incoming" conversations will be required: here some process waits for the operator to initiate a conversation; for example the operating system may have a number of small service processes which wait to be interrogated by the operator when he wants, say, a list of the jobs currently being run; another example of an incoming conversation is to be found after the operator has been unable to reply to a question during an earlier conversation: on his typing "WAIT" the process with which he was conversing would have released the typewriter and then waited for him to restart the interrupted conversation later, possibly on another typewriter.

Thus the envelope that provides the user with a virtual typewriter must take two parameters: one is the name of the conversation and the other specifies whether the conversation is to be incoming or outgoing. The envelope then makes available procedures to read a message, to print a message, and to throw to a new line. The interface, with the necessary constants and types, is given below.

```
monitor module typewriter
    const
        *maxname = 4 {characters per name}
        *maxchar = 36 {characters per message}
    type
        *name = packed array [1 .. maxname] of char
        *typeofconversation = (*outgoing, *incoming)
        *message = record
                        *length: 0 .. maxchar ;
                        *text: packed array [1 .. maxchar] of char
                    end
        *status = (*success, *failure)
    envelope *conversation (name, typeofconversation)
        var *result: status
        procedure *read (var message)
        procedure *print (message)
        procedure *newline
```

The *result* value made available by the envelope is to inform the user whether the data transfer was successful or not.

The file store

The file store is unusual in that the "virtual filestore", or file, that we wish to provide looks very different from the disk store onto which we must map it. For spooling and for intermediate files we wish to provide a sequence of blocks of some fixed length and two procedures, one to read a block from the head of the sequence (and free the space it occupied on disk), and the other to write a block to the tail of the sequence. The way in which these files will be implemented will be described later, but for the moment we may work with the following interface.

monitor module *filestore*
const
 *maxchar = 1023 {*1K characters per block*}
 *maxblock = 500 {*blocks per file*}
type
 *block = **packed array** [0 . . *maxchar*] **of** *char*
 *status = (**success*, **endoffile*)
envelope **file*
 var **result*: *status*
 procedure **write* (*block*)
 procedure **read* (**var** *block*)

Receipt of the status value *endoffile* on reading means that the file was empty, while on writing it means that the file was full (500 blocks of 1K characters in this case). We do not provide a status value *failure* since we shall not attempt to recover from a fault on the disk store; the operating system cannot function while the file store is out of action.

We have also to cater for library files: these differ from the spooled and intermediate files in that they can only be read, not written, and blocks that are read must of course remain on the disk. We therefore provide a second envelope, *libraryfile*, which takes as a parameter the name of the library file—we extend *status* with an extra value *nofile* to cope with attempts to read from non-existent files. We therefore extend the file store interface with the following definitions.

 const **maxname* = 12 {*characters per filename*}
 type
  *status = (**success*, **endoffile*, **nofile*)
  *filename = **packed array** [1 . . *maxname*] **of** *char*
 envelope **libraryfile* (*filename*)
  var **result*: *status*
  procedure **read* (**var** *block*)

This demonstrates that virtual resources of several different types may be mapped onto the real resources of a single type. Indeed, in a more elaborate system we might wish to provide users with envelopes representing sequential files, indexed sequential files and random access files.

Summary
Listing 1 summarizes the complete operating system: it contains one monitor module to administer each type of resource and then the definition of *userprocess*, of which twelve instances are declared. When the operating system begins execution the monitors are initialized and then the twelve user processes are initiated.

Having defined this structure we may now proceed to program, in any order, these monitors and the *userprocess*; in doing so we may well find that we introduce some extra processes to handle peripheral devices, and also some minor service processes and monitors to enable the operator to exercise some control over the system, for example to permit him to stop the user processes in an orderly fashion at the end of the day: this particular monitor, called *switch*, is mentioned in Listing 1 and described in more detail in the next chapter.

Listing 1

```
PROGRAM OPERATINGSYSTEM;

CONST
    MAXUSER = 12 (*USER PROCESSES*);

MONITOR MODULE PROCESSOR = LIST10 IN LIBRARY;
    (*   CONST                                                    *)
    (*      *SLICE = 100 MILLISECONDS                             *)
    (*   ENVELOPE *CPU                                            *)
    (*      PROCEDURE *TIMESLICE                                  *)

MONITOR MODULE MAINSTORE = LIST9 IN LIBRARY;
    (*   CONST                                                    *)
    (*      *MAXCHAR = 102399 I.E. 100K CHARS PER VIRTUAL STORE   *)
    (*   TYPE                                                     *)
    (*      *ADDRESS = 0..MAXCHAR                                 *)
    (*   ENVELOPE *STORE                                          *)
    (*      PROCEDURE *READ (ADDRESS; VAR CHAR)                   *)
    (*      PROCEDURE *WRITE (ADDRESS; CHAR)                      *)

MONITOR MODULE TYPEWRITER = LIST13 IN LIBRARY;
    (*   CONST                                                    *)
    (*      *MAXNAME = 4 CHARACTERS PER NAME                      *)
    (*      *MAXCHAR = 36 CHARACTERS PER MESSAGE                  *)
    (*   TYPE                                                     *)
    (*      *NAME = PACKED ARRAY [1..MAXNAME] OF CHAR             *)
    (*      *TYPEOFCONVERSATION = ( *OUTGOING, *INCOMING )        *)
    (*      *MESSAGE = RECORD                                     *)
    (*               *LENGTH: 0..MAXCHAR;                         *)
    (*               *TEXT: PACKED ARRAY [1..MAXCHAR] OF CHAR     *)
    (*           END                                             *)
    (*      *STATUS = ( *SUCCESS, *FAILURE )                      *)
    (*   ENVELOPE *CONVERSATION (NAME; TYPEOFCONVERSATION)        *)
    (*      VAR *RESULT: STATUS                                   *)
    (*      PROCEDURE *READ (VAR MESSAGE)                         *)
    (*      PROCEDURE *PRINT (MESSAGE)                            *)
    (*      PROCEDURE *NEWLINE                                    *)

MONITOR MODULE CARDREADER = LIST11 IN LIBRARY;
    (*   CONST                                                    *)
    (*      *MAXCHAR = 80 CHARACTERS PER CARD                     *)
    (*   TYPE                                                     *)
    (*      *CARD = PACKED ARRAY [1..MAXCHAR] OF CHAR             *)
    (*      *STATUS = ( *SUCCESS, *FAILURE, *ENDOFFILE )          *)
    (*   ENVELOPE *READER                                         *)
    (*      VAR *RESULT: STATUS                                   *)
    (*      PROCEDURE *READ (VAR CARD)                            *)
```

```
MONITOR MODULE LINEPRINTER = LIST12 IN LIBRARY;
   (*   CONST                                                    *)
   (*      *MAXCHAR = 120 CHARACTERS PER LINE                    *)
   (*   TYPE                                                     *)
   (*      *LINE = PACKED ARRAY [1..MAXCHAR] OF CHAR             *)
   (*      *STATUS = ( *SUCCESS, *FAILURE )                      *)
   (*   ENVELOPE *PRINTER                                        *)
   (*      VAR *RESULT: STATUS                                   *)
   (*      PROCEDURE *PRINT (LINE)                               *)
   (*      PROCEDURE *NEWLINE                                    *)
   (*      PROCEDURE *NEWPAGE                                    *)

MONITOR MODULE FILESTORE = LIST20 IN LIBRARY;
   (*   CONST                                                    *)
   (*      *MAXCHAR = 1023 I.E. 1K CHARACTERS PER BLOCK          *)
   (*      *MAXBLOCK = 500 BLOCKS PER FILE                       *)
   (*      *MAXNAME = 12 CHARACTERS PER FILENAME                 *)
   (*   TYPE                                                     *)
   (*      *BLOCK = PACKED ARRAY [0..MAXCHAR] OF CHAR            *)
   (*      *STATUS = ( *SUCCESS, *ENDOFFILE, *NOFILE )           *)
   (*      *FILENAME = PACKED ARRAY [1..MAXNAME] OF CHAR         *)
   (*   ENVELOPE *FILE                                           *)
   (*      VAR *RESULT: STATUS                                   *)
   (*      PROCEDURE *WRITE (BLOCK)                              *)
   (*      PROCEDURE *READ (VAR BLOCK)                           *)
   (*   ENVELOPE *LIBRARYFILE (FILENAME)                         *)
   (*      VAR *RESULT: STATUS                                   *)
   (*      PROCEDURE *READ (VAR BLOCK)                           *)

MONITOR MODULE SWITCH = LIST2 IN LIBRARY;
   (*   FUNCTION *ON: BOOLEAN                                    *)

PROCESS USERPROCESS = LIST8 IN LIBRARY;
   (*   PROCEDURE RUNUSERJOB                                     *)
   (*      *** DECLARE INSTANCES OF THE VIRTUAL RESOURCE ***     *)
   (*      *** ENVELOPES NEEDED - THESE, TOGETHER, CONSTITUTE *** *)
   (*      *** THE VIRTUAL MACHINE IN WHICH THE USER'S JOB IS *** *)
   (*      *** RUN.                                          *** *)
   (*      BEGIN                                                 *)
   (*         READ TITLE CARD;                                   *)
   (*         REPEAT                                             *)
   (*            LOAD PROGRAM;                                   *)
   (*            RUN PROGRAM                                     *)
   (*         UNTIL JOB FINISHED                                 *)
   (*      END;                                                  *)
   (*   BEGIN                                                    *)
   (*      WHILE SWITCH.ON DO RUNUSERJOB                         *)
   (*   END                                                      *)

INSTANCE
   USER: ARRAY [1..MAXUSER] OF USERPROCESS;

BEGIN
   ***
END.
```

THE USER PROCESS

System Termination

The *userprocess* executes a succession of jobs. As we have seen, its outline form is as follows.

```
process userprocess ;
   procedure runuserjob ;
   begin
      {read title card} ;
      repeat
         {load program} ;
         {run program}
      until {job finished}
   end ;
   begin
      while {system switched on} do runuserjob
   end
```

Let us start by considering the body of the process: it is a loop that should be executed repeatedly until the operator indicates that the system should close down. We therefore introduce a monitor that records whether or not the system is operational. In it we have a process that waits for the operator to stop the system, flags the system as switched off, waits for all the user processes to terminate, and tells the operator that the system has stopped. Listing 2 shows the complete *switch* monitor together with its local *stopper* process and the Boolean function *on* which is invoked by the user processes.

In Pascal string constants must be of the correct length but, for clarity, we have suppressed trailing spaces.

The *stopper* process's two procedures, *waitforoperator* and *telloperator*, illustrate well how the declaration of an envelope instance is used to acquire (and implicitly release) a virtual resource: here the resource is a typewriter used, in one case, for a simple incoming conversation initiated by the operator and, in the other case, for a simple outgoing conversation initiated by the *stopper* process.

Note that we have assumed that disk faults never occur: the entire system relies heavily upon the availability of the file store. Persistent typewriter faults are treated lightly: we can often afford to overlook them, as in the program above. Naturally if all the typewriters or all the cardreaders or all the lineprinters are out of action the system cannot do any useful work: it will merely wait for a peripheral device of the appropriate type to be repaired and returned to use.

Listing 2

```
MONITOR MODULE SWITCH;

   VAR
      OPERATIVE: BOOLEAN;
      STOPCOUNT: 0..MAXUSER;

   INSTANCE
      STOPPED: CONDITION;

   FUNCTION *ON: BOOLEAN;
      BEGIN
         ON:= OPERATIVE;
         IF NOT OPERATIVE THEN
            BEGIN
               STOPCOUNT:= STOPCOUNT + 1;
               IF STOPCOUNT = MAXUSER THEN STOPPED.SIGNAL
            END
      END;

   PROCEDURE SWITCHOFF;
      BEGIN
         OPERATIVE:= FALSE;
         STOPCOUNT:= 0;
         STOPPED.WAIT
      END;

   PROCESS MODULE STOPPER;
      PROCEDURE WAITFOROPERATOR;
         VAR
            M: TYPEWRITER.MESSAGE;
         INSTANCE
            OPERATOR: TYPEWRITER.CONVERSATION
                                  ('STOP', TYPEWRITER.INCOMING);
         BEGIN
            M.LENGTH:= 3;  M.TEXT:= 'OK.';
            OPERATOR.PRINT(M)
         END;
      PROCEDURE TELLOPERATOR;
         VAR
            M: TYPEWRITER.MESSAGE;
         INSTANCE
            OPERATOR: TYPEWRITER.CONVERSATION
                                  ('STOP', TYPEWRITER.OUTGOING);
         BEGIN
            M.LENGTH:= 15;  M.TEXT:= 'SYSTEM STOPPED.';
            OPERATOR.PRINT(M)
         END;
      BEGIN
         WAITFOROPERATOR;
         SWITCHOFF;
         TELLOPERATOR
      END;

   BEGIN
      OPERATIVE:= TRUE;
      ***
   END;
```

Spooling

On entry to the procedure *runuserjob* we must acquire certain resources which are needed to execute the several programs that constitute a job. So at the head of the procedure we would declare the following envelope instances were we not spooling the input and output.

> **instance**
> *printer*: *lineprinter.printer*;
> *reader*: *cardreader.reader*;
> *intermediate*: *filestore.file*;
> *store*: *mainstore.store*;
> *cpu*: *processor.cpu*

However, as we wish to spool the input we shall replace

instance *reader*: *cardreader.reader*

by

> **envelope module** *reader* ;
> **var** **result*: *cardreader.status*;
> **instance** *cardfile*: *filestore.file*;
> **procedure** *spoolinput*;
>   **instance** *reader*: *cardreader.reader*;
>   **begin**
>   {*block together cards from 'reader' and write them to 'cardfile'*}
>   **end**;
> **procedure** **read* (**var** *c*:*cardreader.card*);
>   **begin**
>   {*unblock a card from 'cardfile' and assign it to 'c'*}
>   **end**;
> **begin**
>   *spoolinput*;
>   ***
> **end**

and, to spool the output, we replace

instance *printer*: *lineprinter.printer*

by

> **envelope module** *printer*;
> **var** **result*: *lineprinter.status*;
> **instance** *linefile*: *filestore.file*;
> **procedure** **print* (*l*: *lineprinter.line*);

```
begin
    {block line 'l' for writing to 'linefile'}
end;
procedure *newline;
    begin
        {block newline control character for writing to 'linefile'}
    end;
procedure *newpage;
    begin
        {block newpage control character for writing to 'linefile'}
    end;
procedure spooloutput;
    instance printer: lineprinter.printer;
    begin
        {unblock lines and control characters from 'linefile' and write
        them to 'printer'}
    end;
begin
    ***;
    spooloutput
end
```

Input

The spooled reader envelope presents us with exactly the same interface as does the virtual cardreader, but does so in a different way. It declares an instance of a file and into this it copies the data which it reads from a cardreader. Having done this it releases the cardreader and makes the data available to the user, card by card, from the file. The complete module is shown in Listing 3. As each card is written to the file it is preceded by a control character 'X' and the end-of-file marker is written as the character 'Z'.

Listing 3, although basically simple, is complicated by the details of blocking and unblocking card images and by the need to check for, report, and recover from, failures. The program caters for two types of failure that may occur when the cards are being spooled in: either an attempt to read a card may fail or there may be too many cards to be held in the file. In either case a *report failure* procedure is called with the appropriate string parameter: either 'FAULTY CARDREADER' or 'TOO MANY CARDS'. However, the report, if it is to mean anything to the operator, or to the user who submitted the job, must identify the job to which it relates. We assume that the title card of each deck of cards contains the user's name (in the first twelve columns) and the job's name (in the next twelve columns) in addition to such

Listing 3

```
ENVELOPE MODULE READER;

    VAR
        *RESULT: CARDREADER.STATUS;
        B: FILESTORE.BLOCK;
        J: 0..FILESTORE.MAXCHAR;
        OK: BOOLEAN;

    INSTANCE
        CARDFILE:FILESTORE.FILE;

    PROCEDURE SPOOLINPUT;
        LABEL 9;
        VAR
            C: CARDREADER.CARD;
            USERNAME,
            JOBNAME: PACKED ARRAY [1..MAXNAME] OF CHAR;
            M1, M2: TYPEWRITER.MESSAGE;
        INSTANCE
            READER: CARDREADER.READER;
        PROCEDURE REPORTFAILURE (FAULT: TYPEWRITER.MESSAGE);
            VAR
                M: TYPEWRITER.MESSAGE;
            INSTANCE
                OPERATOR: TYPEWRITER.CONVERSATION
                                       ('USER', TYPEWRITER.OUTGOING);
            BEGIN
                M.TEXT[1..MAXNAME]:= USERNAME;
                M.TEXT[MAXNAME+1..MAXNAME+3]:= ' - ';
                M.TEXT[MAXNAME+4..MAXNAME+FAULT.LENGTH+3]:= FAULT.TEXT;
                M.LENGTH:= MAXNAME+FAULT.LENGTH+3;
                OPERATOR.PRINT(M);
                M.TEXT[1..9]:= ' FOR JOB ';
                M.TEXT[10..MAXNAME+9]:= JOBNAME;
                M.LENGTH:= MAXNAME+9;
                OPERATOR.PRINT(M)
            END;
        BEGIN
            M1.LENGTH:= 17;  M1.TEXT:= 'FAULTY CARDREADER';
            M2.LENGTH:= 14;  M2.TEXT:= 'TOO MANY CARDS';
            READER.READ(C);
            USERNAME:= C[1..MAXNAME];
            JOBNAME:= C[MAXNAME+1..2*MAXNAME];
            J:= 0;
            WHILE READER.RESULT = CARDREADER.SUCCESS DO
                BEGIN
                    B[J]:= 'X';  J:= (J+1) MOD (FILESTORE.MAXCHAR+1);
                    IF J = 0 THEN
                        BEGIN
                            CARDFILE.WRITE(B);
                            IF CARDFILE.RESULT <> FILESTORE.SUCCESS THEN GOTO 9
                        END;
                    IF J+CARDREADER.MAXCHAR-1 <= FILESTORE.MAXCHAR
                    THEN B[J..J+CARDREADER.MAXCHAR-1]:= C
                    ELSE
```

```
        BEGIN
           B[J..FILESTORE.MAXCHAR]:=
                               C[1..FILESTORE.MAXCHAR-J+1];
           CARDFILE.WRITE(B);
           IF CARDFILE.RESULT<>FILESTORE.SUCCESS THEN GOTO 9;
           B[0..J-FILESTORE.MAXCHAR+CARDREADER.MAXCHAR-2]:=
                   C[FILESTORE.MAXCHAR-J+2..CARDREADER.MAXCHAR]
        END;
        J:= (J+CARDREADER.MAXCHAR) MOD (FILESTORE.MAXCHAR+1);
        READER.READ(C)
     END;
    IF READER.RESULT = CARDREADER.ENDOFFILE THEN
       BEGIN B[J]:= 'Z';  CARDFILE.WRITE(B) END;
    IF READER.RESULT = CARDREADER.FAILURE THEN REPORTFAILURE(M1);
  9: IF CARDFILE.RESULT=FILESTORE.ENDOFFILE THEN REPORTFAILURE(M2);
    OK:= (CARDFILE.RESULT = FILESTORE.SUCCESS) AND
                         (READER.RESULT = CARDREADER.ENDOFFILE)
  END;

PROCEDURE *READ (VAR C: CARDREADER.CARD);
   LABEL 9;
   BEGIN
     IF CARDFILE.RESULT = FILESTORE.ENDOFFILE THEN GOTO 9;
     IF B[J] = 'Z' THEN RESULT:= CARDREADER.ENDOFFILE ELSE
        BEGIN
           RESULT:= CARDREADER.SUCCESS;
           J:= (J+1) MOD (FILESTORE.MAXCHAR+1);
           IF J = 0 THEN
              BEGIN
                 CARDFILE.READ(B);
                 IF CARDFILE.RESULT=FILESTORE.ENDOFFILE THEN GOTO 9
              END;
           IF J+CARDREADER.MAXCHAR-1 <= FILESTORE.MAXCHAR
           THEN C:= B[J..J+CARDREADER.MAXCHAR-1]
           ELSE
              BEGIN
                 C[1..FILESTORE.MAXCHAR-J+1]:=
                                   B[J..FILESTORE.MAXCHAR];
                 CARDFILE.READ(B);
                 IF CARDFILE.RESULT=FILESTORE.ENDOFFILE THEN GOTO 9;
                 C[FILESTORE.MAXCHAR-J+2..CARDREADER.MAXCHAR]:=
                       B[0..J-FILESTORE.MAXCHAR+CARDREADER.MAXCHAR-2]
              END;
           J:= (J+CARDREADER.MAXCHAR) MOD (FILESTORE.MAXCHAR+1)
        END;
     9: IF CARDFILE.RESULT = FILESTORE.ENDOFFILE THEN
           RESULT:= CARDREADER.FAILURE
   END;

BEGIN
   SPOOLINPUT;
   IF OK THEN
      BEGIN
         CARDFILE.READ(B);  J:= 0;  RESULT:= CARDREADER.SUCCESS;
         ***
      END
END;
```

information as the name of the library program to be run. The lengths of these names (twelve characters) will be denoted by a constant, *maxname*, declared local to the procedure *runuserjob*.

We shall assume that the *cardreader* monitor will indicate a reader failure only if attempts to rectify the fault have failed; and we shall assume also that the first card—the title card—of each deck of cards will be read without mishap; and furthermore we shall assume that any unread cards at the end of a deck will be skipped before another job tries to use the cardreader. These assumptions we shall justify when we program the *cardreader* monitor.

The manipulation of text is clumsy in Pascal. Here, for legibility, we have used subarray assignments such as

$$m.text[1 \ .. \ maxname] := username$$
$$c := b[j \ .. \ j + cardreader.maxchar - 1]$$

but, before compiling the operating system, we have to rewrite these as loops of character assignments such as

for $i := 1$ **to** *maxname* **do** $m.text[i] := username[i]$

and this tends to be expensive unless the compiler is clever enough both to avoid recalculating the array subscripts and also to make use of whatever multi-character assignment operations are provided by the hardware. Short of adding subarray operations to Pascal, the best solution is to program the text manipulation in machine code.

Another deliberate departure from what is generally considered to be good programming practice is the use of **goto** statements to exit prematurely from a piece of program on detecting a failure. The alternative is to lard the program with tests to determine whether the "success" path or the "failure" path should be followed. This alternative is expensive since, one hopes, failures will only very occasionally arise; it also makes the program longer and more difficult to read.

Output

The development of the spooled printer envelope parallels that of the spooled reader envelope. A file is used to hold the output which is subsequently written to a lineprinter. The complete envelope module is shown in Listing 4. Each line written to the file is prefixed by the control character 'X', *newline* and *newpage* are represented by 'L' and 'P' respectively, and the end-of-file marker is denoted by 'Z'. We use the same abbreviated notation for character manipulation as we did in Listing 3, and also we handle failures in much the same way.

Listing 4

```
ENVELOPE MODULE PRINTER;

   VAR
      *RESULT: LINEPRINTER.STATUS;
      B: FILESTORE.BLOCK;
      J: FILESTORE.MAXCHAR;

   INSTANCE
      LINEFILE: FILESTORE.FILE;

   PROCEDURE *PRINT (L: LINEPRINTER.LINE);
      LABEL 9;
      BEGIN
         IF LINEFILE.RESULT = FILESTORE.ENDOFFILE THEN GOTO 9;
         B[J]:= 'X';   J:= (J+1) MOD (FILESTORE.MAXCHAR+1);
         IF J = 0 THEN
            BEGIN
               LINEFILE.WRITE(B);
               IF LINEFILE.RESULT = FILESTORE.ENDOFFILE THEN GOTO 9
            END;
         IF J+LINEPRINTER.MAXCHAR-1 <= FILESTORE.MAXCHAR
         THEN B[J..J+LINEPRINTER.MAXCHAR-1]:= L
         ELSE
            BEGIN
               B[J..FILESTORE.MAXCHAR]:= L[1..FILESTORE.MAXCHAR-J+1];
               LINEFILE.WRITE(B);
               IF LINEFILE.RESULT = FILESTORE.ENDOFFILE THEN GOTO 9;
               B[0..J-FILESTORE.MAXCHAR+LINEPRINTER.MAXCHAR-2]:=
                           L[FILESTORE.MAXCHAR-J+2..LINEPRINTER.MAXCHAR]
            END;
         J:= (J+LINEPRINTER.MAXCHAR) MOD (FILESTORE.MAXCHAR+1);
      9: IF LINEFILE.RESULT = FILESTORE.SUCCESS
                              THEN RESULT:= LINEPRINTER.SUCCESS
                              ELSE RESULT:= LINEPRINTER.FAILURE
      END;

   PROCEDURE *NEWLINE;
      LABEL 9;
      BEGIN
         IF LINEFILE.RESULT = FILESTORE.ENDOFFILE THEN GOTO 9;
         B[J]:= 'L';   J:= (J+1) MOD (FILESTORE.MAXCHAR+1);
         IF J = 0 THEN LINEFILE.WRITE(B);
      9: IF LINEFILE.RESULT = FILESTORE.SUCCESS
                              THEN RESULT:= LINEPRINTER.SUCCESS
                              ELSE RESULT:= LINEPRINTER.FAILURE
      END;

   PROCEDURE *NEWPAGE;
      LABEL 9;
      BEGIN
         IF LINEFILE.RESULT = FILESTORE.ENDOFFILE THEN GOTO 9;
         B[J]:= 'P';   J:= (J+1) MOD (FILESTORE.MAXCHAR+1);
         IF J = 0 THEN LINEFILE.WRITE(B);
      9: IF LINEFILE.RESULT = FILESTORE.SUCCESS
                              THEN RESULT:= LINEPRINTER.SUCCESS
                              ELSE RESULT:= LINEPRINTER.FAILURE
      END;
```

```
PROCEDURE SPOOLOUTPUT;
   LABEL 9;
   VAR
      L: LINEPRINTER.LINE;
      CH: CHAR;
   INSTANCE
      PRINTER: LINEPRINTER.PRINTER;
   BEGIN
      LINEFILE.READ(B);   J:= 0;
      REPEAT (*PRINT BLOCKS OF LINES UNTIL END OF FILE*)
         CH:= B[J];   J:= (J+1) MOD (FILESTORE.MAXCHAR+1);
         IF J = 0 THEN
            BEGIN
               LINEFILE.READ(B);
               IF LINEFILE.RESULT = FILESTORE.ENDOFFILE THEN GOTO 9
            END;
         IF CH = 'L' THEN PRINTER.NEWLINE ELSE
         IF CH = 'P' THEN PRINTER.NEWPAGE ELSE
         IF CH = 'X' THEN
            BEGIN
               IF J+LINEPRINTER.MAXCHAR-1 <= FILESTORE.MAXCHAR
               THEN L:= B[J..J+LINEPRINTER.MAXCHAR-1]
               ELSE
                  BEGIN
                     L[1..FILESTORE.MAXCHAR-J+1]:=
                                          B[J..FILESTORE.MAXCHAR];
                     LINEFILE.READ(B);
                     IF LINEFILE.RESULT = FILESTORE.ENDOFFILE THEN
                                                           GOTO 9;
                     L[FILESTORE.MAXCHAR-J+2..LINEPRINTER.MAXCHAR]:=
                        B[0..J-FILESTORE.MAXCHAR+LINEPRINTER.MAXCHAR-2]
                  END;
               J:= (J+LINEPRINTER.MAXCHAR) MOD (FILESTORE.MAXCHAR+1);
               PRINTER.PRINT(L)
            END
      UNTIL (PRINTER.RESULT = LINEPRINTER.FAILURE) OR (CH = 'Z');
   9: IF LINEFILE.RESULT = FILESTORE.ENDOFFILE THEN
            BEGIN
               PRINTER.NEWLINE;
               IF PRINTER.RESULT = LINEPRINTER.SUCCESS THEN
                  PRINTER.PRINT('TOO MUCH OUTPUT')
            END
   END;

BEGIN
   J:= 0;   RESULT:= LINEPRINTER.SUCCESS;
   ***;
   B[J]:= 'Z';
   IF LINEFILE.RESULT = FILESTORE.SUCCESS THEN LINEFILE.WRITE(B);
   SPOOLOUTPUT
END;
```

Job Execution

Having programmed the very simple body of the user process, and having programmed the spooling of both the input and the output, we are now left with the body of the procedure *runuserjob*. This consists of three main parts: processing the title card, loading a program, and running a program—in increasing order of complexity.

R. M. McKEAG	EXERCISE 7	MINIPASCAL	

Fig. 3.3

The title card begins with three twelve-column fields containing the user's name, the name of his job and the name of the library file that holds the first program of the job. The user should also place some limit on the resource requirements of his job: this might take the form of the maximum price the user is prepared to pay or it might consist of a separate limitation on each type of resource such as main-store size, amount of lineprinter output, number of disk transfers and processor time. The only one that need worry us is the amount of processor time that a job uses. Normally this will be of the order of half a minute but, to guard against faulty jobs, we must impose some upper limit. If this limit is low we severely restrict the jobs that can be run on the system; this is perhaps sensible, since we are concerned with providing a fast turnround for short jobs and this would be endangered if long jobs were permitted to run; however, as we have two partitions of main store we could reserve one for short jobs and use the other for a mixture of short and long jobs. If, therefore, we set a high upper limit, we must allow each user to set a lesser limit for his job and so a field for this purpose must be set aside on the title card. Here we shall simply have a fixed upper limit of, say, five minutes per job, and we shall leave the extension of the system to provide for long jobs as an exercise for the reader: not only must a time-limit field be set aside on the title card but a scheduler must be introduced to ensure that no more than one long job at a time is occupying main store.

The procedure for processing the title card is shown in Listing 5: it notes the name of the program to be loaded and copies to the output each field, including the rightmost forty-four columns which may contain some information such as instructions to the operator regarding the return of the print-out.

Listing 5

```
PROCEDURE PROCESSTITLECARD (VAR PROGRAMNAME: FILESTORE.FILENAME);

   VAR
      C: CARDREADER.CARD;

   BEGIN
      READER.READ(C);
      PROGRAMNAME:= C[2*MAXNAME+1..2*MAXNAME+FILESTORE.MAXNAME];
      WITH PRINTER DO
         BEGIN
            NEWPAGE;
            PRINT(C[1..MAXNAME]);
            NEWLINE;
            PRINT(C[MAXNAME+1..2*MAXNAME]);
            NEWLINE;
            PRINT(PROGRAMNAME);
            NEWLINE;
            PRINT(C[2*MAXNAME+FILESTORE.MAXNAME+1..CARDREADER.MAXCHAR]);
            NEWLINE;
            NEWLINE
         END
   END;
```

Listing 6

```
PROCEDURE LOADLIBRARYFILEPROGRAM
                    (PROGRAMNAME: FILESTORE.FILENAME; VAR OK: BOOLEAN);

   LABEL 9;

   INSTANCE
      F: FILESTORE.LIBRARYFILE(PROGRAMNAME);

   VAR
      B: FILESTORE.BLOCK;
      A: MAINSTORE.ADDRESS;

   BEGIN
      F.READ(B);
      OK:= (F.RESULT = FILESTORE.SUCCESS);  IF NOT OK THEN GOTO 9;
      A:= 0;
      REPEAT (*LOAD BLOCKS INTO MAIN STORE UNTIL END OF PROGRAM*)
         (*N.B. THIS LOOP ASSUMES THAT THE SIZE OF THE MAINSTORE     *)
         (*     AVAILABLE TO THIS JOB IS A MULTIPLE OF THE FILESTORE  *)
         (*     BLOCK SIZE.                                           *)
         (*COPY BLOCK "B" TO "STORE", STARTING AT ADDRESS "A"*);
         A:= (A+FILESTORE.MAXCHAR+1) MOD (MAINSTORE.MAXCHAR+1);
         F.READ(B)
      UNTIL (A=0) OR (F.RESULT = FILESTORE.ENDOFFILE);
      OK:= (F.RESULT = FILESTORE.ENDOFFILE);
   9: IF NOT OK THEN WITH PRINTER DO
         BEGIN
            NEWLINE;
            PRINT('ATTEMPT TO LOAD PROGRAM FROM ');
            CASE F.RESULT OF
               FILESTORE.SUCCESS:   PRINT('OVERLONG LIBRARY FILE: ');
               FILESTORE.ENDOFFILE: PRINT('EMPTY LIBRARY FILE: ');
               FILESTORE.NOFILE:    PRINT('MISSING LIBRARY FILE: ')
            END;
            PRINT(PROGRAMNAME);
            NEWLINE
         END
   END;
```

Loading programs

Each job consists of one or more programs run in sequence. The name of the
first program is obtained from the title card and, thereafter, each program
names its successor. We need to distinguish between programs loaded from
the library and those loaded from the intermediate file and so we shall write
two similar procedures to handle these two cases. The statement {*load
program*} is thus rendered as:

> **if** *programname* = *'INTERMEDIATE'*
> **then** *loadintermediatefileprogram(ok)*
> **else** *loadlibraryfileprogram(programname,ok)*

where the two procedures are defined as in Listings 6 and 7.

Listing 7

```
PROCEDURE LOADINTERMEDIATEFILEPROGRAM (VAR OK: BOOLEAN);

    LABEL 9;

    VAR
        B: FILESTORE.BLOCK;
        A: MAINSTORE.ADDRESS;

    BEGIN
        INTERMEDIATE.READ(B);
        OK:= (INTERMEDIATE.RESULT = FILESTORE.SUCCESS);
        IF NOT OK THEN GOTO 9;
        A:= 0;
        REPEAT (*LOAD BLOCKS INTO MAIN STORE UNTIL END OF PROGRAM*)
            (*N.B. WE ASSUME                                          *)
            (*        (MAINSTORE.MAXCHAR+1) MOD (FILESTORE.MAXCHAR+1) = 0   *)
            (*COPY BLOCK "B" TO "STORE", STARTING AT ADDRESS "A"*);
            A:= (A+FILESTORE.MAXCHAR+1) MOD (MAINSTORE.MAXCHAR+1);
            INTERMEDIATE.READ(B)
        UNTIL (A = 0) OR (INTERMEDIATE.RESULT = FILESTORE.ENDOFFILE);
        OK:= (INTERMEDIATE.RESULT = FILESTORE.ENDOFFILE);
    9:  IF NOT OK THEN WITH PRINTER DO
            BEGIN
                NEWLINE;
                PRINT('ATTEMPT TO LOAD PROGRAM FROM ');
                IF INTERMEDIATE.RESULT = FILESTORE.SUCCESS
                    THEN PRINT('OVERLONG INTERMEDIATE FILE.')
                    ELSE PRINT('EMPTY INTERMEDIATE FILE.');
                NEWLINE
            END
    END;
```

The statement

$$\{copy\ block\ 'b'\ to\ 'store',\ starting\ at\ address\ 'a'\}$$

occurs in both procedures and presents us with a problem that will recur several times in the construction of this operating system. Strictly speaking we should express this statement as

for $i := 0$ **to** *filestore.maxchar* **do** *store.write* $(a+i,\ b[i])$

where

var $i: 0\ ..\ filestore.maxchar;$

however, this would be expensive. An improvement would be to copy the data en bloc rather than character by character; the only way to achieve this in Pascal is to extend the *mainstore* envelope so that it provides procedures to read and write blocks as well as characters, but we shall find that we also need procedures to read and write card images and line images and other data structures. A still more efficient solution would be to read blocks from the file directly into the user's partition of main store, thereby avoiding the need for block b and the copying; but the strict type-matching rules of Pascal forbid this. We have here a problem that arises over and over again in operating systems: an area of store is to be used to hold data of different types at different times yet Pascal insists that we either reduce all the data to some common type or else enumerate all the possible types—the latter solution is usually impracticable and the former is usually expensive. We have adopted the former solution here, reducing all data stored on files and in the main store to characters. Pools of buffers for holding different types of data pose the same problem, as do communication channels that convey different types of data. P. Brinch Hansen's Concurrent Pascal (*I.E.E.E.Trans. Software Eng.*, **SE-1**, 199–207 (1975)) introduces a *universal* type to describe variables that hold data of several types; a variable of *universal* type has a specified size, and assignments of data to or from the variable are checked only for size compatibility but not for type compatibility. Lacking this useful construct we can instead resort to a few judiciously chosen machine-code instructions to achieve the same effect. Machine code, like **goto** statements and pointers, is potentially dangerous but, if used with care, it can enable us to provide useful constructs that are not available in our high-level language. Parenthetically, it should be remarked that the last sentence is not at odds with the philosophy of structured programming but, rather, an illustration of it.

Running programs

Running a program entails executing the program's instructions one by one until the program terminates or until some resource limit, in this case the five-minute time limit, is reached. The good scheduling of the processor requires that every so often the user process should pause to request permission to embark on its next 100 ms timeslice. So we shall introduce a *coarsetimer*, which is initialized to 5 minutes and decremented as each timeslice is completed, and a *finetimer*, which is initialized each timeslice to 100 ms and decremented as each instruction is executed. The following fragment of program summarizes the control structure, leaving only the innermost loop unelaborated.

const *timelimit* = 5 {*minutes*};
var
    coarsetimer: integer {*timeslices*};
    finetimer: integer {*microseconds*};
    endofjob: Boolean;
    endofprogram: Boolean;
    pc: mainstore.address {*program counter*};
    ok: Boolean;
    coarsetimer := *timelimit* * 60000 **div** *processor.slice*;
    finetimer := 0;
    endofjob := *false*;
repeat {*execute programs until end of job*}
    if *programname* = '*INTERMEDIATE*'
      then *loadintermediatefileprogram*(*ok*)
      else *loadlibraryfileprogram*(*programname,ok*);
    if *ok* **then**
      begin
        endofprogram := *false*;
        pc := 0;
      repeat {*execute timeslices until end of program*}
        cpu.timeslice; *finetimer* := *finetimer*+*processor.slice* *1000;
        repeat {*execute instructions until end of timeslice*}
          {*fetch, decode and execute instruction at address 'pc',*
          updating 'pc' and decrementing 'finetimer' and,
          if appropriate, setting 'endofprogram' or 'endofjob' true}
        until (*finetimer* ≤ 0) **or** *endofjob* **or** *endofprogram*;
        if *finetimer* ≤ 0 **then** *coarsetimer* := *coarsetimer* −1
      until (*coarsetimer* ≤ 0) **or** *endofjob* **or** *endofprogram*;
      if *coarsetimer* ≤ 0 **then with** *printer* **do**
        begin

> *endofjob* := *true*;
> *newline*
> *print* ('*TIME LIMIT EXCEEDED*');
> *newline*
>   **end**
>   **end**
> **until** (**not** *ok*) **or** *endofjob*

Interpretation or execution

Conceptually it is attractive to consider the user's program as being interpreted, instruction by instruction, by the operating system; hence the following formulation of the innermost loop of the above program.

> **repeat**
>   {*fetch, decode and execute instruction at address 'pc', updating*
>   '*pc' and decrementing 'finetimer' and, if appropriate,*
>   *setting 'endofprogram' or 'endofjob' true*}
> **until** (*finetimer* ⩽ 0) **or** *endofjob* **or** *endofprogram*

Unless the compilers guarantee that all user programs are well behaved, and we do not countenance the possibility of hardware failure, we should regard each user program with suspicion and ensure that it cannot corrupt the rest of the system in any way. Interpretation enables us to carry out such checks. Although it is helpful to design the interpreter in Pascal it is not advisable to implement it in Pascal, for several reasons. First, we have the problem of the *universal* type of the main store: we wish to interpret the contents of the store as variable format instructions and as variable-length data values— again we can reduce instructions and data to characters but the cost of the conversion will be excessive, so judicious use of machine code is called for. Second, many of the operations involved in the interpretation can easily, and more efficiently, be accomplished by hardware, for example decoding the instructions and incrementing the program counter and decrementing the timer. Nevertheless, interpretation by software is currently popular: witness the popularity of interpretive forms of Basic or Cobol where processing times and processing efficiency are considered unimportant, or consider the popularity of P. Brinch Hansen's Concurrent Pascal for use even in fields where processor time and efficiency are usually considered crucial. Interpretation by microcode is even more popular and is now used on many computers, often because it is cheaper to develop microcode interpreters than to construct special-purpose hardware; another reason is to enable programs written for one computer to be run on another; yet another is to support several interpreters, each tailored to the requirements of a different language. Traditionally, however, the user program is not interpreted; for speed it is executed directly by hardware. In this case the hardware must be able to cope with several problems. First, it must be able to perform a variety of checks on the behavior of the user program. Second, where such checks fail, it must pass control back to the operating system, together with an indication of the nature of the failure so that an appropriate message can be printed. Third, it must return control to the operating system on the expiry of a time-slice. Fourth, it must recognize "supervisor calls" and return control to the operating system in order that the calls may be translated into operations on the virtual resources allocated to the user process. Often the special-purpose hardware provided to carry out these tasks is barely adequate and very restrictive.

Unless one is aiming to produce a very fast computer, the best solution is probably to design the interpreter in Pascal, hand translate it into microcode and then use what hardware one can to speed it up, for example programmed-logic arrays and read-only memories.

Summary

Listing 8 summarizes the user process which we have developed in this chapter.

Listing 8

```
PROCESS USERPROCESS;
    PROCEDURE RUNUSERJOB;
        CONST
            MAXNAME = 12 (*CHARACTERS PER NAME*);
            TIMELIMIT = 5 (*MINUTES*);
        ENVELOPE MODULE READER = LIST3 IN LIBRARY;
            (*    VAR *RESULT: CARDREADER.STATUS                    *)
            (*    PROCEDURE *READ (VAR CARDREADER.CARD)             *)
        ENVELOPE MODULE PRINTER = LIST4 IN LIBRARY;
            (*    VAR *RESULT: LINEPRINTER.STATUS                   *)
            (*    PROCEDURE *PRINT (LINEPRINTER.LINE)               *)
            (*    PROCEDURE *NEWLINE                                *)
            (*    PROCEDURE *NEWPAGE                                *)
        INSTANCE
            INTERMEDIATE: FILESTORE.FILE;
            STORE: MAINSTORE.STORE;
            CPU: PROCESSOR.CPU;
        PROCEDURE PROCESSTITLECARD = LIST5 IN LIBRARY;
        PROCEDURE LOADLIBRARYFILEPROGRAM = LIST6 IN LIBRARY;
```

```
PROCEDURE LOADINTERMEDIATEFILEPROGRAM = LIST7 IN LIBRARY;
VAR
    PROGRAMNAME: FILESTORE.FILENAME;
    COARSETIMER: INTEGER (*TIMESLICES*);
    FINETIMER: INTEGER (*MICROSECONDS*);
    ENDOFJOB: BOOLEAN;
    ENDOFPROGRAM: BOOLEAN;
    PC: MAINSTORE.ADDRESS (*PROGRAM COUNTER*);
    OK: BOOLEAN;
BEGIN
    PROCESSTITLECARD(PROGRAMNAME);
    COARSETIMER:= TIMELIMIT*60000 DIV PROCESSOR.SLICE;
    FINETIMER:= 0;
    ENDOFJOB:= FALSE;
    REPEAT (*LOAD AND EXECUTE PROGRAMS UNTIL END OF JOB*)
        IF PROGRAMNAME = 'INTERMEDIATE'
            THEN LOADINTERMEDIATEFILEPROGRAM(OK)
            ELSE LOADLIBRARYFILEPROGRAM(PROGRAMNAME, OK);
        IF OK THEN
            BEGIN
                ENDOFPROGRAM:= FALSE;
                PC:= 0;
                REPEAT (*EXECUTE TIMESLICES UNTIL END OF PROGRAM*)
                    CPU.TIMESLICE;
                    FINETIMER:= FINETIMER + PROCESSOR.SLICE*1000;
                    REPEAT (*EXECUTE INSTRS. UNTIL END OF TIMESLICE*)
                        (*FETCH, DECODE AND EXECUTE INSTRUCTION AT    *)
                        (*ADDRESS "PC", UPDATING "PC" AND DECREMENTING*)
                        (*FINETIMER AND, IF APPROPRIATE, SETTING      *)
                        (*"ENDOFPROGRAM" OR "ENDOFJOB" TRUE           *)
                    UNTIL (FINETIMER <= 0) OR ENDOFJOB OR ENDOFPROGRAM;
                    IF FINETIMER <= 0 THEN COARSETIMER:= COARSETIMER-1
                UNTIL (COARSETIMER <= 0) OR ENDOFJOB OR ENDOFPROGRAM;
                IF COARSETIMER <= 0 THEN WITH PRINTER DO
                    BEGIN
                        ENDOFJOB:= TRUE;
                        NEWLINE;
                        PRINT('TIME LIMIT EXCEEDED');
                        NEWLINE
                    END
            END
    UNTIL (NOT OK) OR ENDOFJOB
END;

BEGIN
    WHILE SWITCH.ON DO RUNUSERJOB
END;
```

Exercise 1   Program a variant of the user process which will spool its input from any of the typewriters and will spool its output to a (possibly different) typewriter when requested to do so by the user who submitted the job.

Exercise 2   Devise a simple instruction set for users' programs to execute, and program an interpreter to fetch, decode and execute those instructions.

THE MAIN STORE

Having programmed the user processes we now turn our attention to the resources that they use. Perhaps the most difficult and least typical is the main store. Unlike most resources, which are generally input or output devices, main store offers us many possibilities for devising complicated scheduling algorithms: this is because the main store generally consists of a large number of small units (bytes, words, or pages) and the users' requirements may vary very considerably from one user to another and, indeed, each user's needs may vary dynamically. As store accesses are very frequent it is important that the mapping of a virtual address onto a real address should be extremely fast. If the user has been allocated a single partition of main store, the mapping entails adding the base address of the partition onto the virtual address; but if the user has been allocated several disjoint areas of main store, then the address mapping will also entail looking up a table to find the base address of the partition: the problem is aggravated if a two-level table is used to avoid having to store a large sparse one-level table: to speed the mapping special purpose registers are often introduced to hold the base addresses of the partitions currently being used. Often backing store, such as a drum, is used as an extension to the main store, and the possibilities and problems are multiplied since the scheduling of storage offers more scope for flexibility and complexity and has to be done more frequently, the mapping of addresses may entail one or more data transfers and considerable delays, and more space and time must be expended to keep track of where a program's pages are and which drum and main store page frames are free. To speed the address mapping and to take advantage of special-purpose hardware such as associative stores and page-fault interrupts it is necessary that much of the monitor for administering main store be implemented as efficiently as possible in machine code, microcode or hardware. Much of the design, however, can and should be done in a high-level language.

Fixed Partitions

We have already seen that a simple store-management strategy suffices for the operating system that we are developing here; indeed part of the art of constructing any program is to do so in such a way that simple algorithms suffice. The structure of the *mainstore* monitor module has already been given: it contains a monitor to schedule the two partitions of main store, it contains a monitor for each partition to control the use of that partition, and it defines an envelope each instance of which provides a virtual store: the envelope, by calls upon the scheduler and the appropriate controller, maps operations on the virtual store onto operations on the corresponding partition of real store. Although there are only two partitions of real store there may be any number of virtual stores extant at any moment, all but two of them waiting for a partition to be freed. Listing 9 shows the complete *mainstore* monitor.

The partitions are identified by values of type *msnum* which ranges from 1 to *maxms*. The scheduler is implemented as a monitor since it is accessed by many processes and mutual exclusion is required to prevent two processes from using it simultaneously. It keeps a *pool* of free partitions and has a queue, *freed*, on which, when the pool is empty, processes wait in order of arrival for a free partition; the scheduler's initialization involves assigning all the partitions to the pool.

Each controller is written as a monitor since it is used by many processes, albeit at different times. It contains a partition of 100K characters and provides operations to read and write single characters. We have already seen that we may also need to be able to transfer larger amounts of data, for example when loading a program, block by block, from file store. To provide fast access to store it is necessary that the controller be implemented in hardware and that instructions be available to read and write data values of a variety of sizes without regard for the types of those data values.

Likewise the *read* and *write* procedures of the *store* envelope, perhaps suitably extended to deal with universal types of several sizes, should be implemented in hardware. The variable *ms* should be replaced by a hardware register holding the base address of the partition allocated by the scheduler, and at every read or write operation the content of this register must be added to the virtual address before the main store is accessed.

The design of store-management schemes in a high-level language is beneficial, particularly for more complex algorithms such as those involving paging, since it helps the designer to get the logic right and it suggests to the designer what special-purpose hardware or microcode is required to implement the algorithm efficiently. This approach is also useful if one needs to simulate a new system before the prototype is available, although the cost of doing this may be great.

A More Advanced Example

To illustrate the applicability of this approach to the design of a more elaborate store-management system let us construct a *mainstore* monitor that will permit up to four users' programs to be executed concurrently. The monitor will present the users with the same virtual store as before except that, when declaring an instance of the *store* envelope, a user must specify how much store he needs in units (pages) of, say, 4K characters. A single partition of real store will be allocated to each user but the four partitions will usually overlap one another. We therefore postulate the availability of a backing store—a drum—whose sectors are used to hold pages of users'

Listing 9

```
MONITOR MODULE MAINSTORE;

   CONST
      *MAXCHAR = 102399 (*100K CHARACTERS PER VIRTUAL STORE*);
      MAXMS = 2 (*PARTITIONS*);

   TYPE
      *ADDRESS = 0..MAXCHAR;
      MSNUM = 1..MAXMS;

   MONITOR MODULE MSSCHEDULER;
      VAR
         POOL: SET OF MSNUM;
      INSTANCE
         FREED: CONDITION;
      PROCEDURE *ACQUIRE (VAR MS: MSNUM);
         BEGIN
            IF POOL = [] THEN FREED.WAIT;
            MS:= 1;  WHILE NOT (MS IN POOL) DO MS:= MS+1;
            POOL:= POOL - [MS]
         END;
      PROCEDURE *RELEASE (MS: MSNUM);
         BEGIN POOL:= POOL + [MS];  FREED.SIGNAL END;
      BEGIN
         POOL:= [1..MAXMS];
         ***
      END;

   MONITOR CONTROLLER;
      VAR
         PARTITION: PACKED ARRAY [ADDRESS] OF CHAR;
      PROCEDURE *READ (A: ADDRESS; VAR C: CHAR);
         BEGIN C:= PARTITION[A] END;
      PROCEDURE *WRITE (A: ADDRESS; C: CHAR);
         BEGIN PARTITION[A]:= C END;
      BEGIN
         ***
      END;
   INSTANCE
      MSCONTROLLER: ARRAY [1..MAXMS] OF CONTROLLER;

   ENVELOPE *STORE;
      VAR
         MS: MSNUM;
      PROCEDURE *READ (A: ADDRESS; VAR C: CHAR);
         BEGIN MSCONTROLLER[MS].READ(A, C) END;
      PROCEDURE *WRITE (A: ADDRESS; C: CHAR);
         BEGIN MSCONTROLLER[MS].WRITE(A, C) END;
      BEGIN
         MSSCHEDULER.ACQUIRE(MS);
         ***;
         MSSCHEDULER.RELEASE(MS)
      END;

   BEGIN
      ***
   END;
```

virtual stores when there is contention for use of main store page frames; the drum presents the following interface.

monitor module *drum*
    type **sectornum* = 1 .. 50 {*no. of drum sectors + no. of main store*
                                *page frames ⩾ max. no. of users * max.*
                                no. of pages per user}
    procedure **read* (**var** *page*; *sectornum*) {*reads 'page' from drum*
                                    'sectornum'}
    procedure **write* (*page*; **var** *sectornum*) {*writes 'page' to drum and*
                                  returns 'sectornum'}
    procedure **release* (*sectornum*) {*releases sector, numbered 'sectornum',*
                                  on drum}

where:

    const *pagesize* = 4096 {*characters*};
    type
        charnum = 0 .. *pagesize*−1;
        page = **packed array** [*charnum*] **of** *char*.

Each page frame belongs to a controller monitor which records which user is currently using it and swaps pages to and from drum as necessary—this is known as the *delayed swap technique*. The scheduler monitor allocates a unique identifying number to each user and endeavors to minimize the amount of overlapping of partitions—this is termed the *minimum overlay algorithm*.

    The overall structure of the *mainstore* administration monitor, together with the complete *store* envelope, is as follows.

    monitor module *mainstore*;
        const
            usermax = 4 {*concurrent user programs*};
            storesize = 50 {*pages*};
            *maxchar = 102399; {100*K characters per virtual store*};
        type
            usernum = 1 .. *usermax*;
            pagenum = 0 .. *storesize* − 1;
            *pageqty = 1 .. 25 {*max.partition size ÷ page size*};
            *address = 0 .. *maxchar*;
        monitor module *msscheduler*;
          ⋮

```
procedure *acquire (q:pageqty; var p:pagenum; var u:usernum);
  ⋮
procedure *release (q:pageqty; p:pagenum; u:usernum);
  ⋮
monitor controller;
  ⋮
  procedure *read (u:usernum; n:charnum; var c:char);
    ⋮
  procedure *write (u:usernum; n:charnum; c:char);
    ⋮
  procedure *release (u:usernum);
    ⋮
instance mscontroller: array [pagenum] of controller;
envelope *store (q:pageqty);
  var
    u:usernum;
    p,i:pagenum;
  procedure *read (a:address; var c:char);
    begin
      mscontroller [p+(a div pagesize) mod q].
        read (u, a mod pagesize, c)
    end;
  procedure *write (a:address; c:char);
    begin
      mscontroller [p+(a div pagesize) mod q].
        write (u, a mod pagesize, c)
    end;
  begin
    msscheduler.acquire(q, p, u);
    ***;
    for i:=p to p+q−1 do mscontroller[i].release(u);
    msscheduler.release(q, p, u)
  end;
  begin *** end
```

The scheduler has two functions. One is to allocate unique identifying numbers to users when they are allocated partitions: for this it maintains a pool of free user numbers and a condition queue on which processes wait if the pool is empty. Its other task is to allocate partitions in such a way as to minimize the amount of overlapping: to do this it keeps a count, for each page frame, of the number of users allocated that frame; it can then try all possible positions for a partition and select the position that yields the lowest overlap sum.

```
monitor module msscheduler;
    var
        users: set of usernum;
        count: array [pagenum] of 0 .. usermax;
        p:pagenum;
    instance freed: condition;
    procedure *acquire (q: pageqty; var p: pagenum; var u: usernum);
        var
            sum, min: integer;
            i: pagenum;
        begin
            if users = [   ] then freed.wait;
            u:=1; while not (u in users) do u:=u+1;
            users:=users−[u];
            sum:=0; for i:=0 to q−1 do sum:=sum+count[i];
            p:=0; min:=sum;
            for i:=n to storesize−1 do
                begin
                    sum:=sum−count[i−n]+count[i];
                    if sum < min then
                        begin p:= i−n+1; min:= sum end
                end;
            for i:=p to p+n−1 do count[i]:= count[i]+1
        end;
    procedure *release (q:pageqty; p:pagenum; u:usernum);
    var i:pagenum;
    begin
        for i:= p to p+n−1 do count[i]:= count [i]−1;
        users:= users+[u];
        freed.signal
    end;
    begin
        for p:=0 to storesize−1 do count[p]:=0;
        users:=[1 .. usermax];
        ***
    end
```

The controller for each main store page frame is not too difficult to construct. It must declare the frame in which it is to store pages:

```
var frame: page;
```

it must record which, if any, user currently has a page occupying that frame:

var *owner*: 0 . . *usermax*;

and it must remember, for each user, whether or not a copy of that user's page resides on drum and, if so, in which sector:

> **var** *location*: **array** [*usernum*] **of**
> > **record case** *copy*: *Boolean* **of**
> > > *true:* (*drumsector*: *drum.sector*);
> > > *false*:
> >
> > **end.**

On trying to *read* or *write* a character on behalf of user *u*, the controller must first check whether *owner* = *u* and, if not, invoke a procedure *pagefault* which will bring the required page into main store having first discarded the current page. When a page is written to in main store the copy on drum is no longer valid and its sector can be released by a procedure *releasecopy*. The complete controller is shown below.

```
monitor controller;
   var
     frame: page;
     owner: 0 . . usermax;
     location: array [usernum] of
               record case copy: Boolean of
                   true: (drumsector: drum.sector);
                   false:
               end;
   procedure pagefault (u:usernum);
     begin
       if owner ≠ 0 then with location [owner] do if not copy then
         begin copy := true; drum.write (frame, drumsector) end;
       owner:=u;
       with location [owner] do
         case copy of
             true: drum.read (frame, drumsector);
             false: {clear the frame}
         end
     end;
   procedure releasecopy (u:usernum);
     begin
       with location [u] do if copy then
         begin drum.release (drumsector); copy:= false end
     end;
```

procedure **read* (*u*: *usernum*; *n*: *charnum*; **var** *c*: *char*);
  begin if *owner* ≠ *u* **then** *pagefault*(*u*); *c*: = *frame* [*n*] **end**;
procedure **write* (*u*: *usernum*; *n*: *charnum*; *c*: *char*);
  begin
    if *owner* ≠ *u* **then** *pagefault*(*u*); *frame* [*n*] := *c*;
    releasecopy (*u*)
  end;
procedure **release* (*u*: *usernum*);
  begin if *owner* = *u* **then** *owner*: = 0; *releasecopy*(*u*) **end**;
begin
  for *owner*: = 1 **to** *usermax* **do** *location* [*owner*].*copy*: = *false*;
  owner: = 0;
  ***
end

For efficiency the procedure *releasecopy* need not be invoked on every *write* operation but can be postponed until the next page fault, provided we introduce a Boolean variable to denote whether or not the page has been written to during its sojourn in main store.

One important modification is necessary if the program is to work. If a user of some page frame has to wait for a page to be read from or written to drum, the exclusion on that page frame's *controller* monitor is released. It is necessary, therefore, to delay other users that enter the monitor while the first user is waiting. This can be done simply by declaring within the monitor a *state* variable to denote whether the monitor is *free* or *busy* and a condition *queue* on which processes can wait when they find the monitor busy. Each execution of the *pagefault* procedure should be preceded by:

if *state* = *busy* **then** *queue.wait*; *state*: = *busy*

and the *read* or *write* operation should be followed by:

state: = *free*; *queue.signal*.

Exercise 3   The fixed partition, minimum overlay and delayed swap techniques programmed in this chapter were taken from a survey of store management techniques by Hoare and McKeag (in Hoare and Perrott (1972), pp. 117–51). Program some of the other techniques described in that survey. (Your attention is drawn to Hoare's structured paging system (*Computer J.*, **16**, 209–15 (1973).).

THE PROCESSOR

We have seen that the scheduling of main store can be accomplished at two levels: at the coarser level a limited number of processes is given permission to use the main store, while at the finer level the use of the main store page frames is switched amongst those processes, their pages being transferred between the drum-store sectors and the main-store frames in accordance with their dynamic behavior.

The scheduling of the processor gives us another example of a two-level algorithm. At the finer level the switching of the processor from one process to another is performed by the run-time routines, called the nucleus, that underlie the operating system. Associated with each process is a priority and, whenever the processor is free, it is normally allocated to the highest priority process that is ready to run. Precedence, however, is given to processes executing monitor procedures; this is done for two reasons: firstly because a monitor is a potential bottleneck, and secondly to prevent a process that has been held up by a signaling operation in a monitor from being overtaken by other processes that subsequently enter the monitor. Once a process has been allocated the processor by the nucleus it continues to execute until it voluntarily relinquishes the processor or until it is obliged to wait—on a condition queue, or for an interrupt from some peripheral device, or because it has signaled some other process in a monitor, or because the nucleus has to service some interrupt.

At the coarser level the priorities of the processes can be adjusted to ensure that no process fails to make reasonable progress. Processes that are executing operating-system code, as opposed to interpreting users' programs, make very limited demands upon the processor and can safely be given the highest priority since, when they are allocated the processor, it is known that they will very soon relinquish it again; thus such processes do not unduly delay others and, as many of them are concerned with driving peripheral devices, the efficiency of the entire system depends upon their receiving the processor when they need it. We know nothing, however, about the characteristics of processes interpreting or executing users' programs. Some such programs may do a lot of processing without needing to wait in a monitor or for an interrupt; to ensure that these do not monopolize the processor we shall require them to relinquish the processor voluntarily after performing a certain amount of computation (say a timeslice of 100 ms) and to downgrade their priorities to give other processes a chance. Those programs that make slow progress, either because they frequently wait for data transfers or because they have temporarily been elbowed out by other processes, will be required to upgrade their priorities on the expiry of their timeslices.

We may implement this policy by requiring each user process to reset its priority, thereby delaying itself to a greater or lesser extent, before embarking on each timeslice. It can do this by computing for itself a target time at which it should complete its next timeslice, and from this it subtracts the duration of the timeslice, 100 ms in our system, thus obtaining the latest time at which it can resume processing if it is to meet its target; this value is used as the priority of the process.

The target is computed by adding to the starting time for this timeslice the real time that can be expected to elapse before the timeslice has been completed: if there are n processes competing for 100 ms timeslices, then $100n$ ms should be added to the starting time.

The starting time might be the current real time, i.e. now, or, if we are to compensate (or penalize) processes fully for any past lateness (or earliness), the previous target. We have already seen that some compensation is desirable, but we wish to give greater weight to a process's recent history and we wish to avoid giving too much weight to a short-lived uncharacteristic change in a process's behavior. A simple algorithm with these properties is to take the average of the previous target and the current time as the starting time for the calculation of the new target.

Thus the target is given by:

$$target := (target + time\ now)\ /2 + 100n$$

and the priority is set to:

$$target - 100$$

although since all the timeslices have the same value here we could use the target as the priority. This scheduling algorithm was devised by C. A. R. Hoare.

To implement this scheduler we need to keep track of the number of competing processes, n, which may vary, and we need to record the current real time: to do this we introduce a real-time clock that ticks (i.e. interrupts) with some suitable frequency, say every 20 ms. Thus the monitor to administer the processor contains an envelope, *cpu*, that provides a procedure, *timeslice*, that makes use of a *processcounter* monitor and a *clockcontroller* monitor to determine a target and so set a priority. Care must be taken that variables that are to hold values of real time do not overflow during the period the system is in operation: using units of 1 ms a word length of 36 bits would suffice to measure one year. Listing 10 shows the complete *processor* monitor.

We shall assume that every process is automatically initialized with a priority of zero; if this is not the case then this initialization must be programmed.

Listing 10

```
MONITOR MODULE PROCESSOR;

   CONST
      *SLICE = 100 (*MILLISECONDS*);

   MONITOR MODULE PROCESSCOUNTER;
      VAR
         COUNT: INTEGER;
      PROCEDURE *START;
         BEGIN COUNT:= COUNT + 1 END;
      PROCEDURE *FINISH;
         BEGIN COUNT:= COUNT - 1 END;
      FUNCTION *NUMBER: INTEGER;
         BEGIN NUMBER:= COUNT END;
      BEGIN
         COUNT:= 0;   ***
      END;

   MONITOR MODULE CLOCKCONTROLLER;
      VAR
         CURRENTTIME: INTEGER (*MILLISECONDS*);
      FUNCTION *TIMENOW: INTEGER;
         BEGIN TIMENOW:= CURRENTTIME END;
      PROCEDURE PROCESSTICKSFROMCLOCK;
         CONST
            TICKINTERVAL = 20 (*MILLISECONDS*);
            ETERNITY = FALSE;
         BEGIN
            REPEAT
               (*WAIT FOR A TICK FROM THE CLOCK*);
               CURRENTTIME:= CURRENTTIME + TICKINTERVAL
            UNTIL ETERNITY
         END;
      PROCESS MODULE CLOCKCONTROLLER;
         BEGIN PROCESSTICKSFROMCLOCK END;
      BEGIN
         CURRENTTIME:= 0;   ***
      END;

   ENVELOPE *CPU;
      VAR
         TARGET: INTEGER;
      PROCEDURE *TIMESLICE;
         BEGIN
            TARGET:= (TARGET + CLOCKCONTROLLER.TIMENOW) DIV 2
                                     + PROCESSCOUNTER.NUMBER*SLICE;
            SETPRIORITY(TARGET)
         END;
      BEGIN
         PROCESSCOUNTER.START;  TARGET:= CLOCKCONTROLLER.TIMENOW;
         ***;
         PROCESSCOUNTER.FINISH;  SETPRIORITY(0)
      END;

   BEGIN
      ***
   END;
```

THE CARDREADERS

Many of the resources administered by an operating system are input and output devices; the cardreaders and lineprinters illustrate well some of the problems of administration such as the buffering of successive data transfers and the handling of device failures. The scheduling of such devices is usually straightforward, but we shall encounter more complicated scheduling algorithms when we consider the file store and the typewriters.

We have already specified that the *cardreader* monitor is to make available an envelope, *reader*, which in turn will provide a procedure to *read* a *card* and a *result* value, which might denote *success*, *failure* or, if the four-star terminator has been read, *endoffile*.

We have two cardreaders to administer and these will be identified by values of

$$\text{type } crnum = 1 \ .. \ crmax$$

where

$$\text{const } crmax = 2 \ \{cardreaders\}$$

We shall introduce two controllers, one to handle each cardreader, and a scheduler to match up processes requiring to read decks of cards with cardreaders containing decks of cards ready to be read.

```
monitor module crscheduler
    procedure *acquire (var cr : crnum) ;
    procedure *supply (cr : crnum)
    monitor controller (cr : crnum)
    procedure *read (var c : card ; var s : status)
    instance crcontroller : array [crnum] of controller ((1) (2))
```

The *reader* envelope, which maps a virtual cardreader onto a real cardreader, is easily programmed in terms of calls upon these monitors.

```
envelope *reader ;
    var cr : crnum ; *result: status;
    procedure *read (var c : card) ;
        begin crcontroller [cr].read (c, result) end;
    begin
        crscheduler.acquire (cr) ; result := success;
        ***
    end
```

Note that the envelope does not release the cardreader when it has finished reading the deck of cards: the reason is that the cardreader will often not be immediately ready to be used by some other process, either because it has failed and has to be put right or because it contains no deck of cards and its hopper has to be replenished; in either case we can leave it to the controller to tell the scheduler when the cardreader is ready to be allocated to some user. Note also that we have assumed here that a user will read all the cards of the deck until either the four-star terminator is encountered or until a failure occurs, and we have assumed that it will attempt to read no further. Here we know that these assumptions are justified, but if they were not it would be the duty of the *reader* envelope to carry out the necessary checks.

The scheduler is straightforward to program, requests being dealt with on a first-come, first-served basis and any deck of cards being acceptable to any user.

```
monitor module crscheduler ;
    var pool : set of crnum ;
    instance queue : condition ;
    procedure *acquire (var cr : crnum) ;
        begin
            if pool = [   ] then queue.wait ;
            cr := 1 ; while not (cr in pool) do cr := cr + 1 ;
            pool := pool − [cr]
        end;
    procedure *supply (cr : crnum) ;
        begin
            pool := pool + [cr] ;
            queue.signal
        end;
    begin
        pool := [   ] ;
        ***
    end
```

The controllers are complicated by two factors. One is the need to cope with data transfer failures—we shall defer consideration of that problem for a moment and, meanwhile, glibly assume that failures never occur. The other factor is the need to buffer the input: it would be intolerable if the user had to initiate the input of a card, wait for the completion of the data transfer and then process that card, before beginning the input of the next card. So we declare, local to each controller, a small service process, *crhandler*, whose main task is to read cards into a buffer, from which they can be extracted by the user. A subsidiary task is to inform the scheduler when there is a new deck of cards waiting to be read; note that extra terminator cards may have been inserted between jobs and will have to be skipped.

```
monitor controller (cr : crnum) ;
  var
    buffer : card ;
    result : status ;
    state : (empty, full) ;
  instance
    notfull, notempty : condition ;
  procedure *read (var c : card ; var s : status) ;
    begin
      if state = empty then notempty.wait ;
      s := result ; if s = success then c := buffer ;
      state := empty ; notfull.signal
    end;
  procedure readcardsintobuffer ;
    const eternity = false ;
    procedure readacardintobuffer ;
      begin
        {read a card into 'buffer' from reader 'cr', recording 'success'
          in 'result'} ;
        if buffer [1 .. 4] = '****' then result := endoffile
      end;
    begin
      repeat
        repeat readacardintobuffer until result ≠ endoffile ;
        state := full ; crscheduler.supply (cr) ;
        if state = full then notfull.wait ;
        repeat {read cards until endoffile}
          readacardintobuffer ;
          state := full ; notempty.signal ;
          if state = full then notfull.wait
        until result = endoffile
      until eternity
    end;
  process module crhandler ;
    begin readcardsintobuffer end ;
  begin
    ***
  end
```

The Handling of Faults

Cardreaders are not infallible: they need the attention of operator and engineer from time to time and so, when initiating a transfer, we must be prepared for failure. A fault can occur for any of several reasons: the transfer cannot be started because the reader has been switched off or off-line; or the operator is required to fill the hopper, empty the stacker, attend to a damaged card or position the card weight; or the engineer is needed to replace a broken photoelectric cell or to free a jammed transport mechanism. On detecting any such fault the *crhandler* process reports it to the operator and gives him an opportunity to rectify it. If the fault persists, then the operator is informed and no further attempt will be made to read that file. Thus, when a fault occurs, there is little that the *crhandler* process can do until it is sensible to continue, and only the operator can decide that. So we supply the operator with an interrupt button on each cardreader and it is on this that the *crhandler* process waits before attempting to read further cards.

To report a fault to the operator we shall use a virtual typewriter and output the message *'FAILURE TO READ CARD'* or, if the fault persists, *'FAILURE TO READ FILE'*; in the former case the operator knows he has the opportunity to correct the fault and enable the file to be read satisfactorily, while in the latter case he knows that any remaining cards of the file must be skipped before a new file is submitted. If the precise reason for failure is known, then we can report this to the operator to help him in his diagnosis, but the operating system can rarely make any other use of this information. The body of the procedure *readcardsintobuffer* now runs as follows:

```
begin
  repeat
    awaitoperator ;
    repeat {read files until failure}
      repeat {read until a title card is found}
        readacardintobuffer ;
        if result = failure then
            begin report (M1) ; awaitoperator end
      until result = success ;
      state := full ; crscheduler.supply (cr) ;
      if state = full then notfull.wait ;
      repeat {read cards until failure or endoffile}
        readacardintobuffer ;
        if result = failure then
            begin report (M1) ; awaitoperator ; readacardintobuffer end ;
        state := full ; notempty.signal ;
```

> **if** *state* = *full* **then** *notfull.wait*
> **until** *result* ≠ *success*
> **until** *result* = *failure* ;
> *report* (*M*2) ;
> **until** *eternity*
> **end**

where *M*1 and *M*2 are the messages *'FAILURE TO READ CARD'* and *'FAILURE TO READ FILE'* respectively; these are typed by the procedure *report* which declares an instance of an outgoing conversation and precedes each message by the name *'CR* 1*'* or *'CR* 2*'* as appropriate.

Listing 11 shows the complete *cardreader* administration monitor.

The Use of Machine Code

In the procedure *readacardintobuffer* the statement represented by the comment {*read a card into 'buffer' from reader 'cr', recording the 'success' or 'failure' of the transfer in 'result'*} should be replaced by code to initiate the data transfer from the card reader, by a call on an inbuilt procedure to await the corresponding completion interrupt, and by code to read and store the result of the operation.

In general, machine-code instructions are necessary to initiate operations on peripheral devices since it is undesirable to expect a general-purpose high-level language to support the wide variety of devices that all the operating and real-time systems written in that language might have to support.

The body of the procedure *awaitoperator*, denoted by the comment {*await interrupt from operator on reader 'cr'*}, should be replaced by a call of the same inbuilt procedure as is used when reading a card, but this time to await the arrival of the interrupt from the operator. The effect of this procedure is similar to that of waiting on a condition queue with the corresponding signal coming from the routine that services the interrupt. These routines, *await interrupt* and *service interrupt*, together with the routines to guarantee mutual exclusion on *monitor entry* and *monitor exit*, and the routines to *wait* on and *signal* condition queues, and the routine *set priority* underlie the operating system and manipulate queues of processes and allocate the processor(s) to processes. Together with the queues they manipulate, they form what is termed a *nucleus* and amount to perhaps a few hundred words on most computers, but this figure depends on the number of processes to be supported, on how easy it is to switch a processor from one process to another, on the number of peripheral devices to be supported and on how easy it is to determine the source of an interrupt. The nucleus can be designed in a high-level language such as Pascal and must then be implemented in machine code to take advantage of the architecture of the computer.

Listing 11

```
MONITOR MODULE CARDREADER;

   CONST
      *MAXCHAR = 80 (*CHARACTERS PER CARD*);
      CRMAX = 2 (*CARDREADERS*);

   TYPE
      *CARD = PACKED ARRAY [1..MAXCHAR] OF CHAR;
      *STATUS = ( *SUCCESS, *FAILURE, *ENDOFFILE );
      CRNUM = 1..CRMAX;

   MONITOR MODULE CRSCHEDULER;
      VAR
         POOL: SET OF CRNUM;
      INSTANCE
         QUEUE: CONDITION;
      PROCEDURE *ACQUIRE (VAR CR: CRNUM);
         BEGIN
            IF POOL = [] THEN QUEUE.WAIT;
            CR:= 1;  WHILE NOT (CR IN POOL) DO CR:= CR+1;
            POOL:= POOL - [CR]
         END;
      PROCEDURE *SUPPLY (CR: CRNUM);
         BEGIN POOL:= POOL + [CR];  QUEUE.SIGNAL END;
      BEGIN
         POOL:= [];
         ***
      END;

   MONITOR CONTROLLER (CR: CRNUM);
      VAR
         BUFFER: CARD;
         RESULT: STATUS;
         STATE: (EMPTY, FULL);
      INSTANCE
         NOTFULL,
         NOTEMPTY: CONDITION;
      PROCEDURE *READ (VAR C: CARD; VAR S: STATUS);
         BEGIN
            IF STATE = EMPTY THEN NOTEMPTY.WAIT;
            S:= RESULT;  IF S = SUCCESS THEN C:= BUFFER;
            STATE:= EMPTY;  NOTFULL.SIGNAL
         END;
      PROCEDURE READCARDSINTOBUFFER;
         CONST
            ETERNITY = FALSE;
         VAR
            M1, M2: TYPEWRITER.MESSAGE;
            N: TYPEWRITER.NAME;
         PROCEDURE REPORT (M: TYPEWRITER.MESSAGE);
            INSTANCE
               TW: TYPEWRITER.CONVERSATION(N, TYPEWRITER.OUTGOING);
            BEGIN TW.PRINT(M) END;
         PROCEDURE AWAITOPERATOR;
            BEGIN (*AWAIT INTERRUPT FROM OPERATOR ON READER "CR"*) END;
```

```
PROCEDURE READACARDINTOBUFFER;
   BEGIN
      (* READ A CARD INTO "BUFFER" FROM READER "CR",          *)
      (* RECORDING THE "SUCCESS" OR "FAILURE" OF THE          *)
      (* TRANSFER IN "RESULT"                                 *)
      IF RESULT = SUCCESS THEN
         IF BUFFER[1..4] = '****' THEN RESULT:= ENDOFFILE
   END;
   BEGIN
      N:= 'CR';  N[4]:= CHR(ORD('0') + CR);
      M1.TEXT:= 'FAILURE TO READ CARD';  M1.LENGTH:= 21;
      M2.TEXT:= 'FAILURE TO READ FILE';  M2.LENGTH:= 21;
      REPEAT
         AWAITOPERATOR;
         REPEAT (*READ FILES UNTIL FAILURE*)
            REPEAT (*READ UNTIL A TITLE CARD IS FOUND*)
               READACARDINTOBUFFER;
               IF RESULT = FAILURE THEN
                  BEGIN REPORT(M1);  AWAITOPERATOR END
            UNTIL RESULT = SUCCESS;
            STATE:= FULL;  CRSCHEDULER.SUPPLY(CR);
            IF STATE = FULL THEN NOTFULL.WAIT;
            REPEAT (*READ CARDS UNTIL FAILURE OR END OF FILE*)
               READACARDINTOBUFFER;
               IF RESULT = FAILURE THEN
                  BEGIN
                     REPORT(M1);
                     AWAITOPERATOR;
                     READACARDINTOBUFFER
                  END;
               STATE:= FULL;  NOTEMPTY.SIGNAL;
               IF STATE = FULL THEN NOTFULL.WAIT
            UNTIL RESULT <> SUCCESS
         UNTIL RESULT = FAILURE;
         REPORT(M2)
      UNTIL ETERNITY
   END;
   PROCESS MODULE CRHANDLER;
   BEGIN READCARDSINTOBUFFER END;
   BEGIN
      ***
   END;

INSTANCE
   CRCONTROLLER: ARRAY [CRNUM] OF CONTROLLER((1) (2));

ENVELOPE *READER;
   VAR
      CR: CRNUM;
      *RESULT: STATUS;
   PROCEDURE *READ (VAR C: CARD);
      BEGIN CRCONTROLLER[CR].READ(C, RESULT) END;
   BEGIN
      CRSCHEDULER.ACQUIRE(CR);  RESULT:= SUCCESS;
      ***
   END;

BEGIN
   ***
END;
```

Exercise 4 If we could not assume that the user of a virtual cardreader would read right up to the end of the file (or prior failure) and no further, how should the *reader* envelope be modified to prevent the user from reading too many cards and to skip any unread cards?

Exercise 5 In our operating system any user process is prepared to read any card file since every deck of cards contains a job to be run. If the system were to cater for data files as well as job files, each user process would have to specify the name of the file that it required (either *'JOB'* or the data file name), and each *crhandler* process, on reading a file's title card, would have to supply the scheduler with the name of the file as well as the number of the cardreader. Show how this facility can be added to the *cardreader* monitor. (*Hint:* This is similar to the handling of incoming conversations in the *typewriter* monitor (q.v.).)

THE LINEPRINTERS

The administration of the lineprinters is very similar to that of the cardreaders. Again we identify the devices by values of a subrange:

$$\textbf{type } lpnum = 1 \ . \ . \ lpmax$$

where

$$\textbf{const } lpmax = 2 \ \{lineprinters\};$$

again we have a simple scheduler with procedures *acquire* and *supply*; again we have one controller to handle data transfers on each device; again we have an envelope that maps a virtual device onto the corresponding real devices.

As before, we introduce a small service process, *lphandler*, into each controller, but its interface with the user process is slightly more complicated than was the case with the cardreaders: this is because not only lines must be buffered between them but also control signals, principally *newline* and *newpage*; one other control signal is also required, namely *endoffile*, since the *lphandler* process is unable to detect this event for itself, unlike the *crhandler* which searched the input for a four-star terminator. Thus, to effect the synchronization between the user and the *lphandler*, we need to declare the following variables and queues in the controller monitor.

var
    buffer : *line* ;
    operation : *controlop* ;
    result : *status* ;
    state : (*empty, full*) ;
instance
    notfull, notempty : *condition*

where

type
  controlop = (*linewrite*, *linethrow, *pagethrow, *endoffile) .

In other respects the *lpcontrollers* resemble the *crcontrollers*. In particular, the message *'FAILURE TO PRINT LINE'* is output to the operator in the event of a failure and, after the operator has pressed the interrupt button on the lineprinter, the operation is repeated; if it continues to fail the message *'FAILURE TO PRINT FILE'* is output and the printing of the file is abandoned. These messages are prefixed by the names *'LP 1'* or *'LP 2'* as appropriate. The body of the procedure *printlinesfrombuffer*, which is called by the *lphandler* process, is essentially as follows.

```
begin
  repeat
    awaitoperator ;
    repeat {print files until failure}
      repeat
        {throw to a new page} ;
        if result = failure then
          begin report (M1) ; awaitoperator end
        until result = success ;
        state := empty ; lpscheduler.supply (lp) ;
        if state = empty then notempty.wait ;
        repeat {print lines until failure or end of file}
          printalinefrombuffer ;
          if result = failure then
            begin report (M1) ; awaitoperator ; printalinefrombuffer end ;
          if result ≠ endfile then
            begin
              state := empty ; notfull.signal ;
              if state = empty then notempty.wait
            end
        until result ≠ success
      until result = failure ;
      report (M2)
    until eternity
end
```

The *printer* envelope may now be programmed; it begins by acquiring a printer, it continues by translating calls upon the procedures *print, newline* and *newpage* into calls upon the procedures *print* and *control* of the appropriate controller, and it finishes by sending an *endoffile* control signal to the controller. As with the cardreaders, the task of returning the device to the scheduler for allocation to another user devolves upon the controller's service process because the printer is not usually immediately available to be used again—normally because the last line has still to be printed from the buffer, and occasionally because some failure has to be remedied; in the latter case the *lphandler* process already knows that the file has come to a premature end and so the envelope refrains from sending it an *endoffile* signal.

```
envelope *printer;
  var lp: lpnum; *result: status;
  procedure *print (l: line);
    begin
      if result = success then with lpcontroller [lp] do print (l, result)
    end;
  procedure *newline ;
    begin
      if result = success then with lpcontroller [lp] do
        control (linethrow, result)
    end;
  procedure *newpage ;
    begin
      if result = success then with lpcontroller [lp] do
        control (pagethrow, result)
    end;
  begin
    lpscheduler.acquire (lp); result: = success;
    ***;
    if result = success then with lpcontroller [lp] do
      control (endoffile, result)
  end
```

Listing 12 shows the complete *lineprinter* administration monitor.

Exercise 6 In commercial data processing many files must be printed on special stationery, preprinted invoices or cheques for example. Modify the *lineprinter* monitor so that the user of a virtual lineprinter can specify, in the form of a message to the operator, the special stationery that he requires. The *lphandler* process should type the message and wait for the operator to change the paper; it should also tell the operator when the stationery is no longer required and wait for the paper to be changed back before continuing.

Listing 12

```
MONITOR MODULE LINEPRINTER;

  CONST
      *MAXCHAR = 120 (*CHARACTERS PER LINE*);
      LPMAX = 2 (*LINEPRINTERS*);

  TYPE
      *LINE = PACKED ARRAY [1..MAXCHAR] OF CHAR;
      *STATUS = ( *SUCCESS, *FAILURE, ENDFILE );
      LPNUM = 1..LPMAX;

  MONITOR MODULE LPSCHEDULER;
      VAR
          POOL: SET OF LPNUM;
      INSTANCE
          QUEUE: CONDITION;
      PROCEDURE *ACQUIRE (VAR LP: LPNUM);
          BEGIN
              IF POOL = [] THEN QUEUE.WAIT;
              LP:= 1;   WHILE NOT (LP IN POOL) DO LP:= LP+1;
              POOL:= POOL - [LP]
          END;
      PROCEDURE *SUPPLY (LP: LPNUM);
          BEGIN POOL:= POOL + [LP];   QUEUE.SIGNAL END;
      BEGIN
          POOL:= [];
          ***
      END;

  MONITOR CONTROLLER (LP: LPNUM);
      TYPE
          *CONTROLOP = (LINEWRITE, *LINETHROW, *PAGETHROW, *ENDOFFILE);
      VAR
          BUFFER: LINE;
          OPERATION: CONTROLOP;
          RESULT: STATUS;
          STATE: (EMPTY, FULL);
      INSTANCE
          NOTFULL,
          NOTEMPTY: CONDITION;
      PROCEDURE *PRINT (L: LINE; VAR S: STATUS);
          BEGIN
              IF STATE = FULL THEN NOTFULL.WAIT;
              S:= RESULT;  OPERATION:= LINEWRITE;   BUFFER:= L;
              STATE:= FULL;   NOTEMPTY.SIGNAL
          END;
      PROCEDURE *CONTROL (OP: CONTROLOP; VAR S: STATUS);
          BEGIN
              IF STATE = FULL THEN NOTFULL.WAIT;
              S:= RESULT;  OPERATION:= OP;
              STATE:= FULL;   NOTEMPTY.SIGNAL
          END;
```

```
PROCEDURE PRINTLINESFROMBUFFER;
   CONST
      ETERNITY = FALSE;
   VAR
      M1, M2: TYPEWRITER.MESSAGE;
      N: TYPEWRITER.NAME;
   PROCEDURE REPORT (M: TYPEWRITER.MESSAGE);
      INSTANCE
         TW: TYPEWRITER.CONVERSATION(N, TYPEWRITER.OUTGOING);
      BEGIN TW.PRINT(M) END;
   PROCEDURE AWAITOPERATOR;
      BEGIN (*AWAIT INTERRUPT FROM OPERATOR ON PRINTER "LP"*) END;
   PROCEDURE PRINTALINEFROMBUFFER;
      BEGIN
         CASE OPERATION OF
            LINEWRITE: (* WRITE A LINE FROM "BUFFER" TO PRINTER *)
                       (* "LP", RECORDING THE "SUCCESS" OR       *)
                       (* "FAILURE" OF THE TRANSFER IN "RESULT" *);
            LINETHROW: (* THROW TO A NEW LINE ON PRINTER "LP",   *)
                       (* RECORDING THE "SUCCESS" OR "FAILURE"   *)
                       (* OF THE OPERATION IN "RESULT"           *);
            PAGETHROW: (* THROW TO A NEW PAGE ON PRINTER "LP",   *)
                       (* RECORDING THE "SUCCESS" OR "FAILURE"   *)
                       (* OF THE OPERATION IN "RESULT"           *);
            ENDOFFILE: RESULT:= ENDFILE
         END
      END;
   BEGIN
      N:= 'LP'; N[4]:= CHR(ORD('0') + LP);
      M1.TEXT:= 'FAILURE TO PRINT LINE'; M1.LENGTH:= 22;
      M2.TEXT:= 'FAILURE TO PRINT FILE'; M2.LENGTH:= 22;
      REPEAT
         AWAITOPERATOR;
         REPEAT (*PRINT FILES UNTIL FAILURE*)
            REPEAT
               OPERATION:= PAGETHROW; PRINTALINEFROMBUFFER;
               IF RESULT = FAILURE THEN
                  BEGIN REPORT(M1); AWAITOPERATOR END
            UNTIL RESULT = SUCCESS;
            STATE:= EMPTY; LPSCHEDULER.SUPPLY(LP);
            IF STATE = EMPTY THEN NOTEMPTY.WAIT;
            REPEAT (*PRINT LINES UNTIL FAILURE OR END OF FILE*)
               PRINTALINEFROMBUFFER;
               IF RESULT = FAILURE THEN
                  BEGIN
                     REPORT(M1);
                     AWAITOPERATOR;
                     PRINTALINEFROMBUFFER
                  END;
               IF RESULT <> ENDFILE THEN
                  BEGIN
                     STATE:= EMPTY; NOTFULL.SIGNAL;
                     IF STATE = EMPTY THEN NOTEMPTY.WAIT
                  END
            UNTIL RESULT <> SUCCESS
         UNTIL RESULT = FAILURE;
         REPORT(M2)
      UNTIL ETERNITY
   END;
```

```
PROCESS MODULE LPHANDLER;
   BEGIN PRINTLINESFROMBUFFER END;
BEGIN
   ***
END;

INSTANCE
   LPCONTROLLER: ARRAY [LPNUM] OF CONTROLLER((1) (2));

ENVELOPE *PRINTER;
   VAR
      *RESULT: STATUS;
      LP: LPNUM;
   PROCEDURE *PRINT (L: LINE);
      BEGIN
         IF RESULT = SUCCESS THEN WITH LPCONTROLLER[LP] DO
                                            PRINT(L, RESULT)
      END;
   PROCEDURE *NEWLINE;
      BEGIN
         IF RESULT = SUCCESS THEN WITH LPCONTROLLER[LP] DO
                                            CONTROL(LINETHROW, RESULT)
      END;
   PROCEDURE *NEWPAGE;
      BEGIN
         IF RESULT = SUCCESS THEN WITH LPCONTROLLER[LP] DO
                                            CONTROL(PAGETHROW, RESULT)
      END;
   BEGIN
      LPSCHEDULER.ACQUIRE(LP);   RESULT:= SUCCESS;
      ***;
      IF RESULT = SUCCESS THEN WITH LPCONTROLLER[LP] DO
                                         CONTROL(ENDOFFILE, RESULT)
   END;

BEGIN
   ***
END;
```

THE TYPEWRITERS

Outgoing Conversations

We have already seen that the typewriters can be used for "outgoing" conversations, initiated by processes, and "incoming" conversations, initiated by operators; for the moment we shall consider just the former.

As usual the *typewriter* administration monitor will consist of a scheduler, one controller for each device, and an envelope. As with the cardreaders and lineprinters we shall declare, local to each controller monitor, a process (*twhandler*) to handle the data transfers to and from the device it is controlling and to deal with faults that arise on that device. Faults will be dealt with in the usual way by outputting a message to report the fault, repeating the operation that failed and, if the fault persists, outputting a further message to terminate the conversation; on each occasion the *twhandler* process waits for the operator to press the interrupt button on the typewriter when the fault has been rectified. We shall direct the failure messages to the faulty typewriter: although this seems to be paradoxical it is adequate for several reasons. Firstly, the failure may have occurred on input and the output may be unaffected. Secondly, many of the faults that afflict typewriters are transitory and there is a good chance that the failure message will be printed satisfactorily. Thirdly, the use of another typewriter for reporting faults, if indeed there is another convenient typewriter, may lead to deadlock, which is a more serious problem. Fourthly, if the failure message does not appear the operator will soon realize that his typewriter is lifeless.

We may now program the *typewriter* administration monitor to handle outgoing conversations. First we shall identify the two typewriters by values of

$$\textbf{type } twnum = 1 \ .. \ twmax$$

where

$$\textbf{const } twmax = 2 \ \{typewriters\} \ .$$

Next we program the scheduler with its two procedures to *acquire* a typewriter from, and to *supply* a typewriter to, the pool of free devices.

```
monitor module twscheduler ;
    var pool : set of twnum ;
    instance outgoing : condition ;
    procedure *acquire (var tw : twnum) ;
        begin
            if pool = [   ] then outgoing.wait ;
            tw := 1 ; while not (tw in pool) do tw := tw + 1 ;
            pool := pool − [tw]
        end;
    procedure *supply (tw : twnum) ;
        begin pool := pool + [tw] ; outgoing.signal end ;
    begin pool := [   ] ; *** end
```

The function of the controller monitor is to enable the user process to communicate with the *twhandler* process. This communication consists of the user sending the *twhandler* a signal to *read* a message, to *print* a message, to throw to a *newline* or to *finish* a conversation, and the *twhandler* sending the user a status value to denote the success or failure of the operation; in addition the message that is being input or output has to be buffered. Thus the following variables and queues are required to effect the synchronization between the user and the *twhandler*.

var
    buffer : *message* ;
    operation : *controlop* ;
    result : *status* ;
    state : (*free, busy*) ;
instance
    notbusy, notfree : *condition*

where

type
    controlop = (*textread, textprint, linethrow, finishconversation*) .

The four procedures invoked from the envelope are as follows; in general they indicate the required operation, signal the *twhandler* and wait until it has completed the operation, and then note the status result. A slight complication arises if the result denotes a failure, for then the *twhandler* process must be reactivated to report the failure to the operator.

procedure *∗read* (**var** *m* : *message*; **var** *s* : *status*) ;
    begin
        operation := *textread* ;
        state := *busy* ; *notfree.signal* ;
        if *state* = *busy* **then** *notbusy.wait* ;
        s := *result* ; **if** *s* = *success* **then** *m* := *buffer* ;
        if *s* = *failure* **then begin** *state* := *busy*; *notfree.signal* **end**
    end;
procedure *∗print* (*m* : *message* ; **var** *s* : *status*);
    begin
        operation := *textprint* ; *buffer* := *m* ;
        state := *busy* ; *notfree.signal* ;
        if *state* = *busy* **then** *notbusy.wait* ;
        s := *result* ;
        if *s* = *failure* **then begin** *state* := *busy*; *notfree.signal* **end**
    end;
procedure *∗newline* (**var** *s* : *status*) ;
    begin
        operation := *linethrow* ;
        state := *busy* ; *notfree.signal* ;

```
   if state = busy then notbusy.wait ;
   s := result;
   if s = failure then begin state := busy; notfree.signal end
 end;
procedure *finish ;
  begin
     operation := finishconversation ;
     state := busy ; notfree.signal
end
```

The *twhandler* process spends its entire life executing a procedure of the controller monitor:

```
process module twhandler ;
  begin transfermessagestoandfrombuffer end
```

where:

```
procedure tranfermessagestoandfrombuffer ;
  const eternity = false ;
  var M1, M2 : message ;
  procedure awaitoperator ;
    begin {await interrupt from operator on typewriter 'tw' end ;
  procedure read ;
    begin
       {read a message into 'buffer' from typwriter 'tw', recording
        the 'success' or 'failure' of the transfer in 'result'}
    end;
  procedure print (m : message) ;
    begin
       {print a message from 'm' on typewriter 'tw', recording the
        'success' or 'failure' of the transfer in 'result'}
    end;
  procedure newline ;
    begin
       {throw to a new line on typewriter 'tw', recording the
        'success' or 'failure' of the operation in 'result')
    end;
  procedure performoperation ;
    begin
       case operation of
          textread : read ;
```

```
      textprint : print (buffer) ;
      linethrow : newline ;
      finishconversation : result := endofconversation
   end
end;
begin
   M1.text := 'FAILURE TO TRANSFER MESSAGE.' ;
   M1.length := 28 ;
   M2.text := 'FAILURE TO COMPLETE CONVERSATION.' ;
   M2.length := 33 ;
   repeat
      awaitoperator ;
      repeat {carry on conversations until failure}
         state := free ; twscheduler.supply (tw) ;
         if state = free then notfree.wait ;
         repeat {read and print messages until failure or end of
                 conversation}
            performoperation ;
            if result = failure then
               begin
                  newline; print (M1) ;
                  newline ; performoperation
               end;
            if result ≠ endofconversation then
               begin
                  state := free; notbusy.signal;
                  if state = free then notfree.wait;
               end
         until result ≠ success
      until result = failure ;
      newline ; print (M2)
   until eternity
end .
```

Some care should be devoted to the design of the envelope. As each typewriter will be used to converse with a variety of processes it is important that the operator should be able to distinguish readily between the various conversations, so, on opening a conversation with an operator, a process must preface the exchange of messages by typing some identifying name. Thus when an instance of the *conversation* envelope is declared for an outgoing conversation, the envelope prints the word *'FROM'*, followed by the identifying name, on a new line and indents the subsequent lines of the conversation by four spaces. For example, if the controller of cardreader number two fails to read a card properly, it holds the following, one-sided, conversation with an operator.

FROM CR 2   FAILURE TO READ CARD.

A conversation to report a fault will usually be kept as short as possible but a conversation in which the "operator" is using the typewriter to edit a file, or to run a program interactively, or to browse round an information-retrieval system, will typically consist of many messages being transmitted in each direction.

```
envelope *conversation (n : name) ;
   var
      tw : twnum ;
      FROM, TAB : message ;
      *result : status ;
   procedure *read (var m : message) ;
      begin if result = success then twcontroller [tw].read (m, result) end ;
   procedure *print (m : message) ;
      begin if result = success then twcontroller [tw].print (m, result) end ;
   procedure *newline ;
      begin
         if result = success then twcontroller [tw].newline (result) ;
         if result = success then twcontroller [tw].print (TAB, result)
      end ;
   begin
      TAB.text := '    '; TAB.length := 4 ;
      FROM.text := 'FROM        ': FROM.text [6 .. 9] := n ;
      FROM.length := 13 ;
      repeat
         twscheduler.acquire (tw) ;
         twcontroller [tw].newline (result) ;
         if result = success then twcontroller [tw].print (FROM,result)
      until result = success ;
      ***;
      if result = success then twcontroller [tw]. finish
   end
```

Note that if the envelope is unfortunate enough to acquire a typewriter that is faulty from the start it tries again with another one.

Incoming Conversations

We shall also cater for incoming conversations. Although an incoming conversation is initiated by the operator, the process he wishes to address must be waiting ready to accept the call, if we wish to draw an analogy with the telephone system. To initiate an incoming conversation the operator presses a "call button" on his typewriter; a "switching" process associated with that typewriter is awoken by the resulting interrupt and, after waiting for the current conversation, if any, on that typewriter to finish, types the word 'CALL'; the operator replies with the name associated with the process it is calling; the switching process passes this name and the number of the typewriter to the scheduler; if the named process is waiting it is awoken and continues the conversation but, if it is not, the switching process tells the operator that the call has failed. Thus the switching process plays the rôle of a telephone switchboard operator who accepts calls and routes each to its proper destination. An example of a short incoming conversation is:

$$CALL \quad STOP \qquad OK.$$

We modify the *conversation* envelope so that a process can state whether it is to await an incoming call or engage as soon as possible in an outgoing call. We also test every message read to check whether the operator has typed 'WAIT', this being the signal that the conversation is to be interrupted until he resumes it later as an incoming conversation.

```
envelope *conversation (n : name; outorin : typeofconversation) ;
   var WAIT : message ; *result: status;
      :
      :
   procedure *read (var m : message) ;
      begin
         if result = success then twcontroller [tw].read (m, result) ;
         while (result = success) and (m = WAIT) do
            begin
               twcontroller [tw].finish ;
               twscheduler.await (tw,n) ;
               twcontroller [tw].print (TAB, result) ;
               if result = success then twcontroller [tw].read (m, result)
            end
      end;
      :
      :
   begin
      :
      :
      WAIT.text := 'WAIT' ; WAIT.length := 4 ;
```

```
case outorin of
    outgoing :
    repeat
        twscheduler.acquire (tw) ;
        twcontroller [tw].newline (result) ;
        if result = success then
            twcontroller [tw].print (FROM,result]
        until result = success ;
    incoming ;
    repeat
        twscheduler.await (tw,n) ;
        twcontroller [tw].print (TAB,result)
    until result = success
end;
***;
if result = success then twcontroller [tw]. finish
end
```

The messages *WAIT* and *TAB* are essentially constants and could therefore be moved out of the envelope to a more global position within the *typewriter* monitor. Indeed the same applies to the error messages we have used in the *cardreader*, *lineprinter* and *typewriter* administration monitors.

Turning our attention to the scheduler we note that a new procedure has been introduced, namely *await* which is invoked by a process awaiting an incoming conversation: the process supplies the name associated with the conversation and receives in return the identity of the typewriter on which the conversation is to take place. There must of course be a corresponding scheduler procedure, *call*, which is invoked by a typewriter's switching process on detecting an incoming call; the *call* procedure supplies the scheduler with the identity of the typewriter and the name of the conversation and in return it is informed whether or not there was a process waiting for that particular conversation. The switching process, which is declared local to the controller monitor, takes the following form.

```
process module twswitchingprocess ;
    const eternity = false ;
    var
        m, CALL, FAIL : message ;
        result : status ;
        ok : Boolean ;
    begin
        CALL.text := 'CALL ' ; CALL.length := 5 ;
```

```
    FAIL.text := '          FAILED' ; FAIL.length := 11 ;
    repeat
        awaitcallbutton ; twscheduler.reserve (tw) ;
        print (CALL, result) ;
        if result = success then read (m, result) ;
        if result = success then
            begin
                ok := (m.length = 4) ;
                if ok then twscheduler.call (tw, m.text [1 .. 4,] ok) ;
                if not ok then
                    begin
                        print (FAIL,result) ;
                        if result = success then finish
                    end
            end
    until eternity
    end
```

where *CALL* and *FAIL* can be treated as constants and made more global and the monitor procedure *awaitcallbutton* is:

```
procedure awaitcallbutton ;
    begin {await interrupt from call button on typewriter 'tw'} end.
```

The switching process has now introduced another call on the scheduler, namely *reserve* which resembles *acquire* except that it demands the use of a particular typewriter rather than any typewriter; also it is desirable to give precedence to incoming calls over outgoing calls if the operator is not to be in danger of being locked out. Indeed it is worth noting that any process that produces a lot of output to a typewriter should occasionally pause to input some response from the operator: this gives the operator the chance to stem the flood of output, possibly by typing '*WAIT*' so that he can continue it again later—some such ploy is necessary if the output is appearing on a display screen and is in danger of being scrolled off the screen before the operator has had a chance to read it.

To summarize, the scheduler now has the following procedures:

```
acquire (var twnum)
```

invoked by the user for an outgoing call;

await (**var** *twnum* ; *name*)

invoked by the user for an incoming call;

reserve (*twnum*)

invoked by *twswitchingprocess* in order to accept an incoming call;

call (*twnum* ; *name* ; **var** *Boolean*)

invoked by *twswitchingprocess* to signal an incoming call;

supply (*twnum*)

invoked by *twhandler* after a call.

The scheduler maintains a pool of available typewriters and it has one queue on which user processes wait for *outgoing* conversations (they wait in procedure *acquire* and the signal comes from procedure *supply*), another queue on which user processes wait for *incoming* calls (they wait in procedure *await* and the signal comes from procedure *call*), and an array of queues, one for each switching process to wait on when it needs to use its own *typewriter* (it waits in procedure *reserve* and the signal comes from procedure *supply*). A free typewriter is always offered first to a process on the appropriate *typewriter* queue before it is offered to a process on the *outgoing* queue, thereby giving priority to incoming calls. Subject to that, however, the *outgoing* queue is serviced on a first-come first-served basis. The *incoming* queue is serviced quite differently: processes on it are signaled in turn until one is found that can match the name of the incoming call with its own name or until the queue has been emptied, whereupon all the processes that failed to accept the proffered conversation rejoin the queue; the order of queuing is immaterial.

The scheduler, together with the rest of the *typewriter* administration monitor, is shown in Listing 13.

Listing 13

```
MONITOR MODULE TYPEWRITER;

   CONST
      *MAXNAME = 4 (* CHARACTERS PER NAME *);
      *MAXCHAR = 36 (* CHARACTERS PER MESSAGE *);
      TWMAX = 2 (* TYPEWRITERS *);

   TYPE
      *NAME = PACKED ARRAY [1..MAXNAME] OF CHAR;
      *TYPEOFCONVERSATION = ( *OUTGOING, *INCOMING );
      *MESSAGE = RECORD
                    *LENGTH: 0..MAXCHAR;
                    *TEXT: PACKED ARRAY [1..MAXCHAR] OF CHAR
                 END;
      *STATUS = ( *SUCCESS, *FAILURE, ENDOFCONVERSATION );
      TWNUM = 1..TWMAX;

   VAR
      M1, M2, TAB, WAIT, CALL, FAIL: MESSAGE;

   MONITOR MODULE TWSCHEDULER;
      VAR
         POOL: SET OF TWNUM;
         CALLNAME: NAME;
         CALLTW: TWNUM;
         CALLOK: BOOLEAN;
      INSTANCE
         OUTGOING,
         INCOMING: CONDITION;
         TYPEWRITER: ARRAY [TWNUM] OF CONDITION;
      PROCEDURE *ACQUIRE (VAR TW: TWNUM);
         BEGIN
            IF POOL = [] THEN OUTGOING.WAIT;
            TW:= 1;  WHILE NOT (TW IN POOL) DO TW:= TW+1;
            POOL:= POOL - [TW]
         END;
      PROCEDURE *RESERVE (TW: TWNUM);
         BEGIN
            IF NOT (TW IN POOL) THEN TYPEWRITER[TW].WAIT;
            POOL:= POOL - [TW]
         END;
      PROCEDURE *SUPPLY (TW: TWNUM);
         BEGIN
            POOL:= POOL + [TW];
            IF TYPEWRITER[TW].LENGTH > 0
               THEN TYPEWRITER[TW].SIGNAL
               ELSE OUTGOING.SIGNAL
         END;
      PROCEDURE *AWAIT (VAR TW: TWNUM; N: NAME);
         BEGIN
            INCOMING.WAIT;
            WHILE CALLNAME <> N DO
               BEGIN INCOMING.SIGNAL;  INCOMING.WAIT END;
            TW:= CALLTW;
            CALLOK:= TRUE
         END;
```

```
PROCEDURE *CALL (TW: TWNUM; N: NAME; VAR OK: BOOLEAN);
   BEGIN
      CALLTW:= TW;  CALLNAME:= N;
      CALLOK:= FALSE;  INCOMING.SIGNAL;  OK:= CALLOK
   END;
BEGIN
   POOL:= [];
   ***
END;

MONITOR CONTROLLER (TW: TWNUM);
   TYPE
      CONTROLOP =
                 (TEXTREAD, TEXTPRINT, LINETHROW, FINISHCONVERSATION);
   VAR
      BUFFER: MESSAGE;
      OPERATION: CONTROLOP;
      RESULT: STATUS;
      STATE: (FREE, BUSY);
   INSTANCE
      NOTBUSY, NOTFREE: CONDITION;
   PROCEDURE *READ (VAR M: MESSAGE; VAR S: STATUS);
      BEGIN
         OPERATION:= TEXTREAD;
         STATE:=BUSY;  NOTFREE.SIGNAL;
         IF STATE = BUSY THEN NOTBUSY.WAIT;
         S:= RESULT;  IF S = SUCCESS THEN M:= BUFFER;
         IF S = FAILURE THEN BEGIN STATE:= BUSY; NOTFREE.SIGNAL END
      END;
   PROCEDURE *PRINT (M: MESSAGE; VAR S: STATUS);
      BEGIN
         OPERATION:= TEXTPRINT;  BUFFER:= M;
         STATE:= BUSY;  NOTFREE.SIGNAL;
         IF STATE = BUSY THEN NOTBUSY.WAIT;
         S:= RESULT;
         IF S = FAILURE THEN BEGIN STATE:= BUSY; NOTFREE.SIGNAL END
      END;
   PROCEDURE *NEWLINE (VAR S: STATUS);
      BEGIN
         OPERATION:= LINETHROW;
         STATE:= BUSY;  NOTFREE.SIGNAL;
         IF STATE = BUSY THEN NOTBUSY.WAIT;
         S:= RESULT;
         IF S = FAILURE THEN BEGIN STATE:= BUSY; NOTFREE.SIGNAL END
      END;
   PROCEDURE *FINISH;
      BEGIN
         OPERATION:= FINISHCONVERSATION;
         STATE:= BUSY;  NOTFREE.SIGNAL
      END;
```

```
PROCEDURE TRANSFERMESSAGESTOANDFROMBUFFER;
   CONST
      ETERNITY = FALSE;
   PROCEDURE AWAITOPERATOR;
      BEGIN
         (* AWAIT INTERRUPT FROM OPERATOR ON TYPEWRITER "TW" *)
      END;
   PROCEDURE READ;
      BEGIN
         (* READ A MESSAGE INTO "BUFFER" FROM TYPEWRITER "TW",   *)
         (* RECORDING THE "SUCCESS" OR "FAILURE" OF THE          *)
         (* TRANSFER IN "RESULT"                                 *)
      END;
   PROCEDURE PRINT (M: MESSAGE);
      BEGIN
         (* PRINT A MESSAGE FROM "M" ON TYPEWRITER "TW",         *)
         (* RECORDING THE "SUCCESS" OR "FAILURE" OF THE          *)
         (* TRANSFER IN "RESULT"                                 *)
      END;
   PROCEDURE NEWLINE;
      BEGIN
         (* THROW TO A NEW LINE ON TYPEWRITER "TW",              *)
         (* RECORDING THE "SUCCESS" OR "FAILURE" OF THE          *)
         (* OPERATION IN "RESULT"                                *)
      END;
   PROCEDURE PERFORMOPERATION;
      BEGIN
         CASE OPERATION OF
            TEXTREAD: READ;
            TEXTPRINT: PRINT(BUFFER);
            LINETHROW: NEWLINE;
            FINISHCONVERSATION: RESULT:= ENDOFCONVERSATION
         END
      END;
   BEGIN
      REPEAT
         AWAITOPERATOR;
         REPEAT (* CARRY ON CONVERSATIONS UNTIL FAILURE *)
            STATE:= FREE;  TWSCHEDULER.SUPPLY(TW);
            IF STATE = FREE THEN NOTFREE.WAIT;
            REPEAT (* READ AND PRINT MESSAGES UNTIL FAILURE *)
                   (* OR END OF CONVERSATION               *)
               PERFORMOPERATION;
               IF RESULT = FAILURE THEN
                  BEGIN
                     NEWLINE;  PRINT(M1);  NEWLINE;  PRINT(TAB);
                     PERFORMOPERATION
                  END;
               IF RESULT <> ENDOFCONVERSATION THEN
                  BEGIN
                     STATE:= FREE;  NOTBUSY.SIGNAL;
                     IF STATE = FREE THEN NOTFREE.WAIT
                  END
            UNTIL RESULT <> SUCCESS
         UNTIL RESULT = FAILURE;
         NEWLINE;  PRINT(M2)
      UNTIL ETERNITY
   END;
PROCESS MODULE TWHANDLER;
   BEGIN TRANSFERMESSAGESTOANDFROMBUFFER END;
```

```
PROCEDURE AWAITCALLBUTTON;
    BEGIN
        (* AWAIT INTERRUPT FROM CALL BUTTON ON TYPEWRITER "TW"    *)
    END;
PROCESS MODULE TWSWITCHINGPROCESS;
    CONST
        ETERNITY = FALSE;
    VAR
        M: MESSAGE;
        RESULT: STATUS;
        OK: BOOLEAN;
    BEGIN
        REPEAT
            AWAITCALLBUTTON;  TWSCHEDULER.RESERVE(TW);
            PRINT(CALL, RESULT);
            IF RESULT = SUCCESS THEN READ(M, RESULT);
            IF RESULT = SUCCESS THEN
                BEGIN
                    OK:= (M.LENGTH = 4);
                    IF OK THEN TWSCHEDULER.CALL(TW, M.TEXT[1..4], OK);
                    IF NOT OK THEN
                        BEGIN
                            PRINT(FAIL, RESULT);
                            IF RESULT = SUCCESS THEN FINISH
                        END
                END
        UNTIL ETERNITY
    END;
    BEGIN
        ***
    END;

INSTANCE
    TWCONTROLLER: ARRAY [1..TWMAX] OF CONTROLLER((1) (2));
ENVELOPE *CONVERSATION (N: NAME; OUTORIN: TYPEOFCONVERSATION);
    VAR
        TW: TWNUM;
        FROM: MESSAGE;
        *RESULT: STATUS;
    PROCEDURE *READ (VAR M: MESSAGE);
        BEGIN
            IF RESULT = SUCCESS THEN TWCONTROLLER[TW].READ(M, RESULT);
            WHILE (RESULT = SUCCESS) AND (M = WAIT) DO
                BEGIN
                    TWCONTROLLER[TW].FINISH;
                    TWSCHEDULER.AWAIT(TW, N);
                    TWCONTROLLER[TW].PRINT(TAB, RESULT);
                    IF RESULT = SUCCESS THEN
                        TWCONTROLLER[TW].READ(M, RESULT)
                END
        END;
    PROCEDURE *PRINT (M: MESSAGE);
        BEGIN
            IF RESULT = SUCCESS THEN TWCONTROLLER[TW].PRINT(M, RESULT)
        END;
    PROCEDURE *NEWLINE;
        BEGIN
            IF RESULT = SUCCESS THEN TWCONTROLLER[TW].NEWLINE(RESULT);
            IF RESULT = SUCCESS THEN TWCONTROLLER[TW].PRINT(TAB, RESULT)
        END;
```

```
     BEGIN
        CASE OUTORIN OF
           OUTGOING: BEGIN
                        FROM.TEXT:= 'FROM          ';
                        FROM.TEXT[6..9]:= N;  FROM.LENGTH:= 13;
                        REPEAT
                           TWSCHEDULER.ACQUIRE(TW);
                           TWCONTROLLER[TW].NEWLINE(RESULT);
                           IF RESULT = SUCCESS THEN
                              TWCONTROLLER[TW].PRINT(FROM, RESULT)
                        UNTIL RESULT = SUCCESS
                     END;
           INCOMING: REPEAT
                        TWSCHEDULER.AWAIT(TW, N);
                        TWCONTROLLER[TW].PRINT(TAB, RESULT)
                     UNTIL RESULT = SUCCESS
        END;
        ***;
        IF RESULT = SUCCESS THEN TWCONTROLLER[TW].FINISH
     END;
  BEGIN
     M1.LENGTH  := 28;  M1.TEXT  := 'FAILURE TO TRANSFER MESSAGE';
     M2.LENGTH  := 33;  M2.TEXT  := 'FAILURE TO COMPLETE CONVERSATION';
     TAB.LENGTH := 4;  TAB.TEXT := '    ';
     WAIT.LENGTH:= 4;  WAIT.TEXT:= 'WAIT';
     CALL.LENGTH:= 5;  CALL.TEXT:= 'CALL ';
     FAIL.LENGTH:= 11;  FAIL.TEXT:= '    FAILED';
     ***
  END;
```

Implementation Considerations

This program, despite its moderate length of about 250 lines (about a third of which contain just a single word), provides as powerful and as simple an interface to its users as one could expect of an operating system such as this. Nevertheless the 250 or so lines of code hide a considerable amount of complexity and, unfortunately, further complexity is bound to arise when one considers real typewriters that differ from the "ideal" typewriters postulated here.

For example, although it is usual for cardreaders and lineprinters to have "interrupt buttons" that the operator can use to signal to the operating system that those devices are operable, it is unusual for a typewriter to have such an interrupt button, nor does it normally have a "call button" to enable the operator to initiate an incoming conversation. The effect of these can be achieved by reserving two of the control characters in the typewriter's character set to play the rôles of these two buttons. We then need to introduce into the operating system a routine that will read in each character as it is offered by the typewriter and analyze it to decide whether to pass it on to the process that is waiting for it or else simulate an "operable" or "call button" interrupt. This routine may be a small process in the operating system or, for efficiency, it would probably be incorporated into the nucleus routine that services interrupts.

Likewise, if the machine has no interrupt mechanism one can introduce, for each peripheral device, a small service process that regularly polls the device and, on finding it ready, simulates an interrupt. Again, for efficiency, one would probably replace the family of polling processes by a single process, embedded in the nucleus, to poll all the devices.

A further problem arises from the fact that typewriters work a character at a time, whereas we have assumed that an entire message can be read or printed as a unit. Obviously the *read* and *print* procedures have to be programmed as loops, the only difficulty arising when the *read* procedure tries to detect the end of the message that is being typed: some control character must be set aside to mean "end of message".

With all peripheral devices a serious problem must be faced: if the device does not respond after some suitable interval the operation should be terminated; for example one may be trying to output to a device that has been switched off, or one may be trying to read from a typewriter when the operator has gone to find a cup of coffee. The provision of a time-out mechanism is not difficult in principle although it may be tricky in practice. For the queue associated with each peripheral device we introduce a clock process whose task is to signal that queue at regular intervals of say t seconds. A process waiting for an interrupt from that device would ignore the first n clock signals and would take notice of the $(n + 1)$st, assuming of course that the device had not responded by then. This would give a time-out interval in the range of $nt \ldots (n + 1)t$; in practice n need be no larger than 1 or 2 since the exact duration of a time-out interval is not usually critical. Again, a single clock process servicing all the interrupt queues would be preferable.

The Operators

We began the design of this operating system by considering the users' view of the system. We have yet to consider the operators' point of view. This is perhaps as good a place as any to consider it as the operator is primarily concerned with the peripheral devices and his main channel of communication with the operating system is his typewriter.

The operators begin a session by mounting the disk pack that contains the file store and loading the operating system into the computer. The operating system begins execution but at this stage has no cardreaders, lineprinters or typewriters available to it. The operators can, at any time, press the interrupt button on one of these devices to make it available to the operating system. The operators have two main tasks: to supply the card readers with decks of cards containing jobs to be run—and each of these has to begin with a title card and finish with one or more terminator cards; and to burst the output from the printers and distribute it to the users.

This routine is occasionally interrupted to deal with a message on the typewriter relating to the "failure" of a peripheral device. "Failure" is perhaps too strong a word, for usually the reader will have run out of cards or the printer will have run out of paper and supplies must be replenished. The failure messages that may be received are as follows.

FROM CR n	*FAILURE TO READ CARD.*
FROM LP n	*FAILURE TO PRINT LINE.*
FROM TW n	*FAILURE TO TRANSFER MESSAGE.*

The operator knows that another attempt will be made when he has rectified the fault and pressed the interrupt button on the device. If then the fault persists he will receive one of the following messages.

FROM CR n	*FAILURE TO READ FILE.*
FROM LP n	*FAILURE TO PRINT FILE.*
FROM TW n	*FAILURE TO COMPLETE CONVERSATION.*

The operator knows that the file or the conversation has been abandoned. In the case of a cardreader he must remove any remaining cards of the affected file and later, or on another reader, resubmit the entire file. In the case of a lineprinter he must inform the user for whom the file was being printed or he must resubmit that user's job. Two other failure messages may be printed; these are detected by some user's job and either the job must be resubmitted or else the user informed that his job was unable to run.

FROM USER   name-of-user—FAULTY CARDREADER FOR JOB
name-of-job
FROM USER   name-of-user—TOO MANY CARDS FOR JOB
name-of-job

At the end of the session the operator can stop the system by pressing the call button on a typewriter and, when the word *'CALL'* appears, typing the name *'STOP'*; the system will acknowledge this by typing *'OK'*.

CALL STOP   OK.

Later, when all processing of users' jobs has been completed, the system will output to some typewriter the message:

FROM STOP   SYSTEM STOPPED.

Had the operator inadvertently called up a non-existent program instead of *'STOP'* he would have been informed of his mistake and could have tried again.

CALL STQP   FAILED.

As the system stands the operator is not required to type any messages during a conversation and so he has no occasion to use the *'WAIT'* facility.

Exercise 7   The operators of our system have no way of finding out what jobs have been run, what jobs are currently in the system, what stage each job has reached, and so on. Nor have they any way of telling the operating system that a particular peripheral device is to be removed from service (perhaps for routine maintenance) when it has finished its current task. Nor have they any way of obtaining statistics on the resources used by jobs: turnround times for instance, or run times, or quantities of input and output, or sizes of intermediate files.

Provide one or more of these services. This will usually necessitate writing a monitor in which to record the required information, and a process to print the information when requested to do so by an operator; the *switch* monitor with its *stopper* process in Listing 2 is an example of this.

THE FILE STORE

The file store is the one remaining resource to be considered. Recall that two types of file are to be provided, one to hold spooled and intermediate data, and the other to hold library programs. Both types are sequential; the library files can be read block by block; the other files can be written block by block and read once, block by block, the blocks being discarded as they are read. On reading or writing a block a status result is made available: this will usually be *success* but it may be *endoffile* (the length of a file cannot exceed 500 blocks of 1K characters) or, in the case of an attempt to use a non-existent library file, it may be *nofile*; the possibility of failure is not countenanced.

We have also decided that the actual store onto which the files will be mapped is to be a standard exchangeable disk pack with 200 cylinders of 10 tracks of 3 sectors of 1K characters. Furthermore it was decided that the library would be updated off-line and that, because the users have no permanent files, the dumping and restoration of files are unnecessary.

We may begin the construction of the *filestore* administration monitor with the following definitions for addressing blocks.

const
$CMAX = 200 \ \{cylinders\}$; $TMAX = 10 \ \{tracks\}$; $SMAX = 3$
$\{sectors\}$; $TS = 30 \ \{sectors \ per \ cylinder\}$; $CTS = 6000 \ \{sectors \ per \ disk\}$;
type
$cylinder = 1 \ .. \ CMAX$; $track = 1 \ .. \ TMAX$; $sector = 1 \ .. \ SMAX$;
$address = $ **packed record** c : $cylinder$; t : $track$; s : $sector$ **end**

Two schedulers are required, one to schedule the use of sectors and the other to schedule access to the disk; a monitor to control access to the disk is needed; and two envelopes must be defined to provide users with a *file* and a *libraryfile*.

Because it is simple let us take the disk access controller first; it provides two procedures to *read* and *write* blocks; these may invoke another procedure, *seek*, to move the read/write heads to a different cylinder. The complete *diskcontroller* monitor is shown in Listing 14.

Listing 14

```
MONITOR MODULE DISKCONTROLLER;

VAR
    CYL: CYLINDER;

PROCEDURE SEEK (C: CYLINDER);
    BEGIN
        (* MOVE HEADS TO CYLINDER "C" ON DISK *);
        CYL:= C
    END;

PROCEDURE *READ (A: ADDRESS; VAR B: BLOCK);
    BEGIN
        IF A.C <> CYL THEN SEEK(A.C);
        (* READ A BLOCK INTO "B" FROM SECTOR "A" ON DISK *)
    END;

PROCEDURE *WRITE (A: ADDRESS; B: BLOCK);
    BEGIN
        IF A.C <> CYL THEN SEEK(A.C);
        (* WRITE A BLOCK FROM "B" TO SECTOR "A" ON DISK *)
    END;

BEGIN
    CYL:= 1;
    ***
END;
```

In passing we may note the simplicity of this controller compared with the complexity of the other controllers we have programmed. This is due in part to our assumption of failure-free operation, and in part to the fact that the users operate directly on the device, rather than through the offices of a dedicated device-handling process with the resulting complexities of buffering and synchronization. We avoid the need for a *diskhandler* process by assuming that the device has no existence except when a user is operating upon it. This assumption could not have been made when we were considering the other types of peripheral device, although it might be true of more passive resources such as main store. There are several reasons why device-handling processes may be necessary. One reason is, again, concerned with the failure of devices: a user does not wish to nurse a sick device until it has been restored to health: this the device-handling process can do. Another reason is that we wish to overlap data transfers with processing when using many devices, particularly ones operating on sequential data files: cardreaders and lineprinters fall into this category in most operating systems. Yet another reason is that the device may operate independently of any of the users: the *twswitchingprocess* was incorporated in the typewriter controller for just such a purpose to deal with incoming conversations. Thus considerable simplicity can be gained by assuming failure-free operation provided failures occur infrequently (as in main store) or (as may be the case with typewriters) are not too embarrassing when they do occur.

To avoid excessive numbers of head movements we schedule requests to use the disk according to the number of the cylinder sought rather than first come, first served. To prevent any request from being passed over indefinitely often we use the "elevator algorithm" in which the disk heads sweep across the cylinders, first in one direction and then in the other, selecting the nearest outstanding request in the current direction of travel. Furthermore, when writing a block to disk, we can choose to output it to a sector on, or as near as possible to, the current cylinder, thereby considerably reducing the number of head movements. Thus the algorithm performs as many transfers from and to the current cylinder as possible, it then selects the next *read* operation in the current direction, changing direction if there is none, and finally it performs any outstanding *write* operations. Three queues are therefore required, one for pending *write* operations and the other two for pending *read* operations in each of the upward and downward directions. The scheduler must record whether or not the disk is *busy*, the current cylinder number, *cyl*, and the current direction of travel, *dir*. Each data transfer must be sandwiched between calls of the procedures *starttoread* (or *starttowrite*) and *finish*, in which the elevator algorithm is implemented. Listing 15 shows the complete *diskscheduler* monitor.

Listing 15

```
MONITOR MODULE DISKSCHEDULER;

    TYPE
        DIRECTION = (UP, DOWN);

    VAR
        BUSY: BOOLEAN;
        CYL: CYLINDER;
        DIR: DIRECTION;

    INSTANCE
        WRITE: CONDITION;
        READ: ARRAY [DIRECTION] OF CONDITION;

    PROCEDURE *STARTTOREAD (C: CYLINDER);
        BEGIN
            IF BUSY THEN IF C >= CYL THEN READ[UP].PWAIT(C)
                                    ELSE READ[DOWN].PWAIT(CMAX-C);
            CYL:= C;  BUSY:= TRUE
        END;

    PROCEDURE *STARTTOWRITE (VAR A: ADDRESS);
        BEGIN
            IF BUSY THEN WRITE.WAIT;
            SECTORSCHEDULER.ACQUIRE(A, CYL);
            CYL:= A.C;  BUSY:= TRUE
        END;

    PROCEDURE *FINISH;
        FUNCTION MATCH (DIR: DIRECTION; CYL: CYLINDER): BOOLEAN;
            BEGIN
                IF READ[DIR].LENGTH = 0
                THEN MATCH:= FALSE
                ELSE MATCH:= (READ[DIR].PRIORITY = CYL)
            END;
        BEGIN
            BUSY:= FALSE;
            IF MATCH(UP, CYL)
                THEN READ[UP].SIGNAL ELSE
            IF MATCH(DOWN, CMAX-CYL)
                THEN READ[DOWN].SIGNAL ELSE
            IF (WRITE.LENGTH > 0) AND SECTORSCHEDULER.ANYFREECYLSECTOR(CYL)
                THEN WRITE.SIGNAL ELSE
            BEGIN (* NO OUTSTANDING REQUESTS FOR CURRENT CYLINDER *)
                IF READ[DIR].LENGTH = 0 THEN
                    IF DIR = UP THEN DIR:= DOWN ELSE DIR:= UP;
                IF READ[DIR].LENGTH > 0 THEN READ[DIR].SIGNAL ELSE
                    IF SECTORSCHEDULER.ANYFREEDISKSECTOR THEN WRITE.SIGNAL
            END
        END;

    BEGIN
        BUSY:= FALSE;  DIR:= UP;  CYL:= 1;
        ***
    END;
```

In connection with the scheduling of writing requests several calls are made upon the *sectorscheduler*. The Boolean functions *anyfreecylsector* (*cylinder*) and *anyfreedisksector* are used to ascertain whether or not it is possible to write a block to some specified cylinder or to any cylinder on the disk; thus the scheduler must keep a count of the number of *free* sectors on each cylinder and also the *total* number of free sectors. The procedure *acquire* (**var** *address* ; *cylinder*) is used to obtain a free sector, preferably on some specified cylinder; the search for a free sector will always be successful since it will have been preceded by a check that there is indeed some free sector. If the preferred cylinder has no free sectors, which cylinder should be used? Preferably a cylinder that is close to the specified cylinder, to limit the head movement delay; and perhaps a cylinder that is not almost full so that further head movements can be avoided for a time if a succession of writing operations ensues. The latter consideration is not of great importance to the system we are developing but it is scarcely more difficult or more expensive to program it than to disregard it, provided we can find a cheap way of determining whether or not a cylinder is "almost full": we shall select any cylinder that has at least the average number of free sectors, i.e., any cylinder c for which:

$$free[c] \geqslant total \text{ div } CMAX$$

To find such a cylinder we shall search from the specified cylinder in the direction of the middle of the disk and, if that proves fruitless, search in the other direction; taking the two directions in this order helps to keep the heads away from the edges of the disk and so reduces the possibility of very long head-movement delays. The choice of sector number can also be important, albeit not in this system: on writing a block to a new cylinder it is advisable to choose as low a sector number as possible to reduce rotational delays, while on writing a succession of blocks to a new cylinder it is advisable to choose a succession of sector numbers so that they can subsequently be read during a single revolution of the disk. These techniques are incorporated in the *sectorscheduler* monitor in Listing 16.

Intermediate and Spooling Files

We turn now to the envelope that provides the users with intermediate and spooling files. It must maintain a *table* of the addresses of the sectors occupied by the file it represents and it must count the number of blocks written to the file (*wnum*). When the file is being read it must count how many blocks have been read from the file (*rnum*). Recall that sectors are acquired when blocks are written and that they are to be released when blocks have been read or,

Listing 16

```
MONITOR MODULE SECTORSCHEDULER;

    VAR
        POOL: ARRAY [CYLINDER, SECTOR] OF SET OF TRACK;
        FREE: PACKED ARRAY [CYLINDER] OF 0..TS;
        TOTAL: 0..CTS;
        C: CYLINDER;
        T: TRACK;
        S: SECTOR;

    PROCEDURE *ACQUIRE (VAR A: ADDRESS; CYL: CYLINDER);
        VAR
            DIR: (UP, DOWN);
        BEGIN
            C:= CYL;
            IF FREE[C] = 0 THEN
                BEGIN
                    IF C < CMAX DIV 2 THEN DIR:= UP ELSE DIR:= DOWN;
                    REPEAT (* EXAMINE CYLINDERS UNTIL ONE IS *)
                            (* FOUND THAT IS REASONABLY EMPTY *)
                        CASE DIR OF
                            DOWN: IF C > 1 THEN C:= C-1 ELSE
                                            BEGIN C:= CYL+1;  DIR:= UP END;
                            UP:   IF C < CMAX THEN C:= C+1 ELSE
                                            BEGIN C:= CYL-1; DIR:= DOWN END
                        END
                    UNTIL FREE[C] >= TOTAL DIV CMAX;
                    S:= SMAX
                END;
            REPEAT S:= S MOD SMAX + 1 UNTIL POOL[C,S] <> [];
            WHILE NOT (T IN POOL[C,S]) DO T:= T MOD TMAX + 1;
            A.C:= C;  A.T:= T;  A.S:= S;
            FREE[C]:= FREE[C] - 1;  TOTAL:= TOTAL - 1
        END;

    PROCEDURE *RELEASE (A: ADDRESS);
        BEGIN
            POOL[A.C, A.S]:= POOL[A.C, A.S] + [A.T];
            FREE[A.C]:= FREE[A.C] + 1;  TOTAL:= TOTAL + 1
        END;

    PROCEDURE *RESERVE (A: ADDRESS);
        BEGIN
            POOL[A.C, A.S]:= POOL[A.C, A.S] - [A.T];
            FREE[A.C]:= FREE[A.C] - 1;  TOTAL:= TOTAL - 1
        END;

    FUNCTION *ANYFREECYLSECTOR (C: CYLINDER): BOOLEAN;
        BEGIN ANYFREECYLSECTOR:= (FREE[C] > 0) END;

    FUNCTION *ANYFREEDISKSECTOR: BOOLEAN;
        BEGIN ANYFREEDISKSECTOR:= (TOTAL > 0) END;
    BEGIN
        TOTAL:= CTS;
        FOR C:= 1 TO CMAX DO
            BEGIN
                FREE[C]:= TS;
                FOR S:= 1 TO SMAX DO POOL[C, S]:= [1..TMAX]
            END;
        T:= 1;  S:= SMAX;
        (* NOTE THAT THIS RECORD OF FREE SECTORS MUST BE ADJUSTED, BY  *)
        (* CALLS ON THE PROCEDURE "RESERVE", TO EXCLUDE THOSE SECTORS  *)
        (* OCCUPIED BY BLOCKS OF THE LIBRARY FILES AND DIRECTORY       *)
        ***
    END;
```

for those blocks that are not read, during the finalization of the envelope. The complete *file* envelope is shown in Listing 17.

Listing 17

```
ENVELOPE *FILE;

VAR
    *RESULT: STATUS;
    TABLE: ARRAY [1..MAXBLOCK] OF ADDRESS;
    RNUM,
    WNUM: INTEGER;

PROCEDURE *WRITE (B: BLOCK);
    VAR
        LOCATION: ADDRESS;
    BEGIN
        IF WNUM-RNUM = MAXBLOCK THEN RESULT:= ENDOFFILE ELSE
            BEGIN
                LOCATION:= TABLE[WNUM MOD MAXBLOCK + 1];
                WNUM:= WNUM + 1;
                DISKSCHEDULER.STARTTOWRITE(LOCATION);
                DISKCONTROLLER.WRITE(LOCATION, B);
                DISKSCHEDULER.FINISH
            END
    END;

PROCEDURE *READ (VAR B: BLOCK);
    VAR
        LOCATION: ADDRESS;
    BEGIN
        IF RNUM = WNUM THEN RESULT:= ENDOFFILE ELSE
            BEGIN
                LOCATION:= TABLE[RNUM MOD MAXBLOCK + 1];
                RNUM:= RNUM + 1;
                DISKSCHEDULER.STARTTOREAD(LOCATION.C);
                DISKCONTROLLER.READ(LOCATION, B);
                DISKSCHEDULER.FINISH;
                SECTORSCHEDULER.RELEASE(LOCATION)
            END
    END;

BEGIN
    WNUM:= 0;  RNUM:= 0;  RESULT:= SUCCESS;
    ***;
    WHILE RNUM < WNUM DO
        BEGIN
            SECTORSCHEDULER.RELEASE(TABLE[RNUM MOD MAXBLOCK + 1]);
            RNUM:= RNUM + 1
        END
END;
```

The reason for using the table of sector addresses cyclically is that further blocks may be written to an intermediate file after some blocks have been read from it.

Library Files

Users cannot write to library files: these will already have been written to disk together with their sector address tables. Somewhere on the disk, at some known address, is a directory correlating the names of the library files with the addresses of their sector tables. Thus the initialization of the library file envelope involves "opening" the file by locating the sector table and reading it into main store, provided the file can be found in the directory. Lacking Brinch Hansen's *universal* type we must define the sector table in two ways: physically as a block and logically as a record with a table of addresses and a count of the number of blocks written to the file. Listing 18 shews the *libraryfile* envelope.

Listing 18

```
ENVELOPE *LIBRARYFILE (F: FILENAME);

    VAR
        *RESULT: STATUS;
        LOCATION: ADDRESS;
        SECTOR: RECORD CASE INTERPRETATION: (LOGICAL,PHYSICAL) OF
                        PHYSICAL: (B: BLOCK);
                        LOGICAL: (TABLE: ARRAY [1..MAXBLOCK] OF ADDRESS;
                                  LENGTH: 0..MAXBLOCK)
                END;
        RNUM: 0..MAXBLOCK;
        FOUND: BOOLEAN;

    PROCEDURE *READ (VAR B: BLOCK);
        BEGIN
            IF RNUM = SECTOR.LENGTH THEN RESULT:= ENDOFFILE ELSE
                BEGIN
                    RNUM:= RNUM + 1;
                    DISKSCHEDULER.STARTTOREAD(SECTOR.TABLE[RNUM].C);
                    DISKCONTROLLER.READ(SECTOR.TABLE[RNUM], B);
                    DISKSCHEDULER.FINISH
                END
        END;

    BEGIN
        LIBRARYDIRECTORY.FINDFILE(F, LOCATION, FOUND);
        IF NOT FOUND THEN RESULT:= NOFILE ELSE
            BEGIN
                SECTOR.INTERPRETATION:= PHYSICAL;
                DISKSCHEDULER.STARTTOREAD(LOCATION, C);
                DISKCONTROLLER.READ(LOCATION, SECTOR.B);
                DISKCONTROLLER.FINISH;
                SECTOR.INTERPRETATION:= LOGICAL;
                RNUM:= 0;
                RESULT:= SUCCESS
            END;
        ***
    END;
```

The administration of the library directory is accomplished by a monitor that has one starred procedure, *findfile*. Since there are few library files a linear scan of the table will suffice. On its initialization the monitor reads its directory into main store and instructs the *sectorscheduler* to reserve all those sectors occupied by the library. The *librarydirectory* monitor is shown in Listing 19.

Listing 19

```
MONITOR MODULE LIBRARYDIRECTORY;

   CONST
      HOMEADDRESS = (* DISK ADDRESS OF THE DIRECTORY *);
      MAXFILE = 73 (* MAXIMUM NUMBER OF LIBRARY FILES THAT CAN *)
                   (* BE ACCOMMODATED IN A ONE-BLOCK DIRECTORY *);

   VAR
      DIRECTORY: RECORD CASE INTERPRETATION: (LOGICAL, PHYSICAL) OF
                        PHYSICAL: (B: BLOCK);
                        LOGICAL:  (TABLE: ARRAY [1..MAXFILE] OF
                                          RECORD
                                             NAME: FILENAME;
                                             ADDR: ADDRESS
                                          END;
                                   LENGTH: 0..MAXFILE)
                 END;
      NEXTFILE: 1..MAXFILE;

   PROCEDURE *FINDFILE
             (F: FILENAME; VAR LOCATION: ADDRESS; VAR FOUND: BOOLEAN);
      VAR NEXTFILE: 0..MAXFILE;
      BEGIN
         NEXTFILE:= DIRECTORY.LENGTH;
         REPEAT
            FOUND:= (F = DIRECTORY.TABLE[NEXTFILE].NAME);
            IF FOUND THEN LOCATION:= DIRECTORY.TABLE[NEXTFILE].ADDR
                     ELSE NEXTFILE:= NEXTFILE - 1
         UNTIL FOUND OR (NEXTFILE = 0)
      END;

   PROCEDURE RESERVESECTORSOFFILE (LOCATION: ADDRESS);
      VAR
         SECTOR: RECORD CASE INTERPRETATION: (LOGICAL, PHYSICAL) OF
                        PHYSICAL: (B: BLOCK);
                        LOGICAL:  (TABLE: ARRAY [1..MAXBLOCK] OF ADDRESS;
                                   LENGTH: 0..MAXBLOCK)
                 END;
         NEXTBLOCK: 1..MAXBLOCK;
      BEGIN
         SECTORSCHEDULER.RESERVE(LOCATION);
         SECTOR.INTERPRETATION:= PHYSICAL;
         DISKCONTROLLER.READ(LOCATION, SECTOR.B);
         SECTOR.INTERPRETATION:= LOGICAL;
         FOR NEXTBLOCK:= 1 TO SECTOR.LENGTH DO
            SECTORSCHEDULER.RESERVE(SECTOR.TABLE[NEXTBLOCK])
      END;
```

```
BEGIN
    SECTORSCHEDULER.RESERVE(HOMEADDRESS);
    DIRECTORY.INTERPRETATION:= PHYSICAL;
    DISKCONTROLLER.READ(HOMEADDRESS, DIRECTORY.B);
    DIRECTORY.INTERPRETATION:= LOGICAL;
    FOR NEXTFILE:= 1 TO DIRECTORY.LENGTH DO
        RESERVESECTORSOFFILE(DIRECTORY.TABLE[NEXTFILE].ADDR);
    ***
END;
```

Two points need to be noted about this monitor. Calls upon *diskcontroller.read* need not be sandwiched between calls on the *starttoread* and *finish* procedures of the *diskscheduler* as there is no competition for the disk during this initialization. The other point is that a procedure *reserve* must be added to the *sectorscheduler*.

> **procedure** **reserve* (*a* : *address*) ;
>   **begin**
>   *pool* [*a.c*, *a.s*] := *pool* [*a.c*, *a.s*] — [*a*, *t*] ;
>   *free* [*a.c*] := *free* [*a.c*] — 1 ; *total* := *total* — 1
>   **end**

All the components of the filestore administration monitor can now be combined to produce Listing 20.

Listing 20

```
MONITOR MODULE FILESTORE;

    CONST
        *MAXCHAR  = 1023 (* 1K CHARACTERS PER BLOCK *);
        *MAXBLOCK = 500 (* UP TO 500 BLOCKS PER FILE *);
        *MAXNAME  = 12 (* CHARACTERS PER FILE NAME *);
        CMAX = 200 (* CYLINDERS *);
        TMAX =  10 (* TRACKS *);
        SMAX =   3 (* SECTORS *);

    TYPE
        *BLOCK    = PACKED ARRAY [0..MAXCHAR] OF CHAR;
        *STATUS   = ( *SUCCESS, *ENDOFFILE, *NOFILE );
        *FILENAME = PACKED ARRAY [1..MAXNAME] OF CHAR;
        CYLINDER = 1..CMAX;
        TRACK    = 1..TMAX;
        SECTOR   = 1..SMAX;
        ADDRESS  = PACKED RECORD C: CYLINDER; T: TRACK; S: SECTOR END;
```

```
MONITOR MODULE SECTORSCHEDULER = LIST16 IN LIBRARY;
    (*    PROCEDURE *ACQUIRE (VAR ADDRESS; CYLINDER)                *)
    (*    PROCEDURE *RELEASE (ADDRESS)                              *)
    (*    PROCEDURE *RESERVE (ADDRESS)                              *)
    (*    FUNCTION *ANYFREECYLSECTOR (CYLINDER): BOOLEAN            *)
    (*    FUNCTION *ANYFREEDISCSECTOR: BOOLEAN                      *)

MONITOR MODULE DISKSCHEDULER = LIST15 IN LIBRARY;
    (*    PROCEDURE *STARTTOREAD (CYLINDER)                         *)
    (*    PROCEDURE *STARTTOWRITE (VAR ADDRESS)                     *)
    (*    PROCEDURE *FINISH                                         *)

MONITOR MODULE DISKCONTROLLER = LIST14 IN LIBRARY;
    (*    PROCEDURE *READ (ADDRESS; VAR BLOCK)                      *)
    (*    PROCEDURE *WRITE (ADDRESS; BLOCK)                         *)

MONITOR MODULE LIBRARYDIRECTORY = LIST19 IN LIBRARY;
    (*    PROCEDURE *FINDFILE (FILENAME; VAR ADDRESS; VAR BOOLEAN)  *)

ENVELOPE *LIBRARYFILE = LIST18 IN LIBRARY;
    (*    VAR *RESULT: STATUS                                       *)
    (*    PROCEDURE *READ (VAR BLOCK)                               *)

ENVELOPE *FILE = LIST17 IN LIBRARY;
    (*    VAR *RESULT: STATUS                                       *)
    (*    PROCEDURE *WRITE (BLOCK)                                  *)
    (*    PROCEDURE *READ (VAR BLOCK)                               *)

BEGIN
    ***
END;
```

Implementation Considerations

Listings 1–20 constitute a reasonably complete operating system with only the most machine-dependent parts unelaborated. One task remains to be done and that is to convince ourselves that the space and time overheads of the operating system are acceptably low.

Consider the time overheads first. The amount of computation performed by each routine of the operating system is very limited because we have avoided two dangers. One : the job descriptions are rudimentary—if they were not, the user processes would be engaged in much expensive character processing, although if a library program to interpret the job description were run as part of the user's job the expense would be charged to the user rather than to the operating system. Two : the operating system trusts itself—naturally any supervisor call by a user program must be validated, but in many systems each operating system routine insists on checking the validity of all parameters passed to it by other operating system routines : not only is this expensive but the protection afforded by this precaution is almost invariably inadequate. There is, however, one significantly expensive operation in this system : the copying of data structures when passing parameters on procedure calls and when passing data from one process to another. The former can be mitigated by passing a pointer to the data rather than passing the data themselves: this is potentially unsafe and, although against the spirit of Pascal, can be accomplished by passing parameters by reference rather than by value, thus in the *diskcontroller* monitor the procedure *write* might specify the block to be written as a variable :

procedure *∗write* (*a* : *address* ; **var** *b* : *block*).

The problem of inter-process communication is more difficult : in Pascal Plus processes cannot communicate directly with one another but must pass data through a common monitor. Any amelioration of this problem in Pascal Plus or by resorting to machine code is clumsy and dangerous. A better solution appears to lie with languages, such as Hoare's "Communicating Sequential Process" notation (*Comm. A.C.M.*, **21**, 666-77 (1978)), that permit direct communication between processes. Indeed much copying may be avoided altogether if the data structure is represented as a process, although any saving in time must be offset by the increased time necessary to access that data structure.

In this operating system the file system, with its 1K character blocks, is the main contributor to unnecessary time overheads. It is also the main contributor to the space overheads since each of the twelve users will have up to four files, for each of which it will need space to hold both a sector table and a block, and the *librarydirectory* will need to hold the directory block and will also require another block during its initialization phase. These blocks account for much more than the 56K characters set aside for the operating system. The code of the operating system is limited in size— naturally the precise amount will depend upon the order code and architecture of the computer. The only other substantial data structure is the *pool* of free disk sectors held in the *sectorscheduler*: this is an array of 600 sets, each of 10 members. Describing this data structure, and others, as *packed* may save a useful amount of space, depending on how the standard and packed representations differ from one another. Incidentally, some machine independence is lost when assumptions are made about data representations: for example, it has been assumed in this file system that a packed disk address occupies two characters, thereby enabling a 500 page file to be represented by a sector table of one block. The problem of the 98 1K buffers for the file system can be solved by recognizing that not all the sector tables and not all the blocks will be required simultaneously. For example, the *library directory* needs a second buffer only during its initialization phase, a user engaged in spooling needs only two buffers to hold the sector table and the data of the file that is being read or printed, and a user that is neither spooling nor running needs at most one buffer to hold the sector table of a spooled file. Thus a pool of 31 buffers, each of 1K characters, would suffice and should leave adequate space for the remainder of the operating system : indeed the choice of twelve user processes was somewhat arbitrary, as in a perfectly balanced system six would suffice; extra processes are provided to iron out fluctuations in demand for the use of resources and this number can be reduced to save space or increased to utilize spare space.

Exercise 8   Amend the operating system to use a public pool of buffers, each of 1K characters, in place of the file blocks and sector tables at present declared privately by the user processes. This entails programming a buffer pool and altering those parts of the system that will use the buffers, namely the user processes, the spoolers and the *file* and *libraryfile* envelopes.

Exercise 9   Rewrite the *filestore* monitor to handle disk transfer failures.

Postscript

This operating system and several similar ones have been implemented in Pascal Plus (or its predecessor, PPP) by the author and by D. W. Bustard and have been run on a small ICL 1900 configuration or have been simulated on a large ICL 1900 installation—the simulation involves adding a monitor and an external file to represent each peripheral device (with a pseudo-random-number generator to simulate faults) and a process to represent each operator: the only change to the operating system is to replace the machine code to effect data transfers by calls upon the appropriate peripheral device monitors. The ability to simulate so easily is a great help in developing a system for a configuration whose hardware is not readily available during the testing stage: this is often the case, especially when developing a system to run on a variety of configurations. The ability to simulate the execution of an operating system is also of value when teaching a class of students, since they can then readily modify the system to cope with different configurations, to use different scheduling algorithms, or to provide different services.

Nevertheless, the purpose of this book has not been to "sell" Pascal Plus but to use it to illustrate the application of structured programming to the design of difficult and challenging programs.

BIBLIOGRAPHY

This bibliography lists some of the best books relating to the topics covered in this volume. No attempt is made to list the many excellent papers to be found in such journals as *Acta Informatica*, the *Communications of the A.C.M.*, the *Computer Journal*, the *I.E.E.E. Transactions on Software Engineering* and *Software: Practice and Experience*.

Structured Programming

DAHL, O.-J., DIJKSTRA, E. W. & HOARE, C. A. R., *Structured Programming*, London & New York: Academic Press, 1972.

DIJKSTRA, E. W., *A Discipline of Programming*, Englewood Cliffs, N.J.: Prentice-Hall, 1976.

JACKSON, M. A., *Principles of Program Design*, London: Academic Press, 1975.

WIRTH, N., *Systematic Programming: an Introduction*, Englewood Cliffs, N.J.: Prentice-Hall, 1973.

WIRTH, N., *Algorithms + Data Structures = Programs*, Englewood Cliffs, N.J.: Prentice-Hall, 1976.

Pascal

ADDYMAN, A. M. & WILSON, I. R., *A Practical Introduction to Pascal*, London: Macmillan, 1978.

FINDLAY, W. & WATT, D., *Pascal: an Introduction to Methodical Programming*, London: Pitman, 1978.

JENSEN, K. & WIRTH, N., *Pascal User Manual and Report*, Berlin: Springer, 1974, 2nd edn. 1975.

WELSH, J. & ELDER, J. W. G., *Introduction to Pascal*, Hemel Hempstead: Prentice-Hall, 1979.

Compilers

AHO, A. V. & ULLMAN, J. D., *Principles of Compiler Design*, Reading, Mass. & London: Addison-Wesley, 1977.

BACKHOUSE, R., *Syntax of Programming Languages: Theory and Practice*, Hemel Hempstead: Prentice-Hall, 1979.

GRIES, D., *Compiler Construction for Digital Computers*, New York: Wiley, 1971.

ROHL, J. S., *An Introduction to Compiler Writing*, London: Macdonald & Jane's; New York: American Elsevier, 1975.

Operating Systems

BRINCH HANSEN, P., *Operating System Principles*, Englewood Cliffs, N.J.: Prentice-Hall, 1973.

BRINCH HANSEN, P., *The Architecture of Concurrent Programs*, Englewood Cliffs, N.J.: Prentice-Hall, 1977.

HOARE, C. A. R. & PERROTT, R. H. (eds.), *Operating Systems Techniques*, London & New York: Academic Press, 1972.

McKEAG, R. M. and WILSON, R. (ed. HUXTABLE, D. H. R.), *Studies in Operating Systems*, London & New York: Academic Press, 1976.

INDEX